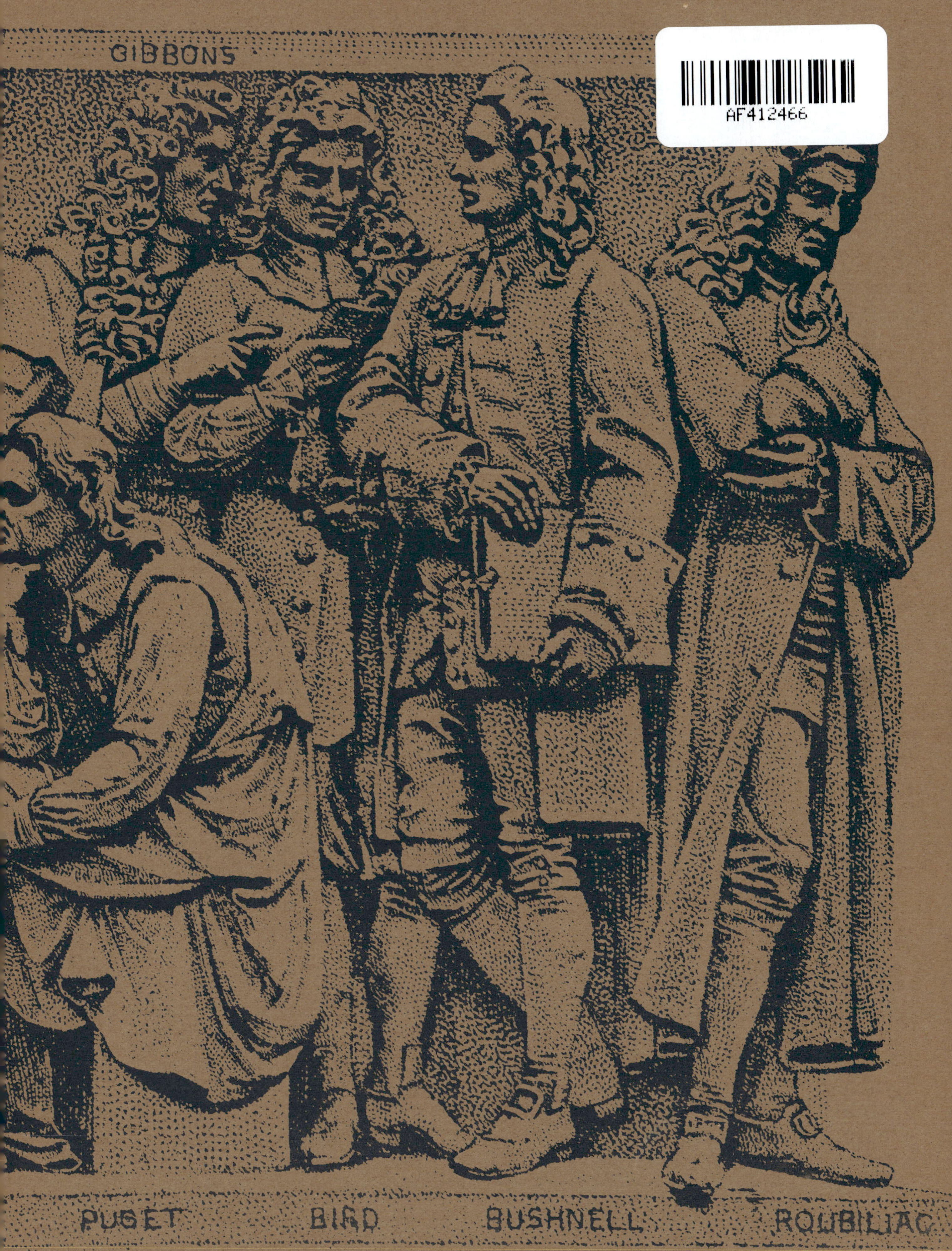

GIBBONS
PUGET
BIRD
BUSHNELL
ROUBILIAC

(*End-papers*) Sculptors. Detail of the west side of the podium, Albert Memorial, by J. B. Philip. From *The Albert Memorial, Hyde Park* by James Dafforne, London, 1878.

(*Title-page*) Detail of two cherubs, from William Kent's design for the monument to Sir Isaac Newton in Westminster Abbey. (See No. 48)

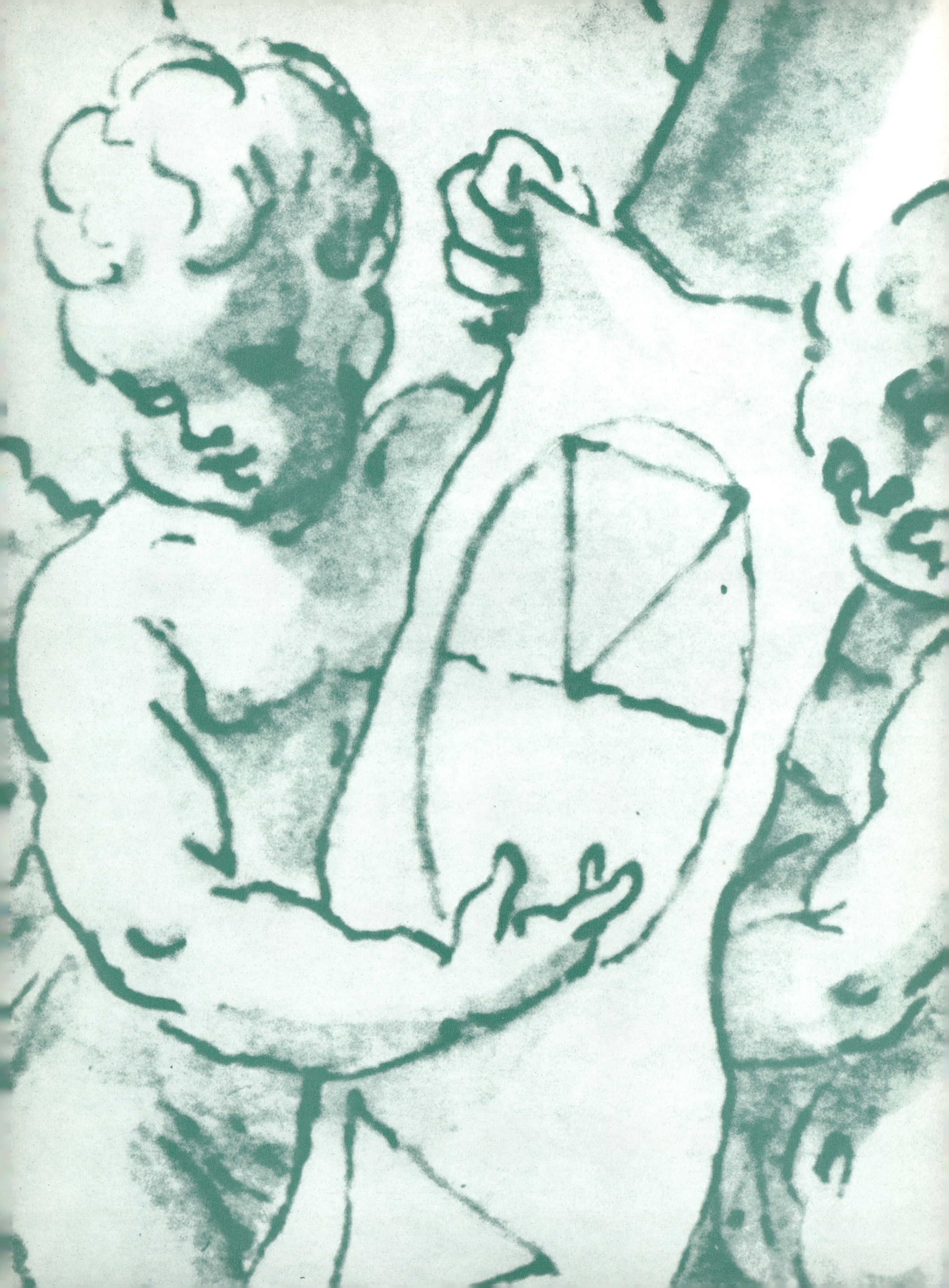

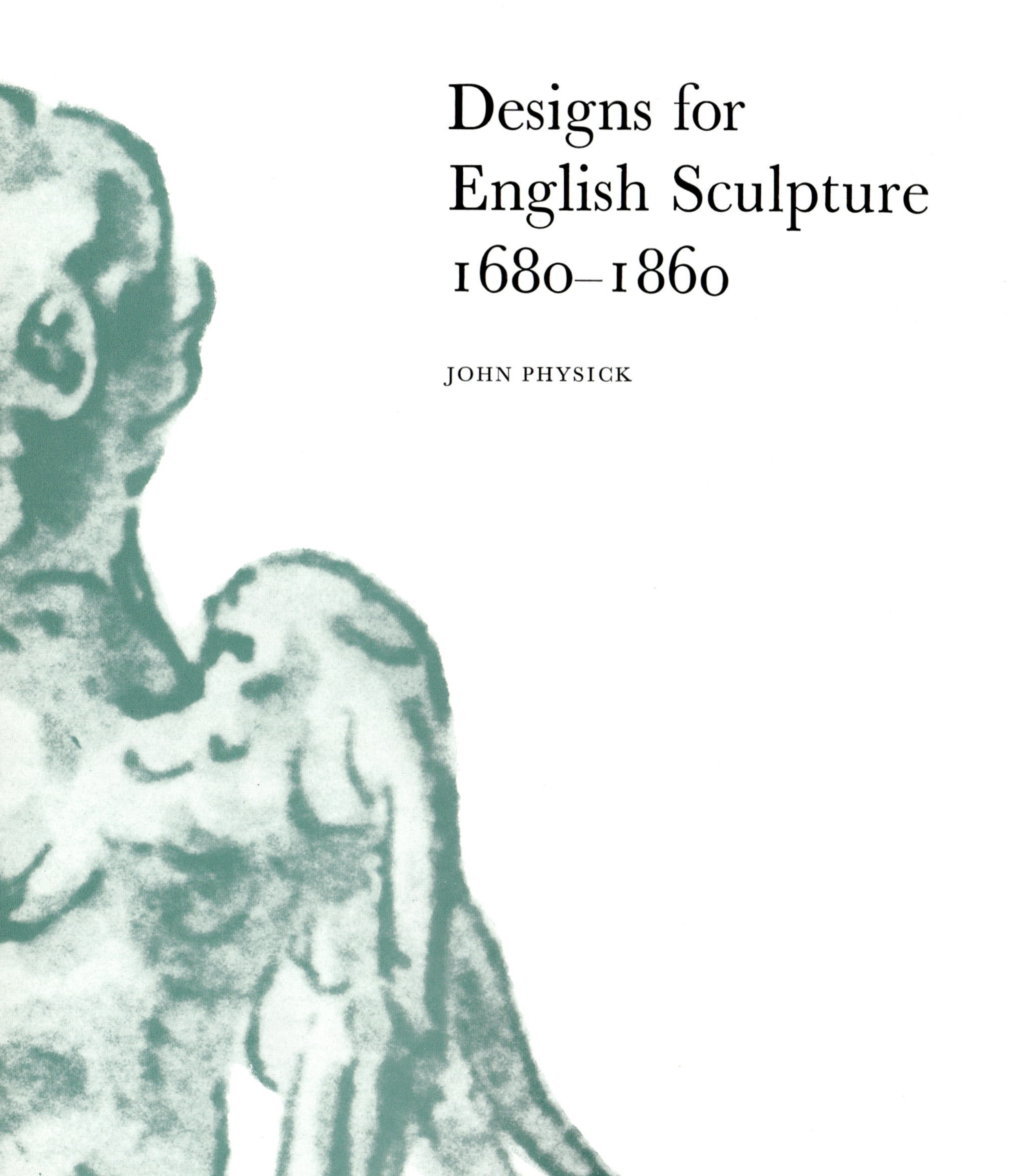

VICTORIA AND ALBERT MUSEUM

# Designs for English Sculpture 1680–1860

JOHN PHYSICK

LONDON: HER MAJESTY'S STATIONERY OFFICE 1969

SBN 11 290028 3*

Designed by HMSO/Alan Stephens

Printed in England for Her Majesty's Stationery Office
by Butler and Tanner Ltd, Frome and London

# Foreword

The almost total disregard for late 17th and 18th century sculpture until after the Second World War, was a legacy of 19th century antiquarianism which devoted itself to praising the virtues of gothic art; and also, no doubt, because such sculpture was nearly always for sepulchral monuments. This rejection is reflected in the amazingly low prices paid during the 19th century by the South Kensington Museum for unidentified and usually anonymous designs for sculpture—a drawing by John Nost for 3 shillings, or a group of 60 designs by Michael Rysbrack, Sir Henry Cheere, John Francis Moore and others for only £1. 5 shillings. The collection of drawings in the then newly-formed Museum benefited greatly by what it was able to acquire from a local dealer, Mr. E. Parsons of Brompton Road, who seems to have specialised in such material.

The revival of interest in post-Reformation sculpture was pioneered by Mrs. Katharine Esdaile, and she inspired Mr. Rupert Gunnis to compile his *Dictionary of British Sculptors 1660–1851*, which was published in 1953. This book, in its turn, has since been the means whereby many of our designs have been identified. By the end of 1966, due largely to research by Mr. John Physick, the Department of Prints and Drawings was in a position to stage the first exhibition devoted entirely to drawings of this hitherto completely unexplored field. The present book is a record of some of the material in that exhibition drawn from the Museum's collection, with the addition of a few drawings which were lent by the British Museum and the Bodleian Library, Oxford. Many of the designs have subsequently been exhibited at the Ashmolean Museum, Oxford, and the Central Museum and Art Gallery, Northampton.

JOHN POPE-HENNESSY  *Director*

# Contents


List of Illustrations   *page ix*
Introduction   *page 1*
Catalogue   *page 45*
Index   *page 199*

## ACKNOWLEDGEMENTS

Most of the illustrations showing sculpture are from the negatives of
the Royal Commission on Historical Monuments (England); the
National Monuments Record; the Warburg Institute (from the series
made by Mr. Helmut Gernsheim); and of Mr. Bruce Bailey, of
Northampton; and are reproduced with permission. Other photographs are reproduced with the permission of the British Museum,
the Bodleian Library, Oxford, the Ministry of Public Building and
Works, the Royal Institute of British Architects, and Mr. Brian
Gould.

# List of Illustrations


1  "Queen Margaret of Valois" c. 1300, Lincoln Cathedral.
Photograph: *National Monuments Record.*

2  The Sondes monuments c. 1584 and c. 1618, Throwley, Kent.
Photograph: *author.*

3  Design for the monument of Edward VI, Bodleian Library, Oxford, (Gough Maps 45, no. 63).
Photograph: *Bodleian Library.*

4  Design for the monument to Elizabeth, Countess of Shrewsbury, Smythson Collection.
Photograph: *Royal Institute of British Architects.*

5  Design for the monument to Robert Adam (unexecuted), by Joseph Nollekens, R.A.   E.4369–1920.

6  Design for the monument to Mrs. Cox, Kilkenny Cathedral, by Peter Scheemakers. (Bequeathed by Rupert Gunnis, J.P.   E.961–1965.)

7  Design for a monument, perhaps related to that to Sir Thomas Wendy, Haslingfield, Cambridgeshire, by William Stanton.   D.1105–1898.

8  Design for the monument to the Duke of Queensberry, Durisdeer, Dumfries-shire, by John Nost, in the Bodleian Library, Oxford (MS. Gough Drawings a.2, fol. 132).
Photograph: *Bodleian Library.*

9  Statue of William III, Portsmouth Dockyard, attributed to John Nost.
Photograph: *Ministry of Public Building and Works.*

10  Statue of William III, Wrest Park, attributed to John Nost.
Photograph: *Mr. Bruce Bailey.*

11  Design for a statue of Neptune, probably for Chatsworth, Derbyshire, by Caius Gabriel Cibber.   E.668–1949.

12  Detail of the monument to James Craggs, Westminster Abbey, by G. B. Guelfi. Photograph: *Warburg Institute.*

13  Design for the monument to Lord Foley, Great Witley, Worcestershire, by J. M. Rysbrack.   4910.1.

14  Design for the monument to Harriot Bouverie, Coleshill, Berkshire, by J. M. Rysbrack.   E.448–1946.

15  Monument to the Duke of Newcastle, Westminster Abbey, by Francis Bird.
Photograph: *Warburg Institute.*

16  Model for the monument to the Duke of Montagu, Warkton, Northampton-shire, by L. F. Roubiliac.   A.6–1947.

17  Design for the monument to Samuel Tufnell, Pleshey, Essex, by Sir Henry Cheere, Bart.   4910.29.

18  Design for an unidentified monument, by Sir Henry Cheere, Bart.   4910.37.

19  Detail from the design for the monument to Elizabeth Grigg, St. Katherine's Chapel, Regent's Park, London, by Joseph Nollekens, R.A.   E.4367–1920.

20  Design for the monument to Mrs. Howard, of Corby, Wetheral, Cumberland, by Joseph Nollekens, R.A. (Bequeathed by Rupert Gunnis, J.P.   E.958–1965.)

21  Design for the monument to Lady Warburton, St. John's, Chester, by Edward Pierce.   3436.421.

22  Monument to Lady Warburton, St. John's, Chester.
Photograph: *National Monuments Record.*

23  Design for the monument to Christopher Clitherow, Pinner, Middlesex, by William Stanton. D.1129–1898.

24  Monument to Christopher Clitherow, Pinner, Middlesex.
Photograph: *Royal Commission on Historical Monuments (England).*

25  Design for the monument to Sir John Roberts, Bart., St. Mary's, Bromley, Poplar, London, by William Stanton. E.959–1965.

26  Monument to Sir John Roberts, Bart., St. Mary's, Bromley, Poplar, London.
Photograph: *Royal Commission on Historical Monuments (England).*

27  Design for the monument to Lady Brownlow, St. Nicholas's, Sutton, Surrey, by William Stanton. D.1104–1898.

**28** Design for the figures of Pallas and Apollo, Chatsworth, Derbyshire, by Caius Gabriel Cibber. E.946–1965.

**29** Apollo on the Grand Staircase, Chatsworth, Derbyshire. Photograph: *National Monuments Record.*

**30** Design for a statue of William III, by John Nost. 9145.

**31** Design for a fountain at Hampton Court, with a figure of William III, by John Nost (British Museum, No. 1964-12-12-7). Photograph: *British Museum.*

**32** The Diana Fountain, Bushey Park, Middlesex. Photograph: *Royal Commission on Historical Monuments (England).*

**33** Design for the monument to the Duke of Newcastle, Westminster Abbey, by John Nost (Bodleian Library MS. Top. Gen. a.7, fol. 22). Photograph: *Bodleian Library.*

**34** Design for the chimney-piece in the Queen's Gallery, Hampton Court, from the workshop of John Nost. 3436.330.

**35** Chimney-piece in the Queen's Gallery, Hampton Court, by John Nost. Photograph: *Royal Commission on Historical Monuments (England).*

**36** Design for the monument to Sir William Russell, St. Dunstan-in-the-East, London, by Edward Stanton. D.1099–1898.

**37** Monument to Sir William Russell, St. Dunstan-in-the-East, London. Photograph: *National Monuments Record.*

**38** Design for the monument to Jane and Edward Bray, Great Barrington, Gloucestershire, by Christopher Cass. 3436.424.

**39** Monument to Jane and Edward Bray, Great Barrington, Gloucestershire. Photograph: *National Monuments Record.*

**40** Design for the monument to James Craggs, Westminster Abbey, by James Gibbs. E.3641–1913.

**41** Monument to James Craggs, Westminster Abbey, by G. B. Guelfi. Photograph: *National Monuments Record.*

**42** Design for an unidentified monument by J. M. Rysbrack. E.434–1946.

**43** Design for the monument to Marwood Turner, Kirkleatham, Yorkshire, by James Gibbs. E.3643–1913.

**44** Design for the monument to Sir Ambrose Crowley, Mitcham, Surrey, by James Gibbs. 4910.52.

**45** Monument to Sir Ambrose Crowley, Mitcham, Surrey, probably by J. M. Rysbrack. Photograph: *National Monuments Record.*

**46** Design for the statue of Inigo Jones, Chiswick House, Middlesex, by William Kent. 8933.103.

**47** Statue of Inigo Jones, Chiswick House, Middlesex, by J. M. Rysbrack. Photograph: *Mr. Brian Gould.*

**48** Design for the monument to Sir Isaac Newton, Westminster Abbey, by William Kent. E.424–1946.

**49** Design for the monument to Sir Isaac Newton, Westminster Abbey, by J. M. Rysbrack (British Museum, No. 1859-7-9-100). Photograph: *British Museum.*

**50** Monument to Sir Isaac Newton, Westminster Abbey, by J. M. Rysbrack. Photograph: *Warburg Institute.*

**51** Design for the monument to Earl Stanhope, Westminster Abbey, by William Kent. 8933.251.

**52** Design for the monument to Earl Stanhope, Westminster Abbey, by J. M. Rysbrack (British Museum, No. 1859-7-9-99). Photograph: *British Museum.*

**53** Monuments to Sir Isaac Newton and Earl Stanhope, Westminster Abbey. Plate from Ackermann's *History.*

**54** Monument to Earl Stanhope, Westminster Abbey, by J. M. Rysbrack. Photograph: *Warburg Institute.*

**55** Design for the monument to the Rev. Thomas Busby, Addington, Buckinghamshire, by J. M. Rysbrack. 4235.

**56** Detail of the monument to the Rev. Thomas Busby, Addington, Buckinghamshire. Photograph: *Mr. Bruce Bailey.*

**57** Design for the monument to Lord King, Ockham, Surrey, by J. M. Rysbrack. 4910.8.

**58** Detail of the monument to Lord King, Ockham, Surrey. Photograph: *National Monuments Record.*

**59** Design for the monument to Nicholas Rowe, Westminster Abbey, by J. M. Rysbrack. E.441–1946.

**60** Monument to Nicholas Rowe, Westminster Abbey. Photograph: *Warburg Institute.*

**61** Design for the monument to Sir Watkin Williams Wynn, Ruabon, Denbighshire, by J. M. Rysbrack. E.426–1946.

List of Illustrations

**62** Monument to Sir Watkin Williams Wynn, Ruabon, Denbighshire. Photograph: *National Monuments Record.*

**63** Design for the monument to Charlotte and Mary Pochin, Barkby, Leicestershire, by J. M. Rysbrack. 4230.

**64** Monument to Charlotte and Mary Pochin, Barkby, Leicestershire. Photograph: *Mr. Bruce Bailey.*

**65** Design for the monument to the Dukes of Beaufort, Badminton, Gloucestershire, by J. M. Rysbrack. 4910.45.

**66** Monument to the Dukes of Beaufort, Badminton, Gloucestershire. Photograph: *National Monuments Record.*

**67** Design for a chimney-piece, Teddesley Hall, Staffordshire, incorporating the relief of Charity, by J. M. Rysbrack. E.465–1946, A.58, 59–1953.

**68** Design for the chimney-piece in the hall, Teddesley Hall, Staffordshire, by J. M. Rysbrack. E.462–1946.

**69** Chimney-piece in the hall, Teddesley Hall, Staffordshire. Photograph: *National Monuments Record.*

**70** Design for the monument to Sir James Reade, Hatfield, Hertfordshire, by J. M. Rysbrack. 4910.31.

**71** Design for the monument to Sir James Reade, Hatfield, Hertfordshire, by J. M. Rysbrack. E.1183–1965.

**72** Monument to Sir James Reade, Hatfield, Hertfordshire. Photograph: *Mr. Bruce Bailey.*

**73** Design for the monument to Admiral Vernon, Westminster Abbey, by J. M. Rysbrack. E.433–1946.

**74** Monument to Admiral Vernon, Westminster Abbey. Photograph: *Warburg Institute.*

**75** Design for the monument to Lord Somers, North Mimms, Hertfordshire, by Peter Scheemakers. D.1060–1887.

**76** Monument to Lord Somers, North Mimms, Hertfordshire. Photograph: *Mr. Bruce Bailey.*

**77** Design for the monument to Sir Samuel Ongley, Old Warden, Bedfordshire, by Peter Scheemakers. 8949.

**78** Monument to Sir Samuel Ongley, Old Warden, Bedfordshire, by Peter Scheemakers and Laurent Delvaux. Photograph: *Mr. Bruce Bailey.*

**79** Design for the monument to Ann Colleton, All Hallows-by-the-Tower, London, by Peter Scheemakers. D.1035–1887.

**80** Monument to Ann Colleton, All Hallows-by-the-Tower. Photograph: *National Monuments Record.*

**81** Design for the monument to Lord Aubrey Beauclerk, Westminster Abbey, by Peter Scheemakers. D.1058–1887.

**82** Monument to Lord Aubrey Beauclerk, Westminster Abbey. Photograph: *Warburg Institute.*

**83** Design for the monument to the Duke of Argyll and Greenwich, Westminster Abbey, by L. F. Roubiliac. 8381.

**84** The monument to the Duke of Argyll and Greenwich, Westminster Abbey; and detail, Eloquence. Photographs: *Warburg Institute.*

**85** Design for the monument to Philip de Sausmarez, Westminster Abbey, by Sir Henry Cheere, Bart. 4910.25.

**86** Monument to Philip de Saumarez, Westminster Abbey. Photograph: *Warburg Institute.*

**87** Design for the monument to Sir Edmund Prideaux, Bart., Westminster Abbey, by Sir Henry Cheere, Bart. 8933.2.

**88** Monument to Sir Edmund Prideaux, Bart., Westminster Abbey. Photograph: *Warburg Institute.*

**89** Design for the monument to David Polhill, Otford, Kent, by Sir Henry Cheere, Bart. 4910.41.

**90** Monument to David Polhill, Otford, Kent. Photograph: *Mr. Bruce Bailey.*

**91** Design for a chimney-piece by Sir Henry Cheere, Bart. D.715(13)–1887.

**92** Chimney-piece in the Dining Room, Picton Castle, Pembrokeshire. Photograph: *National Monuments Record.*

**93** Design for a chimney-piece by Sir Henry Cheere, Bart. D.715(23)–1887.

**94** Design for the monument to Jonas Hanway, Westminster Abbey, by J. F. Moore. 4910.22.

**95** Monument to Jonas Hanway, Westminster Abbey. Photograph: *National Monuments Record.*

**96** Design for the monument to Lord Hawke, North Stoneham, Hampshire, by J. F. Moore. 4910.4.

**97** Monument to Lord Hawke, North Stoneham, Hampshire. Photograph: *National Monuments Record.*

**98** Design for the monument to Thomas Steavens, Preston-on-Stour, Gloucestershire, by Thomas Scheemakers. 8408.14.

**99** Monument to Thomas Steavens, Preston-on-Stour, Gloucestershire. Photograph: *Mr. Bruce Bailey.*

**100** Design for the monument to Elizabeth Bacon, Linton, Cambridgeshire, by Joseph Wilton, R.A. E.504–1964.

**101** Monument to Elizabeth Bacon, Linton, Cambridgeshire. Photograph: *Mr. Bruce Bailey.*

**102** Design for the monument to Archbishop Tillotson, Sowerby, Yorkshire, by Joseph Wilton, R.A. E.1184–1965.

**103** Monument to Archbishop Tillotson, Sowerby, Yorkshire. Photograph: *Mr. Bruce Bailey.*

**104** Design for a statue of Alderman Beckford, Guildhall, London, by Nathaniel Smith. 4910.12.

**105** Model of the statue of Alderman Beckford, by Nathaniel Smith. A.48–1928.

**106** Design for the monument to Robert Child, Heston, Middlesex, by Robert Adam. E.973–1965.

**107** Monument to Robert Child, Heston, Middlesex, by Peter van Gelder. Photograph: *National Monuments Record.*

**108** Design for the monument to Sir Robert Cunliffe, Bart., Bruera, Cheshire, by Joseph Nollekens, R.A. E.4354–1920.

**109** Detail of the monument to Sir Robert Cunliffe, Bart., Bruera, Cheshire. Photograph: *National Monuments Record.*

**110** Design for the monument to Captains Bayne, Blair and Lord Robert Manners, Westminster Abbey, by Joseph Nollekens, R.A. E.4379–1920.

**111** Monument to the three Captains, Westminster Abbey. Photograph: *Warburg Institute.*

**112** Design for the monument to Mary Irby, Whiston, Northamptonshire, by Joseph Nollekens, R.A. E.4361–1920.

**113** Monument to Mary Irby, Whiston, Northamptonshire. Photograph: *Mr. Bruce Bailey.*

**114** Design for the monument to Mrs. Coke, Tittleshall, Norfolk, by Joseph Nollekens, R.A. E.4358–1920.

**115** Monument to Mrs. Coke, Tittleshall, Norfolk. Photograph: *National Monuments Record.*

**116** Design for the monument to the Duke of Dorset, Withyham, Sussex, by Joseph Nollekens, R.A. E.4378–1920.

**117** Monument to the Duke of Dorset, Withyham, Sussex. Photograph: *National Monuments Record.*

**118** Design for the monument to Ann Whytell, Westminster Abbey, by John Bacon, R.A. E.1548–1931.

**119** Monument to Ann Whytell, Westminster Abbey. Photograph: *Warburg Institute.*

**120** Design for the monument to Captain Rogers, Lymington, Hampshire, by John Bacon, R.A. E.1547–1931.

**121** Monument to Captain Rogers, Lymington, Hampshire. Photograph: *Mr. Bruce Bailey.*

**122** Design for the monument to Admiral Sir George Pocock, Westminster Abbey, by John Bacon, R.A. E.1534–1931.

**123** Monument to Admiral Sir George Pocock, Westminster Abbey. Photograph: *National Monuments Record.*

**124** Design for the sculpture in the tympanum of the pediment of East India House, London, by John Bacon, R.A. E.1953–1889.

**125** Design for the monument to William Mason, Westminster Abbey, by John Bacon, R.A. E.1529–1931.

**126** Monument to William Mason, Westminster Abbey. Photograph: *Warburg Institute.*

**127** Design for the memorial to Lord Nelson, St. Paul's Cathedral, by James Paine the Younger. 8520.10.

**128** Design for the monument to Charles James Fox, Westminster Abbey, by Thomas Stothard, R.A. 7344.

**129** Design for a colossal statue of Britannia at Greenwich, by John Flaxman, R.A. E.950–1965.

**130** View of Greenwich, with the proposed statue of Britannia, by William Blake.

**131** Design for the "National Cup", by John Flaxman, R.A. D.379–1886.

**132** Design for the monument to Dr. Warton, Winchester Cathedral, by John Flaxman, R.A. 7345.

**133** Monument to Dr. Warton, Winchester Cathedral. Photograph: *National Monuments Record.*

**134** Design for the monument to General Simcoe, Exeter Cathedral, by Joseph Flaxman, R.A. 8967A.

**135** Monument to General Simcoe, Exeter Cathedral. Photograph: *Mr. Bruce Bailey.*

**136** Design for the monument to Captain Cooke, Westminster Abbey, by John Bacon the Younger. 8417.7.

**137** Monument to Captain Cooke, Westminster Abbey. Photograph: *National Monuments Record.*

*List of Illustrations*

**138** Design for the monument to Anna Rhodes, St. James's, Hampstead Road, London, by John Bacon the Younger.   E.1556–1931.

**139** Monument to Anna Rhodes, St. James's, Hampstead Road, London. Photograph: *National Monuments Record*.

**140** Designs for decorative plaques, by John Gibson, R.A.   D.1333–1898.

**141** Design for the monument to Lord Nelson in Trafalgar Square, London, by L. W. Collmann.   8595s.

**142** The equestrian statue of the Duke of Wellington, for the Arch at Hyde Park Corner, by James Wyatt the Younger. E.1896(146)–1948.

**143** The equestrian statue of the Duke of Wellington, formerly at Hyde Park Corner, and now at Aldershot, by M. C. Wyatt. Photograph: *author*.

**144** Design for the monument to the Duke of Wellington, St. Paul's Cathedral, by Alfred Stevens.   1119–1884.

**145** Competition model for the monument to the Duke of Wellington, St. Paul's Cathedral, by Alfred Stevens. 44–1878.

**146** Monument to the Duke of Wellington, St. Paul's Cathedral. Photograph: *Royal Commission on Historical Monuments (England)*.

**147** Design for the memorial to the Prince Consort, Kensington Gardens, by Sir G. G. Scott, R.A.   E.2601–1962.

**148a** The Albert Memorial, Kensington Gardens. Photograph: *National Monuments Record*.

**148b** Detail of the Albert Memorial; sculptured group 'Asia' by J. H. Foley, R.A. Photograph: *National Monuments Record*.

**149** Design for a glass-house to enclose the Albert Memorial, by J. Wills, drawn by A. Bedborough. Library Photograph 77,200.

**150** Design for the Albert Memorial by James Fergusson, F.R.S. D.1094–1886.

**151** Design for the Albert Memorial by Joseph Durham, A.R.A.   9150F.

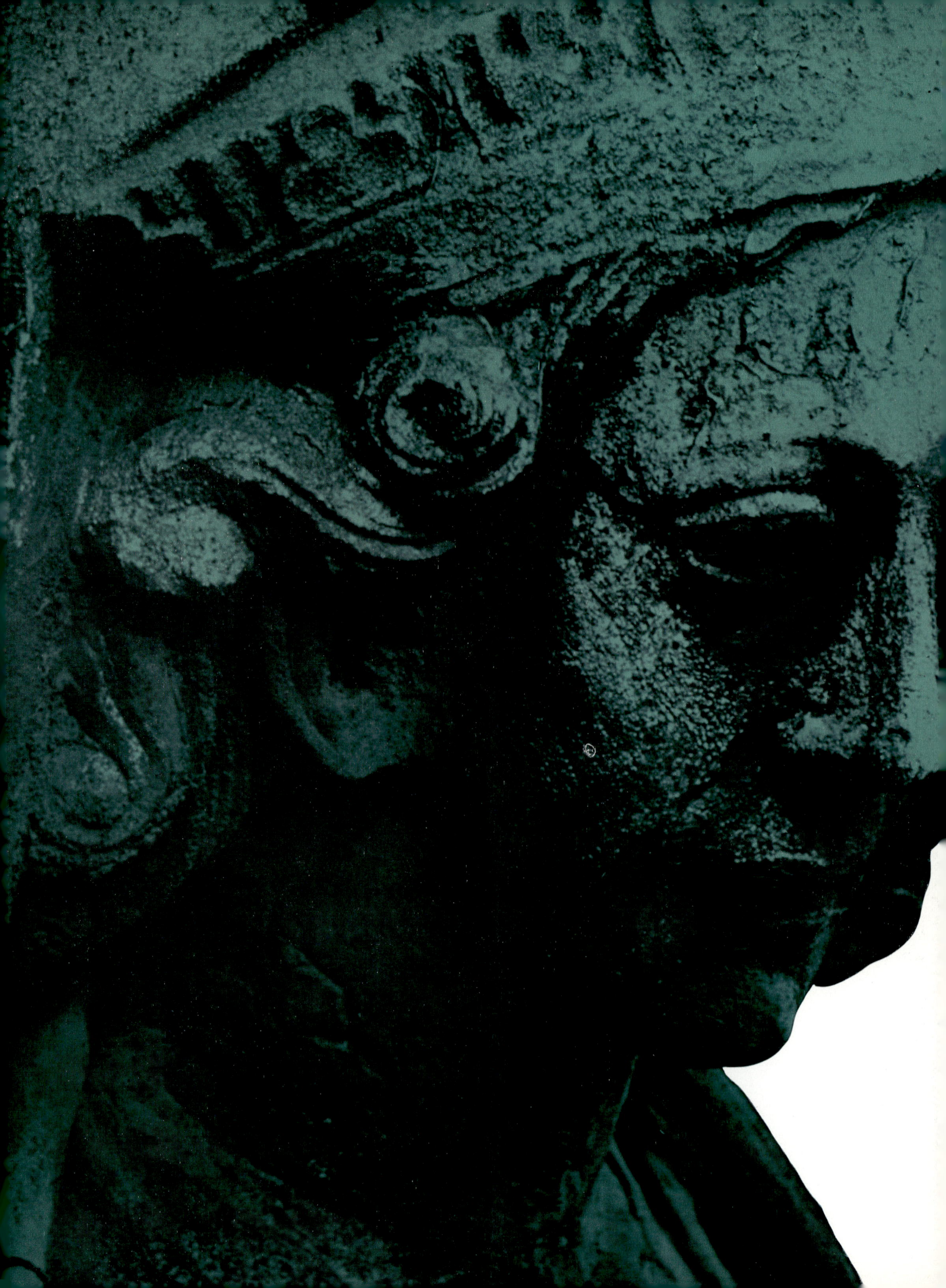

# Introduction

## I

DURING THE MIDDLE AGES sculpture in England was a facet of a lively and flourishing art, which was in one way or another nearly always ecclesiastical, whether it was concerned with architecture, painting, sculpture or stained glass. The carved decoration of cathedrals and parish churches was closely linked with the architecture, as at Wells where the cathedral façade was a great array of brightly coloured figures of saints standing in tiers of niches, or as at Lincoln where the beautiful figure, called Queen Margaret of Valois, c. 1300, looks down from the south side of the choir (fig. 1). There were flashes of earthy humour in the minor sculpture of such details as gargoyles and roof-bosses. Within the churches, the wood-carved ornament on misericords, poppy-heads and bench-ends showed biblical figures, genrescenes such as a scolding wife, or a schoolboy being birched, or perhaps an illustration of a well-known fable; and there were also the carved fonts, altar-pieces and so on.

The deliberate policy of destruction of religious imagery after the Reformation and during the Commonwealth, has fortunately left relatively untouched the large number of recumbent effigies on tombs. These were sometimes of bronze, particularly for royal monuments, for instance that of Henry III (died 1272), by William Torel at Westminster, or that to the Black Prince (died 1376) in Canterbury Cathedral; and in stone, or alabaster from the quarries of Derbyshire and Nottinghamshire, for the medieval nobility. With the rise of the middle classes during the 16th century, these monuments became much more numerous; there was also a greater use of colour and gilding, and the display of heraldry became increasingly lavish and prominent. It was just at this time that the influence of the Renaissance began to be felt in this country.

The Reformation, and the dissolution of the monasteries by Henry VIII, caused a complete change in traditional patronage, and the demand for sculpture of a purely religious significance, like much else, disappeared. The climate of the British Isles being what it is, there was never any great desire for garden or other outdoor sculpture in the form of fountains and decorative figures; so from the middle of the 16th century a major part of the energies of English sculptors was directed to the lucrative business of producing sepulchral monuments.[1]

---

[1] This period has been covered by Sir J. G. Mann's "English Church Monuments 1536–1625", in *Walpole Society*, Volume 21, 1933.

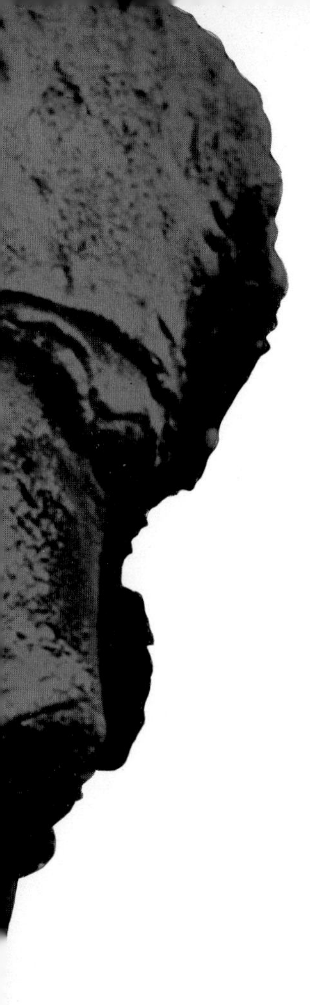

Fig. 1
"Queen Margaret of Valois",
Lincoln Cathedral. c. 1300.
(Photo: *National Monuments Record*)

The recumbent effigies began to vary their attitudes; they propped themselves on one elbow, or rose and knelt, husband and wife often facing each other over prayer-desks, as may be seen on the monuments to the Sondes family at Throwley in Kent (fig. 2),[1] which are early examples on free-standing tombs and, according to Hasted, were originally surmounted by canopies; and on the mural monument to the Pitman family (1627), at Woodbridge, Suffolk, where they are arranged in tiers.

From about this time, we begin to find the names of some of the craftsmen, Gerard Johnson,[2] for instance; William Cure and his son Cornelius; and Epiphanius Evesham who was, says Dr. Whinney, 'the first English-born sculptor of any personality'.[3] Alabaster, now losing its purity of colour as the quarries became worked out, was gradually being replaced by the imported white marble from Italy which was popular with the craftsmen of the London School; this was comprised very largely of foreigners from the Low Countries who were bringing new ideas with them. As figures of saints, angels and other religious sculptures were now no longer in favour, a new symbolism emerged, with representations of the Virtues, and Death was seen in many guises—skulls, bones, hour-glasses, urns, scythes, and mourning cherubs were all brought into service.

A few agreements exist for the erection of monuments of the 16th and early 17th centuries. There is at this date often no mention of a drawn design. When Vertue described Henry VIII's monument at Windsor (designed by Benedetto da Rovezzano for Cardinal Wolsey) which was destroyed in 1646, he used the words "true draught" and "moddel" when referring to the original design.[4] These words are ambiguous because the "draught" could well have been a three-dimensional representation, and this is probably confirmed by a description in Vasari's life of Baccio Bandinelli, "fece ancora un bellissimo modello di legno, e le figure de cera, per una sepoltura al Rè d'Ingilterra, la quale non sortì poi l'effetto da Baccio, ma fù date a Benedetto da Rovezzano scultore, che le fece di metallo".[5]

Contracts for two royal monuments still exist, those to the Countess of Richmond, and to her grandson, Henry VIII. The contract for the tomb of the Countess of Richmond, mother of Henry VII, in Henry VII's

[1] Dame Cycyllye Sondes (died 1584), and Sir Thomas Sondes (died 1592). The effigies suffered at the time of the Commonwealth when their hands and feet were lopped off.
[2] Garret Jansen of Amsterdam, who came to London in 1567.
[3] Margaret Whinney, *Sculpture in England 1530–1840* (Pelican History of Art), 1964.
[4] Vertue Note-books, I, *Walpole Society*, Volume 18, 1930, page 41.
[5] *Delle Vite de più Eccelenti Pittori, Scultori et Architetti* by Giorgio Vasari, Volume I, Part 3, Bologna, 1647, page 427. Benedetto da Rovezzano's marble sarcophagus was eventually incorporated in the tomb of Lord Nelson in the crypt of St. Paul's Cathedral.

   Early foreign designs in the Department of Prints and Drawings include those by (possibly) Il Bambaia for a monument to Gaston de Foix (died 1512), by Leone Leoni for the monument to Jacopo de' Medici, Marquis of Marignano, in Milan Cathedral, completed 1564, and Guglielmo della Porta for the monument in St. Peter's, Rome, to Pope Paul III (died 1549).

Fig. 2
The Sondes monuments, Throwley, Kent. c. 1584 and 1618.
(Photo: *Author*)

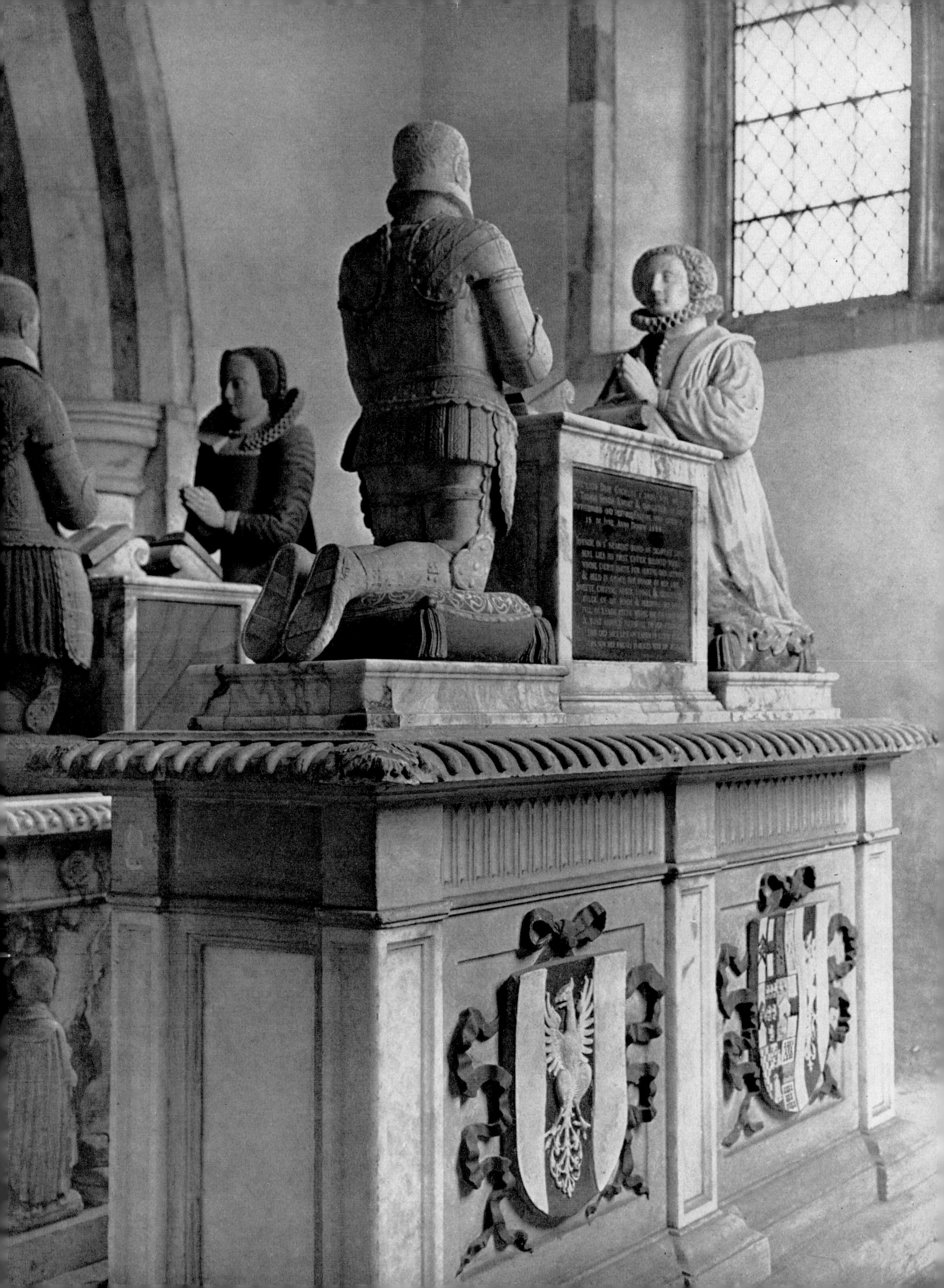

Chapel at Westminster, is preserved among the muniments of St. John's College, Cambridge.[1] The Countess of Richmond died in 1509 at Westminster, and probate of her will, dated 1508, was granted in October 1512. Nearly a year before this, however, and two years after the Countess's death, her executors contracted with "Petir Thoryson of florence graver" to erect a monument to her memory. This contract like others of the 16th century went into very great detail, and showed also that a design had been drawn:

"This endenture betwene the Right Reuerende faders in Criste Richard Bisshop of Winton, John Bishop of Roffen, Charles Seymour, knighte, lorde Herbert, Chamberleyn to our soueraigne lord the king, Thomas Lovell, knight, Henry Marney, knight, John Seint John, knight, Henry Horneby and Hugh Asheton, clerkes and Excecutours . . . and Petir Thoryson of florence graver on that other partie; Witnesseth that the said Petir hath couenaunted and bargayned to make . . . A Tabernacle of copper with an ymage lying in the same Tabernacle and a best called an yas [? yale] lying at the fote of the same Tabernacle, With like pillers, bases, chaptrels, gablettes, crokkettes, anelled, fynials, orbs, housings, Scocheons, graven with porte-coleyses and Roses, all of copper and in the like makyng length and brede according to A patron drawen in a Cloth the which is sealed with the seale of the said Petir and subscribed at the oon end with his owne hand, and is remayning in the custodye of the said executours."

This part of the contract refers to the recumbent effigy of the Countess who lies with her feet on a yale, under a horizontal bronze canopy.

Torrigiano also agreed to make the tomb-chest

"of good, clene and hable towche stone with all such workmanship in the same as shalbe according to a patrone drawen and kerven in Tymbre and signed with thand and sealed with the seale of the said Petir and remaynyng in thandes of the said executours And shall also grave or do to be graven wele, clenly, werkemanly and sufficiently viij sufficient and clenly scucheons in such places of the same Tombe or case and with such armes as shalbe assigned by the said executours, And also at his owne costes shall make or do to be made wele clenly and werkemanly such borders graven all of copper about the creest, lydger or edge of the same Tombe with such scriptures the letters thereof graven outwardes as shalbe assigned by the same executours . . . And also that the same Tabernacle, ymage, beest, tombe or case and other the premisses shalbe wele and sufficiauntly wrought made graven and gilded after the fourme abouesaid and also shalbe sufficiauntly framed ioyned fixed and set up in the south Isle of the Kinges new chapell at Westminster outhisside the first day of feūer the which shall be in the yere of our lord M¹.Vᶜ.xij."

---

[1] R. S. Scott, "On the Contract for the Tomb of the Lady Margaret Beaufort . . ." In *Archaeologia*, Volume 66, 1915, pages 365–76.

The executors agreed to pay the sculptor four hundred pounds, but held "Petir and Leonard fristobaldi and John Cawalcant merchauntes of florence" as sureties for five hundred pounds in case the work was not completed, and then the contract ended with "In witness whereof the said parties to these endentures chaungeably have set their seales yoven the xxiij day of Novembre the third yere of the Reigne of King Henry the viij[th] permi Piero Torrigiani Schultore fiorintino."

Thus from this contract we learn that there were drawn designs for the figure of the Countess of Richmond, the architectural niche in which she lies, and the tomb-chest, as well as a wooden model for the latter, but there is no indication that they were from the hand of Torrigiano. From other documents at St. John's College[1] it would seem that they were not, but that the sculptor was working from the designs of some-one else, who first made three drawings of alternative schemes, and finally the two copies of the design selected:

"firste for making iij patrons in paper for her Tombe eche of theym diuerse facions   summa   13s. 4d."

"Item for ij patrons made in cloth beyng the length of her tombe wrought with colours whereof the one Remayned in the executours handes and the other in Master Petirs handes at xl s. the pece . . . £4. Summa totalis £4 13s. 4d."

"Memorandum payd by Morgan Mores on monnday the iij[de] daye of nouember the iij[rd] yere of the raigne of Kyng Henrie the viij[th] for his boot hyre from London to Mortlake and frome thens to London Whyen he and the franchmen was with my lord chamberlayne with the pateron of my ladeys Towme   2s. 4d."

"Memorandum that I Maynarde Vewike of London paynter haue ressauid the vij daie of february the thrid yere of the reigne of kynge Henry the viij of the Reuerend father in God John bushop of Rochester thre poundes sterlyng in parte of payement of a more some for a certen table and ij patrones drawen for my ladie the kynges grandamm tombe . . ."

"First paide the xxviij day of December in the iiij yere of the reigne of King Henry the viij[th] to M. Garter the king of haroldes for makyng and declaryng my ladies armes in viij scochyns for my ladies tombe and deliuerede to the florentyne   13s. 4d."

"Item paide the xxij[th] day of Junij in the v[th] year of the reigne of Kinge Henry the viii[th] to Maynarde the paynter for makinge the picture and image of the seide ladye   33s. 4d."

"Item paide to the seid Maynard the xvj[th] day of Marche in the fifte yere of the reigne of the seid Kynge for making of diuerse patrons for my ladies tombe.   £4. 13. 4d."

---

[1] R. S. Scott, *loc. cit.*

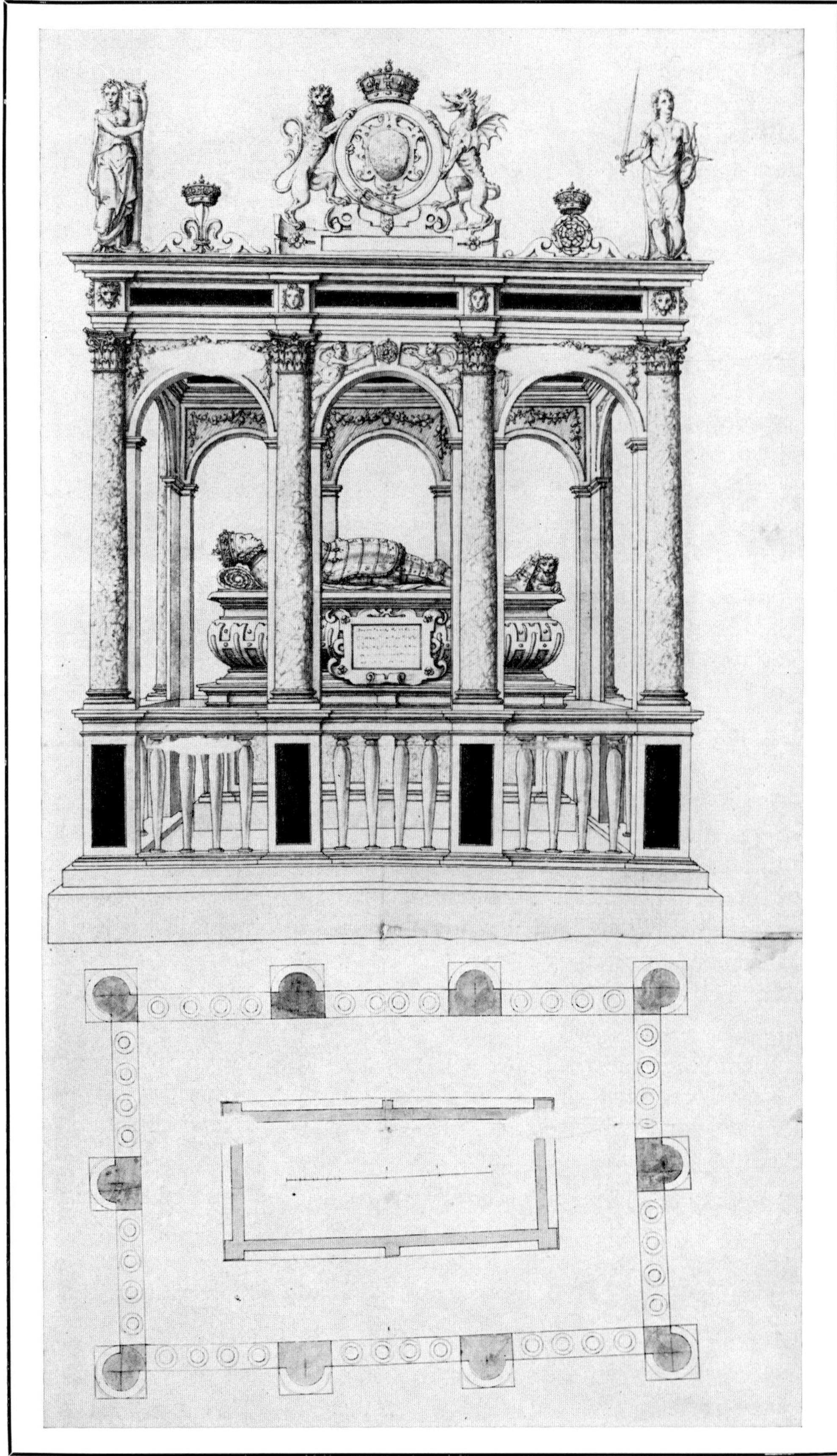

Fig. 3
Design for the monument to
Edward VI (d. 1553), perhaps
by Cornelius Cure.
(*Bodleian Library, Oxford*)

While the tomb of Henry vii's mother was being made by Torrigiano Henry viii turned his attention to the monument of his father. The first design for this was not suitable; there is in the British Museum[1] a manuscript "Estimate of ye Charge for ye makynge of a Tomb for Kinge H. 7, to be erected in his Chappell in Westminster, wch Plott was afterward disliked by Kinge H. viii, & altered accordinge as it now standes, in an⁰.———." It is not known what this monument was really like, but there were to be recumbent effigies of Henry vii and his Queen, as well as a kneeling statue of the King and four kneeling "Lordes", to be of bronze, and twelve little figures around the tomb also. Models of these figures were to be made of wood by "Lawrence Ymber, Karver" and among other craftsmen who estimated for the monument were "Humfray Walker, Founder", "Nicholas Ewen, Coppersmithe & Gilder", "John Bell, John Maynard, Peintres", "Robert Vertue, Robart Jenins, & John Lobons, ye Kinges iij M$^r$. Masons".

In 1512 Torrigiano signed the contract for the present monument to Henry vii which was completed before 1518, when Henry viii decided that the same sculptor should make a larger monument for himself and Katherine of Aragon. Another contract, dated January 5th, 1518, was drawn up;[2] in this it was stated that Torrigiano under the direction of Cardinal Wolsey "shall wtyn the space of foure yeres next comyng aftr the date of this Endenture make or cause to be made & pfyghtly fynysshed in alle things as it shall appteyne anothir Tombe or sculptur' of like whit marebill & of black toucheston of the same our said most dradd sov$^r$aign Lorde the Kyng and the most excellent princesse Kateryn his most derist Quene & wif . . ." The monument was to be greater "by the iiij$^{th}$ parte than ys the said Tombe whiche the saide Petre before made & fynysshed for the same Kyng Henry the vij$^{th}$ . . .", and Torrigiano was to make a "patrone or example" which would probably have been a model rather than a drawing. As far as is known, nothing came of this monument (the contract is only a draft, and is not signed) which might later have been a source of some embarrassment to Henry viii at the time of his divorce from Katherine.

In 1581 two craftsmen of the Burton-on-Trent School undertook to make the monument at Somerton, Oxfordshire, to Thomas Fermor, who had died during the previous year. There was no mention of a drawing in the contract, but the tomb itself was described in great detail, and still followed the conventional stock pattern of the early part of the century. The figures were also from stock designs, and the

---

[1] Reproduced in *The History and Antiquities of the Abbey Church of St. Peter, Westminster* by E. W. Brayley, and J. P. Neale, Volume 1, 1818, page 55.

[2] "Transcript of a Draft of an Indenture of Covenants for the erecting of a Tomb to the Memory of King Henry the Eighth, and Queen Katherine his wife, found among the Papers of Cardinal Wolsey, in the Chapter House at Westminster", *Archaeologia*, Volume 16, 1809, pages 84–8.

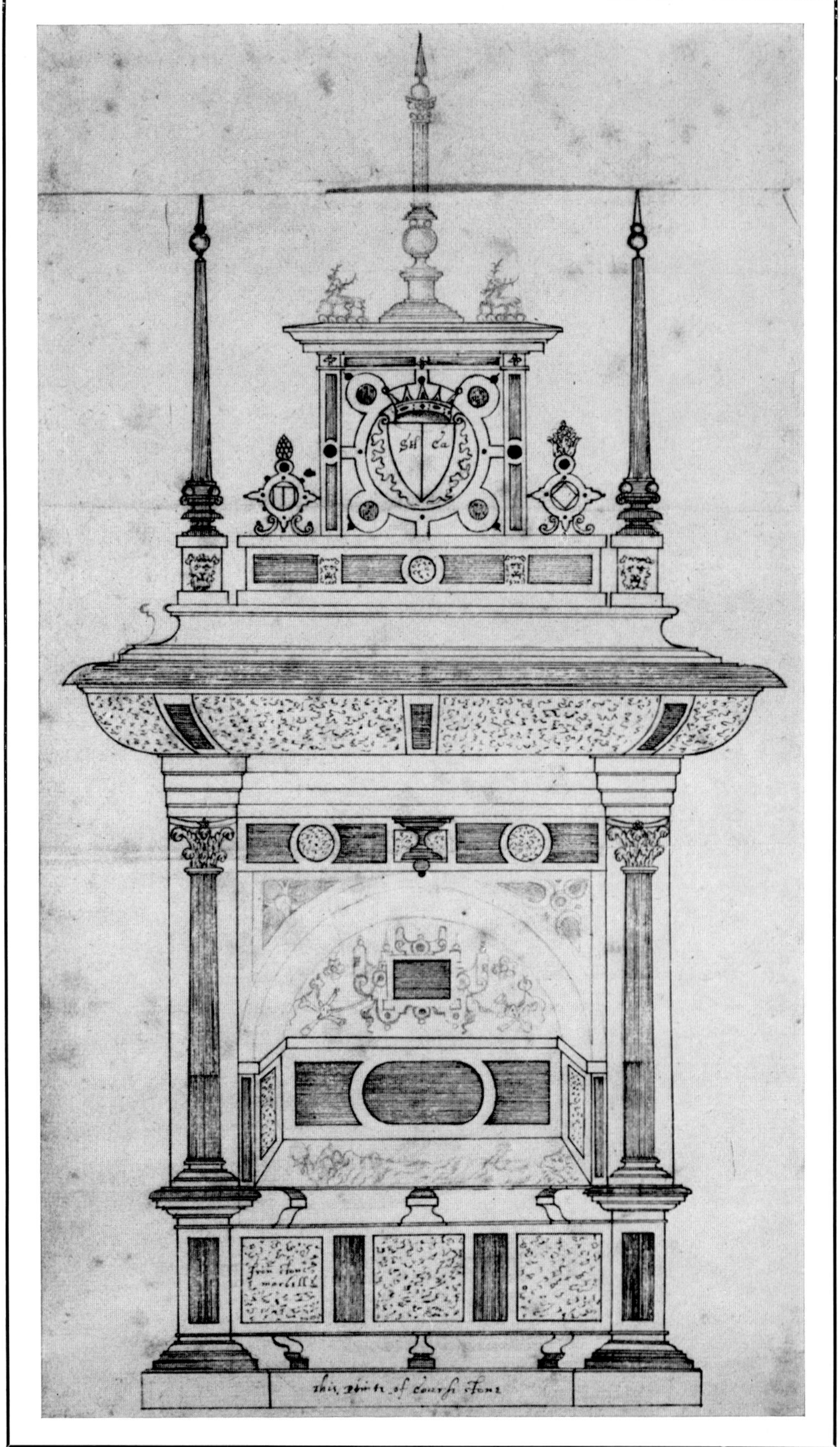

Fig. 4
Design for the monument to
Elizabeth, Countess of
Shrewsbury, Derby Cathedral.
c. 1607.
(*Smythson Collection, R.I.B.A.*)

agreement is interesting in that it shows the methods used by two crafts-men of the Burton School of alabaster workers.[1]

Richard Roiley and his son Gabriel,[2] "Tumbe" makers, agreed with Sir George Shirley, Bart., of Staunton Harold, executor of Thomas Fermor, "artyficially cunningly decently and substancially to devise, work, sett up, and p'fectly and fully finish at Somerton . . . before the Feaste of Pentecoste commonly called Witsontide next ensewinge ye date herof, at or neare ye grave of ye said Thomas Fermor there, a very faire Tumbe of very good faire well chosen and durable Alabaster stone, containeing in lengthe six foote and a halfe by ye standard, and of ye breadth of fower Feete by the standard, and of ye height of five Foote by ye standard, with two endes and one [*formerly* two, *but changed*][3] uttermost syde all throughe out adwrought gilded engraved portraited and sett forth all as hereafter enseweth:—That is to saie, ye said Richard and Gabriel Roiley . . . will worke . . . and place . . . on ye uppermoste p'te of ye said Tumbe . . . a very faire decent and well p'portioned picture or portraiture of a gentleman representing . . . Thomas Fermor wth furniture and ornaments in armour, and about his necke a double cheyne of gold wth creste and helmette under his head, with sword and dagger by his side, and a lion at his feete . . . and on . . . the uttermoste parte of the uppermoste parte . . . a decent and p'fect picture or portraiture of a faire gentlewoman wth a Frenchehood, edge and abilliment, wth all other apparell furniture, jewells ornamentes and thinges in all respectes usuall, decent, and semely, for a gentlewoman."

The Roileys further agreed to put on the side of the tomb-chest "decent and usuall pictures of, or for, one sonne or [*sic*] two daughters . . . wth their severall names of Baptism over or under ye said picture, severally and orderly wth scutcheons in their handes, whereof ye said sonne to be pictured in armour and as liveinge, and ye one of ye said daughters to be pictured in decent order and as liveinge, and ye other daughter to be pictured as dieinge in ye cradle or swathes".

The agreement then continued to list the heraldry to be displayed, the wording of the epitaph which was to be in "one rower of greate and faire gilt engraven letters", and to set down the arrangements for getting the sculpture from Burton to Somerton. For all of this Shirley agreed to pay the Roileys the "full somme of Forty poundes of lawful mony of England".

That this monument was to conform to the accepted pattern is

---

[1] *The Archaeological Journal*, Volume 8, 1851, pages 185, 186.

[2] "It would appear that the Royleys stifled all competition and their practice of constant repetition quickly brought about a decline in their artistic qualities as can be seen in the later monuments. By 1590 the standard of Burton workmanship was deplorable . . ."
S. A. Jeavons, F.S.A., "The Monumental Effigies of Staffordshire, Part III", *Transactions of the Birmingham Archaeological Society*, Volume 71, 1955, page 1.

[3] This alteration might indicate that the original proposal had been for the monument to be free-standing, but that this was later changed so that it might be placed against the wall of the church.

conveyed by the statement that the figures of the son and daughters as weepers on the side of the tomb-chest were to be the "usuall pictures", and it is also apparent that the recumbent effigies of husband and wife were not going to be portraits, but only representative figures; portraits, in fact, are not often to be found until the Restoration.

It would seem that drawn designs ("plotts") began to come into more general use during the 16th century, although as has been the custom since, three-dimensional models were made as well.[1] Vertue saw[2] a "draught of a Monument—for King Edw. 6.—on a sheet of paper. his figure cumbent laying on his back on a tomb stone, and a skrreen of iron rails round it. on the back of this paper is writ by the hand of Ld Burghly 2 plotts for the Monumt of K. Ed. 6 and Qu. Mary." There is a large design for the monument to King Edward VI in the Bodleian Library, Oxford (fig. 3).[3] It is by an unidentified artist who may have been Cornelius Cure.

The monument to the Earls of Sussex at Boreham, Essex, was ordered by the will of Thomas, the third Earl (died 1583), in which he also directed that the bodies of his parents and grandparents should be removed to Boreham from London. Among his papers Vertue found an "agreement made by Sr. Christ. Wray . . . for erecting and finishing a Tomb or Monument in memorial to the late Earle of Sussex . . . his monument ordered . . . and directed before his death of white alabaster. touch & other stones. according to the plott thereof".[4] An early "plott" to survive is in the Smythson collection for the monument to Elizabeth, Countess of Shrewsbury ("Bess of Hardwick")[5] (died 1607), in All Saints' Cathedral, Derby (fig. 4);[6] while a design played an important part in the agreement for the monument to Roger, 5th Earl of Rutland (died 1612) and his wife Elizabeth (the daughter of Sir Philip Sidney), at Bottesford, in Leicestershire. The agreement[7] was between William Saxton of London, and "Nicholas Johnson[8] of the parish of St. Saviours in the borough of Southwarke in ye Countie of London Tomb maker". Johnson was to erect within one year, in 1619, a "Monument or Tomb for the late Erle of Rutland and the Countess his late wife in such manner Fashion and forme and of such stuffe according to the plott thereof as is already drawen sett forth

---

[1] For an early 17th-century monument Vertue saw "a busto-Moddel as big as the Life. in bak'd clay of Isaac Oliver (painter), only the head with the ruff under it. suppos'd to be the Moddel for his Monument which was lost in the ruins of the Fire of London. (he was buried in the Church in Blackfryers.)." Vertue Note-books, I, *Walpole Society*, Volume 18, 1930, page 68.

[2] Vertue Note-books, III, *Walpole Society*, Volume 30, 1955, page 113.

[3] Gough Maps 45, no. 63. See *Architectural Drawings in the Bodleian Library*, Bodleian Picture Book No. 7, with an introduction by Howard Colvin, 1952.

[4] Vertue Note-books, IV, *Walpole Society*, Volume 24, 1936, page 143.

[5] Reproduced as Plate 19b to "English Church Monuments 1536–1625" by Sir J. G. Mann, *loc. cit.*, and is now in the collection of the Royal Institute of British Architects.

[6] Plate 19a, *loc. cit.*

[7] Lady Victoria Manners, "The Rutland Monuments in Bottesford Church", *Art Journal*, 1903, pages 335, 336.

[8] Nicholas Johnson was the son of Gerard Johnson.

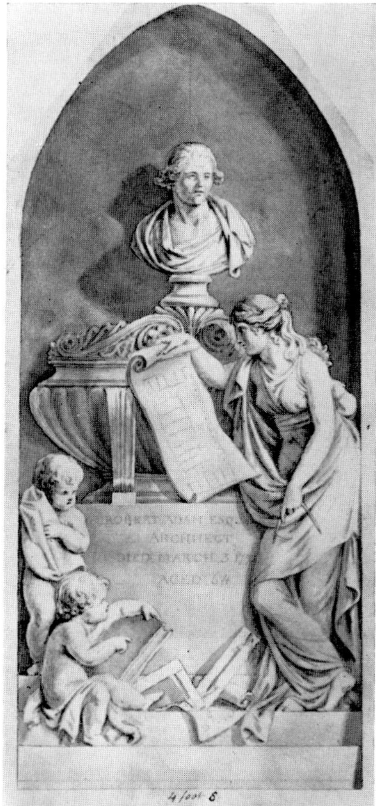

Fig. 5

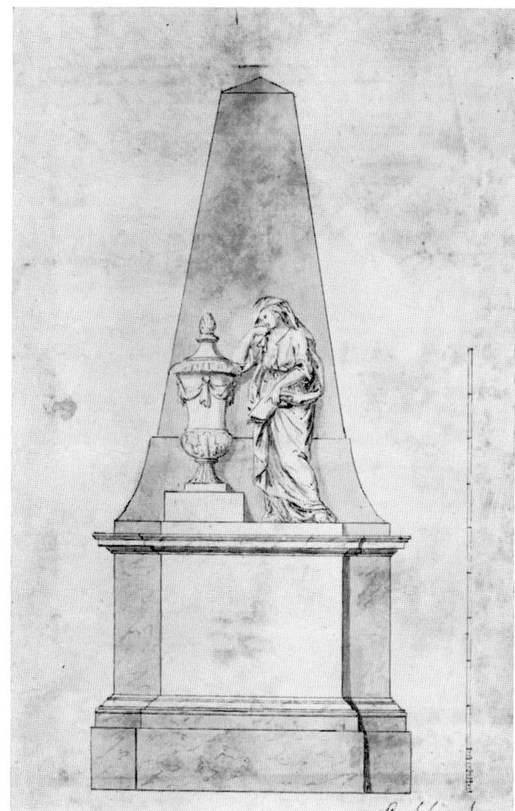

Fig. 6

Fig. 5
Unexecuted design by Joseph
Nollekens, R.A., for a monument to
Robert Adam, probably intended
for Westminster Abbey. c. 1792.

Fig. 6
Design by Peter Scheemakers, for
the monument to Mrs. Cox,
Kilkenny Cathedral. d. 1746.

and shewen by the said Nicholas Johnson to . . . William Saxton w'ch plott is now in the Custodie and Keepinge of the said William Saxton . . . And it is the trew entent and meanyng of both the said parties . . . that all such Cullours as are . . . culloured black in the said plott to be of Touchstone in the said Tombe. And that all the white cullours therein to be of Allabaster. And that all the Redd Cullours therein to be of Rance. And all the yellowe cullours to be gylded of rich gold . . ."

A late 16th-century drawing which, though not for a carved monument, is of importance as it is a rare design for a tomb incorporating three engraved brass figures by Gerard Johnson.[1] The monument is to John Gage and his two wives Elizabeth and Margaret, in West Firle church, Sussex, where it was erected in 1595 by order of John Gage himself (he did not die until 1598). Of particular interest are the many remarks about the work which both Johnson and Gage wrote in the margins of the drawing.

Johnson noted that "This Stone to be of Marble enlayed, the pictures and Stouchions wth the epitaphe to be of Brasse. Md that all the marble appteyninge to thes thre platts are to be of Mr. Gage his

[1] "The Gage Monuments, Firle" by W. H. Godfrey in *Sussex Notes and Queries*, Volume 2, 1928–29, pages 175–7, and plate facing page 176. This drawing and others by Gerard Johnson are still in the possession of the family.

owne, and I woulde have the p̄fitt Length and Bredth of the Largest Stone wch must serve for this purpose sent upp wth all the inscriptions that must be in everye Tombe."

John Gage took pains to ensure that his wives were shown dressed as he wished them to be and, as his comment shows, he sent the sculptor a box containing a head-dress so that it could be used as a model, as well as suggesting alterations to his wives' dresses:

"Where you have sett owte my two wyves wth long heare wyered, my request is that they shall be both attired wth frenche hoodes and cornetts some heare shewed under the cornetts, the pattren of the cornett I have sent yō by this berer in a boxe bowed and dressed as it should stand upon their heades. their gownes to be made lose and not girded wth no girdle wthowt vardingales and close before and to be so longe as may cover some p̄te of their feete . . ."

From other inscriptions it seems that this drawing passed between John Gage and Gerard Johnson two or three times before everything was settled.

Johnson, however, was not the only man who, primarily a carver, produced an engraved brass; that to Sir Edward Filmer (died 1638) and his wife,[1] at East Sutton, Kent, is signed by Edward Marshall (1598–1675), Master-mason to the King from 1660, and father of the better known Joshua Marshall.[2]

The College of Arms in London owns a book of sketches by Maximilian Colt (died after 1645),[3] who designed the monument to Queen Elizabeth I in Westminster Abbey. But on the whole these 16th- and early 17th-century designs are extremely rare.

Besides designs, however, there are still in existence two important documents relating to the early years of the 17th century. They are the account-book and the note-book of Nicholas Stone (c. 1587–1647),[4] in Sir John Soane's Museum, and together they constitute an extremely valuable record of the output of a sculptor who was Master-mason to James I and Charles I. But for the work of this period generally, these two books are isolated and notable examples of great importance.

Until the later 17th century it is unusual to find a signature on a

---

[1] Reproduced as Plate 37 in the *Catalogue of Brasses and Incised Slabs* by Muriel Clayton, Victoria and Albert Museum, 1929.

[2] "The Sculptor and the Brass" by Mrs. Esdaile in *Transactions of the Monumental Brass Society*, December, 1935, pages 49–56; "Signed Monuments in Kentish Churches" by Rupert Gunnis in *Archaeologia Cantiana*, Volume 62, 1949, page 76. Mrs. Esdaile lists other brasses which she considered to be the work of sculptors, among whom were Epiphanius Evesham and Nicholas Stone. It has been suggested that Edward Marshall was the brother of the 17th-century engraver William Marshall, but M. Corbett and M. Norton in *Engraving in England in the Sixteenth and Seventeenth Centuries: The Reign of Charles I*, 1964, can find no evidence to support this.

[3] The tomb of the 7th Earl of Shrewsbury is reproduced in colour as the frontispiece to *English Church Monuments 1510–1840* by Mrs. Esdaile, 1946.

[4] W. L. Spiers, "The Note-book and Account Book of Nicholas Stone", *Walpole Society*, Volume 7, 1919.

piece of sculpture, and consequently the entries in Stone's account-book are of great help in attributing work by Stone which otherwise would be unknown, such, for instance, as the following which relates to his monument to Lady Digges, at Chilham in Kent.[1]

"Agreed with the Right Wor¹¹ Ser Dudly Diges of Chellem in Kent Knight this 25th of August 1631 for to make and set up 1 monument in a new Chapell now to be Bulte by him and that I have geven order and derickins to the workmen: . . . the monement is to be a pillar blak and whit marbell with an orne on the tope thar of and at the bases on the pedestall to set 4 Status of the vertues for which he is to paye the some of 150£ . . ."[2]

If only there were more books like these by other sculptors (perhaps there are, but they have not yet been discovered), they would also be very helpful in tracing monuments and sculptors so far not recognised, and they would probably assist in putting names to those 17th-century designs which have survived.

[1] W. L. Spiers, *loc. cit.*, page 85.
[2] A typical pre-war attitude to renaissance monuments is revealed by "an unhappy group (which should be removed) of four white figures sitting round a black column, in memory of Lady Digges". Arthur Mee, *Kent*, 1936.

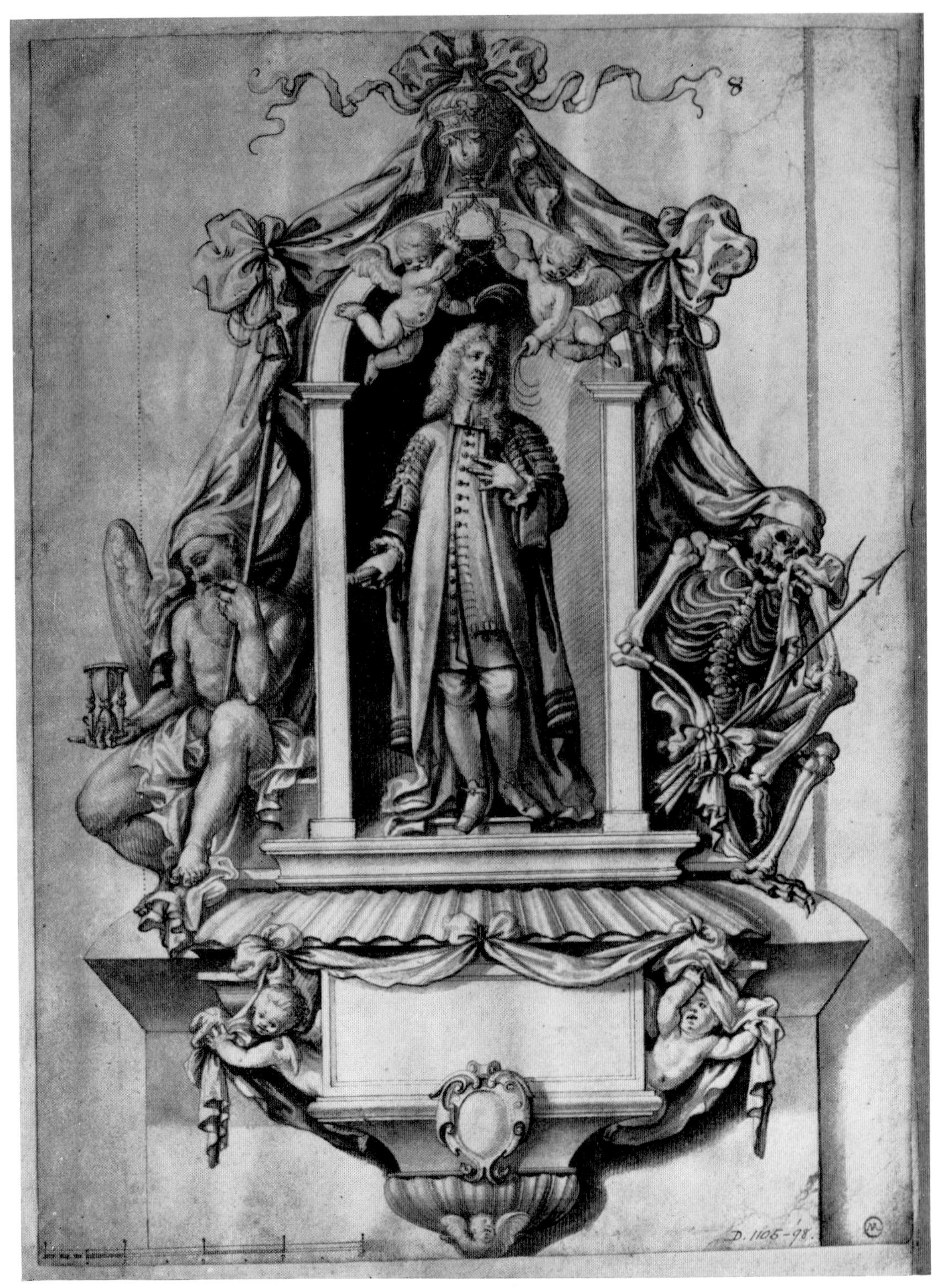



14

## II

THE PLATES IN THIS BOOK have been drawn from a total collection of more than one thousand drawings for English sculpture in the Department of Prints and Drawings, and this is probably the largest single group of them in existence. For more than one hundred years the Museum has been collecting these drawings as examples of design, although during this time very little was known of most of them— neither the name of the sculptor who drew them, nor the location of the finished work. This is not really surprising for very few of them were signed, which meant that there was nothing to help identification except an approximation of date; and it must be remembered that throughout the British Isles there are many thousands of monuments and other sculpture of the 17th and 18th centuries. Almost until the Second World War work of this period was largely ignored, and such photographs that were taken were nearly always of a medieval knight, a roof-boss, a capital, or some other piece of gothic carving.

A pioneer worker in the field of renaissance sculpture in England during this time of indifference and neglect, when even the Royal Commission on Historical Monuments ignored anything after 1714,[1] was Mrs. Katharine Esdaile, and her book *English Monumental Sculpture since the Renaissance*, published as long ago as 1927, brought many new sculptors and their work to the attention of the general public for the first time.

But not until 1953 was there any way in which the Museum could begin to identify the drawings in its possession, except for a small number which were for well-known monuments, and not even all of these were recognised. In 1953, however, the late Rupert Gunnis published his *Dictionary of British Sculptors 1660–1851*, which covers the whole of the period represented by our designs. Gunnis's book, which at once received the status of a standard work, was important in three ways—it listed hundreds of sculptors, many of whom were completely unknown hitherto; all of their signed work which Gunnis had found; and the location of this work. Thus, at last, it became possible to start the long task of attempting to identify the Museum's sculpture drawings.

The first thing which had to be done was to recognise the drawings by the various artists concerned. Some of the draughtsmen, for instance Rysbrack, with his mannered style of drawing and scribble to indicate lettering, were instantly recognisable (see fig. 63). It was surprising to note some of their former attributions, a Rysbrack chimney-piece turned up as by Thomas Sandby, while Henry Keene was credited with a chimney-piece which is probably by Scheemakers. This sorting has, to a large extent, now been achieved, though there are many drawings of the late 17th century on scraps of paper, which are not

Fig. 7
Design by William Stanton, perhaps for the monument to Sir Thomas Wendy, Haslingfield, Cambridge-shire. c. 1673.

---

[1] The Royal Commission now has discretion to consider work up to 1850.

proving to be a simple matter.[1] However, this work has been comparatively easy when compared with that of trying to identify the finished sculpture to which the designs relate. In some cases, such as William Kent's designs (although originally attributed to Rysbrack) for the monuments to Sir Isaac Newton and Earl Stanhope in Westminster Abbey (figs. 48 & 51), there was no problem; but for the majority there was still the handicap of no adequate photographic reference material, and church guide-books largely made only passing reference, if any, to 18th-century monuments. Few of them were described in the detail necessary for our purpose.

Even today sculpture of the later 17th century and afterwards, is frequently treated with contempt. In the south transept of Elmley Castle church in Worcestershire are two monuments separated by about seventy years. The earlier, of c. 1631, is a pretty, quite conventional work in alabaster, with three recumbent effigies, to Sir William Savage, his son and wife. The current guide-book to the church describes this monument in detail and states that it is "one of the finest and most beautiful examples of alabaster carving in the world, and certainly the best in this country". However, only a few feet away on the other side of the transept, is a fine work by William Stanton of 1700, commemorating the first Earl of Coventry who died in 1699.

The Coventry monument was destined for the neighbouring church of Croome d'Abitot, where it would have been a fitting companion for Grinling Gibbons's carving there. Lord Coventry, though, in his old age married one of his servants named Grimes (or Graham). She commissioned Stanton to carve the memorial with its reclining figure under a large architectural canopy, and almost life-size angels, but Lady Coventry indulged in a spurious genealogy for herself, which she allowed Stanton to include among the heraldry. This infuriated her son-in-law, the second Earl, so much, that he refused to permit the erection of the monument in Croome.[2] As the guide-book complains Elmley church "became the repository of this white marble effigy . . . blocking what must have been a very beautiful stained glass window . . . It would not be putting it too strongly to say that the Church could well do without this marble monstrosity, which stands in such stark and brazen contrast to the delicate and exquisite Savage memorial on the opposite wall."[3]

The photographs in the useful collection of the National Monuments Record are filed topographically by county and parish, which thus made a systematic search through their prints so lengthy as to be quite impracticable. Rupert Gunnis was acutely aware of this problem, and

---

[1] As the collection has grown haphazardly, there are of course omissions, a noticeable absentee being Grinling Gibbons, and many sculptors of the early nineteenth century such as Chantrey are also not represented.
[2] John Physick, "Tracing the work of William Stanton", *Country Life Annual*, 1968, page 88.
[3] *The Story of Elmley Castle, Worcestershire* (2nd Edition), 1967, by the Rev. R. H. Lloyd, page 32.

began to build his own photograph library, with a classification by sculptor, to which he generously allowed the Department of Prints and Drawings to have unlimited access.[1] But even the most enthusiastic of collectors is not able to have everything photographed, so that with a few of the designs identification had to be made from some distinctive feature, such as the heraldry depicted.[2] However, hundreds of drawings still await further study.

The fact that there happens to be a drawing for a monument or sculpture does not, it must be remembered, mean that a finished work necessarily exists (fig. 5). The drawing may be only a very early preliminary design, or an alternative for a project which was considerably modified in its later stages, or even rejected altogether;[3] and often in the case of monuments many years could pass between the death of a person and the completion of the work.[4] In cases like this it has been a matter of chance whether the design happened to be recognised, albeit in some cases only tentatively. Examples which may be cited are the design for the monument to Marwood William Turner at Kirkleatham, Yorkshire (fig. 43), which was not executed from the proposal of James Gibbs, and the design for the monument, quite different in its final form, to Lord Somers, at North Mimms, Hertfordshire (fig. 75) by Peter Scheemakers. Rysbrack in some cases prepared up to six different designs of a monument for his client to select from.

A few of the drawings are inscribed with notes, or perhaps with an agreement between the sculptor and his client; one of these,[5] bearing *May 14th. 1747. This is the Model referred to in an Agreement bearing even Date herewith between me and Michael Rysbrack excepting the Arms are to be double* and signed by Thomas Pochin, gave little trouble once Gunnis's book had appeared. Although he did not list a monument to Thomas Pochin, there was one at Barkby, Leicestershire, to Charlotte Pochin. A short search revealed that Pochin had had two wives, Mary (died 1732) and Charlotte (died 1736), and that "In Memory of Them the said Tho: Pochin, Esq. caused this Monument to be erected, intending it both for them and himself", which explains Pochin's insistence, as recorded above, on two coats of arms instead of only the one originally suggested by Rysbrack (fig. 63).

[1] The Gunnis collection of photographs is now housed at the Courtauld Institute of Art; he bequeathed his collection of sculptors' drawings to the Victoria and Albert Museum, as well as many pieces of sculpture.

[2] This was the case with the drawing for the Wogan monument by John Francis Moore, at Redenhall, Norfolk, No. 4910.14.

[3] A drawing by Joseph Nollekens in the Douce Bequest to the Ashmolean Museum, Oxford, is on the back of a letter, "Lady Bowyer's Comp[ts] to Mr. Nollikins, and begs he will be so good as to call on her tomorrow Morn[g] before twelve o'clock, as she has just heard from her Son & some other friends that the smallest of the two designs is best approved, and she wishes to have some conversation with Mr. Nollikins about it". E4389–1920, in the Department of Prints and Drawings, is one of the designs for Sir George Bowyer's monument at Radley, Berkshire, and is inscribed *May the 29th 1801 Lady Bowyers with [. . .] recd. 130 Guineas.*

[4] See the bill dated 1802 for the monument to Henry Kent at Potterne who died in 1769, on page 22.  [5] No. 4230.

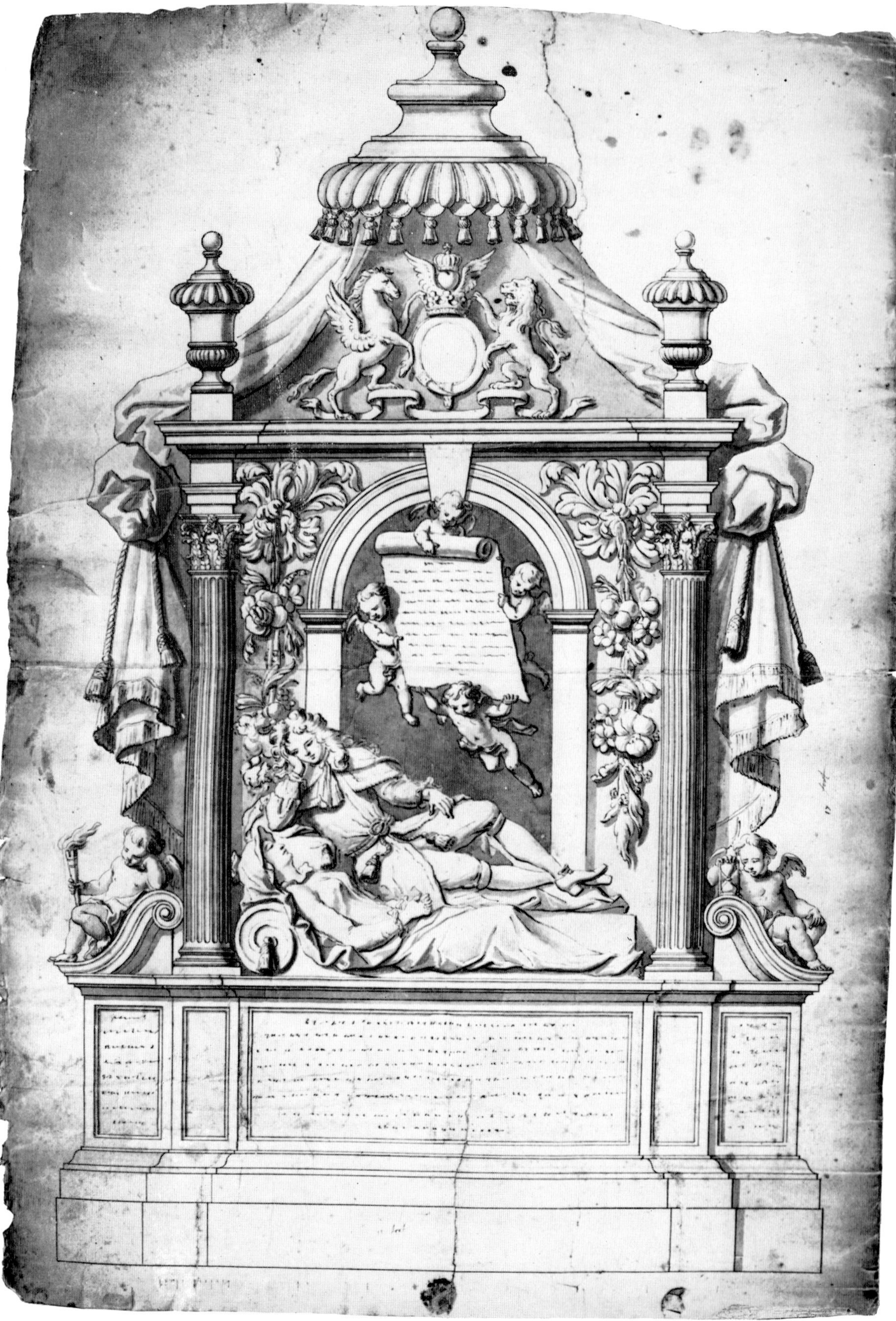

Another design, by Peter Scheemakers, is inscribed on the back *I agree to pay Mr. Scheemaker one hundred and forty* (originally written as *twenty*, but altered) *pds. Stg. for the monument to be erected according to the drawing on the other side—and to lett him take his own time to execute it—at London the 15th of May 1766—as witness my hand Ad: Gordon*. This is the design for the monument to Henrietta, Duchess of Gordon (1682–1760) in the ruined cathedral at Elgin.[1]

But not all clients were quite so accommodating as Lord Adam Gordon who let Scheemakers have unlimited time to complete the work. In Sevenoaks Public Library and Museum is a contract between Sir Henry Cheere and Charles Polhill which is much more demanding:

"Whereas Charles Polhill Esqr Agrees to pay Henry Cheere Six Hundred Pounds for a monument to the late Charles Polhill Esqr his Uncle Deceas'd the will of his said Uncle Expressly requiring the said monument to be Completely finish'd and Erected in the Parish Church of Otford in the County of Kent within two years from the Decease of his said Uncle wch. will be in September one thousand Seven Hundred & Fifty Seven, the said Henry Cheere agrees to Compleat the said Monument One Month before the said time & on Condition the said Charles Polhill agrees to pay the said Henry Cheere the full sum of Six Hundred Pounds."

This agreement was written out by Cheere himself—at the end of which the cautious Polhill added the rider, *as soon as the said monument shall be Completed*, dating it *Dec: 15: 1755*. Cheere received his money in two instalments, £300 was paid on January 17th, 1757, and the final payment was made on April 26th, 1758.

One of the hazards encountered in identifying the drawings is that a name written on a design need not refer at all to the person being commemorated. It may be that of an executor, or someone else, who was only commissioning the work. An instance of this is found on a drawing (fig. 6) bequeathed to the Museum by Rupert Gunnis,[2] by Peter Scheemakers, for a monument to be executed by "Order of the Revd. Thomas Foster", and the sculptor was paid by the Hon. Edward Southwell. The monument, when eventually tracked down, was found in Kilkenny Cathedral, to a Mrs. Cox, and it is now so mutilated that it bears but little resemblance, and that perhaps only to a willing eye, to the original design.

Mutilation of monuments does, of course, increase the difficulties experienced in the recognition of their designs, and there are several instances in Westminster Abbey of works which have been altered. That to James Craggs, for one, has been shorn of its plinth and background, and removed from the south aisle of the nave to a window-



[1] E.165–1942.

[2] E.961–1965; see "Some Irish Memorials (VIII, the Foster Memorial)" by Rupert Gunnis in the Irish Georgian Society's *Quarterly Bulletin*, Volume IV, No. 1, January to March, 1961, page 15.

ledge in the chapel beneath the south-western tower (figs. 40 & 41). Monuments and other sculpture in parish churches are nowadays protected as much as possible from destruction or damage by Diocesan Advisory Committees, who act as watchdogs; but they do not have any control over what may go on in a cathedral or certain other churches.

Westminster Abbey is, owing to its unique place in the history of this country, virtually the national museum of sculpture, no matter what the enemies of its "monstrous monuments" may say; work by every major sculptor may be seen there, and this has inevitably led to much overcrowding and consequent damage to the fabric of the building. So, for more than a century, monuments have been moved around, or reduced in size, whenever this has been thought necessary.[1] After some mural paintings were discovered in the south transept, the monuments to Nicholas Rowe by Rysbrack (fig. 60) and John Gay were transported up into the triforium.

During recent years one incomprehensible alteration has taken place. In 1757 "Athenian" Stuart designed (and Peter Scheemakers carved) for the East India Company, the monument to Admiral Watson which stands in the triforium arcade of the north transept. The admiral, in a toga, is between the figures of Calcutta and a captive Indian. To give cohesion to his composition Stuart had made use of the gothic arches and pillars of the triforium by overlaying them with carved palm-trees between and above the figures. These trees have now been removed in order, presumably, to reveal yet more of the already abundant triforium arcade, but at the cost of having reduced Admiral Watson's monument to three isolated and unco-ordinated pieces of sculpture.[2] It is quite certain that an alteration so disastrous in its result would not have been made to a work of the 17th century or earlier.

Reference to the illustrations shows that very few of the designs incorporate any kind of architectural setting, and those which do are

[1] "The Rev. Mr. Hughes & Twining called.—The Chapter of Westminster Abbey disapproving the placing the monuments lately finished by Flaxman & Bacon in between the pillars of the nave of the Abbey, have addressed the Lords of the Treasury against such innovations as contributing to destroy the effect of the building." (Joseph Farington's *Diary*, March 13th, 1806). These monuments were those to Captains Harvey and Hutt, and to Captain Montague, and they have now been moved to other positions.

[2] In 1869 the First Commissioner of Works asked the Society of Antiquaries of London to provide him with a list of Royal or historical tombs and monuments which "it would be desirable to place under the protection and supervision of the Government, with a view to their proper custody and preservation". The *Report of the Sepulchral Monuments Committee* was published by Her Majesty's Stationery Office in 1872, in which the Society voiced the opinion that "It may, for instance, be said that no such protection and supervision can be needed in Westminster Abbey where, under the superintendence of the present Dean (a member of the Committee) much care and attention to the condition of the monuments are known to be given. Practically, however, it is impossible to ascertain what particular monuments are specially exposed to danger from malicious injury, neglect or misdirected zeal for 'Church restoration'. The custodians of these objects are constantly changing, and with a change of men comes a change of taste."

531 monuments in England and Wales were listed; included were those to James Craggs (No. 141), Nicholas Rowe (No. 323), John Gay (No. 328) and Admiral Watson (No. 370).

Chantrey's monument to James Watt has recently been removed from the Abbey to the Transport Museum at Clapham.

nearly all for Westminster Abbey (fig. 87)—a notable exception is the drawing by Thomas Scheemakers, for his monument which was designed by "Athenian" Stuart, at Preston-on-Stour, Gloucestershire (fig. 98).[1] The reason for this is that it was usual for eighteenth-century sculptors to supply the monument only. Often they did not know where it would be placed in the church,[2] and John Thomas Smith in his biography of Joseph Nollekens, R.A., noted at the end of the century:

"There is one truly lamentable disadvantage to which works of our best Sculptors are frequently exposed, namely the want of a good light, wtihout which their labours cannot be viewed with that essential assistance which the painter's production can in most instances pro-pure . . . The sculptor . . . unaided by colours, has perhaps either too much or too little light for his monument; and is often obliged to erect where there is hardly any at all, or they insist on having it as near as possible to their pew, which has always gone with the mansion they reside in; thus enshrouding themselves in their own primitive impor-tance in the parish, at the same time, perhaps, being totally ignorant of the effect of a masterpiece of art, upon which they have expended a considerable sum; or not in any way evincing an interest for the fame of the artist employed, whose reputation has invited travellers to visit the church, which is often a great pleasure for the tourist. I remember Flaxman, after he had put up his monument to the memory of Lord Mansfield, in Westminster Abbey, applied to the Dean to cover a small portion of a window with a grey colour, in order to shut out an unpleasant glare of light, but the Dean, to the great mortification of the Sculptor, would not comply with the request; Nollekens seldom knew, nor indeed did any of the English Sculptors of former days care, in what part of a country church their monuments were to be placed; they received the measurements from the carpenter, who was not at all times very correct, without any notice of the aspect, or stating whether that space were over or under a window, or against a pier, or near the altar, receiving a vertical light, or a diagonal one: and upon this carelessly measured order, the sculptor proceeded, never dreaming that his work was to be placed close to the vestry-door in a dark corner. Then, too, when it was up, the plasterer was to adorn it with a *neat jet-black border* of a foot in width! so that it would match ostentatiously with a monument on the opposite side, in an equally forlorn position, belonging to a family with whom the relatives of the last deceased had been for ages inveterately at variance; whilst to crown the whole of the

---

[1] The church at Preston-on-Stour was rebuilt by Edward Woodward (c. 1697–1766) between 1753 and 1757, and is an early example of 18th-century gothic (see H. M. Colvin, *A Biographical Dictionary of English Architects, 1660–1840*, page 697). Stuart's classical monument was designed to be placed within an existing 'gothic' decorative frame, c. 1780.

[2] "Although doubtlessly intended for an eye-level position, the monument to Field-Marshal Wade was placed at window height, and Roubiliac is said to have wept when he saw how his work had been treated." (*The history of the Abbey Church of St. Peter's Westminster*, published by R. Ackermann, 1812, Volume 2, page 37.)

unhappy injury to Art, the putting up was generally entrusted to a mason,[1] who upon his return to London, was rarely questioned as to where it was erected, or as to *how it looked*."

There are hundreds of such forlorn works throughout the country; Guelfi's monument to the Duchess of Richmond[2] is in such a gloomy chapel at Deene, Northamptonshire, that it can hardly be seen, while George Rennie's large figure of the first Lord Harris in the north chapel at Throwley, Kent, is set in front of such very large windows, that it appears usually only in silhouette. The bill from the unnamed mason for erecting Nollekens's monument to Dr. Henry Kent (died 1769), at Potterne, Wiltshire, for which we possess the design,[3] is among the Nollekens sketches in the Douce Bequest to the Ashmolean Museum, Oxford, and is dated July 3rd, 1802:

| | | | |
|---|---|---|---|
| To Coach Hire to and from Devises and Traveling Expenses | 3. | 17. | 0. |
| To Board and Lodging at Pottern | 0. | 14. | 6. |
| To Liquor &c at the Church | 0. | 6. | 0. |
| To Scaffolding, Mortar Lime | 0. | 7. | 0. |
| Pd. for Help | 0. | 15. | 0. |
| Pd. the Saxton | 0. | 2. | 0. |
| Paid for Carriage of the Cases as p Acct | 1. | 17. | 6. |
| To a File | 0. | 0. | 6. |
| To 7 days | 1. | 8. | 0. |
| | 9. | 7. | 6. |

| | £. | s. | d. |
|---|---|---|---|
| Receiv'd | 10. | 4. | 0. |
| Contents of this Bill | 9. | 7. | 6. |
| By Cash Acct | £0. | 16. | 6. |
| Paid Monday July the 5. | | | |

---

[1] Michael Sidnell (working 1714–45), signed the monument to Edward Colston (1729), in All Saints', Bristol. This monument, however, was designed by James Gibbs and according to his *Book of Architecture* the figure was by Rysbrack. Sidnell was probably only the mason who erected the monument, and perhaps executed the architectural background.

[2] Guelfi's terracotta model for the bust of the Duchess is in the Department of Architecture and Sculpture, A.19-1957.

[3] E.4441-1920.

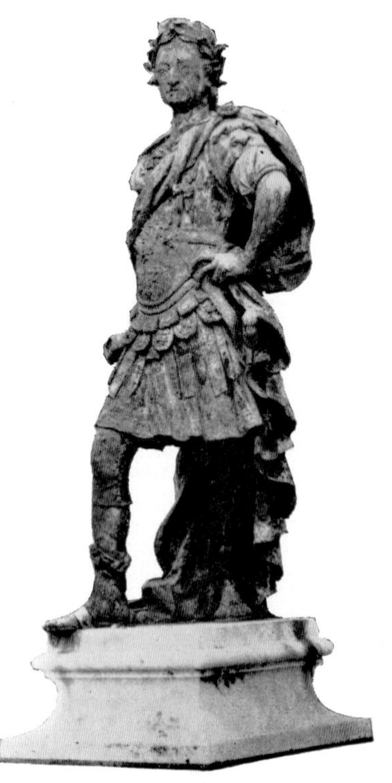

Fig. 9
Statue of William III, attributed to John Nost, Portsmouth Dockyard. (Photo: *Ministry of Public Building and Works*)

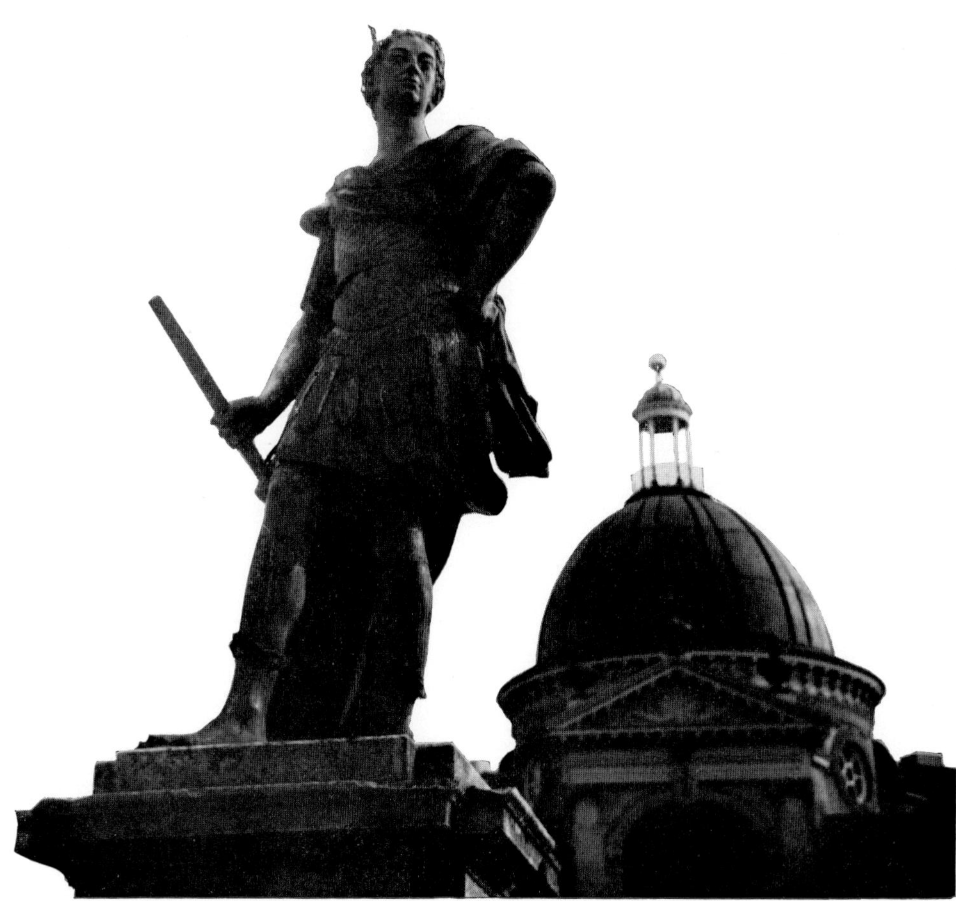

Fig. 10
Statue of William III, attributed to
John Nost, Wrest Park, Bedfordshire
(Photo: *Mr. Bruce Bailey*)

# III

AMONG THE EARLIEST DRAWINGS in the collection is the design by
Edward Pierce, who died in 1695, for the monument to Lady Warburton (fig. 21) which is in St. John's Church, Chester. In medieval
sculpture it was not uncommon to use a skeleton or a corpse to repre-
sent mortality; an example of this is to be seen at Ewelme, Oxfordshire, where Alice, Duchess of Suffolk (Chaucer's grand-daughter),
who died in 1477, lies realistically on a sumptuous monument surrounded by shield-bearing angels, but beneath, visible through arches,
is her skeleton lying in its shroud. The portrait of John Donne's
shrouded figure, rising from an urn on the Day of Resurrection—for
which Donne himself, wearing only a winding-sheet, stood to be
painted—was used by Nicholas Stone as his model for the well-known
monument retrieved from old St. Paul's Cathedral.[1] But Lady Warburton's monument displays a living skeleton which stands upright,

[1] When Sir Ralph Verney was considering a monument to Lady Verney for Middle
Claydon, Buckinghamshire, he wrote, September 23rd, 1651, about an arch "over her
Statue . . . in a Winding Sheet, with her hands lift upp, set uppon an Urne or Pedestall
. . . see Dr Dunns and other Tombes at Pauls or Westminster or elsewhere before you
speak with the Workmen". Mrs. Esdaile, "William Wright of Charing Cross, Sculptor",
*Reports* of the Architectural and Archaeological Society of the County of Lincoln, Volume
42, 1937, page 221.

and modestly holds its shroud in front, upon which is lettered the epitaph.[1] During the 17th and early 18th centuries, the skeleton became a familiar piece of symbolism and occurs again, for instance, on William Stanton's design (fig. 7) which may have been used as the model for the monument to Sir T. Wendy (1673) at Haslingfield, Cambridgeshire, and at Shoreditch, London, where Francis Bird's two skeletons tear apart a living oak tree on the extraordinary monument to Elizabeth Benson, 1710,[2] although eventually the skeleton became personified as Death itself, as in Roubiliac's Nightingale monument in Westminster Abbey. The drawing by Pierce forms part of a group, others are in the British Museum,[3] the Ashmolean Museum and Sir John Soane's Museum, which until recently were attributed to William Talman,[4] the seventeenth-century architect who was, from 1689 until 1702, Comptroller of the King's Works, but it is now known that Pierce bequeathed his drawings to Talman.[5] During the rebuilding after the Great Fire, Pierce was active in London, and was concerned with many of Wren's churches, and at St. Paul's Cathedral.[6]

John Nost, who died in 1729, came from Malines to England, and in 1686 was employed by Arnold Quellin as his foreman. When he later set up on his own account he had a flourishing business in lead garden-figures, and on the death of Quellin, married his widow. Few of his drawings are yet known; until a few years ago the only one which could confidently be given to him, was the documented design in the Bodleian Library, Oxford, for the monument to the Duke of Queensberry (1711), at Durisdeer in Dumfries-shire (fig. 8). Recently, however, a drawing in the Victoria and Albert Museum for a statue of King William III probably for Hampton Court, has come to light (fig. 30); two lead statues of the King, at Wrest Park, Bedfordshire,[7] and in Portsmouth Dockyard, may also be related to this design (figs. 9 & 10). Two more of Nost's drawings have been acquired by the British Museum (fig. 31), and the Bodleian Library (fig. 33). A design for the chimney-piece in the Queen's Gallery at Hampton Court Palace (fig. 34), for which Nost



---

[1] In the church of S. Giacomo alla Lungarna, Rome, Bernini's monument to Ippolito Merenda (died 1636) consists of a flying, winged skeleton holding a lettered shroud in front of it

[2] Reproduced on Plate 50 of *East London*, Royal Commission on Historical Monuments, 1930.

[3] Edward Croft-Murray and Paul Hulton, *Catalogue of British Drawings*, Volume 1, published by the British Museum, 1960, pages 451–5, Plates 241–5.

[4] H. M. Colvin, *Dictionary*, pages 456, 593. Some have the three interlaced Ts, the mark of the Talman collection. See also "William Talman", by Margaret Whinney in the *Journal of the Warburg and Courtauld Institutes*, Volume 18, 1955, page 138.

[5] H. M. Colvin, *Leeds Art Calendar*, No. 51, 1963, page 4. "Several drawings of Edw. Pierce a curious Architect & Carver. a great assistant of Sr Christo Wren. J. Talman", Vertue Note-books, 1, *Walpole Society*, Volume 18, 1930, page 69.

[6] In 1678 Pierce employed five assistants, which was the same number as that of Cibber's workmen. William Stanton had a larger establishment with nine men working for him (D. Knoop and G. P. Jones, *The London Mason in the Seventeenth Century*, 1935, pages 20, 21).

[7] Ascribed to Andrew Carpentière in *Bedfordshire* (etc.) by Nikolaus Pevsner, 1968.

Fig. 11
Design for a statue of Neptune, perhaps for Chatsworth, by Caius Gabriel Cibber.

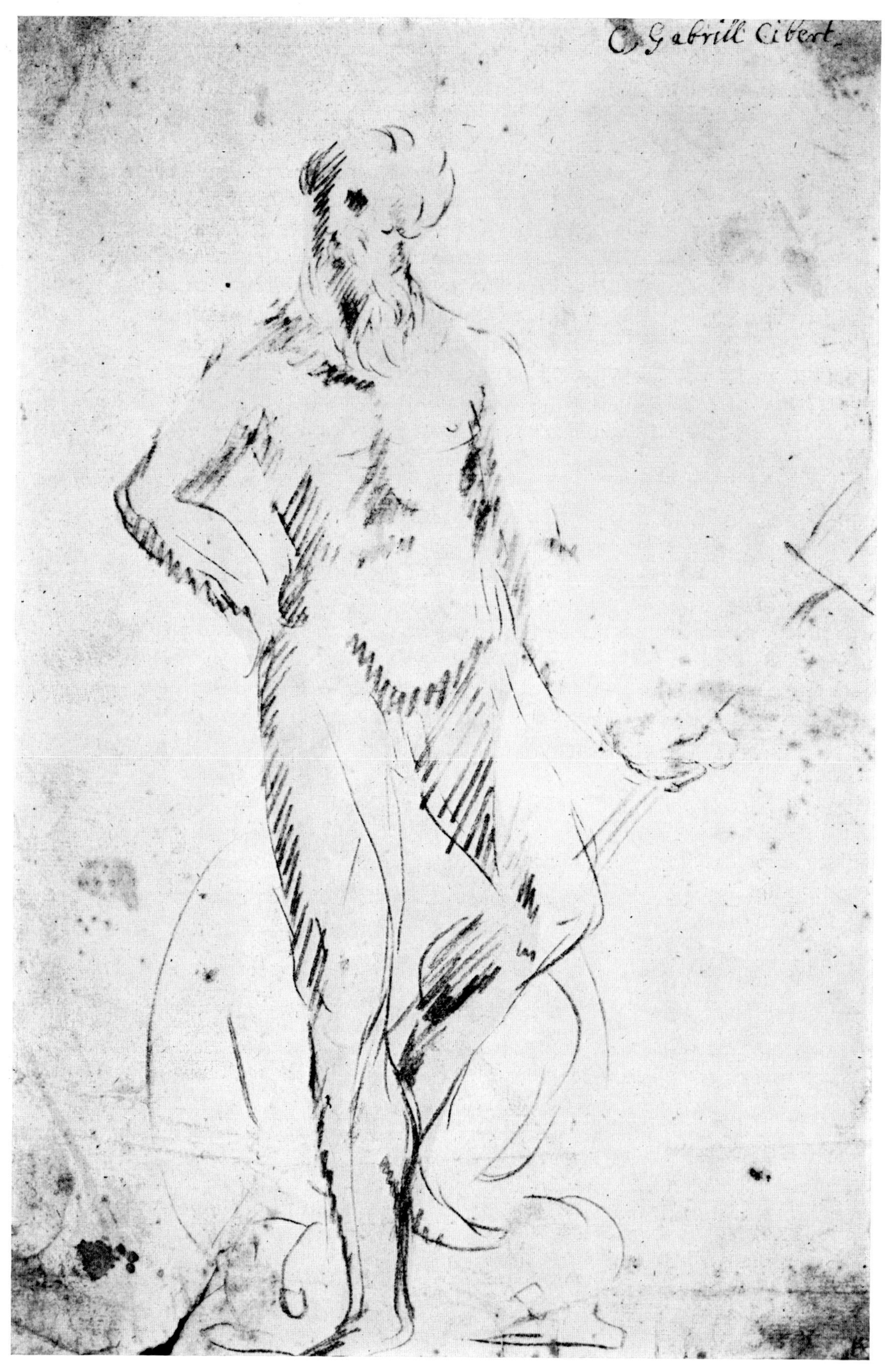

Gabrill Cibert

was paid £235, is so badly drawn, that it must have been the work of one of his many assistants.



Another important figure at the end of the 17th century was the Dane, Caius Gabriel Cibber (1630–1700). He was first employed in this country by John, the son of Nicholas Stone. After Stone's death in 1667, Cibber worked on his own, until he became known as one of the foremost sculptors of this country, and this success culminated in his appointment as Sculptor to William III in 1693. Among those he worked with was William Talman, who was then building Chatsworth, for which Cibber designed fountain figures (fig. 11), as well as decorative carvings for the House, such as the figures of Pallas and Apollo which stand in niches on the Grand Staircase (fig. 28). Well known for his relief on the Monument in the City to the Great Fire, Cibber must have had, in common with his contemporaries, a trade in sepulchral monuments; but none, other than the Sackville monument at Withyham, Sussex, seems to be known.[1] There is among the Isham Papers, now in the Northamptonshire Records Office, a design, dated 1670, for a plain mural tablet, apparently unexecuted, for a monument in Lamport Church.

A volume of designs in the Department of Prints and Drawings was acquired in 1898 as the work of Cibber. But for a variety of reasons it is now considered that the drawings were more likely to have been the work of members of the Stanton family, master-masons of Holborn.[2] This family of masons and sculptors was rescued from obscurity by Mrs. Esdaile,[3] and it seems quite probable that the best known of them, William Stanton (1639–1705), was a far more accomplished sculptor than has yet been recognised (fig. 27).[4] His son Edward (1681–1734) was a rather more pedestrian statuary than his father, but was capable of producing a large number of monuments which are quite competent (fig. 37). Edward Stanton was appointed Mason to Westminster Abbey, and took Christopher Horsnaile the Elder as his partner in the family business.

---

[1] "Yesterday I receued a letter from Lin Regis that my marble was arrived thear, from whence I doe intend to get it caried up the river to wansor, for that hath more water than at stamford, and bring it by land to thither. I shall go in Ester wick to Lin, and when I have soe taken care, how to send the marble I will then come to Belvoir to do the models of my Lords father and mother and Lord George which are the three designd, in the monuments, as I take it, in the mean time I promised my sone Colly to se bevoir castle in the holly days . . . P.S. I have two rare stones for two gladiators bigger than the liffe, which I have begone at Ketton, of which my Lord shall have the refusall . . . Exton 7th April 1682." Lady Victoria Manners, *loc. cit.*, page 339. The monument to the eighth Earl of Rutland (died 1679) at first ordered from Cibber, c. 1681, was two or three years later commissioned from Grinling Gibbons instead. (See *Grinling Gibbons* by David Green, 1964, page 154, and Gunnis Papers.) In 1678 Cibber was employing five assistants (D. Knoop and G. P. Jones, *The London Mason in the Seventeenth Century*, 1935, page 69).

[2] John Physick, "Tracing the work of William Stanton", *Country Life Annual*, 1968, page 88.

[3] "The Stantons of Holborn", *Archaeological Journal*, Volume 85, 1928, page 149.

[4] In 1678 it appears that probably the largest mason's establishment in London was that of Stanton who employed nine assistants, and in 1694 he had eight men working for him (D. Knoop and G. P. Jones, *The London Mason in the Seventeenth Century*, 1935, page 20).

Another of the master-masons of this period at the end of the seventeenth century who also turned his hand to carving was Christopher Cass (1678–1734). He was employed for work on St. Alfege, Greenwich, St. Luke, Old Street, St. Anne, Limehouse, and many other buildings including St. Martin-in-the-Fields, where he carved the royal achievement in the tympanum of the pediment of the west front. Outside London Cass worked at Cambridge on the Senate House designed by James Gibbs, at Canons, near Edgware, Middlesex, then being built for the Duke of Chandos, and in all probability at Blenheim. He is known to have been at Woodstock, Oxfordshire, in about 1720, because the design for the monument to the Bray children at Great Barrington, Gloucestershire, was addressed to him at the George Inn at Woodstock (fig. 38). Although there is no conclusive evidence that Cass either drew the design or carved the monument, this drawing is the only one that can, so far, be definitely linked with him in any way.

Whatever we might think nowadays of the work of Nost, Cibber, Francis Bird and other sculptors who ornamented London's buildings and streets during the 17th and early 18th centuries, they came in for criticism in about 1728. There is in the Museum's library an unpublished manuscript by an unidentified Frenchman who visited London and southern England at that time.[1] Of London sculpture he had this to say:

"Je n'oserois presque, Monsieur, vous parler des statües erigées dans la ville de Londres. Comme je vous ay deja prevenu de leur mechante sculpture j'apprehende que cet article ne soit inutile. Je vous ay deja parlé de la statüe en pied de Charles I sur un piedestal au milieu de la bourse. Le meme Charles I est en bronze a cheval dans le Carrefour de Charing-Cross qui regarde le palais Withehal. Le piedestal en est fort elevé et chargé de sculpture. Cette figure est entourée d'une petite balustrade de fer tres simple. L'ouvrage en general n'en est pas beau. Il y â encor dans le Stocks-Market une statue equestre plus mauvais de Charles II qui terrasse un Ennemi; elle est de pierre toute noircie, et elevée sur un mauvais piedestal, au bas duquel se voit une espece de fontaine qui ne joue jamais. Le meme Roy, Comme je crois vous l'avoir deja fait remarquer, est en pied dans le quarré de Sohò, dans un bassin d'eau accompagnée des quartre principaux fleuves d'Angleterre, la Tamise, la Saverne, la trente, et l'humber. Cette figure est moins mauvaise que l'equestre, Mais les fleuves sont trop petits pour la place.

On voit la figure en pied de Jacques II dans une cour du palais Withehal en face de banquet-housse; elle est de bronze et assez belle. On a eté obligé de l'entourer de planches; la populace ayant deja cassé le baton royal qu'il tenoit a la main. La Reine Anne est mise en face de l'Eglise de St. Paul dans la petite place qui est vis a vis, comme vous l'aurez deja Remarqué, accompagnée de quatre figures representant

---

[1] "Voiage D'Angleterre D'Hollande Et de Flandre fait en l'année 1728" (L.1255, 1.7.1912).

les quatre Royaumes. Ce seroit vous tromper Monsr. que de vous dire que cela est beau. La meme Reine se voit en pied, dans une niche dans un petit Quarré au dessus du parc appellé Queen Square. Je ne vous parleray point de toutes les figures qui se voient a la Bourse, a l'hotel de ville, a temple Baar et autres portes de la ville, ainsi qu'aux portes de Withehal. C'est encor pire que les autres et l'air les a demy rongéz. Je finirai par la figure equestre de Georges 1 en plomb doré que l'on a posé dans le milieu du Quarre de Grosveneur: Cette figure n'est pas mal, mais elle paroit un peu trop petitte. Les Anglois aimoient tant ce Roy, qu'ils ont mis sa figure en pierre de 17 pieds de haut, elevée sur la tour d'une eglise dans le Marché de Bloomsbury."

After the accession of the Hanoverians to the throne of England in 1714, there was an immigration into this country, during the second and third decades of the 18th century, of a group of sculptors who were for the next fifty years to dominate the sculpture of England. Two of them, Michael Rysbrack and Giovanni Battista Guelfi, were intimately connected with the Palladian circle of the Earl of Burlington. Guelfi, in fact, was brought to this country from Rome by the Earl himself in about 1714/5, who employed him in making statues for Burlington House in London, and Chiswick House, Middlesex.[1]

Guelfi's most important work with its far-reaching influence, was probably the monument to James Craggs (died 1721) (fig. 12), in Westminster Abbey, which is now only a fragment of the original. It was designed by James Gibbs, whose drawing is illustrated in fig. 40.[2] This figure leaning on a large urn became a popular one with later 18th-century sculptors and, although adapted, it may be seen in many other statues, as at Stoke Bruern, Northamptonshire, where the figure of Sir George Cooke (died 1740), perhaps by Sir Henry Cheere, stands in the gardens of Stoke Park; in Peter Scheemaker's William Shakespeare in Westminster Abbey, which was designed by William Kent (1740); and in the figure of Peace on the monument to Ann Whytell (1791) by John Bacon, R.A., also in Westminster Abbey (fig. 119).[3]

Vertue did not think very highly of Guelfi as he considered him opinionated and his work often defective, and when Guelfi at last departed for Italy in 1734, Vertue thought that Burlington was not altogether sorry to see him go.

John Michael Rysbrack (1694–1770) came to London from Antwerp

---

[1] M. I. Webb, "Giovanni Battista Guelfi", *Burlington Magazine*, Volume 97, 1955, pages 139, 260.

[2] It is perhaps worth noting here that up to this period the functions of mason, architect and sculptor had been, to a large extent, overlapping; one man, William Stanton, for instance, tried his hand at all three trades. Even during the 18th century Gibbs, Kent, Taylor and Adam, known primarily for their buildings, all produced designs for works of sculpture.

[3] It is quite possible that Gibbs adopted the pose from an antique statue which he had seen during the period he was the pupil of Carlo Fontana in Rome. There is, for instance, in the Vatican a figure of a youth, perhaps Ganymede, who has his legs crossed in the same manner, and who leans on a tree trunk (reproduced on Plate 179 of *Die Skulpturen des Vaticanischen Museums* by Georg Lippold, Volume 3(2), Berlin, 1956).

in 1720.[1] He worked first of all for James Gibbs, and it is probable that he carved the monument to Sir Ambrose and Lady Crowley (c. 1727) at Mitcham, Surrey, which Gibbs had designed and whose drawing is in the Museum (fig. 45). Gibbs was, according once again to Vertue, rather an unfair employer who gave Rysbrack quite a lot of work "but has always done it for his own advantage not for Encouragement. that the poor Man has oppend his mind to me & told me of his extravagant exactions on his labour that he could not possibly live had not other business come in to help him of more proffit. an instance of this is now in the monument to Mr Prior which he [Rysbrack] is now about the statues at lenght as big as the life representing poesi. he [Gibbs] will give him no more than 35 pounds for each statue to be cut in Marble. when others have above a hundred pounds, & Gibbs is to have of My Lord Harley, upwards of a hundred pounds for each of these statues. many other things of this kind he has done by him. 'tis an unreasonable gripeing usuage to a most Ingenious Art. (in his way) far more merrit than Gibbs ever will be Mr. of."[2] The monument to Prior in Westminster Abbey designed by Gibbs, and carved by Rysbrack, with a bust by Coysevox, prompted the following lines:

> *While Gibbs displays his elegant Design*
> *and Rysbrakes Art doth in the Sculpture shine*
> *with due composure & proportion just*
> *adding new lustre to the finisht bust*
> *Each Artist here perpetuates his Name*
> *and shares with Prior an immortal Fame.*[3]

[1] No. 4910.52. "(October 1720) came into England. Michael Rysbracht Statuary. (son of . . . Rysbracht of Antwerp an excellent Landskape painter.) his moddels in Clay are very excellent & shows him to be a great Master *tho' young* (about 26 years old.) he is of Antwerp & there & at Brussells has lived till he came to England. he was recommended to Mr. Gibbs. Architect." Vertue Note-books, I, *Walpole Society*, Volume 18, 1930, page 76.

[2] Vertue Note-books, III, *Walpole Society*, Volume 22, 1934, page 17.

[3] Vertue Note-books, VI, *Walpole Society*, Volume 30, 1955, page 19.

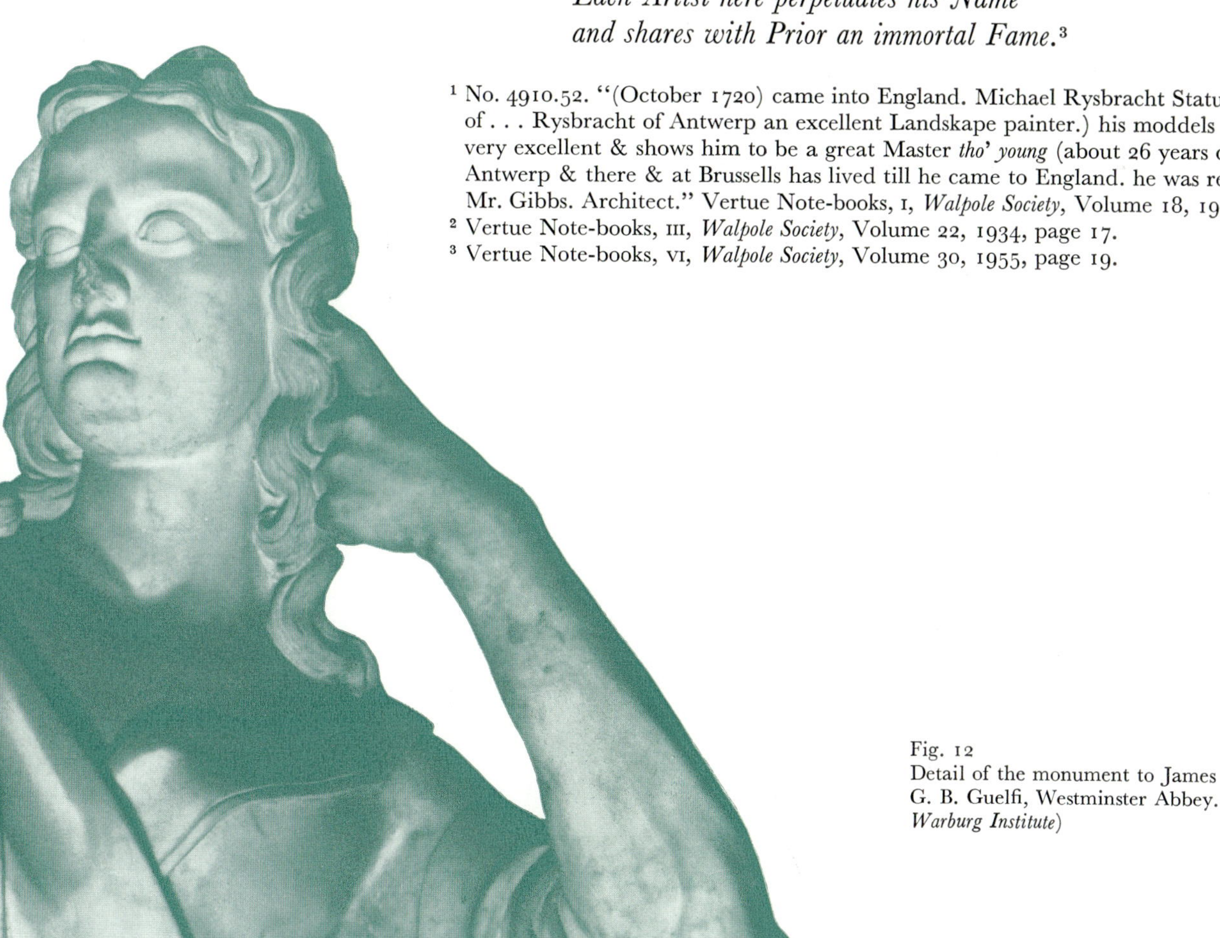

Fig. 12
Detail of the monument to James Craggs by G. B. Guelfi, Westminster Abbey. (Photo: *Warburg Institute*)

Rysbrack was, however, soon drawn into the Burlington group in which was also the architect and designer, William Kent.[1] The latter designed the figure of Inigo Jones at Chiswick House (fig. 46), which seems hitherto not to have been noticed, and the monuments in Westminster Abbey nave to Sir Isaac Newton (fig. 48), and Earl Stanhope (fig. 51), all of which were carved by Rysbrack. But besides his large architectural and sculptural compositions—the Dukes of Beaufort at Badminton, Gloucestershire (fig. 65), and Lord Foley (died 1733) at Witley, Worcestershire (fig. 13),[2] Rysbrack was equally able when producing chimney-pieces (Teddesley Hall, Staffordshire, figs. 67 & 68)[3] and small mural monuments such as those to the Rev. Thomas Busby (1753), at Addington, Buckinghamshire (fig. 55), and Baldwin Duppa at Hollingbourne, Kent,[4] in which he conducted a successful business. In these smaller works Rysbrack was not averse from using the same symbolism in more than one of them; the little cherub holding the snake of eternity appears on the Busby monument, as well as identically on that to Harriot Bouverie at Coleshill, Berkshire (fig. 14),[5] and in Canterbury Cathedral on John Sympson's monument.

But although he was the most successful sculptor of the first half of the eighteenth century, Rysbrack had a rival in Peter Scheemakers (1691–1781). The exact date when Scheemakers came to England does not yet appear to be known, but he is recorded as working for Francis Bird (then the leading British sculptor) before 1720. While he was Bird's assistant he met another immigrant, Laurent Delvaux, also a Fleming who was working for the same master. Scheemakers and Delvaux soon teamed up and carried out a number of works together, including the monuments to Lewis, Earl of Rockingham (1725)[6] at Rockingham, Northamptonshire, and to Sir Samuel Ongley (1726) (fig. 77), at Old Warden, Bedfordshire. The two men sign these works jointly, but the drawings and probably the designs are by Peter Scheemakers alone. The memorial to William Shakespeare (1740) which Kent designed for Westminster Abbey,[7] where it is in Poets'

---

[1] M. I. Webb, *Michael Rysbrack, Sculptor*, 1954, *passim*.

[2] No. 4910.1. The church at Witley incorporates ceiling paintings, and painted glass windows, which were bought by the second Lord Foley in 1747 from the Duke of Chandos's chapel at Canons, Middlesex (see F. J. B. Watson, "A Venetian Settecento Chapel in the English countryside" in *Arte Veneta*, Volume 8, 1954, pages 295–302).

[3] E.462–1946. Teddesley Hall was demolished in 1954, after having been occupied by the army during the Second World War.     [4] E.455–1946.

[5] E.448–1946. Both drawing and monument are reproduced as Plates 33 and 34 of *Michael Rysbrack, Sculptor*, by M. I. Webb, 1954.

    Besides two designs probably for the monument to the Duke of Argyll in Westminster Abbey, the Cottonian Collection in the City Museum and Art Gallery at Plymouth, contains at least eight other unrecorded drawings for monuments by Rysbrack, one of which is another version of that to Sir Watkin Williams Wynn at Ruabon, Denbighshire, for which the Department of Prints and Drawings possesses the drawing as executed, E.426–1946. Presumably Rysbrack prepared at least six designs as that at Plymouth is number 4, while that in the Victoria and Albert Museum is number 6.     [6] No. 8408.1.

[7] James Gibbs designed a monument to Shakespeare also; there is a drawing in the Department of Prints and Drawings, E.3640–1913, and another in the Ashmolean Museum, Oxford.

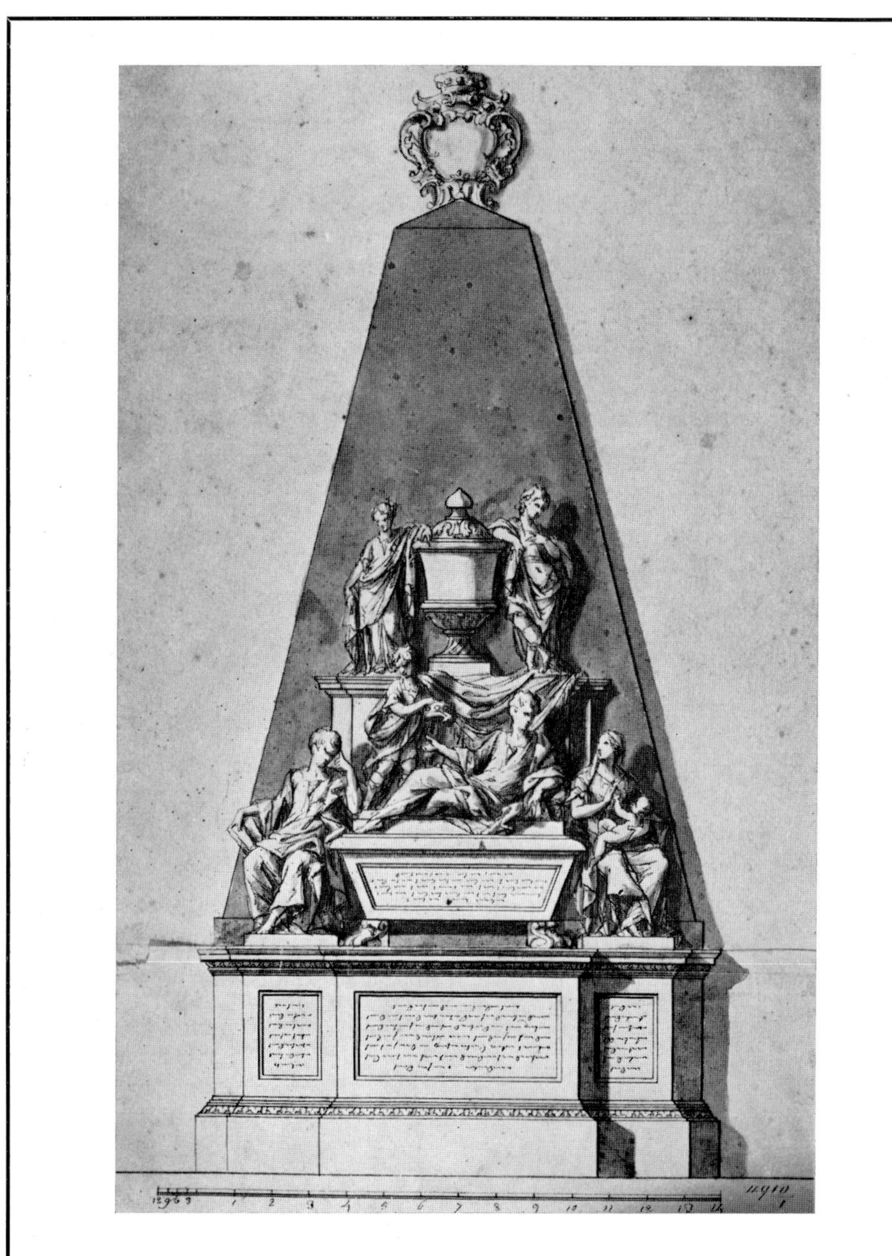

Fig. 13
Design by Michael Rysbrack, for
the monument to Lord Foley,
Great Witley, Worcestershire.
c. 1733.

Corner, brought Scheemakers to the summit of his career. Vertue recorded the "great and unproportiond exultation of that statue of Shakespeare erected in Westminster Abbey . . . so much spoke of in all conversations and publick print. Which has effectually established his [Scheemakers's] Credit & reputation—and at the same time obliterated in some degree that of Rysbrakes. insomuch that he feels the effect in the decline of Busines . . . Rysbrake has long been at the top of fortunes wheel here."[1]

Scheemakers frequently appears among the pages of the Vertue

[1] Vertue Note-books, III, *Walpole Society*, Volume 22, 1934, page 116.

Note-books, sometimes when he quotes someone else's flattering remarks:

> *Great Shakespears statuary's skill is known.*
> *In living sculpture and figured stone*
> *on each bold Figure, almost life bestows,*
> *and each beholders breast with rapture Glows*
> *Postures unforced his chisel does command*
> *and nature seems obedient to his hand.*[1]

But the general picture, however, seems to have been one of Vertue's dislike. When he wrote about the Duke of Newcastle's monument in the Abbey by Gibbs and Francis Bird (fig. 15), Vertue remarked that it had been criticised by a "little animal", whom he later revealed as being Scheemakers, who had told the Earl of Oxford that Bird's allegorical figures "disgracd it" and should be removed.[2]

Both Rysbrack and Scheemakers were eventually overshadowed by the last and most distinctive of the foreigners, this time a Frenchman from Lyons, Louis François Roubiliac (1702?–1762). Roubiliac arrived here in about 1732, after a period during which he had been a pupil of Balthasar Permoser, probably at Dresden, and his first master in England may have been either Benjamin or Thomas Carter, the brothers who are noted for their chimney-pieces.[3] Roubiliac then became an assistant to Henry Cheere, and it was at this time that he carved the figure of Handel for Vauxhall Gardens, in 1738,[4] on the recommendation of Cheere. The seated and very informal Handel was immensely popular with visitors to the London pleasure-garden, but this was not sufficient to allow Roubiliac to break through the barrier against him of better-known and established sculptors in London at the time—his master Henry Cheere, Rysbrack and Scheemakers. So he had to content himself with carving busts and other

[1] *Ibid.*, page 122. "Daily post. March. 1743/4. Sr. The Pediment of the Mansion House of the Lord Mayor of London being ready to be carvd with Emblems as they are expressd in the Model gave birth to the following lines . . .' that sort of Puff beforehand—for Scheemakers did not take effect. for altho' he made a Moddell & design so did others—a design by *Rysbrack.* and *Gravelot.* and *Shears* & Rubillac all these Foreigners was opposed by Carter a young Englishman Cittizen & son of a Mason . . . when the Common Councill of the Citty put it to the Vote amongst them . . . they had 8 in ten for their Country man & a Cittizen." Vertue wrote Carter instead of Taylor, for it was Sir Robert Taylor who was awarded the commission.

[2] "This little fellow since he has done Shakespear Mont thinks himself above all others—and tells several such bold face storys of his own assurance without reserve. and the truest is when he sayes I am a little impudent fellow, no matter? I can't help it." Vertue, *loc. cit.*, page 108. "When the Committee offerd to Mr. Scheemakers to make a Moddell anew [for the Mansion House pediment], in opposition to Carter [*sic*]. (he answered) he was not under the necessity to turn prize-fighter—he thought he had done workes enough to shew his merrit." Vertue, *loc. cit.*, page 122.

[3] The two Carters also carved monuments; a joint work (together with a relief by their assistant John Eckstein) designed by Robert Adam, is that to Col. Townshend (died 1759), with Red Indian caryatids, in Westminster Abbey. See also "The Carters, Georgian Sculptors" by Rupert Gunnis, *Architectural Review*, Volume 123, 1958, page 334.

[4] Terence Hodgkinson, "Handel at Vauxhall", *Victoria and Albert Museum Bulletin*, Volume 1, 1965, No. 4, page 1.

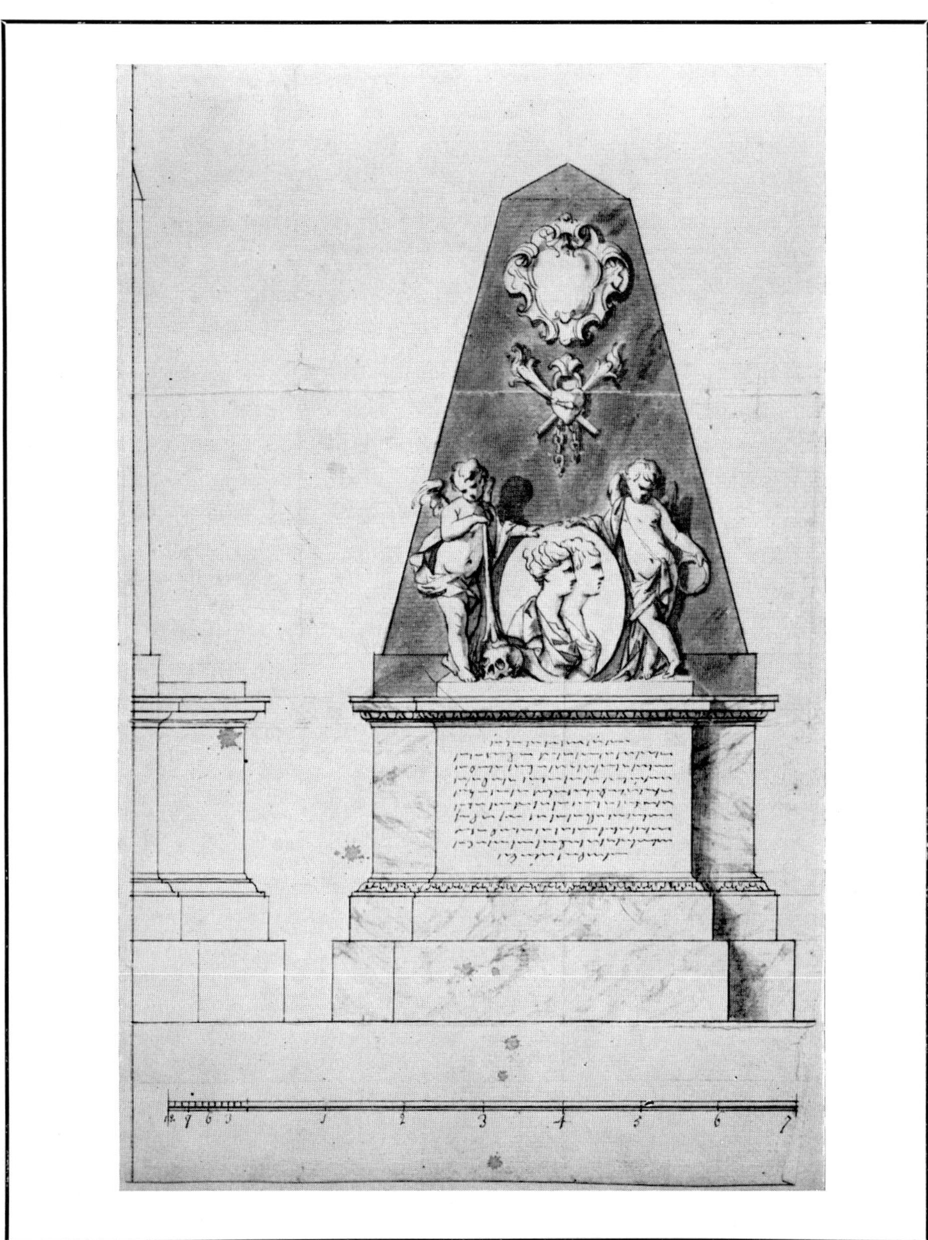

Fig. 14
Design by Michael Rysbrack, for
the monument to Harriot Bouverie,
Coleshill, Berkshire. c. 1751.

minor work, and generally building up his reputation until he received
the commission to carve the monument to the Duke of Argyll and
Greenwich in Westminster Abbey in 1745, and in the same year he
was appointed lecturer in sculpture at the St. Martin's Lane Academy.
The large design for the Argyll monument which Roubiliac signs
(fig. 83) is a little earlier than his terracotta model, which is now in the
Department of Architecture and Sculpture.[1] The monument itself was
finished by 1749 and unveiled in the south transept of the Abbey on
May 18th of that year (fig. 84), establishing at last Roubiliac's position
as an important sculptor working in a rococo manner completely

[1] Reproduced as fig. 11 of "Some eighteenth-century designs for monuments in Westminster
Abbey", *Victoria and Albert Museum Bulletin*, January, 1967.

different from any which had so far been seen in London.[1] As a result he received many commissions for his dramatic conceptions such as the monuments to the 2nd Duke and Duchess of Montagu (fig. 16),[2] both at Warkton, Northamptonshire, the amazing resurrection of General Hargrave, with its crumbling cenotaph (1751)[3] and the skeleton Death aiming his spear at Lady Nightingale,[4] which are in Westminster Abbey.

Roubiliac's master, Sir Henry Cheere, Bart. (1703–1781) had been an apprentice of Robert Hartshorne in 1718. He started his own business in 1726, and for a while was in partnership with Henry, the brother of Peter Scheemakers.[5] Cheere developed his own particular form of rococo monument and other sculptural work, making use of coloured marbles, and he was the first to indicate these by various colour washes in his drawings. A large number of Cheere's monuments, even if not signed, are quite distinctive enough to be attributed to him and his studio; he favoured wreathed urns, delicately carved garlands, winged cherub-heads—often in threes—rococo flaming lamps, acanthus leaves, busts on pedestals with fish-scale decoration, and lion-paws to support a sarcophagus (figs. 17, 18, 87, 89). In addition, Cheere was much in demand for his chimney-pieces, long forgotten, but many of which are just beginning to be recognised again with the assistance of our drawings. These chimney-pieces were decorated with charming little reliefs of pastoral scenes—farmyards, milk-maids, shepherds, children skating or lighting fires, sheep, goats and other animals—which caught the fancy of a number of patrons, so that throughout the country chimney-pieces of this type are found in many a library and drawing-room (figs. 91 & 93). Cheere was created a baronet by George III in 1766 in recognition of his services in public life.

It has been suggested that the Cheere drawings in the Museum are by three different people, one of whom was Richard Hayward (1728–1800).[6] Hayward was Cheere's assistant for some time, being apprenticed



---

[1] "Nollekens spoke highly of his talents,—said He worked '*con amore*', was an enthusiast in his profession & often dissatisfied with his works, which he wd. frequently destroy & begin the subject again." (Joseph Farington's *Diary*, February 1st, 1803.)

    An interesting comparison may be made between Roubiliac and his contemporaries like Rysbrack. It is evident from the catalogues of Rysbrack's various sales that he produced a large number of drawings for his various projects. Roubiliac seems to have left almost none, and it would appear from Nollekens's remarks that he preferred to work directly on models instead.

[2] One model for the Duke's monument is in the Department of Architecture and Sculpture, A.6–1947, whilst another, and that for the Duchess's monument are both in Westminster Abbey. Mrs. Esdaile, *The Life and Works of Louis François Roubiliac*, 1928, Plates XVII, XVIII.

[3] Even Roubiliac did not shrink from using a similar design more than once; the monuments to General Hargrave, and to Mary Myddelton at Wrexham, Denbighshire, are both on the same theme (see Mrs. Esdaile, *op. cit.*, plate XXXVI).

[4] The model is also in Westminster Abbey. (Mrs. Esdaile, *op. cit.*, Plate XLVIII.)

[5] M. I. Webb, "Henry Cheere, Henry Scheemakers and the Apprenticeship Lists", *Burlington Magazine*, Volume 99, 1957, page 119. John Nost's son, John (died 1787) was apprenticed to Henry Scheemakers on October 17th, 1726.

[6] M. I. Webb, "Henry Cheere, Sculptor and Businessman and John Cheere", *Burlington Magazine*, Volume 100, 1958, pages 232–40, 274–9.

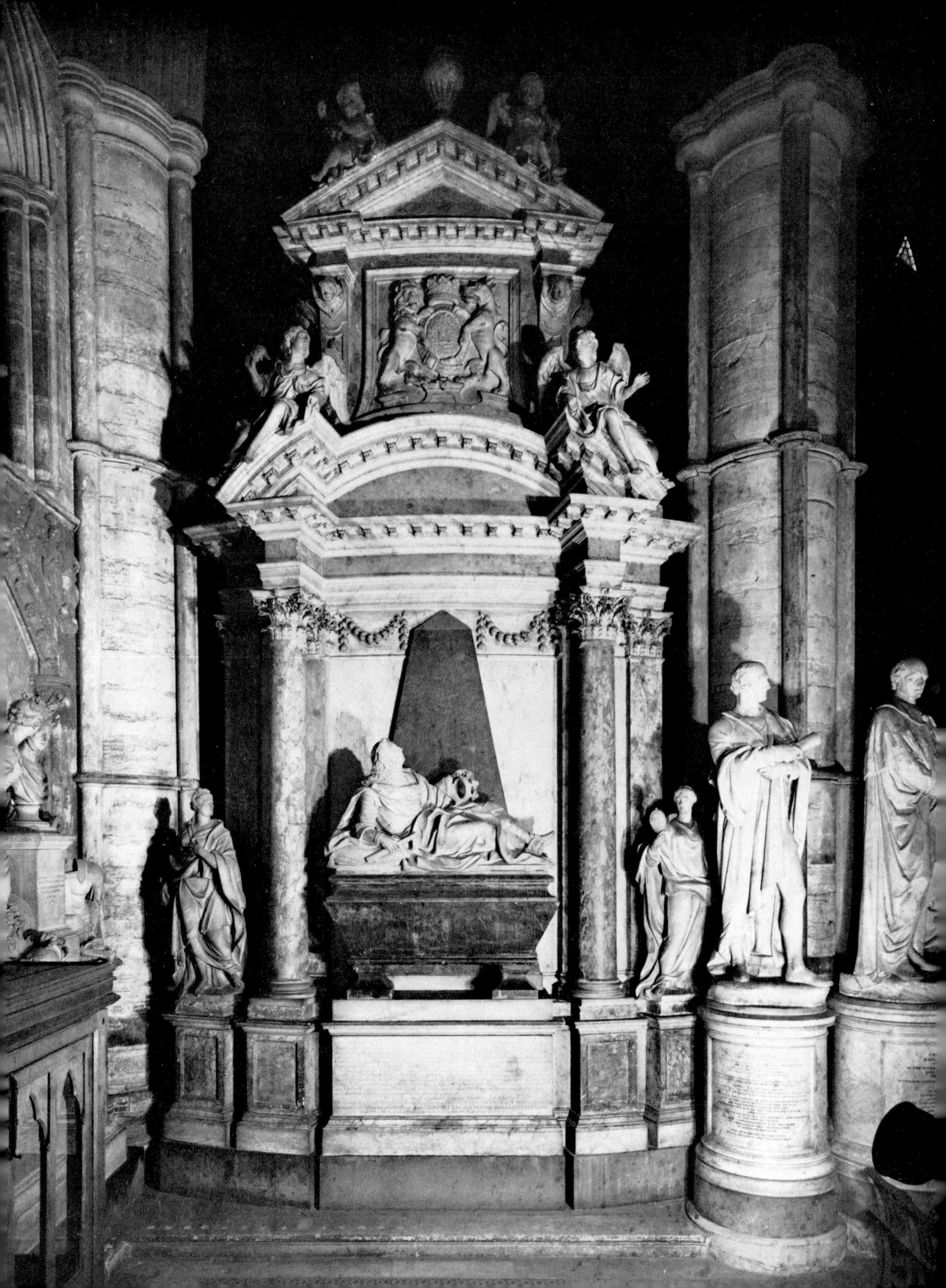

to him for seven years on June 29th, 1742,[1] but I think that there is no doubt that all the drawings are by the same hand, before and after Hayward's service with Cheere, who was, however, so active in spheres other than sculpture that he must have had many assistants and craftsmen working for him on much of the carving for which he was responsible. Of one of Cheere's assistants, William Collins, J. T. Smith wrote "Gainsborough's friend, Collins, of Tothill-fields, was indeed the most famous modeller of chimney-tablets, of his day, but his figures were mostly clothed, and exhibited pastoral scenes, which were understood by the most common observer; such, for instance, as a shepherd's boy eating his dinner under an old stump of a tree, with his dog begging before him; shepherds and shepherdesses seated upon a bank, surrounded by their flocks; anglers, reapers, &c. as may be seen in numerous chimney-pieces, executed in the early part of the last century, and which are still to be found in houses erected about that time".[2] Even in America, the drawing-room of George Washington's house at Mount Vernon, Virginia, has a chimney-piece with a central sculptured panel of a milkmaid with sheep and cows. This might be by Cheere, and is based on one of his designs in the Museum's collection.

Joseph Wilton, R.A. (1722–1803) was in 1768, one of the three founder-members of the Royal Academy who were sculptors.[3] As a youth he had been apprenticed to Laurent Delvaux in Flanders, for whom he worked until 1744, when he went on to Paris to study with the French sculptor Jean-Baptiste Pigalle. Some years later he journeyed to Rome and Florence where he remained until 1755. Wilton was a friend of Cipriani and Sir William Chambers, and he was appointed Coach-carver to George III; in this capacity he would have worked on the new State coach which was made for George III's coronation in 1762;[4] he was appointed Sculptor to the King in 1764. Besides busts and monuments Wilton produced quite a lot of archi-

---

[1] Gunnis says that Hayward was apprenticed to Christopher Horsnaile the Younger, and became free of the Masons' Company in 1749, but an entry in the Apprenticeship lists at the Public Record Office records that "1742 June 29 Henry Cheere of St. Margts Westmr Carver takes Richd. son of Mary Hayward of Weston, Warwk 7 years £105" and is quoted by Mrs. Webb, *loc. cit.*, 1958, page 274.

[2] For example, Nos. 144, 145 in the exhibition of the Society of Artists, 1761, were two bas-reliefs for chimney-pieces, "a clown and country girl" and "boy keeping sheep".

[3] The two others were Agostino Carlini, R.A. (died 1790), and William Tyler, R.A. (died 1801).

[4] "I also remember, one Sunday morning going with my father and Mr. Nollekens to see the studio of the late Joseph Wilton, Esq., R.A., father of the present Lady Chambers and friend of Barretti. Wilton on his return from his travels, brought Capitsoldi and Cipriani to this country . . . We viewed his works, and the model of King George the Third's state-coach, a most beautiful little toy exquisitely adorned with ornaments, modelled in wax by Capitsoldi and Voyers, the panels being painted in water-colours by Cipriani . . ." [The model, owned by the Coachmakers' and Coach-harness Makers' Company, was exhibited, July, 1968, at Fishmongers' Hall, in the exhibition of City treasures.] J. T. Smith, *Nollekens and his Times.* It is often presumed that Sir William Chambers married Wilton's daughter, Fanny, but it was Sir Robert Chambers (1737–1803), an Indian judge, who married her in 1774. She died in 1839.

tectural decoration, much of it to the design of Chambers, for Somerset House, and chimney-pieces for Blenheim Palace, Milton Abbey, Dorset,[1] and Peper Harrow House, Surrey, among others. However, when he inherited a substantial sum of money from his father, and no longer had the necessity of earning his living, much of his earlier promise disappeared, although he continued to exhibit at the Royal Academy until 1783. His extravagant living brought him into financial difficulties, which caused him to sell his property by auction in 1786, though this did not save him from being declared bankrupt in 1793. Wilton had been appointed Keeper of the Royal Academy in 1790, and he retained this position for thirteen years, until his death in 1803.

The rise of neo-classicism in England became apparent in sculpture at about the beginning of the last quarter of the 18th century. Its chief exponent at this time was Joseph Nollekens, R.A. (1737–1823) who, after being apprenticed to Peter Scheemakers, studied in Rome between 1760 and 1770. As a fashionable sculptor he obtained a large number of orders for busts and monuments, and this enabled him to leave a fortune of some £200,000 when he died. The portrait busts of William Pitt and Charles James Fox were so popular that Nollekens was repeatedly asked for copies, and it is reported that more than fifty replicas of each were made at £150 a time.

Nollekens's biographer, J. T. Smith, presents an unflattering account of him, his household, and his miserly habits; certainly many of his drawings in the Museum are on scraps of paper or on the backs of letters. Smith has recorded that "whenever [Nollekens] was not engaged on modelling, he employs himself, particularly in the evening, in making designs upon the backs of letters, and other scraps of paper for every description of monument of the simple kind, such as a female weeping or entwining festoons of flowers over an urn, or a child with an inverted torch (fig. 19), and for one and the same monument I have known him make half a dozen or more trials.[2] Quantities of the sketches were purchased at his auction by Mrs. Palmer who, having so many of his works, at one time had the idea of building a room for their reception . . . These sketches were often in pencil, or sometimes finished in Indian-ink, but many of his later ones were drawn only with charcoal; he kept them always to hand, to show a gentleman who had lost his wife, or a lady who had been deprived of her husband or child; and he has often been heard to say, when he received an order for a monument, 'You see I take 'em when the tear's in the eye' " (fig. 20).

Other artists of this period of the late 18th century, whose designs are in the Museum, include the relatively unknown John Francis Moore

---

[1] His design for the Library chimney-piece at Milton Abbey is in the Department of Prints and Drawings, E.495–1964.

[2] There are at least four drawings in the Museum which relate to the Salusbury monument at Great Offley, Hertfordshire.

(died 1809), who came to England from Hanover in about 1760. His drawings, which often show a confusion of styles, are noteworthy for their colour at a time when the cold contrast of white marble against sombre grey or black was fashionable, as illustrated in those designs for the monuments to Admiral Hawke (fig. 96) at North Stoneham, Hampshire, or to Jonas Hanway (fig. 94), in Westminster Abbey.[1] The architect Robert Adam also turned his hand to designing monuments and worked especially with Peter Van Gelder from Amsterdam, who earlier had been employed by Thomas Carter. Adam and Van Gelder are probably best known for their theatrical group, set in a large classically-decorated niche, commemorating the Duchess of Montagu (died 1771), at Warkton, Northamptonshire, which must have been influenced by the two earlier monuments of Roubiliac, but a small work of their collaboration is represented by Adam's design in the Museum for the monument to Robert Child of Osterley Park, which is in Heston Church, Middlesex (fig. 106). A drawing by Thomas (1740–1808), the son of Peter Scheemakers, is for the monument to Thomas Steavens at Preston-on-Stour, Gloucestershire (fig. 98). Although it was designed by "Athenian" Stuart, the drawing is one of a group by Thomas Scheemakers in the Department of Prints and Drawings.

With the end of the 18th century, and the beginning of the 19th century, we come to the work of three prolific sculptors, John Bacon, R.A. (1740–1799), his son John (1777–1859), and John Flaxman, R.A. (1755–1826).

In his early days John Bacon, R.A., worked for Wedgwood, and was later appointed the chief designer for the Coade Artificial Stone Manufactory at Lambeth. Both he and his son were extremely successful with their stock designs of monuments which repeated time and time again women mourning, urns, willow-trees, pelicans, and allegorical figures of Faith, Hope, Charity, Religion, and so on. These monuments are to be found in nearly every church in this country, and as far away as the West Indies.[2] They have also been copied endlessly and badly by inferior craftsmen[3] of the 19th century, the result being the distaste of the sentimentality into which they deteriorated, which is still provoked by them to this day. The success of the elder Bacon did not, perhaps naturally, endear him to his fellow sculptors. Some thought him unscrupulous, whilst others considered that he tried to influence the King, George III. Joseph Farington, who loved to record gossip, noted in his diary on Christmas Eve, 1798, "The King told Wyatt that

---

[1] Moore also designed chimney-pieces. See John Harris, "Fonthill, Wiltshire", *Country Life*, November 24th, 1966, page 1373.

[2] Mrs. Lesley Lewis, F.S.A. "English Commemorative Sculpture in Jamaica", *Commemorative Art*, November, 1965–February, 1967.

[3] The London statuaries were somewhat contemptuously called the "New Road" School, because many were centred on what is now Marylebone and Euston Roads, to be within easy reach of the Regent Canal. (Ann Cox-Johnson, [Ann Saunders] *Handlist of painters, sculptors and architects associated with St. Marylebone, 1760–1960*, 1963.)

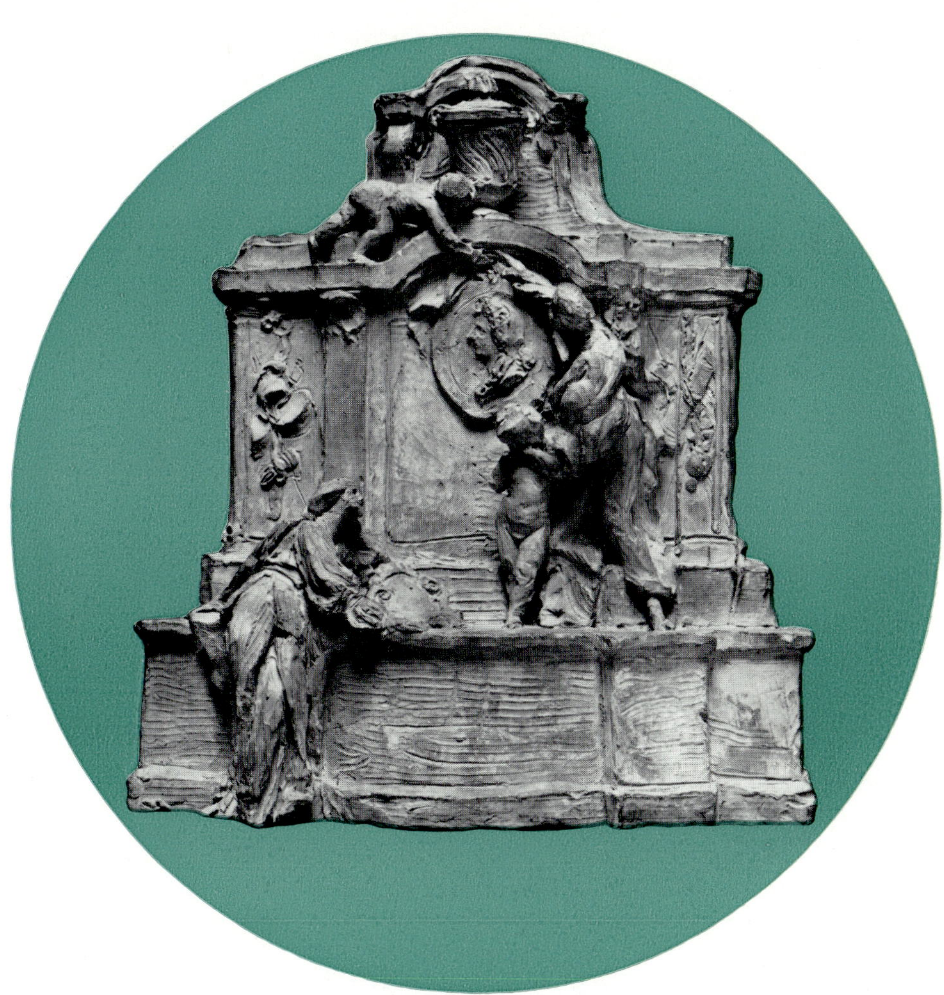

Fig. 16
Model by L. F. Roubiliac, for the
monument to the Duke of Montagu,
Warkton, Northamptonshire. 1749.

after the monuments that have last been voted by Parliament, Bacon went to His Majesty and expressed his hope that he might be fixed upon to execute *them all* for a reason that all the monuments that have been erected in St. Paul's were by him. The King replied that that seemed to be a reason why He should not do any of those now to be ordered."

In 1797/9 Bacon designed the sculpture for the pediment of East India House in the City of London, which was then being rebuilt to the designs of Richard Jupp[1] and Henry Holland, but he died before he had finished, and the sculpture was completed by his son (fig. 124); the cost was £2,342.

John Bacon the Younger was neither so accomplished a draughtsman nor sculptor as his father had been. He took a young sculptor named Charles Manning into partnership in 1808, and it seems that although he was to leave the business entirely to Manning, who died in 1812, and after that to his son Samuel, all the work was to be produced in Bacon's name. Bacon died a rich man in 1859, and most of his money

---

[1] The Department of Prints and Drawings possesses many of Jupp's architectural drawings relating to the rebuilding.

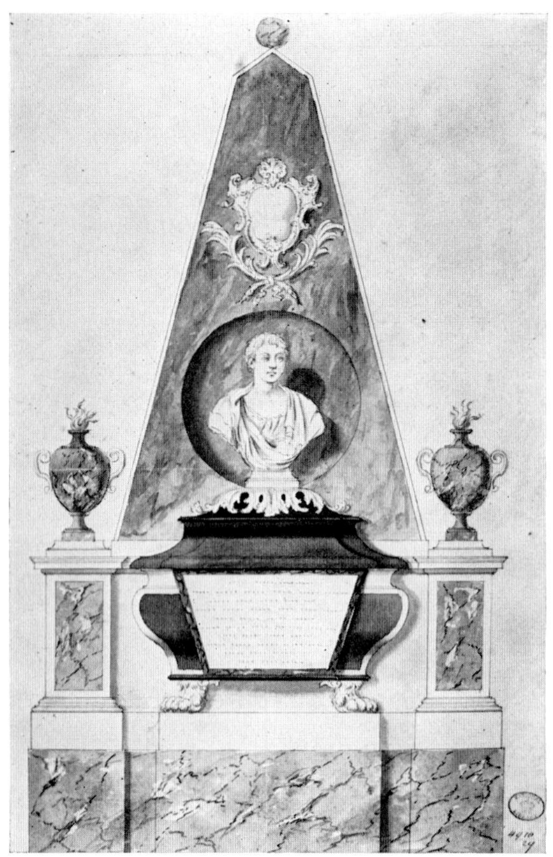

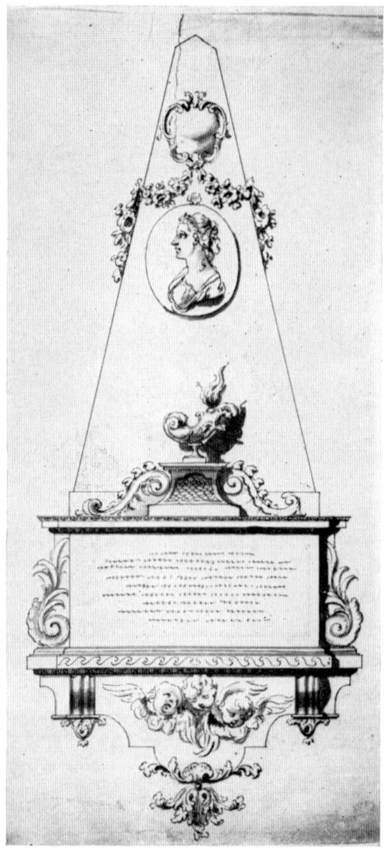



**Fig. 17**             **Fig. 18**

---

must have come from the proceeds of the lamentable and abysmal monumental tablets which the Mannings mass-produced for him.

On the other hand John Flaxman, R.A., was a man of parts—sculptor, illustrator, designer of metalwork, some of it for George IV, and designer for Wedgwood's pottery, and he seems to have been the only English sculptor with a reputation outside this country. He was able to adapt himself to work both in the classical and gothic idioms, gothic for instance in the monument to General Simcoe at Exeter (fig. 134), and the "National Cup" for George IV (fig. 131).[1] In 1799 in order to commemorate the victories of the Royal Navy over the French it was suggested that there should be a national memorial. Flaxman came along with the bizarre suggestion that an enormous Britannia, more than 200 feet high, should be placed on Greenwich Hill next to the Observatory, and looming over the Hospital,[2] so that it could be seen from miles around and serve to remind travellers to London on the Thames, or on the Dover Road, of the triumph of the

[1] Shirley Bury, "The lengthening shadow of Rundell's", *The Connoisseur*, March, 1966, page 155.

[2] Peter Hollins (1800–1886) must have been influenced by Flaxman's project, because his entry in the competition held in 1839 for the Nelson memorial in Trafalgar Square incorporated a 120 feet high statue of Britannia.

40

Navy (fig. 129); his large model is now in Sir John Soane's Museum,[1] and his published *Letter* of explanation was illustrated by William Blake.

During the nineteenth century English sculpture was in rather a sorry state. Much of its minor sculpture is of high quality and attractive, but major public works so often failed to achieve their purpose, due perhaps to everyone concerned being overwhelmed with a sense of the importance of the occasion; they tried too hard to produce the best and the most worthy, which in the end, eluded them.

There was a tendency for the Government to give these important commissions unannounced to a sculptor of its choice and not through competition. Not unnaturally this aroused resentment and suspicion, directed at one time against Baron Marochetti, who was accused of obtaining the Prince Consort's influence on his behalf. Undoubtedly without foundation: one must suspect, however, that there was some-one behind him. There was bitter criticism, for instance, of his Crimean War monument for Scutari, commissioned and made in secrecy, and not announced until it had been finished and the Baron asked for £17,000 to pay for it. Lord Harrington asked in Parliament why Marochetti had been chosen for the work, and who had in fact chosen him, as this had led to talk of "undue influence". For the Government Lord Panmure replied that they had been guided by the Baron's reputation, and that the responsibility of the choice was his own, but no one believed this.

The climax came a little later when the Government decided to erect in St. Paul's Cathedral, a monument to the Duke of Wellington. E. H. Baily, John Foley, John Gibson and Baron Marochetti were asked to produce models. Gibson and Marochetti declined, and those models made by Bailey and Foley were rejected. At once it was rumoured that this was a "job" and that Marochetti had been given the commission anyway, as he "preferred to rely on his private influence". Baily wrote to the Government to say that to give the work to one who had not competed would be a "wrong of many kinds". A little later an open letter was sent to the First Commissioner of Works, Sir Benjamin ("Big Ben") Hall, signed by twenty-two sculptors including E. H. Baily, P. MacDowell, W. Calder Marshall, J. Foley, William Behnes and Matthew Noble, in which they stated that there was not a "dearth of genius among the sculptors of England" and asked if the patronage of the nation could be "exercised with more care and

---

[1] Flaxman's model was exhibited at the Royal Academy in 1801. Nothing came of the scheme but the monument to Lord North at Wroxton, Oxfordshire, incorporates the design. The idea of a naval memorial must have been kept alive, for "Robert Smirke (jnr) [Sir Robert Smirke, R.A., F.R.S., F.S.A. (1781–1867)] shewed me His design for the Trafalgar Monument to be placed on Greenwich Hill neer Hampstead [*sic*. i.e. Flamsteed] House. He sd. the sum allowed is £11,000—he reckoned upon it being completed in 6 or 7 years." *The Farington Diary*, July 10th, 1817.

discrimination" although they wished to guard against any imputation of an "illiberal jealousy" towards foreigners.

The Department of Prints and Drawings possesses very little in the way of preliminary designs for projects of the period, and cannot claim to be representative. There is nothing by Chantrey, Lough, Foley, Carew, but there are E. H. Baily's designs for metalwork,[1] and the drawings by John Gibson are nearly all early works made while he was apprenticed to S. and T. Franceys, the Liverpool statuaries (fig. 140). However, four much publicised national works are represented, and as might be expected from the situation and feeling prevailing at the time, most of them had stormy histories of indecision, jealousy, suspicion and criticism. They are the statue of the Duke of Wellington at Hyde Park Corner (fig. 142), the Nelson memorial in Trafalgar Square (fig. 141), the monument to Wellington in St. Paul's Cathedral (fig. 144), and the memorial to the Prince Consort in Kensington Gardens (figs. 147, 150, 151).

Matthew Cotes Wyatt, assisted by his son James, made the enormous statue of Wellington for Decimus Burton's arch at Hyde Park Corner. It took more than six years to achieve, and when placed in position was called a national scandal and the sculptors were told within a few weeks that it had been "irrevocably decided by Her Majesty and the Government that the Equestrian Statue should be removed from the Arch".[2] No-one was satisfied with the Nelson monument in Trafalgar Square, and argument about the lions went on for many years. The result of the competition of the Wellington monument in St. Paul's was uproar, and the monument itself took more than sixty years to complete; it is undoubtedly the masterpiece of Alfred Stevens, and the only one entered for the competition which got away from the conventional figures of Britannia, War, Peace, Fame and like symbolism. A comparison with John Nost's design (fig. 33) for the Duke of Newcastle's monument of nearly a century and a half earlier, or with that to Queen Elizabeth in Westminster Abbey, shows that Stevens was not nearly as unconventional as was thought in 1858, and his monument follows in a tradition of Renaissance forerunners. The Albert Memorial which cost nearly £120,000 has been an object of ridicule or praise since its completion in 1876—an object of amusement or the supreme achievement of Sir George Gilbert Scott and High Victorian art,[3] with its mosaics by Clayton and Bell, and sculpture by Armstead, MacDowell, Foley, Theed, Weekes and others.[4] In spite of the lavish praise be-

[1] Charles Oman, "A problem of artistic responsibility: the firm of Rundell, Bridge & Rundell", *Apollo*, March, 1966, pages 174–83.

[2] Letter to Matthew Cotes Wyatt from Lord Morpeth, in the Victoria and Albert Museum Library.

[3] Charles Handley-Read, "The Albert Memorial re-assessed", *Country Life*, December 14th, 1961.

[4] Baron Marochetti was asked to make the large seated figure of Prince Albert, but both of the models he produced before his death were considered unsuitable, and the commission was given to Foley instead.

stowed by the *Art Journal* on the proposal by J. Wills to enclose the whole structure within an ornate gothic glass-house as high at St. Paul's Cathedral (fig. 149), nothing came of his scheme.

The drawing by Scott (fig. 147) shows quite clearly that although the sculpture was by many different people, Scott had indicated the form it was to take, and the various sculptors have followed his intentions closely. It is also apparent that the pedestals of the four main groups, the Continents, were to be decorated with low reliefs; that on the right of the design for instance, beneath Asia, is shown as a representation of the 1851 Exhibition. The Memorial suffered some damage during the Second World War when the cross was blown off; it was replaced on a different axis, as photographs taken before the War show that its position then agreed with this design.

THERE ARE NO BOOKS which deal solely with the drawings of sculptors during the period covered by this book, although these drawings are sometimes referred to in some of the works listed by Dr. Margaret Whinney in the bibliography of her *Sculpture in Britain 1530–1840*, to which should be added an occasional mention in the pages of *Country Life*.

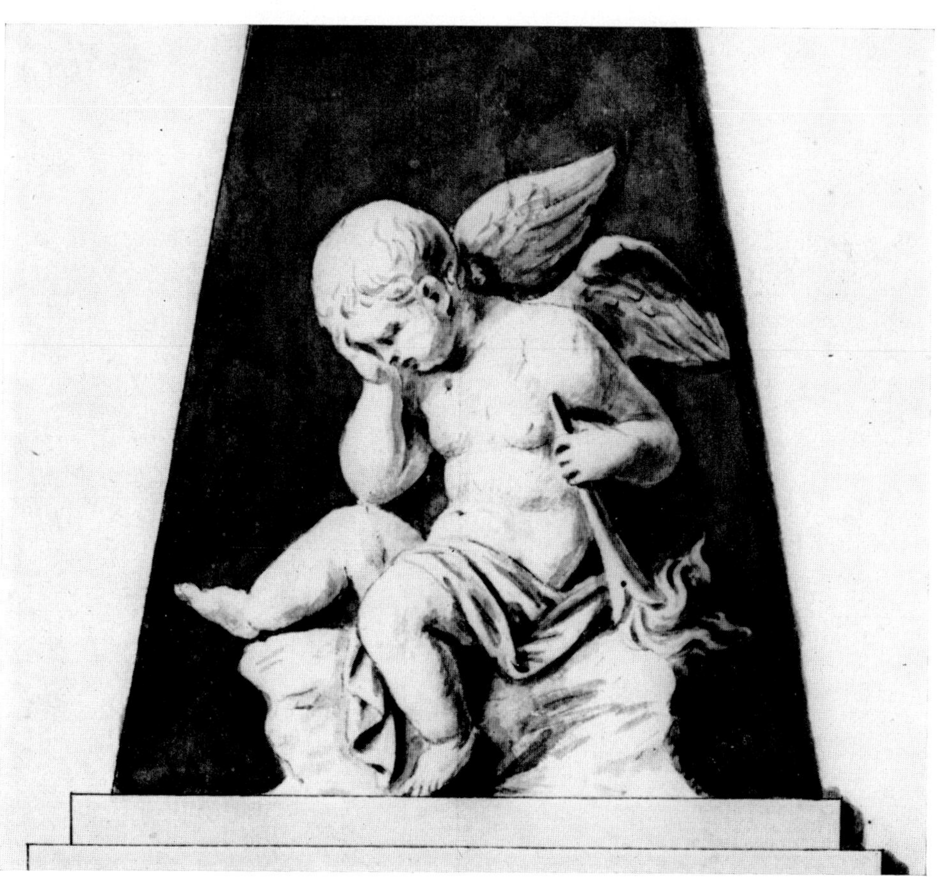

Fig. 19
Detail of a design by Joseph Nollekens, R.A., for the monument to Elizabeth Grigg, St. Katherine's Chapel, Regent's Park, London.

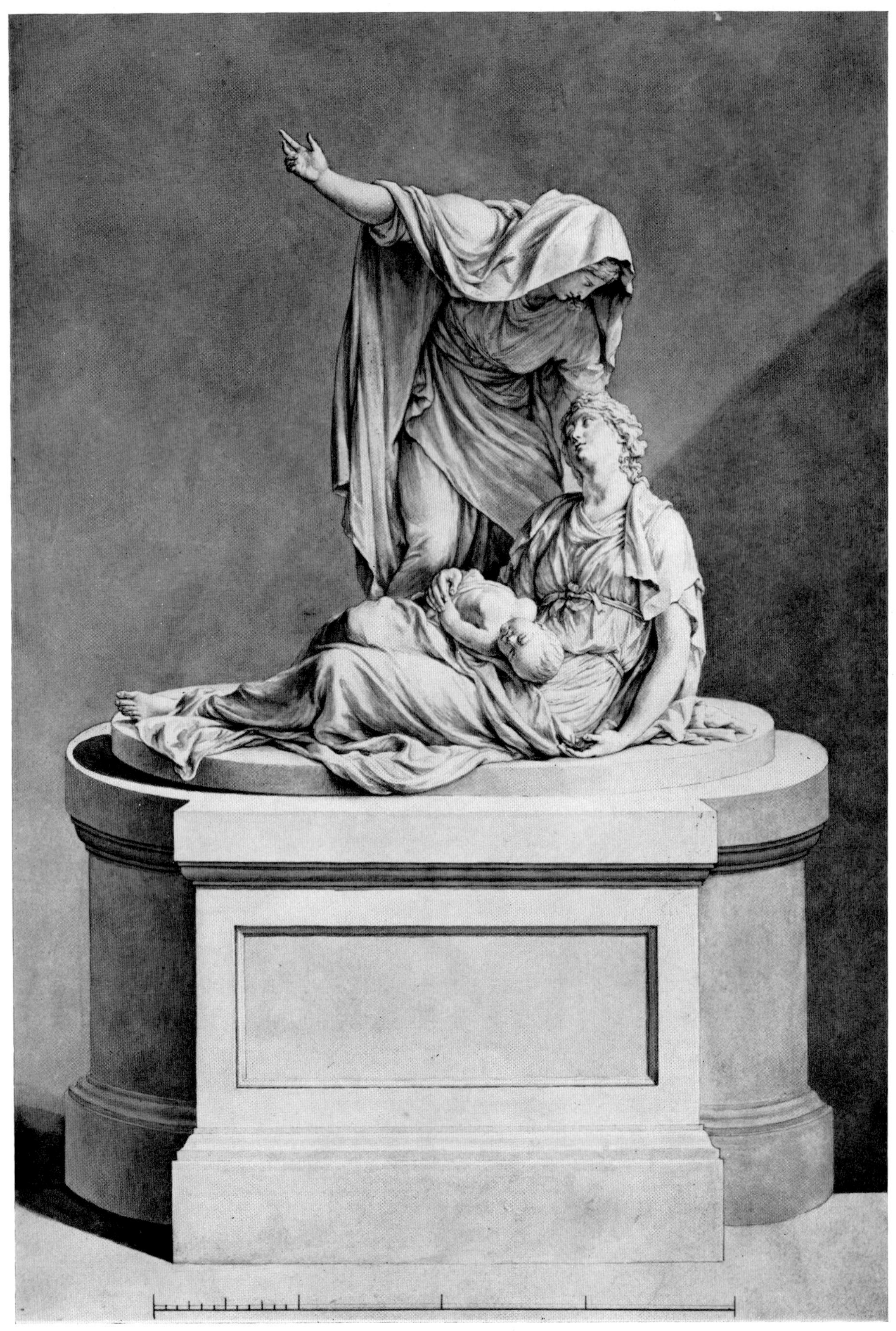

Fig. 20
Design by Joseph
Nollekens, R.A., for t
monument to Mrs.
Howard, of Corby,
Wetheral, Cumberla
c. 1789.

# Catalogue

# EDWARD PIERCE *or Pearce (died 1695)*

*Figure 21 (right):*  Design for the monument to Lady Warburton (died 1693–4), in St. John's Church, Chester.
Pen and ink and wash, 17 × 10 inches. No. 3436.421.

*Figure 22 (below):*  Monument to Lady Warburton (died 1693–4), in St. John's Church, Chester.
Photograph: *National Monuments Record.*

---

**21**  This drawing was at one time in the collection of John Talman (1677–1726), son of the architect William Talman to whom it was formerly attributed. It was later in the possession of Sir John Soane's assistant, Charles James Richardson (1806–1871), and bought from him in 1863. Other designs by Pierce are in the British Museum and Sir John Soane's Museum.

(See H. M. Colvin, *A Biographical Dictionary of English Architects, 1660–1840*, pages 456, 593.)

**22**  "M.S. of Diana Warburton, wife and relict of Sir George Warburton, of Arley, in Cheshire, bart. who survived her husband 17 years, in an unmarried state, with true mourning, fasting and prayers. She was daughter of Sir Edward Bishop, of Parham, in Sussex, Knight and Baronet, and in her minoritie had had a virtuous and severe education, so as she became a great exemplar of all Christian graces and virtues, and adorned every relation she stood in. She was a loving and loyal consort, a tender and indulgent parent, a compassionate mistress to her servants, a most accomplished friend, cheerful in her family, obliging to strangers, a daily almoner to the poor, fervent and composed in her devotion, both in public and private, a patron to the clergy, and a generous benefactor to the church, and all places of her abode. She was of a quicke and piercing understanding, of a deep apprehension and discerning judgment, of great evenesse of mind and calmness of spirit in all events; aspiring after things only solid, improving, and rational; just in her actions, candid in all her censures, ready to forgive injuries, and never prone to doe any; delighted to see good in others, commended and encouraged it in all; her religion was not a bare shew or empty noise, but solid, substantial, even, and uniform; humble and patient in her sickness, and in the midst of pain without murmuring and despondency submitted herself to God, and with great constancy of mind and cheerfulness of spirit, resigned herself to Him in one continued act of devout prayers and praises, of heavenly meditations and discoursings, suitable to the entertainment of a departing soul, on the 13th of March, anno domini 1693."

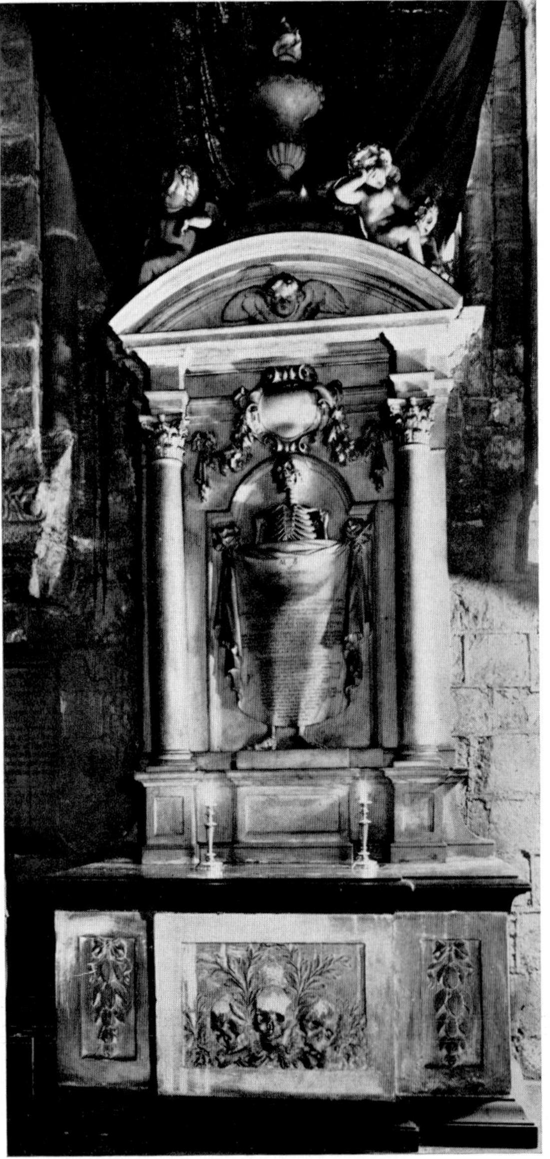

Fig. 22

46

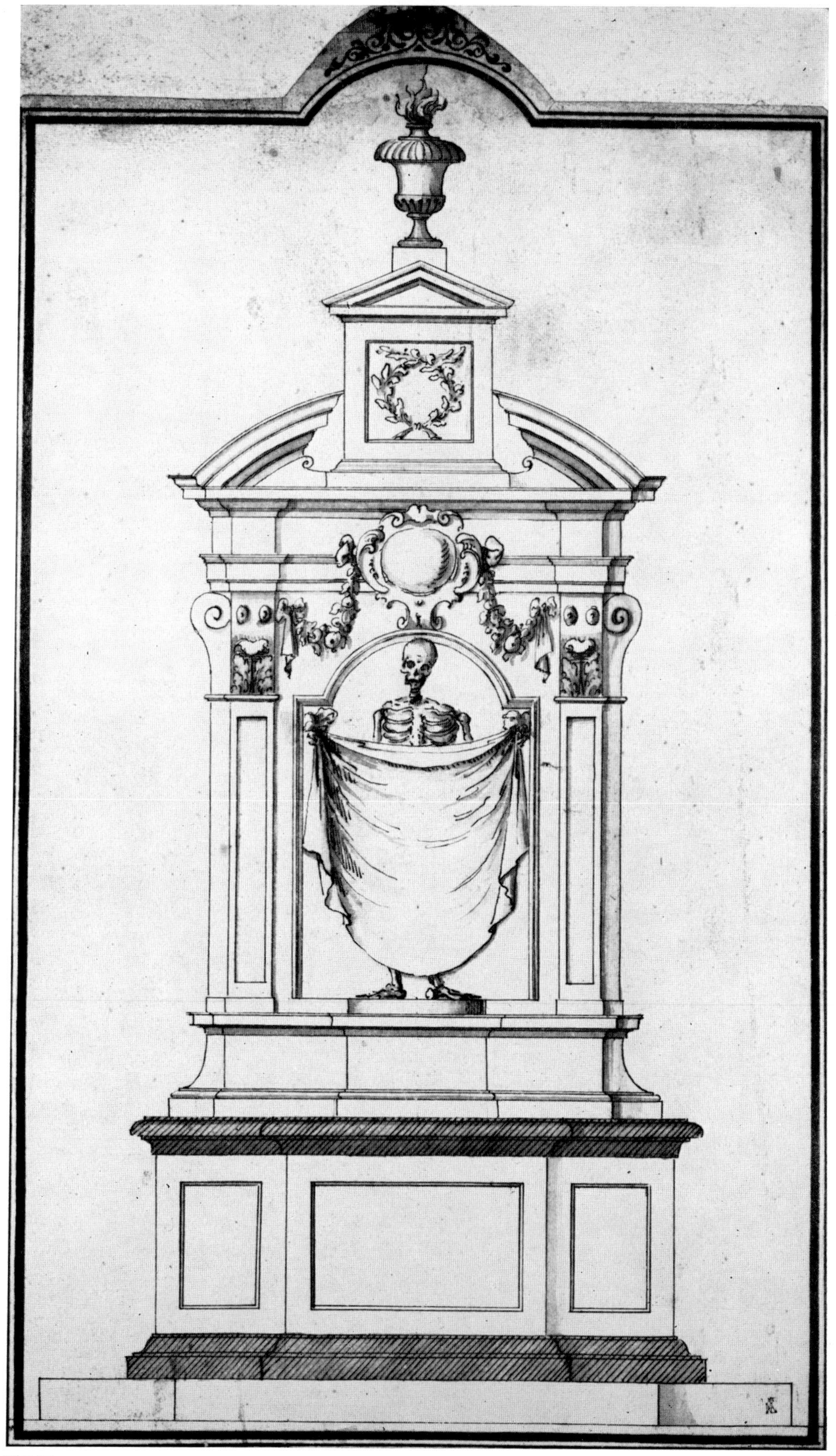

Fig. 21

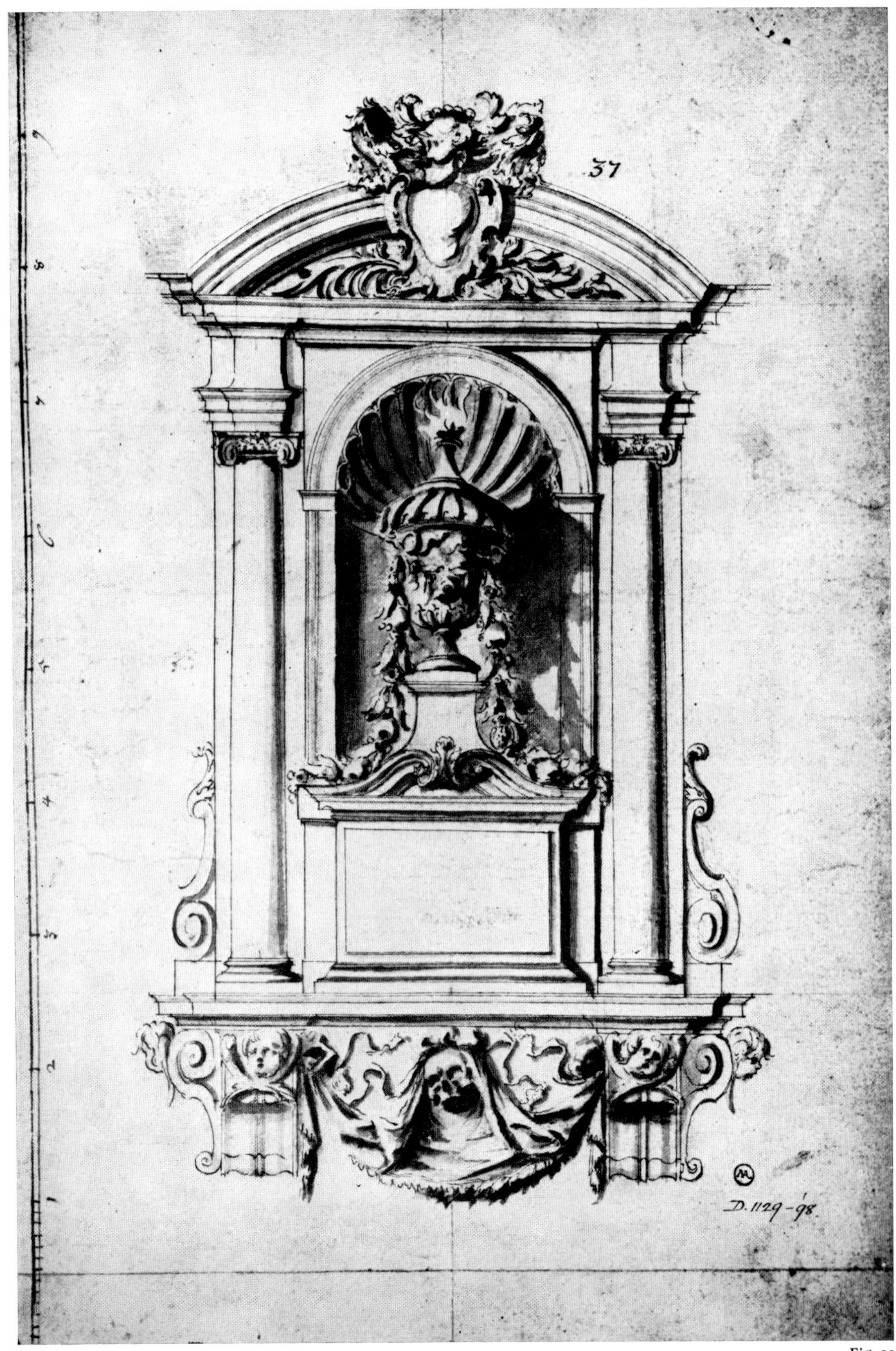



Fig. 23

# WILLIAM STANTON (*1639–1705*)

*Figure 23 (left)*:   Design for the monument to Christopher Clitherow (died 1685), at Pinner, Middlesex.
Inscribed with a scale in feet.
Pen and ink and wash, 10 × 6 inches. No. D.1129–1898.

*Figure 24 (below)*:  Monument to Christopher Clitherow (died 1685), at Pinner, Middlesex.
Photograph: *Royal Commission on Historical Monuments (England)*.

---

**23**  This drawing was formerly attributed to Caius Gabriel Cibber, and is one of 44 so attributed, which were bought from Mr. E. Parsons, of Brompton Road, on May 28th, 1898, for £3. 10. od. They had previously been sold at Messrs. Sotheby and Wilkinson's on November 27th, 1861, for £1. 3. od.

**24**  "Near this place lyeth ye body of Christopher Clitherow of Pinnar Esq. ye Son of Christopher Clitherow and Jane his Wife, and Grandson of Sr. Christopher Clitherow Ld. Mayor of London.

He lived a very honest man, a loyall Subject & a good Christian in a corrupt, Seditious wicked Age & went to his reward ye 12th of May in ye Year of our Ld. 1685 and of His Age the 32d."

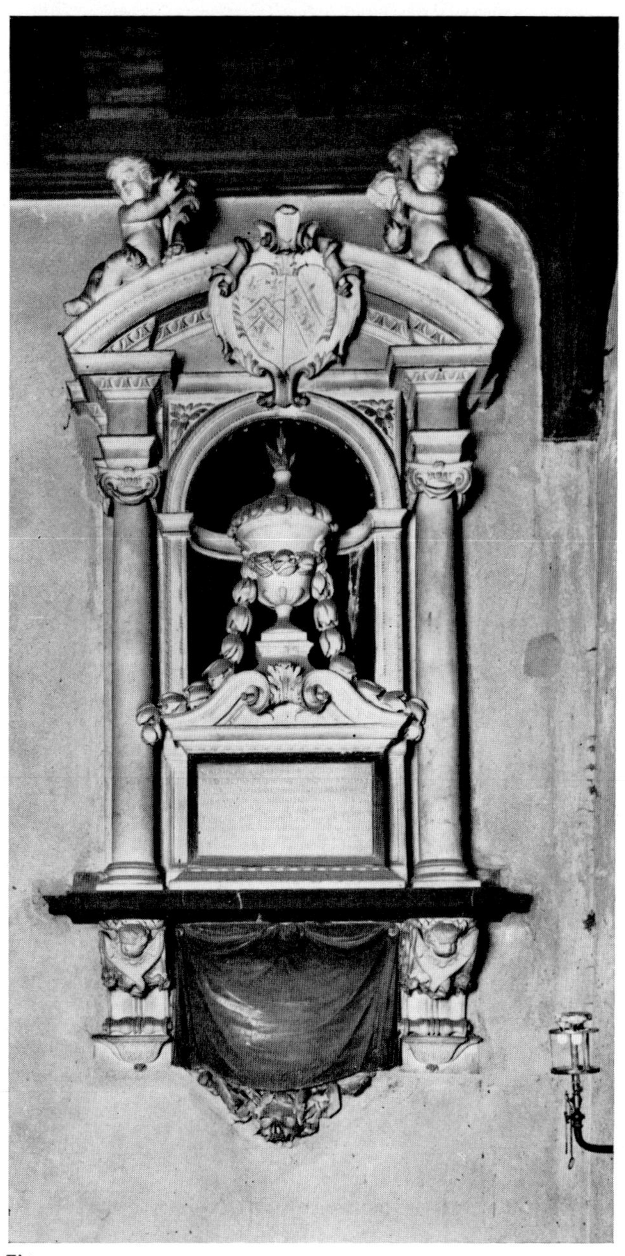

Fig. 24

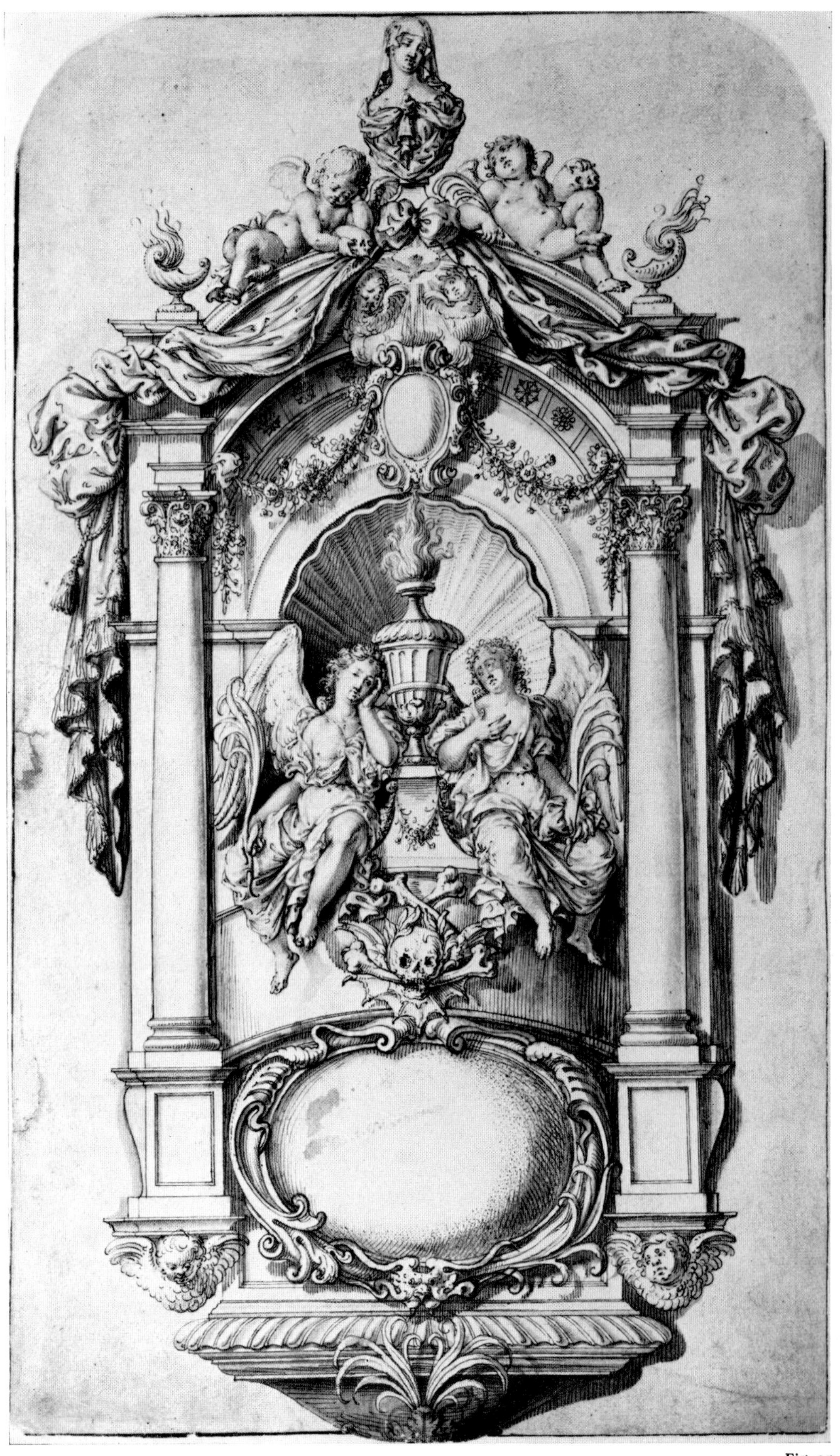

Fig. 25

# WILLIAM STANTON (*1639–1705*)

*Figure 25* (*left*):　Design for the monument to Sir John Roberts, Bart. (died 1692), in St. Mary's Church, Bromley, Poplar, London.
Pen and ink and wash, size of sheet $16\frac{1}{4} \times 9\frac{3}{4}$ inches. No. E.959–1965.

*Figure 26* (*below*):　Monument to Sir John Roberts, Bart. (died 1692), in St. Mary's Church, Bromley, Poplar, London.
Photograph: *Royal Commission on Historical Monuments (England)*.

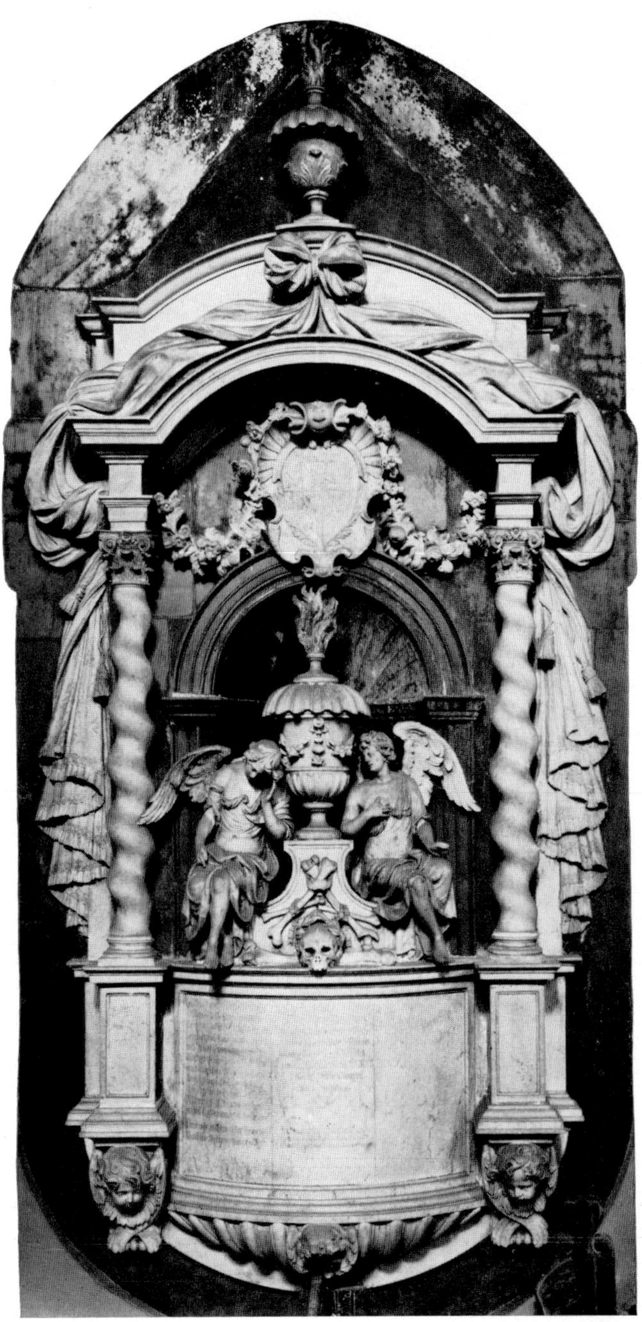

**Fig. 26**

**25**　This drawing was bequeathed to the Museum by Rupert Gunnis, J.P.

**26**　The whole work was destroyed by bombing during the Second World War. The epitaph, however, had been recorded in *Monumenta Anglicana* by John Le Neve, Volume 3, 1718, "In this vault lyeth the body of Dame Mary Roberts, daughter of William Amy Merchant of *Exon* & late wife of Sir Jo. Roberts of *Bromley* Bart. by whom she had 4 sons and 5 daughters all dyed young. She dyed 21 Sept. 1690. In the same vault lyeth buried Sr. J. Roberts Bart. Patron of this Church who dyed 14. Dec. 1692. to whose memory his Relict Dame Deborah Roberts being his 2d. wife caused this inscription."

It is possible that the design was intended for a monument to Mary, Lady Roberts, as it incorporates a bust of a woman, and that when Sir John died two years later, the sculptor adapted the monument to meet this new circumstance.

# WILLIAM STANTON (*1639–1705*)

*Figure 27 (right):*  Design for the monument to Dorothy, Lady Brownlow (died 1700), in St. Nicholas's Church, Sutton, Surrey.
Pen and ink and wash, $12\frac{7}{8} \times 8\frac{3}{4}$ inches. No. D.1104–1898.

---

**27**  This drawing was formerly attributed to Caius Gabriel Cibber; see fig. 23.

"Joyning to the *North* wall of the Chancel is a beautiful, Marble Monument railed in, whereon lies, at full length, a Lady leaning on her left Arm, and by her three Children, two weeping, and one pointing to a Glory surrounded with Cherubims on a Curtain, on the Top two Cupids with Golden Trumpets; on each side two Urns, and on an oval Tablet underneath is the following Inscription: *Here lyes the body of Dame Dorothy Brownlowe, Wife of Sr.* William Brownlowe *of* Belton *in the County of* Lincoln, Bart. *eldest Daughter and Coheiress of* Sir Richard Mason Knight *& Clerk Controler of the Green-Cloath to* King Charles *and* King James 2d. *and of Dame* Anne *his Wife who departed this Life the 13 day of* January, *Anno Domini 1699/1700 in the 34 Year of her Age . . .*" (*The Natural History and Antiquities of the County of Surrey* by John Aubrey, 1718, Volume 2, page 124).

William Hone visited the church in 1831 when he saw "Dame Dorothy Brownlow's gorgeous marble monument beside the altar. She is represented in a recumbent posture, with three sorrowing infants about her, and four cherubs above, in a sort of hasty pudding, garnished with slices of gilt gingerbread" (quoted by Edward Walford in *Greater London*, Volume 2, page 209).

The church was rebuilt during the 19th century, and as the monument is now behind the organ, it can no longer be seen. A photograph of the head of Lady Brownlow appeared in the *Sutton and Cheam Herald* for August 18th, 1966, and shows that the monument is now in a very dirty condition. (See John Physick, "Tracing the work of William Stanton", *Country Life Annual*, 1968.)

Between c. 1679 and 1726, William Stanton and his son Edward produced several monuments to members of the Brownlow family. They are in Belton and Old Somerby churches in Lincolnshire. The earliest is that to Sir John (d. 1679) and his wife Alicia (d. 1676), a standing architectural work, in which are two half-effigies holding hands. Others commemorated are Elizabeth, Lady Brownlow (d. 1684), Sir John

(d. 1697), Alice, Lady Brownlow (d. 1721), and William Brownlow (d. 1726). In addition, William Stanton was the master-mason during the building of Belton House from 1685. Ann, the younger sister of Dorothy, Lady Brownlow, married Charles Gerard, 2nd Earl of Macclesfield, in 1683. She became the mistress of Richard Savage, 4th Earl Rivers, and was divorced by Lord Macclesfield in 1698, when their two children Ann (Savage) (born 1695) and Richard (Savage) (born 1697) were declared illegitimate. The monument to Lord Rivers's father, the 3rd Earl, c. 1694, with a reclining figure in contemporary dress, in the parish church of Macclesfield, Cheshire, is also the work of William Stanton.

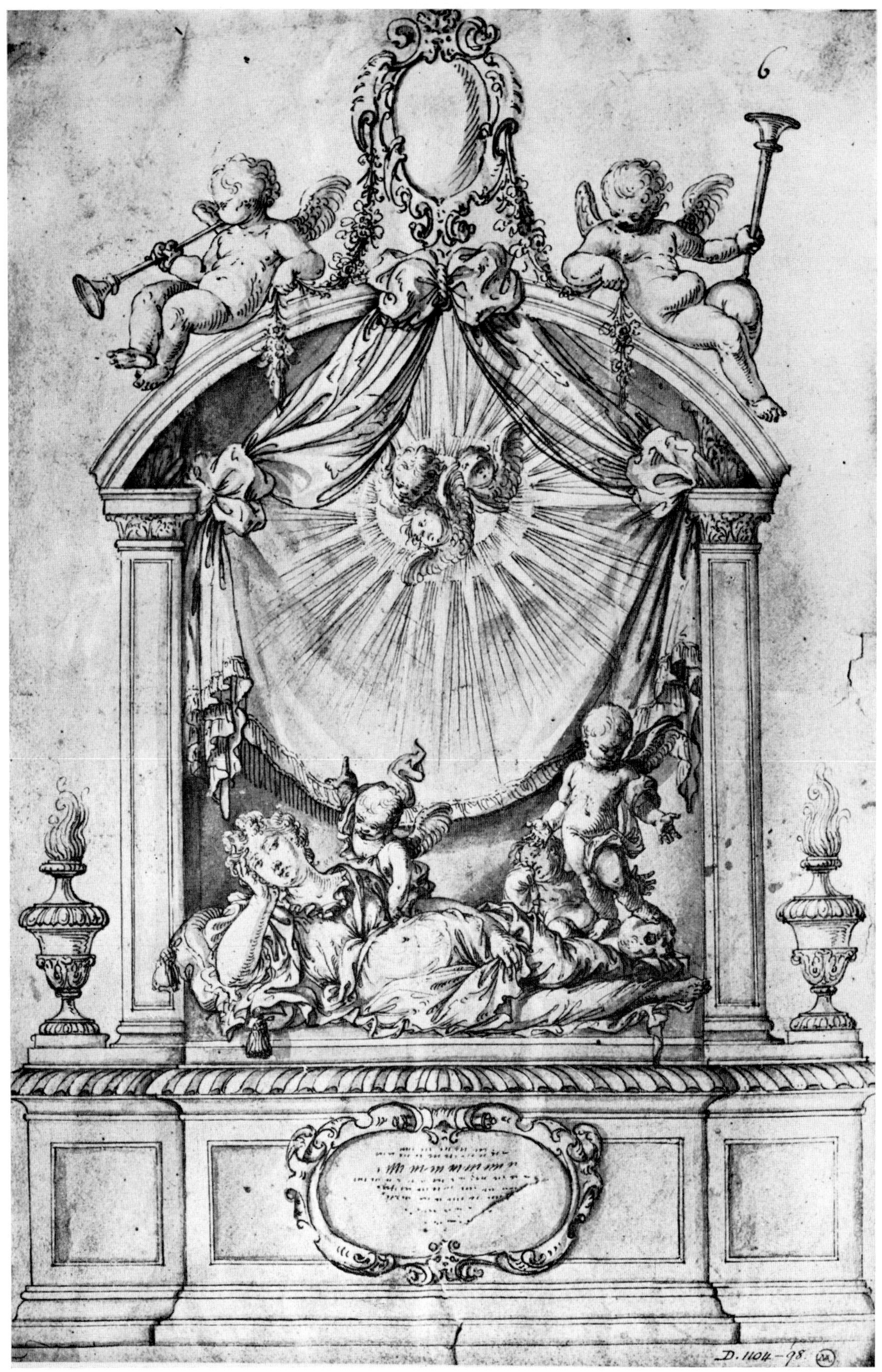

Fig. 27

*Figure 28* (*below*): Design for the statues of Pallas and Apollo on the Grand Staircase, Chatsworth, Derbyshire.
Signed *C* and *CGC*. Inscribed *Two figures in Niches on the Grand Stairs at Chatsworth*.
Pen and ink, size of sheet $10\frac{1}{8} \times 13\frac{3}{8}$ inches. No. E.946–1965.

*Figure 29* (*right*): The figure of Apollo on the Grand Staircase, Chatsworth, Derbyshire.
Photograph: *National Monuments Record*.

---

**28** This drawing was bequeathed to the Museum by Rupert Gunnis, J.P.

**29** Among the Chatsworth Accounts is an entry, dated August 17th, 1688, "Receaved then of James Whildon in full for making three figures, vizt. Pallas, Apollo & the Triton, by his Lordps especiall order the sum of fifty-poundes. I say receaved the said summ of £50. 0. 0. C. Gabriel Cibber" (H. Faber, *Caius Gabriel Cibber 1630–1700, his life and work*, 1926, page 50). Francis Thompson in his *History of Chatsworth* (1949, page 124) suggests that these figures were originally made for the gardens.

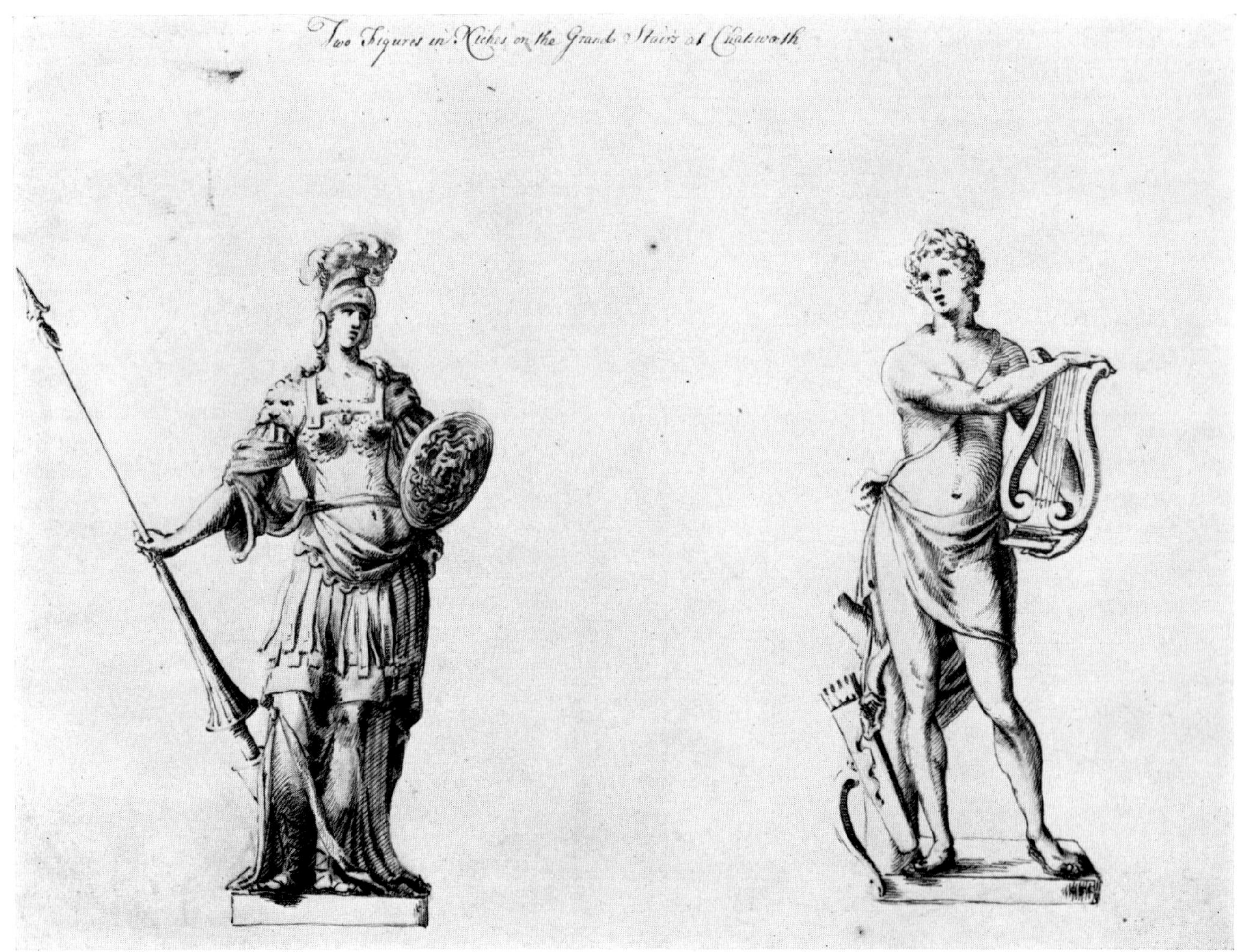


Fig. 28

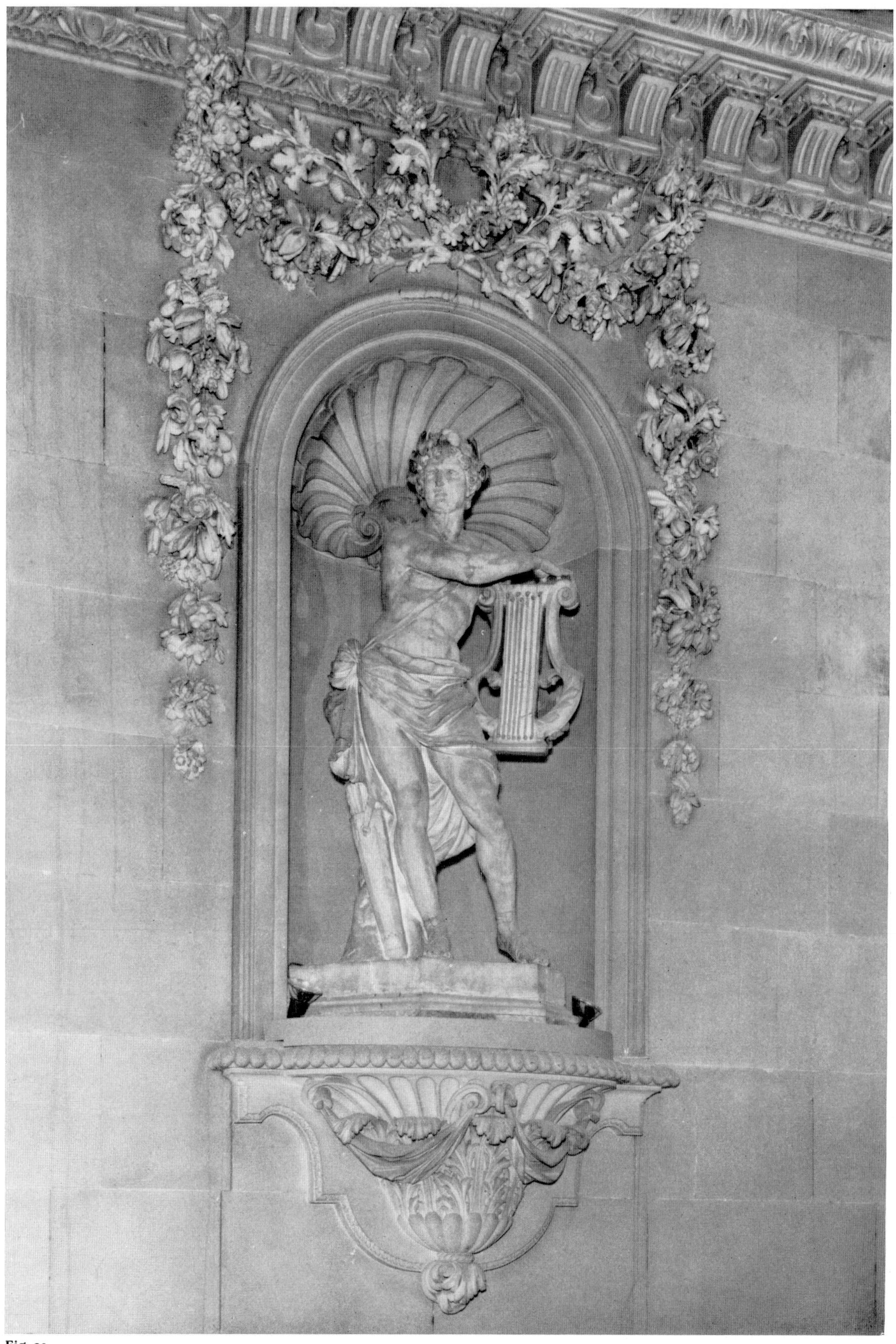

Fig. 29

*Figure 30* (*below*): Design for a statue of King William III, flanked by two Continents.
Pen and ink and wash, 19½ × 7⅛ inches. No. 9145.

*Figure 31* (*right*): Design for a fountain at Hampton Court, Middlesex, with a statue of King William III.
Pen and ink and wash, 20¼ × 12⅝ inches. British Museum, No. 1964–12–12–7.

---

**30**  This design was acquired by the Museum in 1883, as by an unidentified artist, for 5 shillings.

**31**  At the end of the 17th century John Nost made several drawings of a figure of William III for the "marble fountain" for which he received £2. He also made models for a fountain, one of which had "four mermaids, each sitting on a dolphin and four shells between them, and four dolphins in the middle, supporting a large shell". An alternative design consisted of "four figures of young men each sitting on a dolphin and four swans between them, a pedestal of four scrowles in the middle and a Mercury on top of it" (Public Record Office, Works 5/52).

It may have been the intention that the statue of William III had a Continent at each of the corners of the pedestal, but there is the possibility that it may have had a companion statue of Queen Mary II, which would have had the other two Continents.

The fountain design has obviously some relationship with the so-called Diana Fountain which was, at that time, in the Privy Garden. It was not moved to Bushey Park, where it still is, and raised on its rusticated stone base until about 1712.

Statues of William III attributed to John Nost, one recently repaired and gilded, in Portsmouth Dockyard, the other in the grounds of Wrest Park, Bedfordshire, are illustrated as figures 9 and 10.

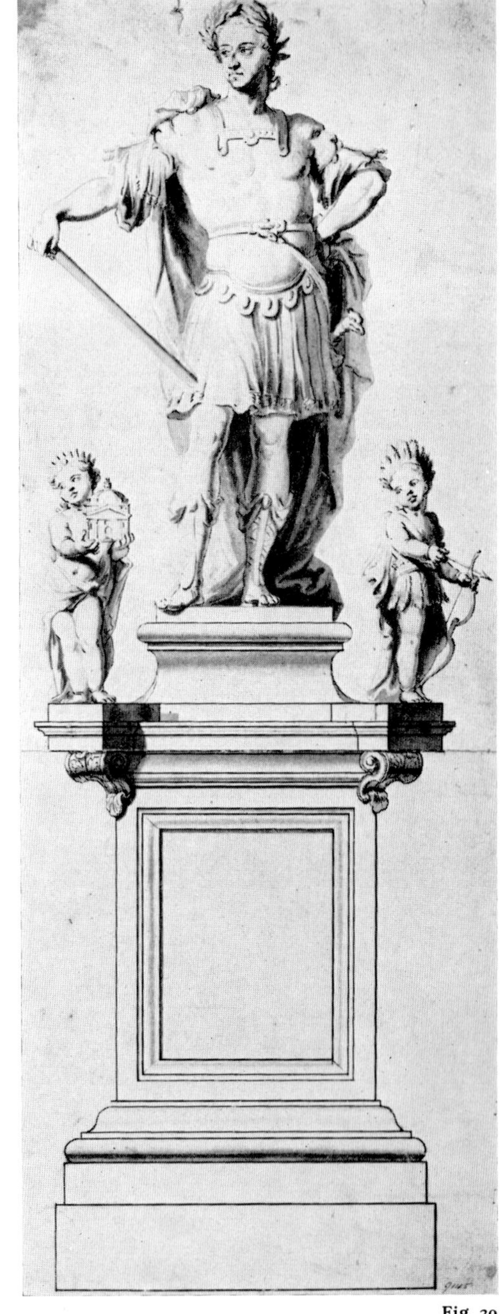

Fig. 30

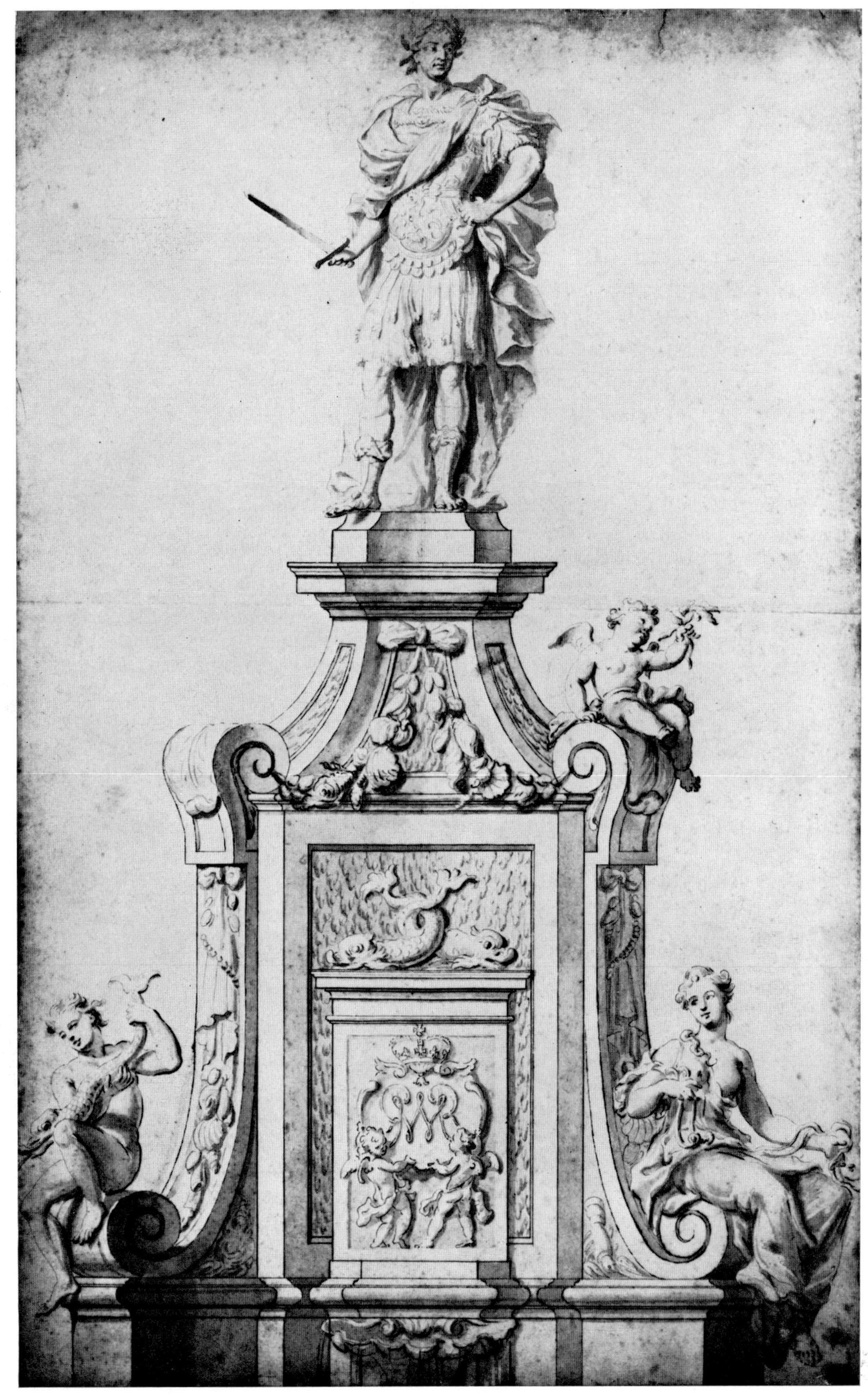

Fig. 31

# FRANCESCO FANELLI (*worked 1608–1665*)



*Figure 32 (right):* The Diana Fountain, in Bushey Park, Middlesex, the figures are before 1640.
Photograph: *Royal Commission on Historical Monuments (England).*

---

**32** The fountain was probably made for Charles I, and an engraved view by Sutton Nicholls, published during the last decade of the 17th century, of the South Front of Hampton Court, with the Privy Garden, shows the fountain as it then was, without its high base. The attribution to Fanelli appears to derive from the statement by John Evelyn in his diary. An inventory made of the Palace and its gardens in 1659 includes:

"One large fountaine of black marble with a curbe of Eight cants about it of the same marble lined with lead.

Fower scollop basins  
Fower Sea-monsters } of brass about the  
Three scrowles { Fountaine  
Fower boyes holding Dolphins

One large brasse Statue on the top of the Fountaine called Arethusa."

In June, 1662, John Evelyn noted that "In ye garden is a rich and noble fountaine, with syrens, statues, &c. cast in copper by Fanelli, but no plenty of water", and a year later another visitor, the Duke of Monconys, also thought the fountain was worth describing, "A fountain composed of four syrens in bronze, seated astride dolphins, between which was a shell, supported on the foot of a goat. Above the syrens on a second tier, were four little children, each seated, holding a fish, and surmounting all a large figure of a lady—all the figures being of bronze, but the fountain itself and the basin of marble" (quoted in E. Law, *The History of Hampton Court Palace*, Volume 2, page 244).

It is quite probable that the fountain was altered between 1689 and 1696, and took the form which it has in Sutton Nicholls's engraving, and which it retains today at the top of the tall pedestal, as Edward Pierce was paid £1,262. 3s. for "carving done about the ffountaine in P. G. [Privy Garden] carving 8 scrowles & 4 festoons with shells and sev^ll foot of sup. in the gt. stones under the Cornish" (Pipe Rolls 4, *Wren Society*, Volume 4, page 32).

In 1699/1700 Henry Wise constructed the basin in Bushey Park, "In the digging and sinking the Bason of 400 ft Diameter and 5 ft deep are contained 21,005 solid yards, the charge of digging and carting it into the low grounds between the Lyme trees and other low places with ye charge of working and levelling the grounds & sowing it with hay seed . . . at 12d per solid yard £1,050. 5. 0." (Treasury Papers, Volume lxvii, no. 14). William Talman, in a "Memorial" of work to be carried out at Hampton Court, dated December 19th, 1699, and entered on January 18th, 1699/1700, had estimated "To make a pedestall of Portland Stone for a Diana in brass to stand on being 3 ft 6 in. high and 2 ft 6 in. square; & 4 pannels, each to be carved with Emblems will come to £20; & to do the same in marble will come to abt £60" (Treasury Papers, Volume lxvii, no. 12). If this was for the high pedestal, work must have ceased at the death of William III in 1702, because it was not until 1712 and 1713 that work began on the reconstruction, mending and gilding of the fountain, which included the "figure of Diana at the top, and the four nymphs, and four boys with dolphins in their hands, and four large shells" (Treasury Papers, Volume clxxxii, no. 18).[1]

An undated pencil sketch in Sir John Soane's Museum, reproduced as an inset to Plate 4 of Volume 4 of the *Wren Society*, shows a plan of the Privy Garden, with what appears to be the fountain in the centre.

---

[1] The Diana Fountain, and a newly discovered related design by Edward Pierce, are to be discussed by John Harris in a forthcoming issue of the *Burlington Magazine.*



Fig. 32 ▶

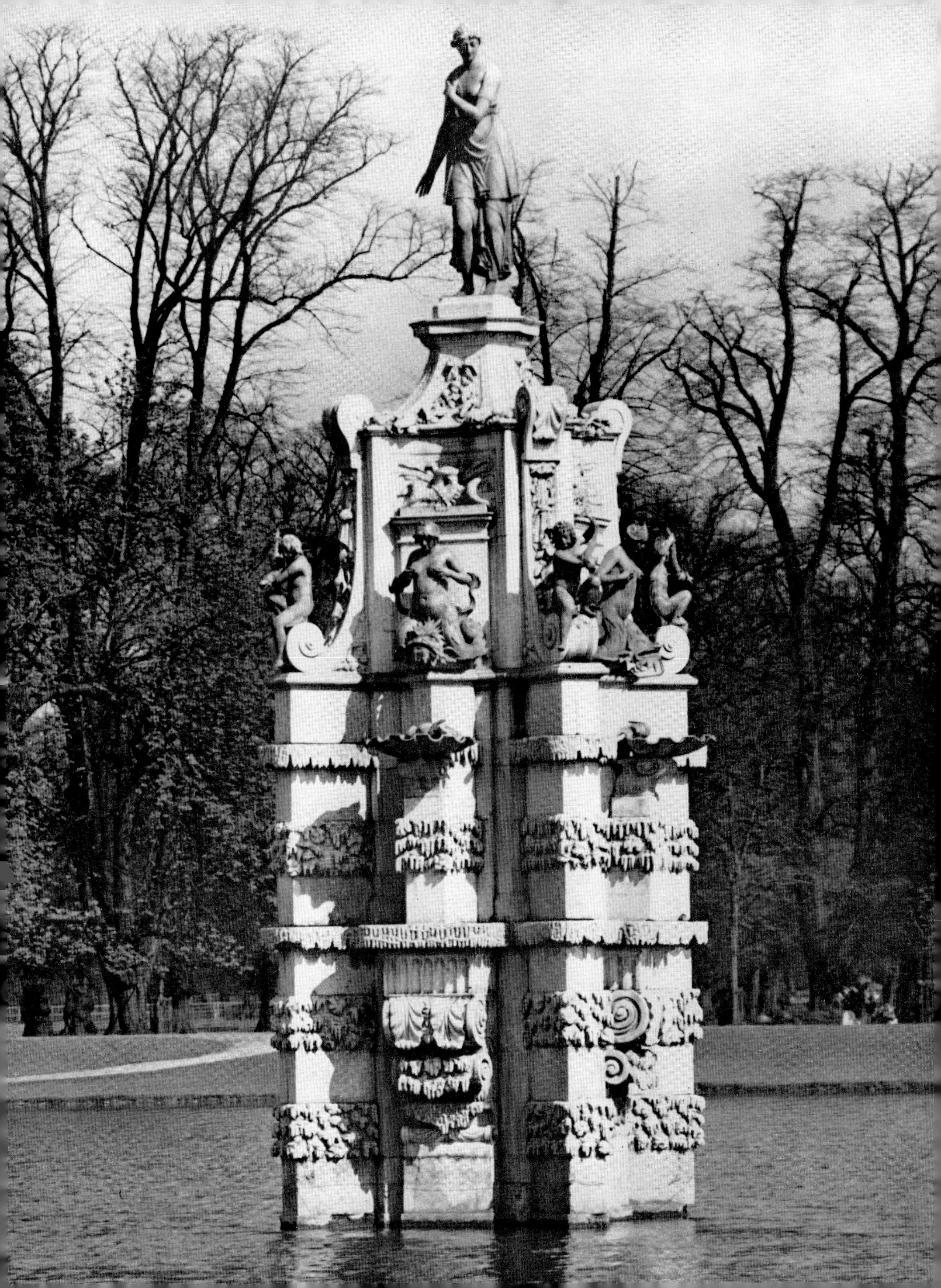

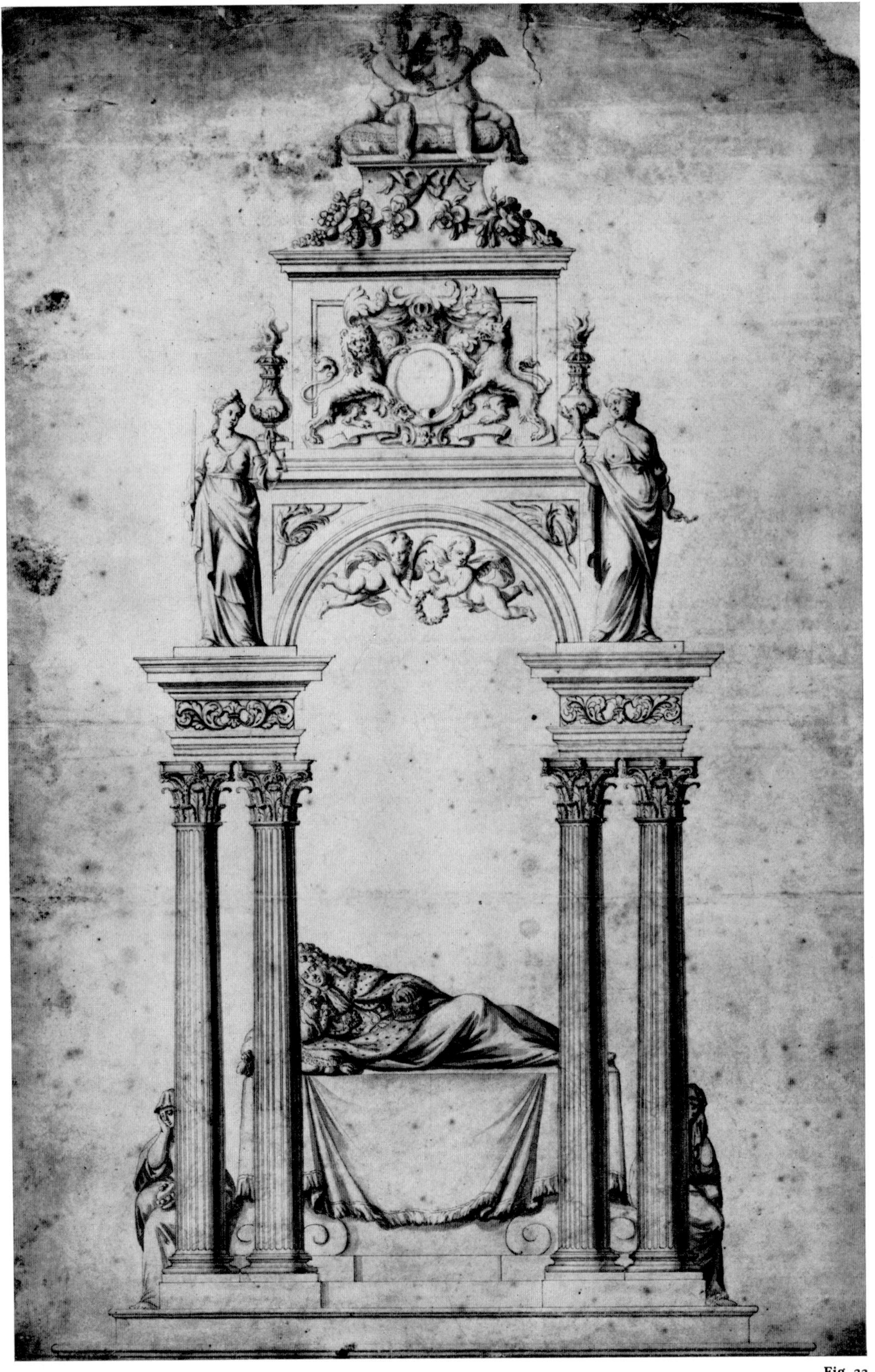

*Figure 33 (left):*    Design for the monument to John Holles, Duke of Newcastle, K.G. (died 1711), for Westminster Abbey.
Pen and ink and wash, $25\frac{7}{8} \times 15$ inches. Bodleian Library, Oxford, MS. Top. Gen. a.7. fol. 22.

*Figure 34 (p.62):*    Design for the chimney-piece in the Queen's Gallery, at Hampton Court Palace. Inscribed *Hampton Court* and with a scale in feet.
Pen and ink and wash, $8\frac{3}{4} \times 5\frac{3}{4}$ inches. No. 3436.330.

*Figure 35 (p.63):*    The chimney-piece in the Queen's Gallery, Hampton Court Palace.
Photograph: *Warburg Institute.*

---

**33**  This design, hitherto unrecorded, was recognised as the work of Nost only recently, at the time of its acquisition by the Bodleian Library. It has been definitely established from the heraldic supporters, the ducal coronet, and the Garter, as being an unexecuted project for the Duke of Newcastle's monument. The monument as it stands in Westminster Abbey today, is the work of Francis Bird, after the design of the architect James Gibbs, and was erected in the north transept in 1723 (see fig. 15). A design by Gibbs is in the Ashmolean Museum, Oxford. (See also Volume 12 of the *Wren Society*, 1935, Plate XXXIII.)

The inscription on Bird's monument reads:
"To the memory of John Holles, *Duke of Newcastle,* Marquis and Earl of Clare, Baron Haughton, of Haughton, and Knight-Companion of the most Noble Order of the Garter, whose Body is here deposited under the same Roof with many of his noble Ancestors and Relations, of the Families of *Vere, Cavendish,* and Holles, whose Eminent Virtues he inherited, and was particularly distinguished for his Courage, Love to his Countrey, and Constancy in Friendship; which Qualities he exerted with great Zeal and Readiness, whenever the Cause of Religion, his Country, or Friends required Him. In the Reign of Queen Anne, he filled, with great capacity and Honour, the several Employments of Lord Keeper of the Privy Seal, and Privy Councellour, Lord Lieutenant and *Custos Rotulorum* of the Counties of Middlesex and Nottingham, and of the County of the Town of Nottingham, and of the East and North Ridings of the County of York, Lord Chief Justice in Eyre, North of Trent, and Governour of the Town and Fort of Kingston-upon-Hull; to all of which Titles and Honours his personal Merit gave a Lustre, that needed not the Addition of the great Wealth he possessed. He was born the 9th of January 1661/2, and Dyed the 15th. of July, 1711. He married the Lady Margaret, third Daughter and Heir to Henry Cavendish, Duke of Newcastle, whom he left Issue one only Child, the Lady Henrietta Cavendish Holles Harley, who caused this Memorial of Him to be Erected in the year of our Lord 1723. *Jacobo Gibbs Architecto.*"

**34**  This drawing, as by an unidentified artist, was formerly in the possession of Sir John Soane's assistant, Charles James Richardson (1806–1871), and was acquired by the Museum in 1863. Although a preliminary design for the chimney-piece, it is not in the same hand as drawings by John Nost, and must have been the work of one of his assistants. The hand is similar to that of the design for the monument to the Bray children at Great Barrington, Gloucestershire (see fig. 28).

There is another design almost certainly for this chimney-piece by a very similar hand, in a volume of drawings probably connected with Thomas Fort (died 1745), who was Clerk of the Works at Hampton Court between 1714 and 1745. Mr. Howard Colvin drew my attention to this book which is in the Library of the Ministry of Public Building and Works (Q. 914.21:725, 171, 17978[1]).

**35**  In about 1700 Nost was paid £235 for the chimney-piece with the "Triumph of Venus", in what was then called the King's Gallery (David Green, *Grinling Gibbons*, 1964).

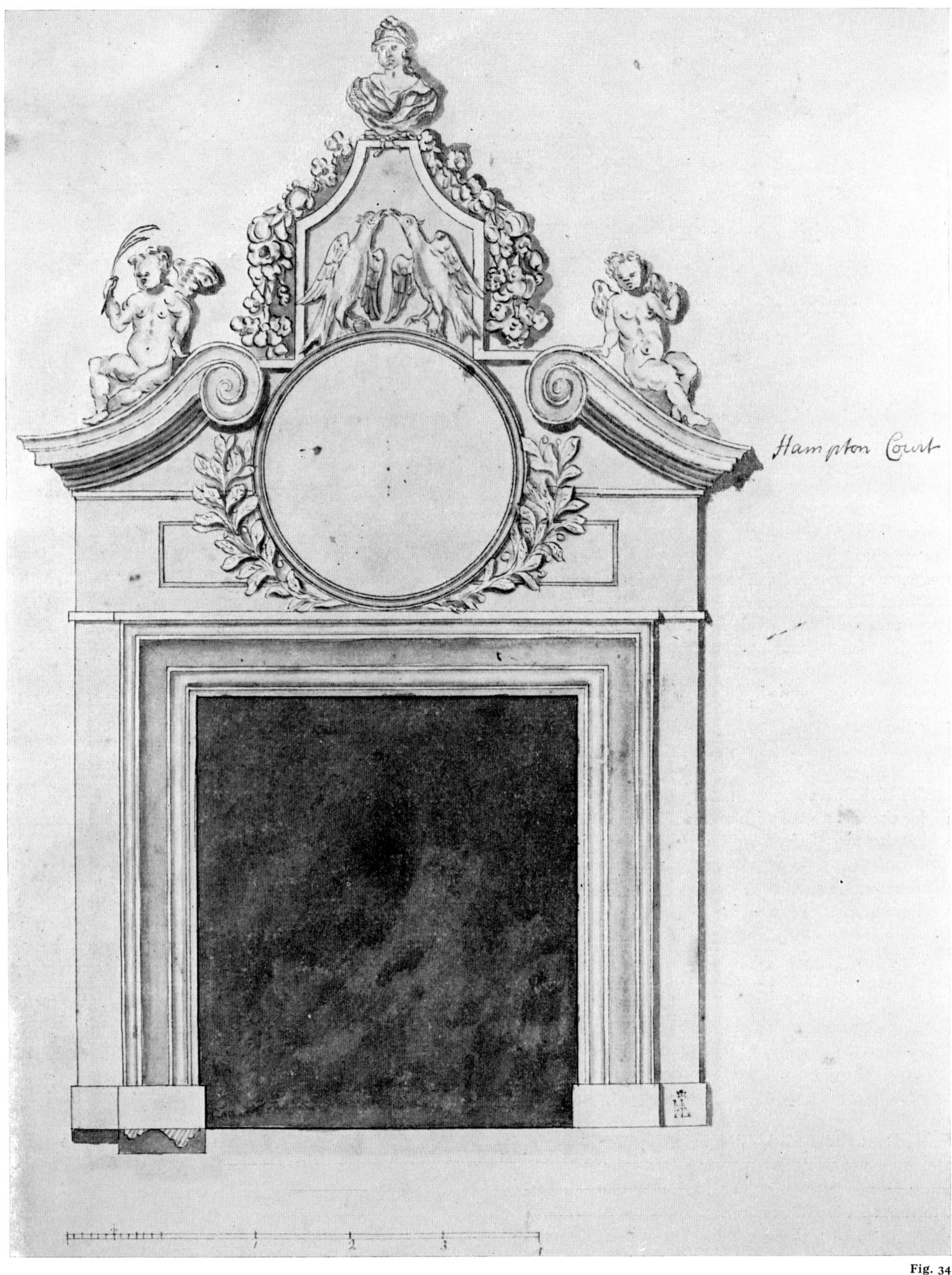



C2

**Fig. 34**

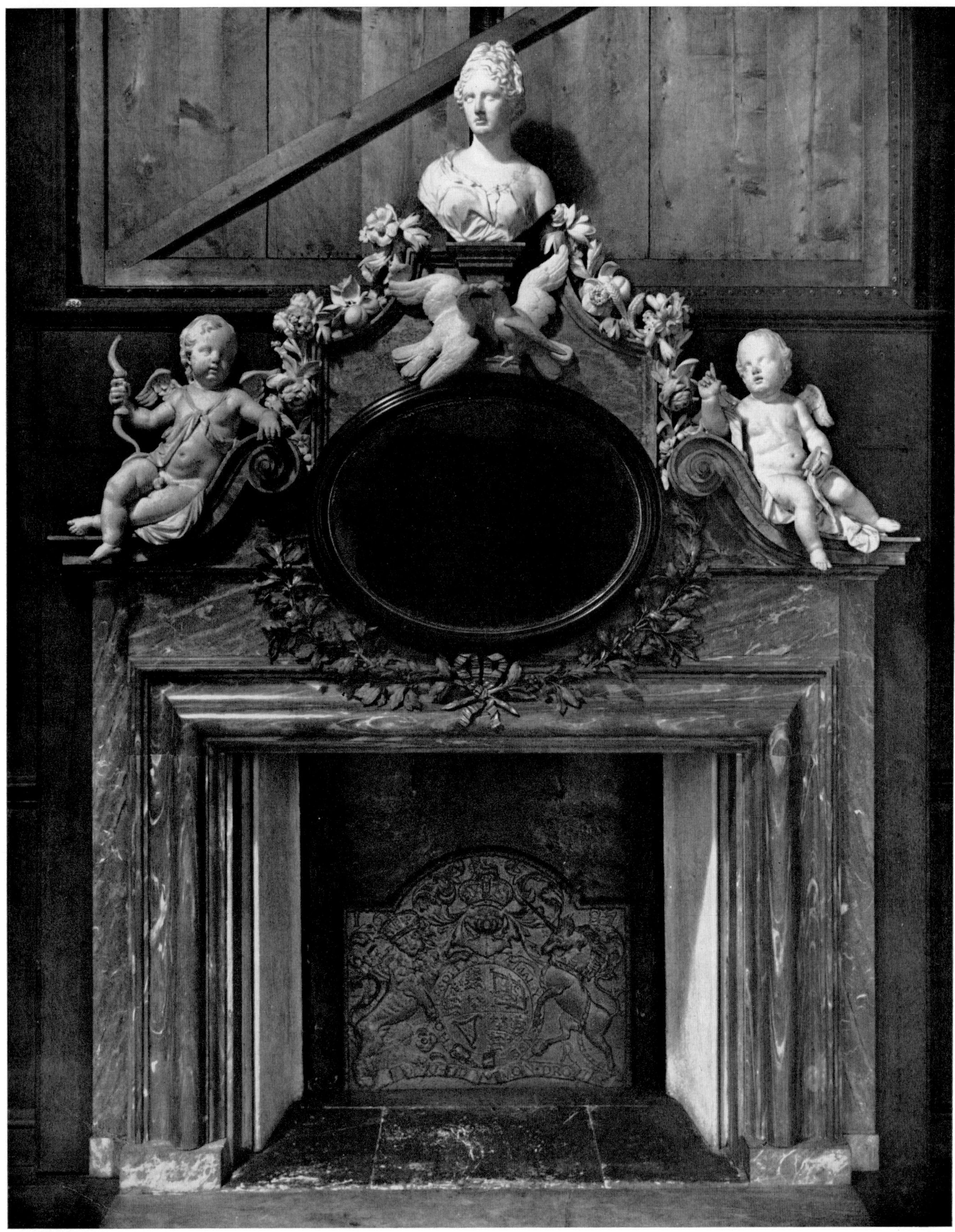

Fig. 35

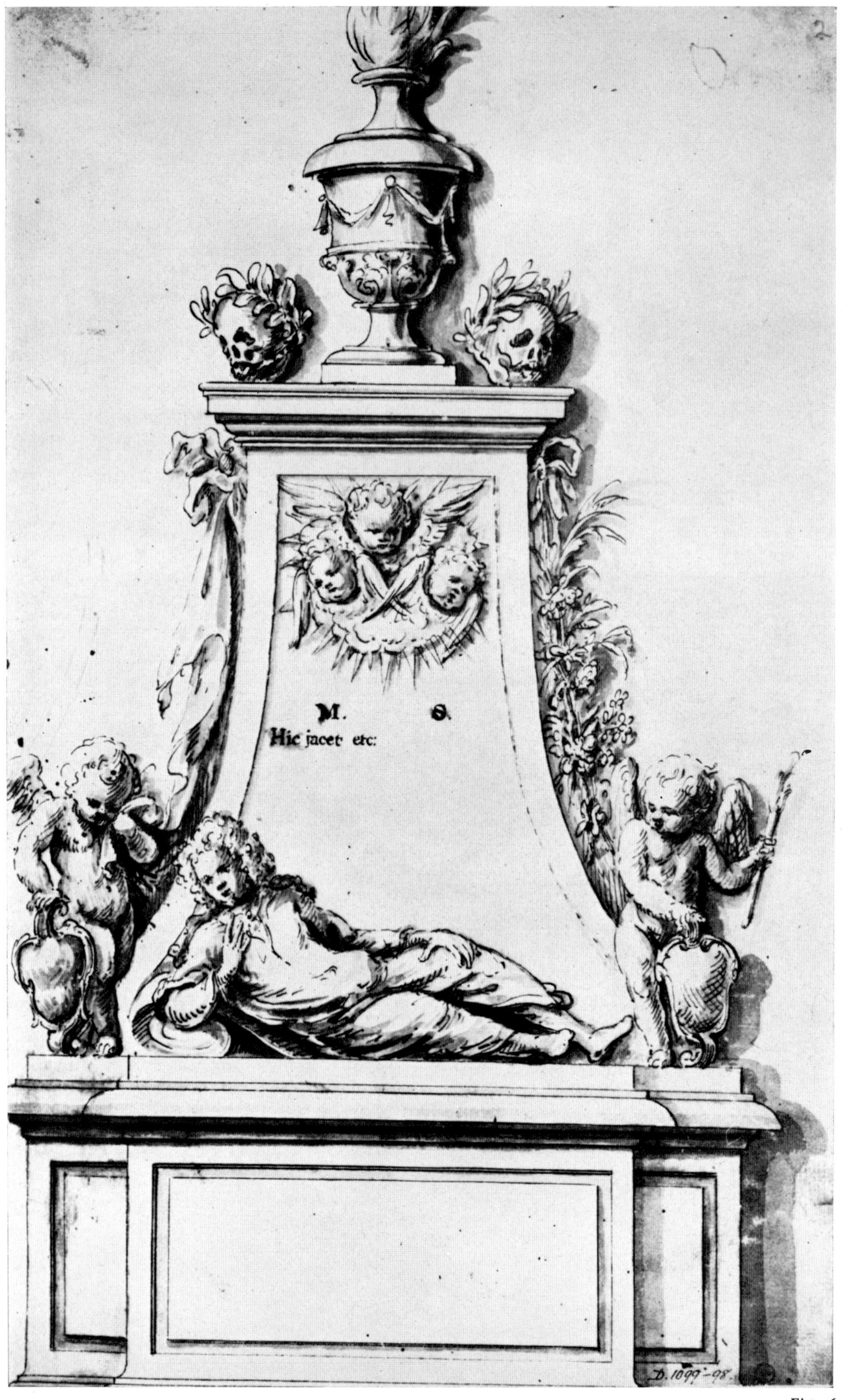


Fig. 36

# EDWARD STANTON (*1681–1734*)

*Figure 36 (left):*  Design for the monument to Sir William Russell (died 1705), in the church of St. Dunstan-in-the-East, London.
Pen and ink and wash, $14\frac{1}{8} \times 8\frac{1}{4}$ inches. No. D.1099–1898.

*Figure 37 (below):*  Monument to Sir William Russell (died 1705), formerly in the church of St. Dunstan-in-the-East, London.
Photograph: *National Monuments Record.*

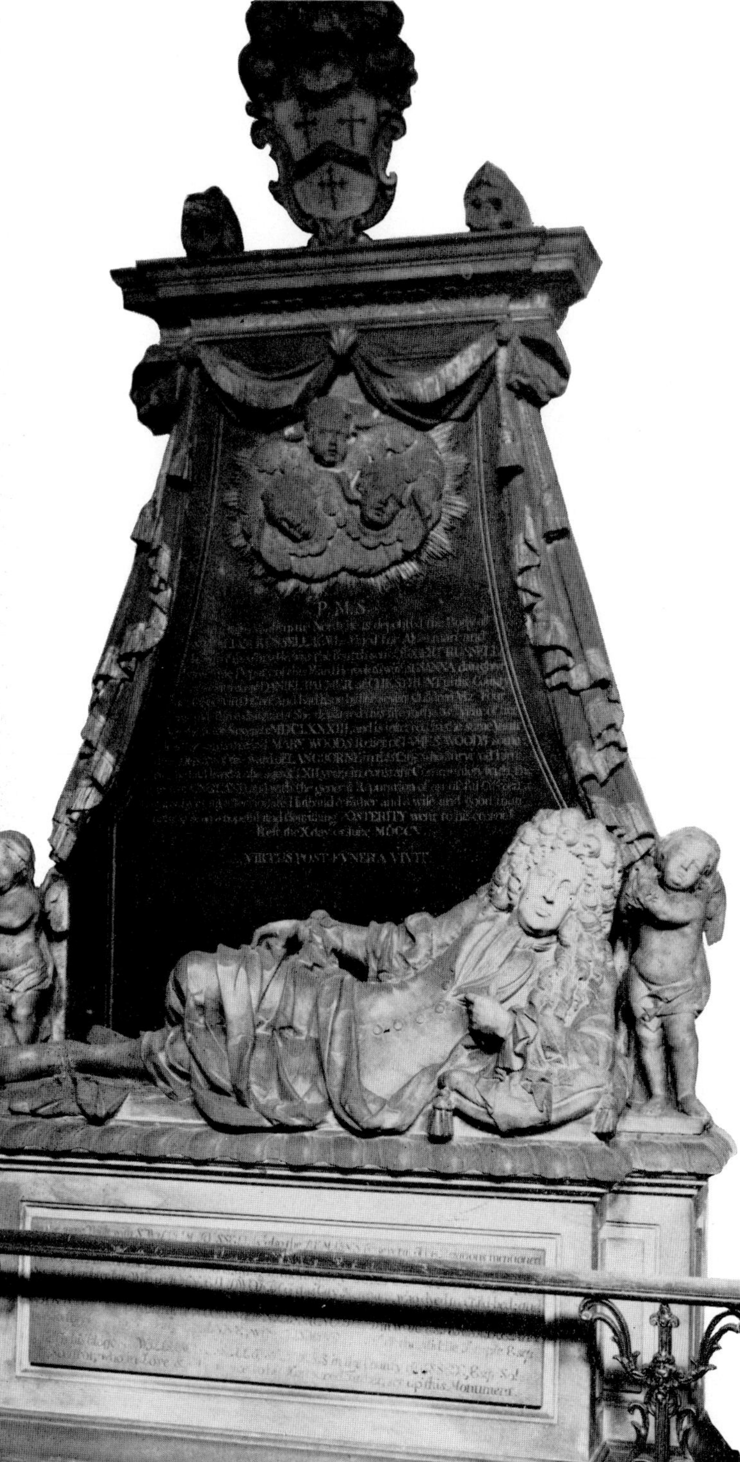

Fig. 37

**36**  This drawing was formerly attributed to Caius Gabriel Cibber, see fig. 23. The identification of this design with the Russell tomb was first made by Mr. Edmund Esdaile.

**37**  The church of St. Dunstan-in-the-East was severely damaged in air raids during September 1941, in the Second World War, but the monument escaped with relatively light damage. The church has now been cleared, and all that remains of the monument is the outline of its background in the plaster on the south aisle wall. It is not now remembered what became of the sculpture.

John Le Neve recorded the epitaph in *Monumenta Anglicana,* Volume 4, 1717:

"M.S. In a fair Vault in the North Ile is deposited the Body of *Sir William Russel,* who fined for Alderman and Sheriff of this City. He was the fourth son of *Robert Russel,* some time Deputy of this Ward. He took to Wife *Susanna,* Daughter and sole Heiress of *Daniel Palmer* of Cheshunt in the County of Hertford, Gent. and had Issue by her 7 Children: (She departed this Life in the 35th. Year of her Age the 18th. of Nov. 1683, and is interr'd in the same Vault) He afterwards married *Mary Wood,* Relict of *James Wood,* some time Deputy of the Ward of Langbourn in this City, who survived him, after he had lived to the Age of 68 Years in constant Communion with the Church of England; and with the general Reputation of a useful Citizen, a loyal Subject, an affectionate Husband and Father, and a wise and good Man; having seen a hopeful and flourishing Posterity, went to his Eternal Rest the 10th Day of *June* 1705. Virtus post funera vivit."

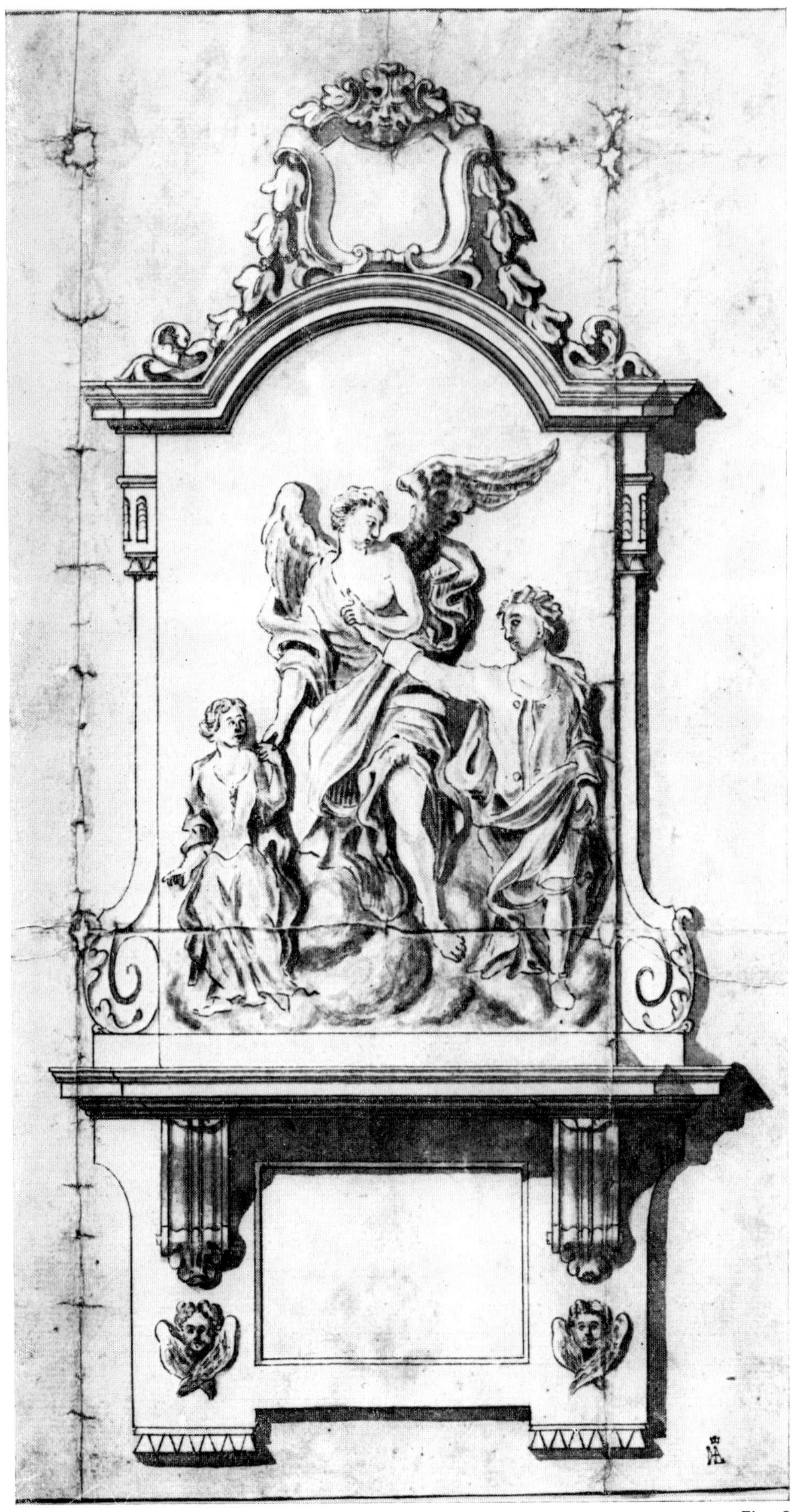

# CHRISTOPHER CASS (*1678–1734*)

*Figure 38 (left):* Design for the monument to Jane (died 1711), and Edward (died 1720), children of Sir Edmund Bray, at Great Barrington, Gloucestershire. Inscribed on the back *To Mr Chri Cass to be left att the George Inn; in Woodstock Oxfordshire.* Pen and ink and wash, size of sheet 12 × 7⅜ inches. No. 3436.424.

*Figure 39 (below):* Monument to Jane (died 1711) and Edward Bray (died 1720), at Great Barrington, Gloucestershire.
Photograph: *National Monuments Record.*

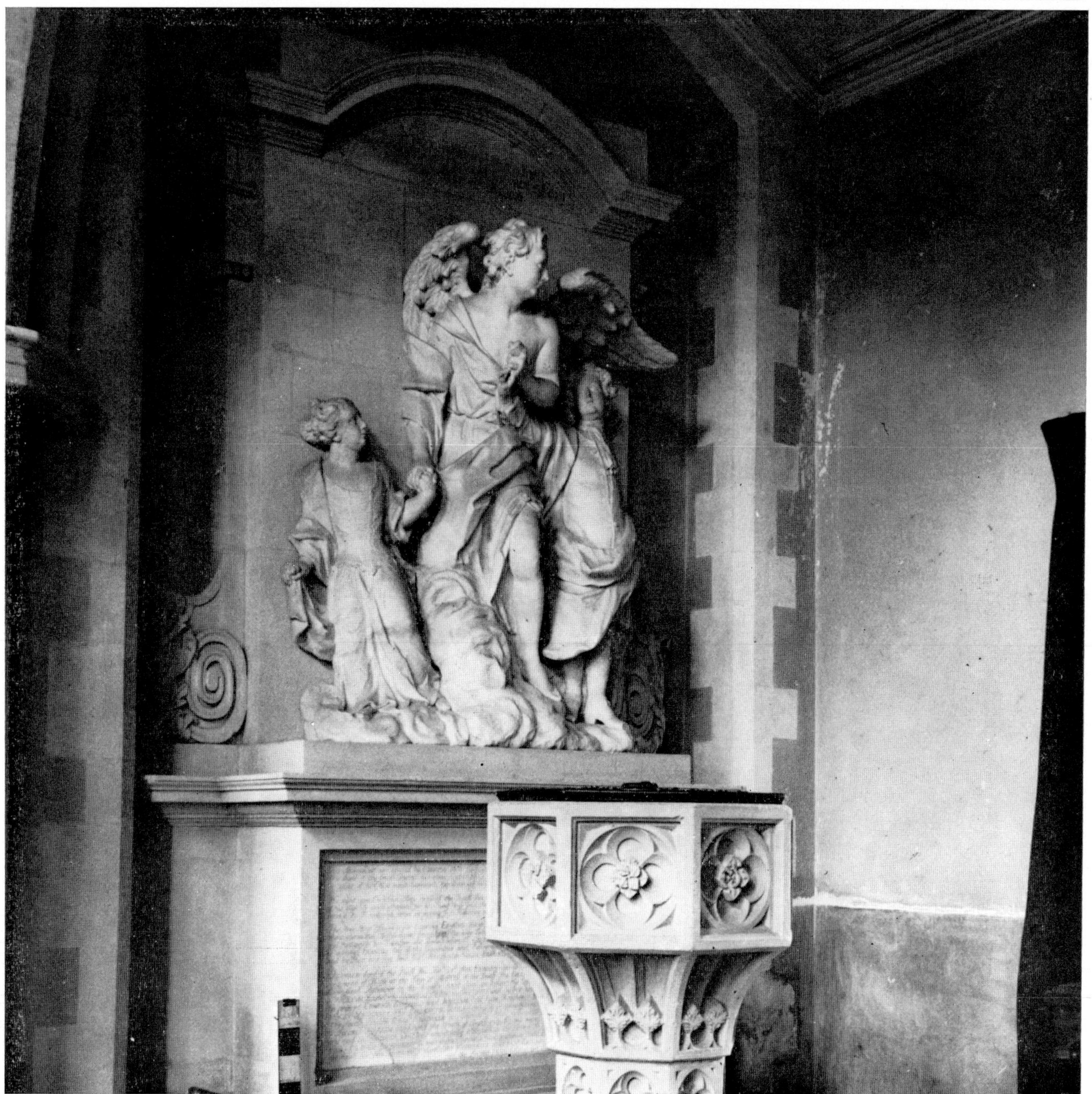

**Fig. 39**

**38**   This drawing was formerly in the possession of
Sir John Soane's assistant, Charles James Richardson
(1806–1871), from whom it was bought by the Museum,
as by an unidentified artist, in 1863. (See John
Physick, *Country Life*, August 1st, 1957.)

Although this design was sent to Cass at Woodstock,
there is no certainty, of course, that it was drawn by
him. There are several designs for chimney-pieces in
the collection (which also were once in the possession
of C. J. Richardson until 1863) for Hampton Court,
Canons, Middlesex, and Gidea Hall, Essex, which
might be by the same hand as this design for the Bray
monument (see fig. 34). Mr. Howard Colvin has
drawn my attention to a volume of drawings in the
Ministry of Public Building and Works Library
(Q.914.21:725.171, 17978 [1]), which could also be by
the same artist, and which might be connected with
Thomas Fort (died 1745), Clerk of the Works at
Hampton Court from 1714 to 1745, and who worked
at Canons for the Duke of Chandos between 1720 and
1723 (see H. M. Colvin, *A Biographical Dictionary of
English Architects 1660–1840*, page 210).

**39**   Above the figures is carved the inscription:
"I say unto you that in heaven their angels do always
behold the face of my Father which is in Heaven."

"This monument was erected by Edmund Bray Esq.
and Frances his Wife, in memory of Their dear children Jane and Edward. She died of the Small pox at
her Aunt Catchmay's in Gloucestershire, on Monday
the one and twentieth of May 1711 in the eighth
Year of her Age, much lamented. Her extreme good
qualities having engaged the Affections of all that
knew Her.

He dyed upon Christmas Day 1720 of the Small pox
at the Royal Academy at Angiers, in France, in the
fifteenth year of his Age, so much esteemed for his
Good Sense and Fine Temper that every Gentleman
of the Academy (Foreigner as well as Briton) seem'd
to rival each other in paying Just Honours to his
Memory; and the Beautys of His Person were Equal
to those of his Mind. . ."

The rest of the inscription lists a number of other
members of the Bray family, descendants of Edmund
Bray (died 1620), many of whom also had died from
smallpox, or as the inscription puts it "the Same fatal
Distemper to this ffamily".

(See Ida M. Roper, *The Monumental Effigies of
Gloucestershire*, 1931, pages 668–70.)

## JAMES GIBBS (*1682–1754*)

*Figure 40 (p.70):* Design for the monument to James Craggs, P.C. (1686–1721), Secretary of
State, designed for the south aisle of the nave, Westminster Abbey.
Inscribed with a scale in feet.
Pen and ink and wash, $9\frac{5}{8} \times 7\frac{1}{8}$ inches. No. E.3641–1913.

## GIOVANNI BATTISTA GUELFI (*active 1714–34*)

*Figure 41 (p.71):* Monument to James Craggs, P.C. (1686–1721), Secretary of State, now on a
window-ledge in the Chapel beneath the south-west tower, Westminster Abbey.
Photograph: *National Monuments Record.*

**40**  This drawing was part of Lot 229 at the sale held
by Messrs. Sotheby's on November 18th, 1913.

**41**  Ann, Mrs. John Newsham, the sister of Craggs,
asked Alexander Pope to act on her behalf during the
negotiations with Guelfi over the monument. Pope
wrote to her on July 9th, 1724, to say that the Italian
had not yet finished the clay model, which was not a
good likeness, and he wondered whether another
sculptor should be asked also to make a model. He
probably consulted the monument's designer, because
Gibbs wrote to Pope telling him that Rysbrack's house
was at the end of Bond Street, in Lord Oxford's grounds,
and that Gibbs would wait for Pope at about five in
the afternoon of the Thursday following at Williams's
Coffee House.

All, however, must have gone well with Guelfi's
model because on August 8th Pope was able to write
to Mrs. Newsham to tell her that he had paid Guelfi
£60, and as he liked the work, he had told the
sculptor to go ahead. Two months later the marble
had been bought and Pope had composed the epitaph.
We do not learn any more until three years later, on
October 30th, 1727. On that day Pope informed
Mrs. Newsham that he had been to Burlington House
(where Guelfi was working), and that the monument
was boxed and waiting to be taken to the Abbey.
Guelfi had as assistant Francis Bird, and everything

was obviously not in harmony between them as
Guelfi had sent two letters in one day to Pope com-
plaining about Bird. In the midst of the argument,
Guelfi took to his bed, leaving a slightly annoyed Pope
to write that he wished "to God it were once well set
up", and when it was, he was sure it was going to be
the finest figure in the Abbey. Bird must have got to
work because only a month later Pope was able to
write: "At last I have seen the statue up, and the
statuary [Guelfi] down at the same time. The poor
man has not been out of bed since. I sent part of the
money to him and offered him more, which he refused,
till he has been at the Abbey to do some little matter more
to the hair (as I understand) and feet. The inscription
on the urn is not done yet, though they promised two
months ago, and had the draught; but yesterday they
sent to me again for it, which I can't conceive the
meaning of, for I read it scored on in the Abbey. I
have sent it once again to Mr. Bird this day, however."

In 1728 the monument was still causing trouble and
Pope withheld some of the payment from Guelfi, as he
was not yet entirely satisfied with the workmanship in
concealing a joint on the urn, and he let Guelfi know
that he would not be paid until the work was done
properly.

(See *The Correspondence of Alexander Pope*, edited by
George Sherburn, 1956.)

A terracotta model by Guelfi for the figure is in Sir
John Soane's Museum.

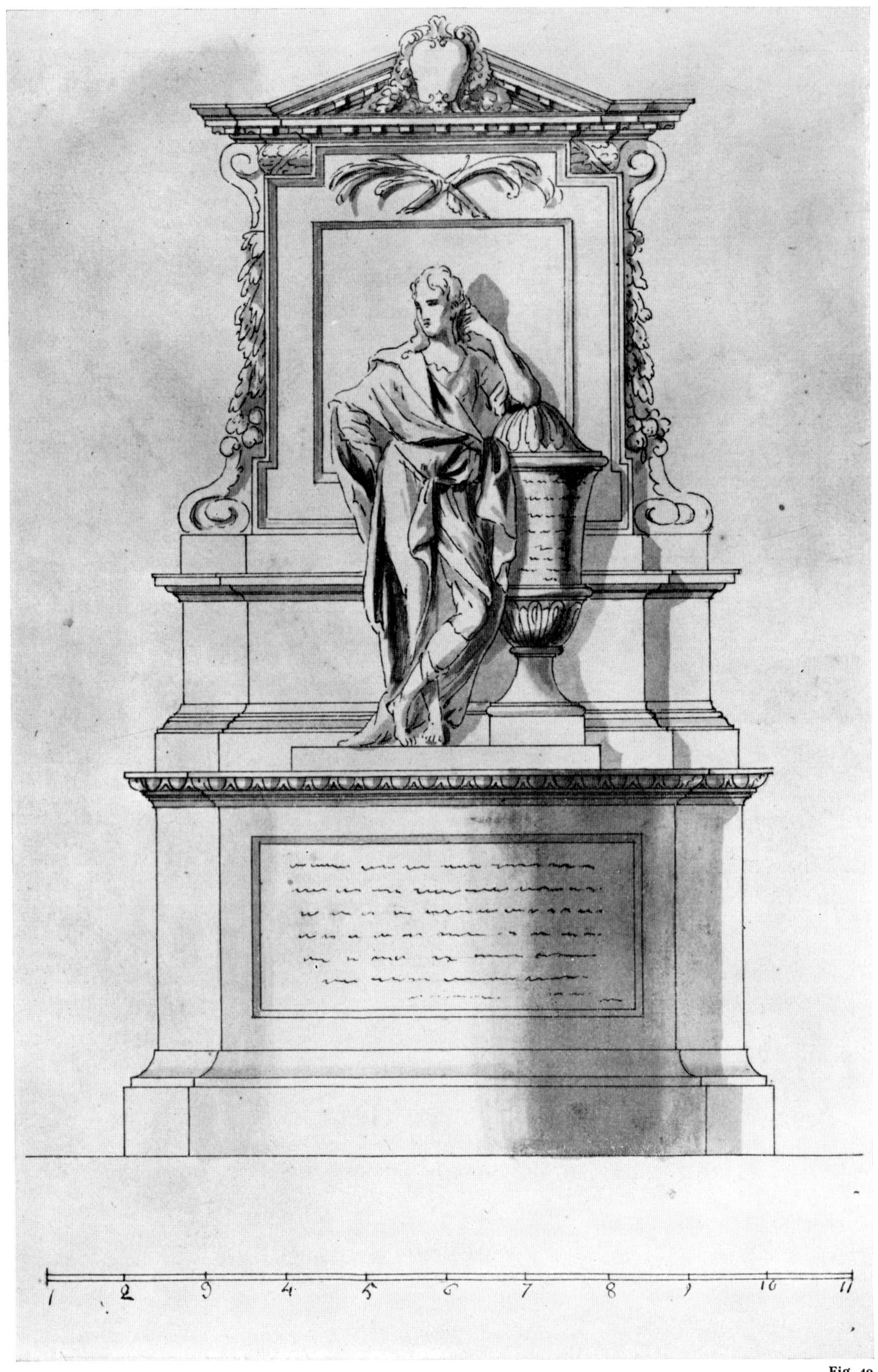



Fig. 40     Fig. 41 ▶

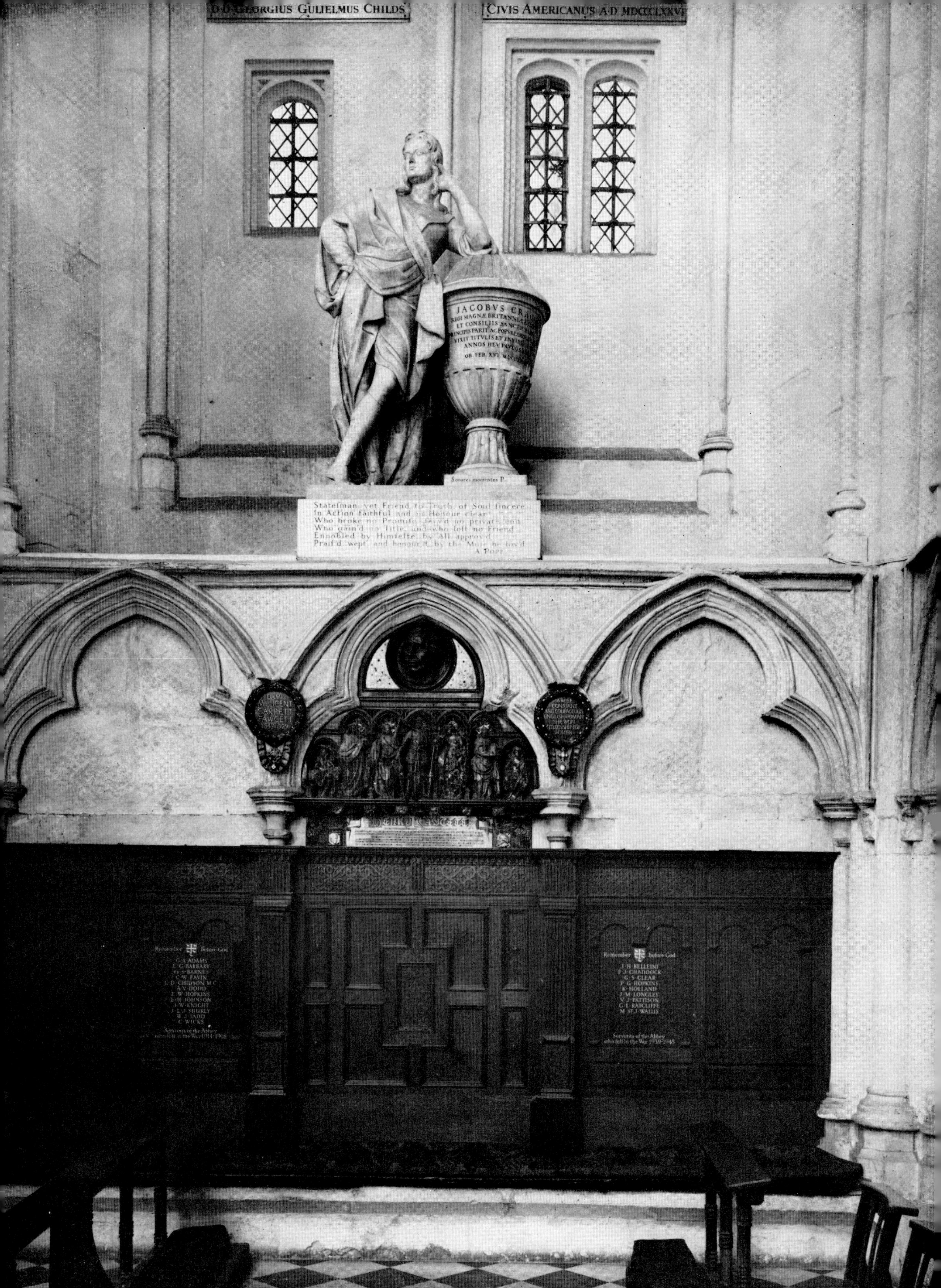

D·D· GEORGIUS GULIELMUS CHILDS
CIVIS AMERICANUS A·D MDCCLXXVI
JACOBVS CRAGGS
REGI MAGNÆ BRITANNIÆ
ET CONSILIIS SANCTIORIBVS
PRINCIPIS PARITER AC POPVLI AMOR
VIXIT TITVLIS ET INVIDIA MAIOR
ANNOS HEV PAVCOS XXXV
OB FEB XVI MDCCXX
Sorores mœrentes P.
Statesman, yet Friend to Truth, of Soul sincere
In Action faithful and in Honour clear
Who broke no Promise, serv'd no private end
Who gain'd no Title, and who lost no Friend
Ennobled by Himselfe, by All approv'd
Prais'd, wept, and honour'd by the Muse he lov'd
A. POPE
DAME
MILLICENT
GARRETT
FAWCETT
Remember before God
G. A. ADAMS
E. G. BARRABY
C. A. BARNE
C. W. EAVIS
F. D. CHIDSON M.C.
A. V. DODD
F. W. HOPKINS
E. H. JOHNSON
J. W. KNIGHT
J. E. T. SHURLY
W. J. TADD
C. WICKS
Servants of the Abbey
who fell in the War 1914-1918
Remember before God
J. H. BELLERN
F. J. CHADDOCK
G. S. CLEAR
P. G. HOPKINS
K. HOLLAND
J. M. LONGLEY
V. J. PATTISON
G. L. RATCLIFFE
M. ST. J. WALLIS
Servants of the Abbey
who fell in the War 1939-1945

# JOHN MICHAEL RYSBRACK (*1694–1770*)

*Figure 42 (right):*   Design for a monument, with a profile, influenced by James Gibbs's design of
the monument to James Craggs.
Inscribed *£625* and with a scale in feet. On the back is *No. (4) £625 The
Height 14 ft 10 in 6 pts Width 8. 5. 0. Projection 2. 9. 0.*
Pen and ink and wash, $14\frac{3}{4} \times 10\frac{1}{4}$ inches. No. E.434–1946.

---

**42**   The price quoted, and the dimensions, are virtually
the same as those given on the design for the monument to Admiral Vernon in Westminster Abbey (see
fig. 73), which is numbered *2*. This drawing may be
an alternative for Vernon's monument.

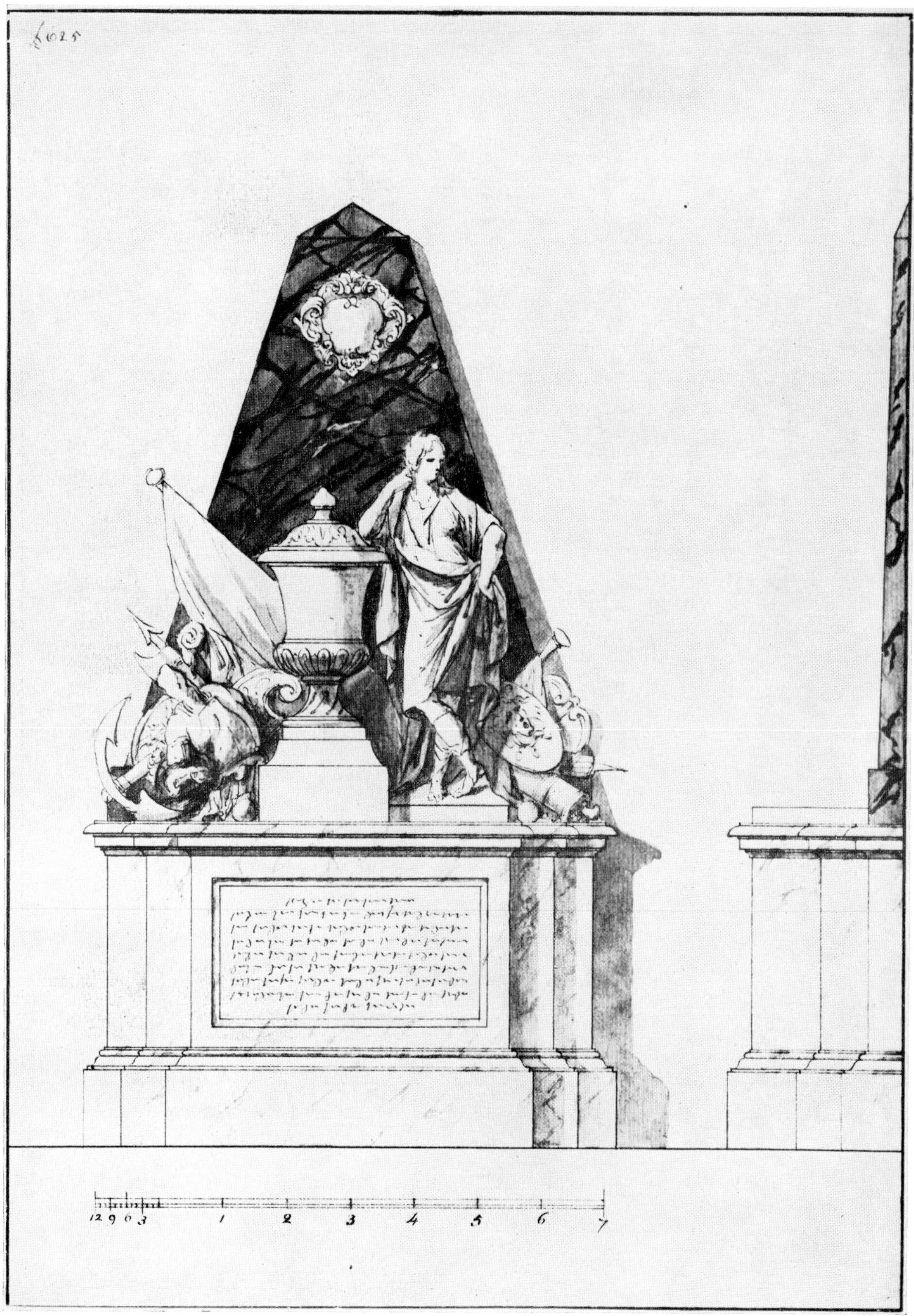

Fig. 42

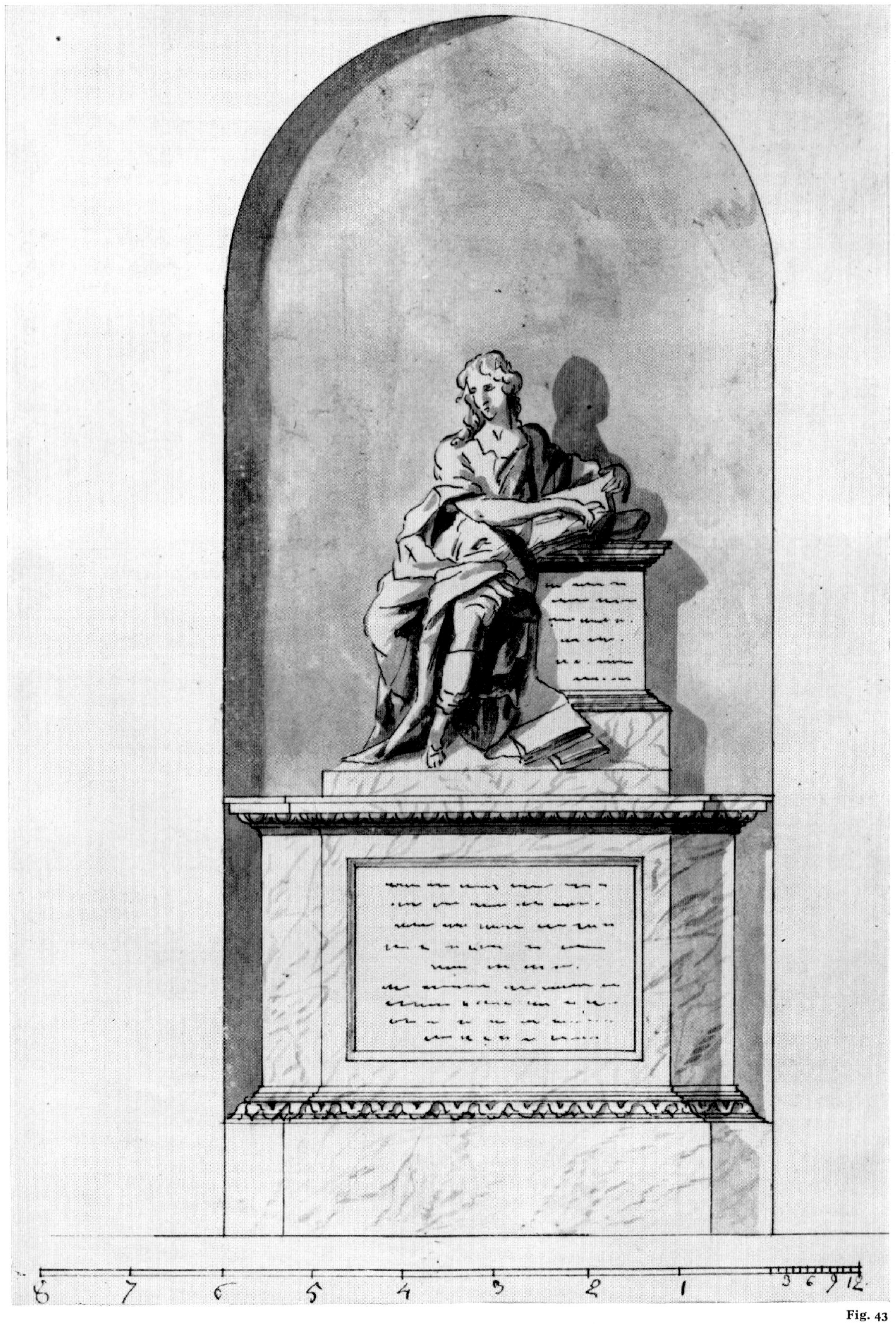

Fig. 43

# JAMES GIBBS (*1682–1754*)

*Figure 43 (left):*  Design for the monument to Marwood William Turner (died *1734*), in the
Mausoleum at Kirkleatham, Yorkshire.
Inscribed with a scale in feet.
Pen and ink and wash, $9\frac{1}{2} \times 6\frac{5}{8}$ inches. No. E.3643–1913.

---

**43**  This drawing was part of Lot 229 at the sale held by Messrs. Sotheby's on November 18th, 1913.

The Mausoleum was designed by Gibbs, and a section of the proposed building, in the Ashmolean Museum, Oxford (Gibbs Collection, II, 94), shows an identical figure seated in a round-headed niche. The existing monument to Marwood Turner was, however, carved by Peter Scheemakers, whose signed design is in the Kirkleatham Parish records. (See A. C. Taloy, "Kirkleatham" in *Architectural Review*, Volume 124, 1958, pages 247–50.)

*Figure 44 (p.76):*  Design for the monument to Sir Ambrose Crowley (c. *1659–1713*), and his
wife Mary (died *1727*), Mitcham, Surrey.
Pen and ink and wash, $7\frac{3}{4} \times 4\frac{1}{2}$ inches. No. 4910.52.

---

**44**  This drawing was one of 60 "by Rysbrack" bought from Mr. B. Quaritch, on January 25th, 1867, for £1. 5s.

James Gibbs designed several monuments, many of which appear as engraved plates in his *Book of Architecture*, 1728.

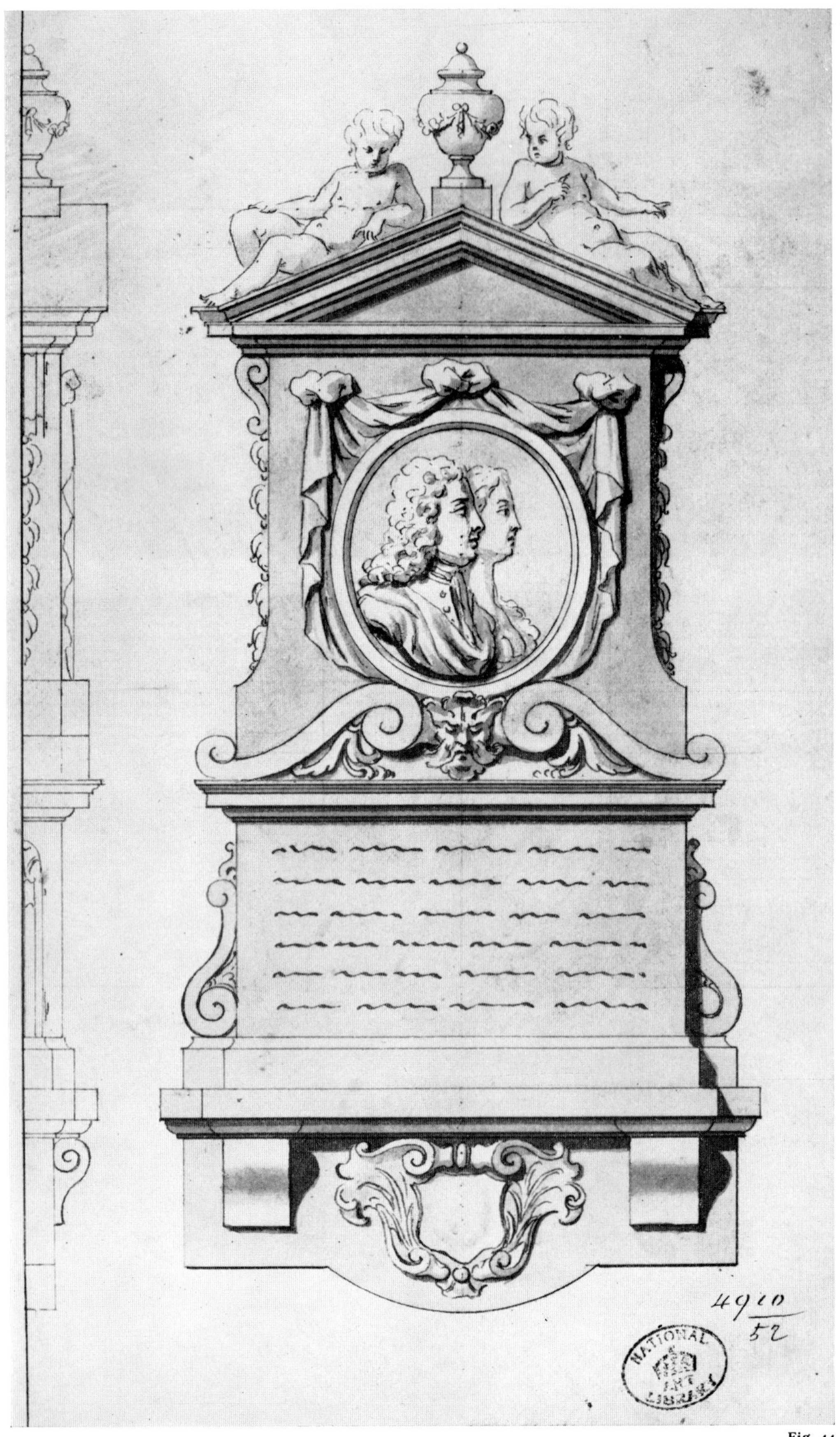



Fig. 44

*Figure 45 (below):* Monument to Sir Ambrose Crowley (c. 1659–1713), and his wife Mary (died
1727), Mitcham, Surrey.
Photograph: *National Monuments Record.*

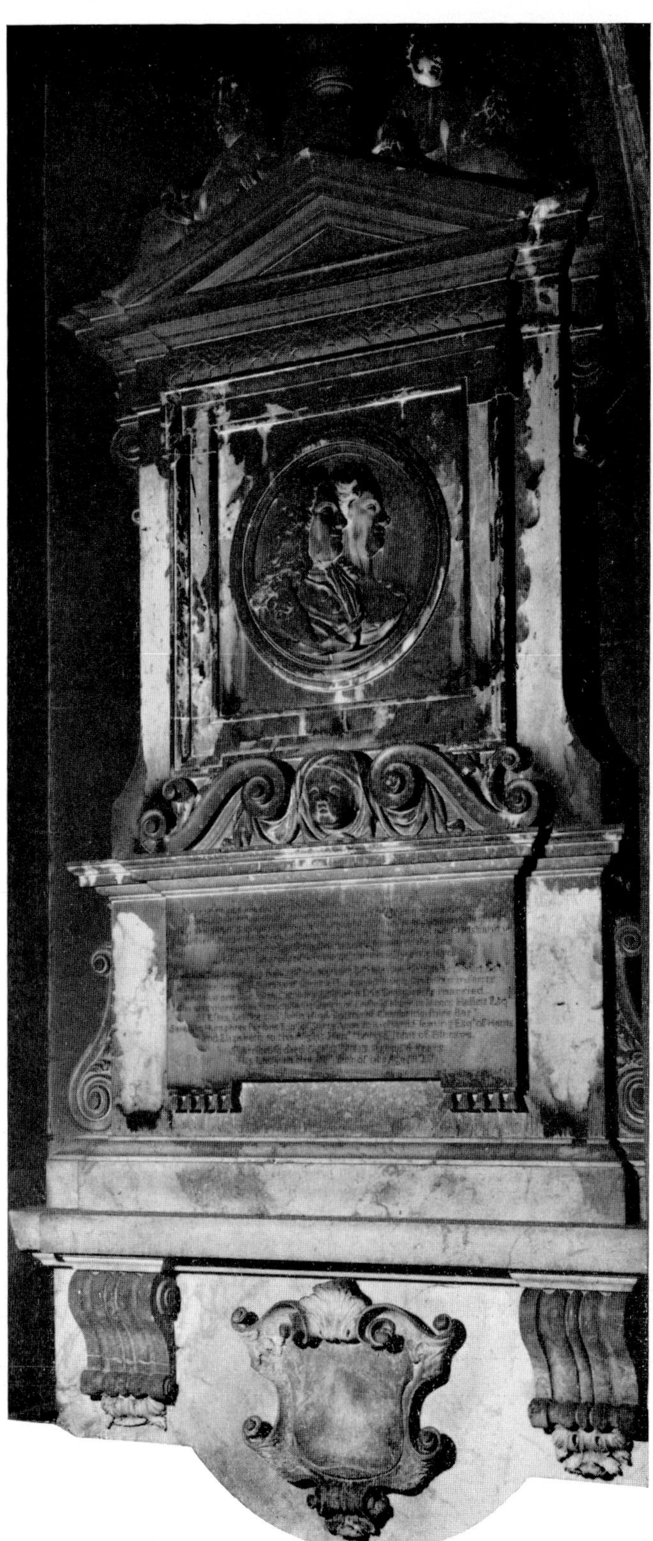

**45** "Near this place are deposited the remains of Sir *Ambrose Crowley* Knight, citizen and Alderman of *London,* whose numerous family and great estate were the present awards of an indefatigable practice of true Christianity, and particularly a boundless liberality towards the poor, many hundreds of whom he continually employed. Near him lies ye body of Dame *Mary* his wife, ye daughter of *Charles Owen* Esq., a younger son of ye family of Condor. She buried seven children infants, and saw one sone, *John Crowley* Esq. and five daughters married. *John* was married to *Theodosia Gascoign* of Enfield; *Mary* to *James Hallett* Esq. of *Essex; Lettice* to Sir *John Hind Cotton* of *Cambridgeshire* Bart.; *Sarah* to *Humphry Parsons* Esq. of *Surry; Anna* to *Richard Fleming* Esq. of *Hants.* and *Elizabeth* to the Right hon. Lord *St. John of Bletsoe.* Sir *Ambrose* died Oct. 11, 1713, aged 54 years; his lady in the 63d year of her age, 1727."

**Fig. 45**

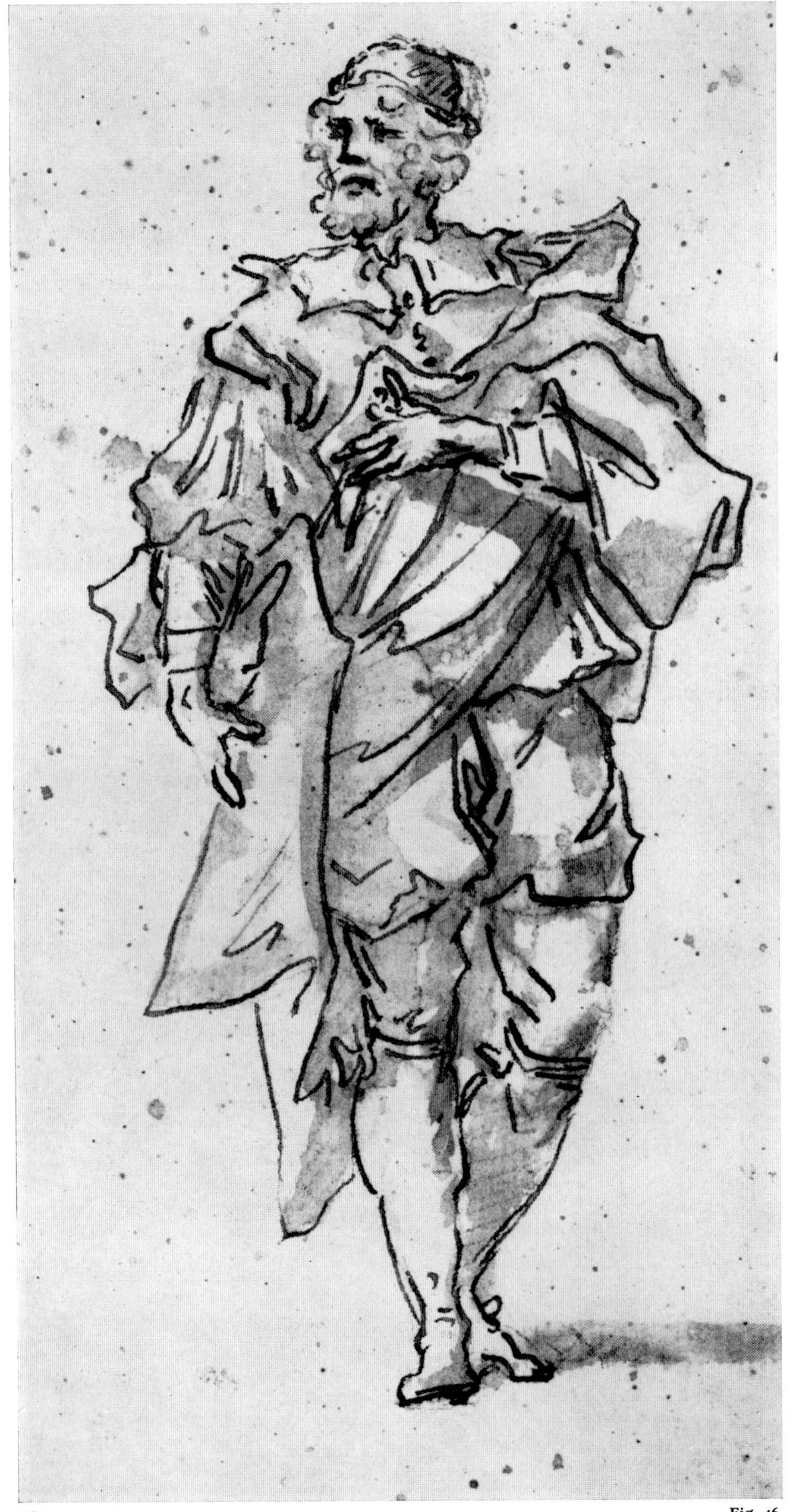



Fig. 46

# WILLIAM KENT (*1685?–1748*)

*Figure 46 (left):*   Design for the statue of Inigo Jones at Chiswick House, Middlesex.
Pen and ink and wash, $5\frac{3}{4} \times 2\frac{7}{8}$ inches. No. 8933.103.

---

# JOHN MICHAEL RYSBRACK (*1694–1770*)

*Figure 47 (below):* Statue of Inigo Jones at Chiswick House, Middlesex.
Photograph: *Mr. Brian Gould.*

---

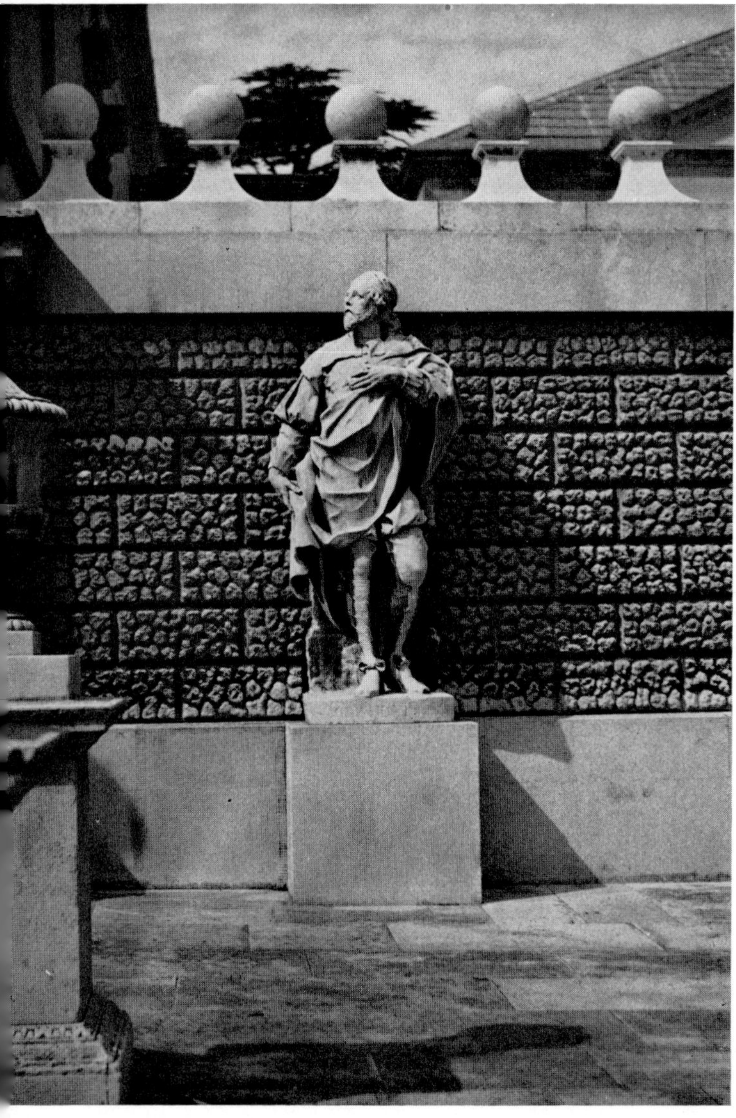

Fig. 47

**46**  This drawing was part of a miscellaneous collection of sculpture designs, numbering 738, bought from Mr. E. Parsons of Brompton Road, on September 11th, 1882, for £25 as "apparently the work of J. Bacon".

The figure of Inigo Jones was also carved in ivory, by Verskovis, and stands on the pediment of a hanging cabinet made for Horace Walpole in 1743, which is now in the Museum's collection, w.52–1925.

**47**  See *Michael Rysbrack, Sculptor* by M. I. Webb, 1954, pages 101–12.

There is in the Victoria and Albert Museum Library an unpublished manuscript (L.1255, 1.7.1912) by an unknown Frenchman, dated 1728. He visited London and southern England recording his impressions of towns and country-houses. Of English sculpture he was, in general, highly critical, but at newly-built Chiswick House he considered "Le jardin â beaucoup de gout dans sa disposition. Les extremitez des allées sont terminees par des Rotondes et de petits pavillons d'une jolie forme et toute differente. Ou voit dans un de ces batimens, deux figures assez bonnes d'*Inigo Jones* et de *Pallade*."

*Figure 48* (*below*)*:* Design for the monument to Sir Isaac Newton (died 1727), in Westminster
Abbey.
Signed *W Kent* and inscribed with a scale in feet.
Pen and ink and wash, $11\frac{3}{4} \times 5\frac{1}{4}$ inches. No. E.424–1946.

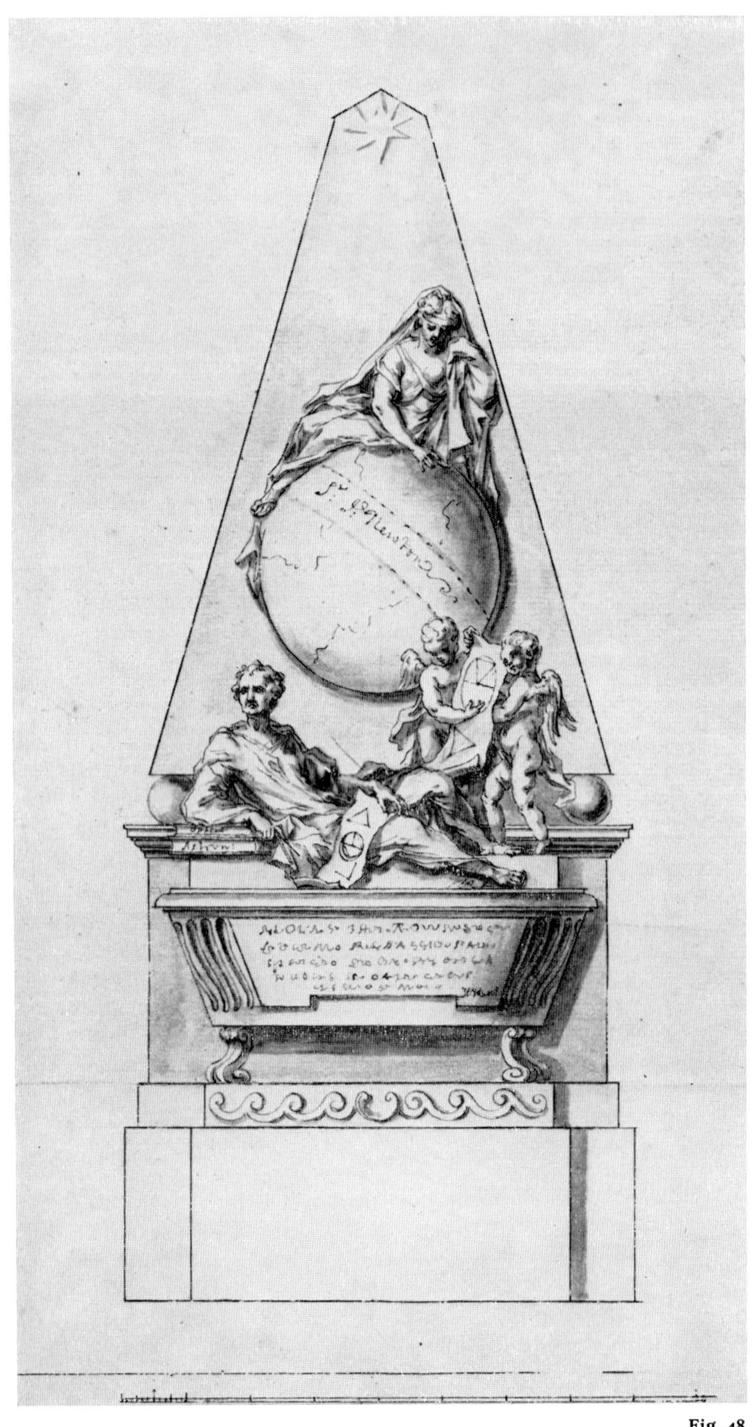

**Fig. 48**

# JOHN MICHAEL RYSBRACK (*1694–1770*)

*Figure 49 (below):* Kent's design, adapted by the sculptor, for the monument to Sir Isaac Newton
(died 1727), in the nave, Westminster Abbey.
Pen and ink and wash, $11\frac{1}{2} \times 6\frac{3}{8}$ inches. British Museum, No. 1859-7-9-100.

*Figure 50 (below):* The monument to Sir Isaac Newton (died 1727), against the nave screen,
Westminster Abbey.
Photograph: *Warburg Institute.*

---

**49**  Rysbrack's terracotta model of Newton's figure is
in the Victoria and Albert Museum, Department of
Architecture and Sculpture, A.1–1938. It is reproduced
as fig. 4 of "Some eighteenth century designs for monuments in Westminster Abbey" by John Physick, *Victoria
and Albert Museum Bulletin*, January, 1967. A model of a
reclining man holding a book, in the Cottonian Collection of the City Art Gallery and Museum at Plymouth, is stated to be for the figure of Newton for this
monument.

**50**  The critical Frenchman who travelled around
southern England in 1728 (see fig. 47), later made an
addition to his account of Westminster Abbey, stating
that "ou travailloit au tombeau du fameux Newton
en marbre blanc, rien ne repond moins à l'idée de ce
grand homme".

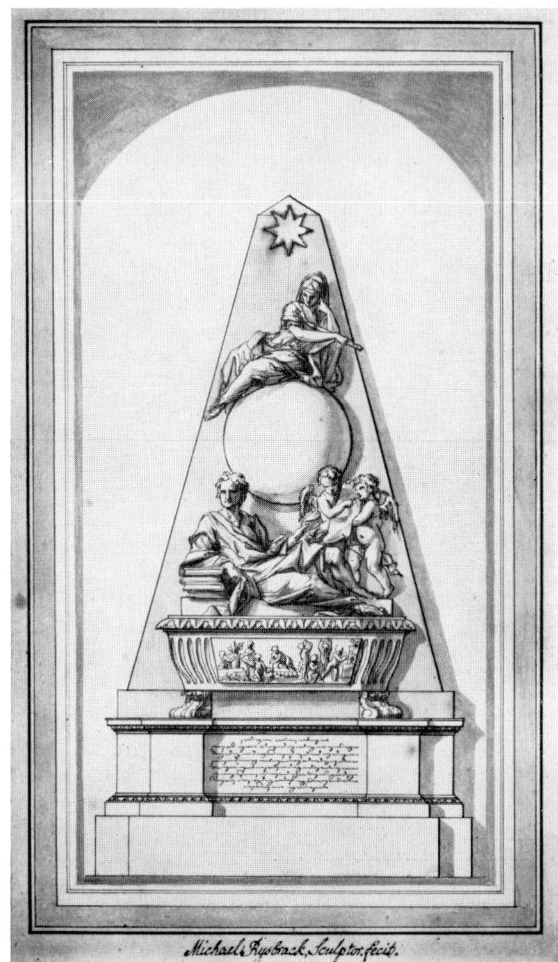

**Fig. 49**

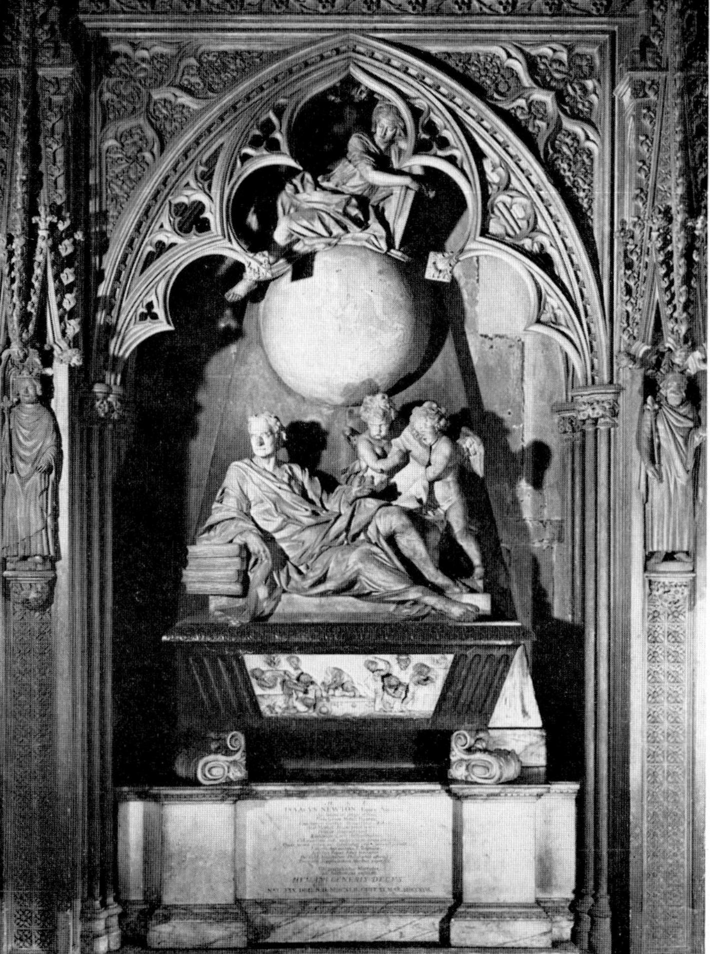

**Fig. 50**

"""

*Figure 51 (below):* Design for the monument to James, 1st Earl Stanhope (c. 1674–1721), in Westminster Abbey.
Inscribed with a scale in feet.
Pen and ink and wash, size of sheet $15\frac{3}{8} \times 10\frac{3}{8}$ inches. No. 8933.251.

---

**51**　This drawing was part of a miscellaneous collection of sculpture designs, numbering 738, bought from Mr. E. Parsons, of Brompton Road, on September 11th, 1882, for £25, as "apparently the work of J. Bacon", it was subsequently attributed to J. M. Rysbrack.

Attached to the design is another piece of paper with an alternative suggestion for the treatment of the tented canopy, which was that executed.

Of these two designs by William Kent, Vertue records "Mr Kents payments for his work & drawings

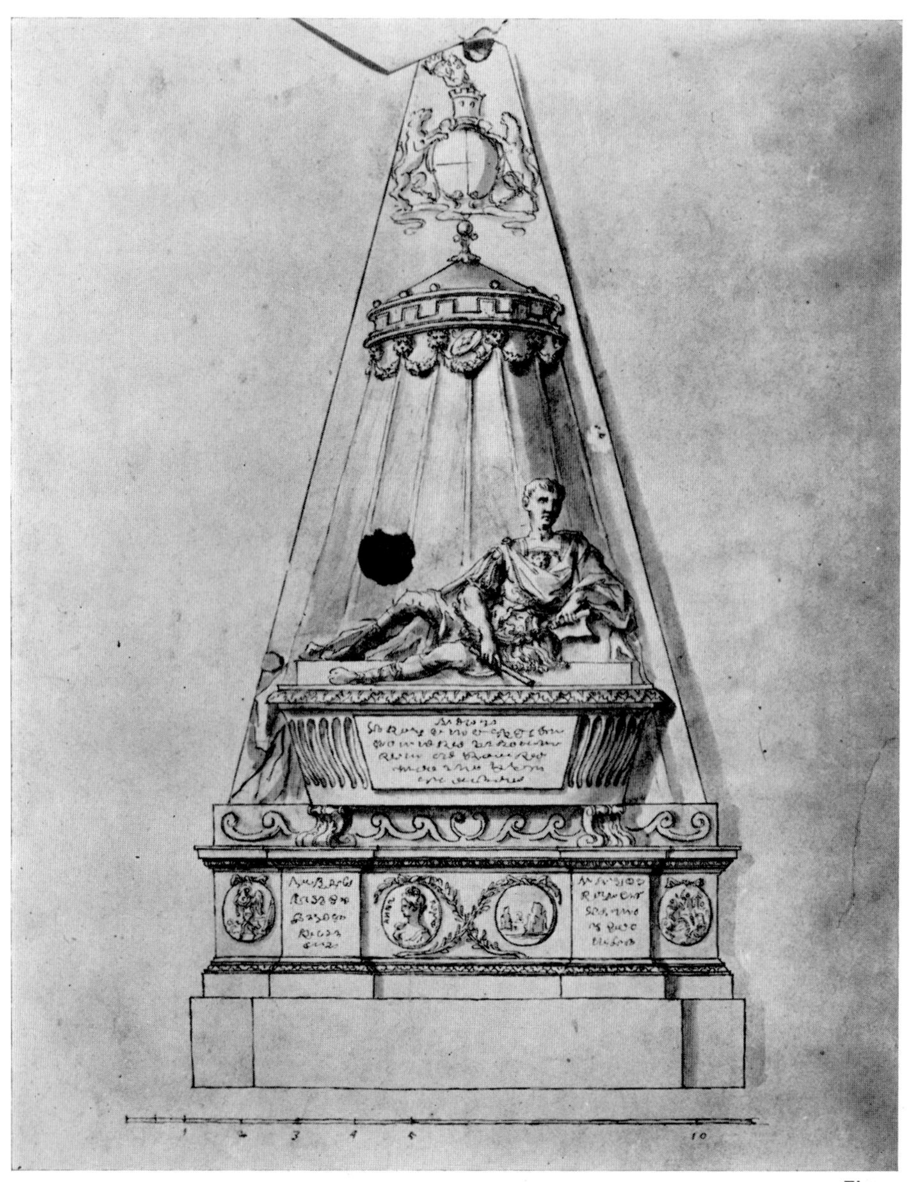

Fig. 51

# JOHN MICHAEL RYSBRACK (*1694–1770*)

*Figure 52 (below):* Kent's design, adapted by the sculptor, for the monument to James, 1st Earl
Stanhope (c. 1674–1721), in the nave, Westminster Abbey.
Pen and ink and wash, $11\frac{1}{2} \times 6\frac{1}{2}$ inches. British Museum, No. 1859-7-9-99.

especially were high enough commonly.—two
particulars I know—the sketch designs for the monument at Westminster. of Sir Isaac Newton. 50£.£. also
that draught or sketch of Ld Stanhopes monument
also. 50 pounds.[1]

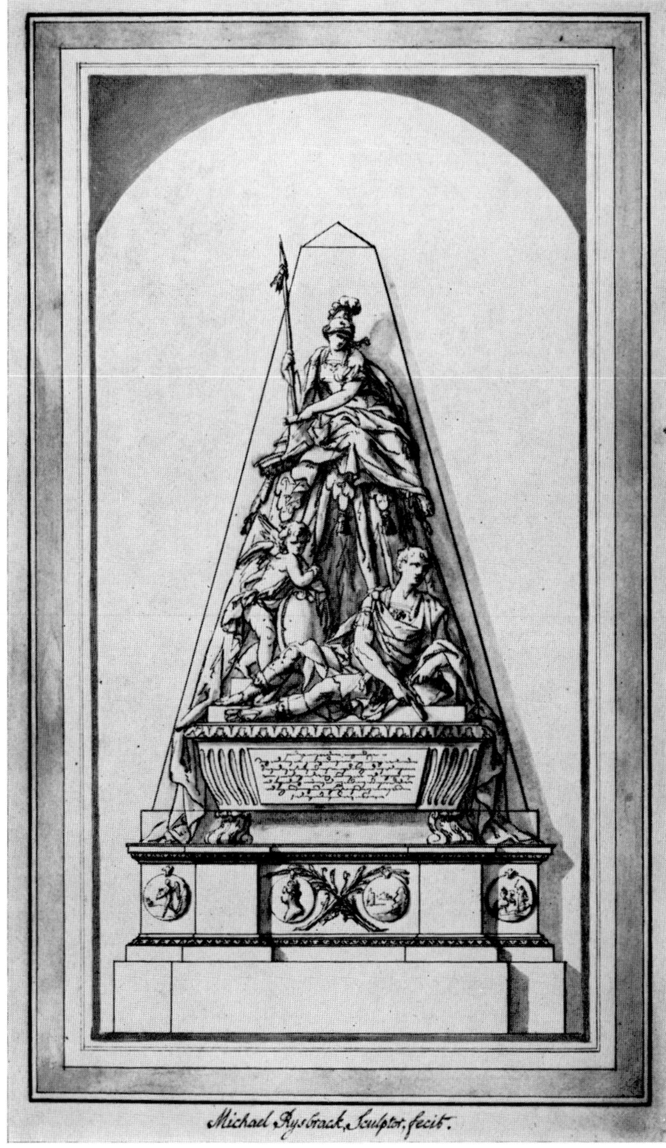


Fig. 52

But Vertue it seems did not have a very high opinion
of Kent's powers as a draughtsman for he wrote,
"April 1731. Sett up in Westminster Abbey the
Monument of Sr. Isaac Newton. a noble and Elegant
work of Mr. Michael Rysbrack. much to his
Reputation. tho the design or drawing of it on paper
was poor enough, yet for that only Mr. Kent is hon-
oured with his name on it (Pictor et Architect
inventor) which if it had been delivered to any other
Sculptor besides Rysbrack, he might have been glad
to have his name omitted."[2]

But what exactly was Kent's part in the design of the
Stanhope monument? We know that Vertue recorded
that Kent was paid £50 for his drawing, but in an
account book appear these two rather puzzling
entries:[3]

1731 May ist    Paid Mr. Knight in part for designing
Earl Stanhope's monument £21.

1733 June 3rd    By paid Mr. Kent in Full for
Designing said monument  £26. 5.

Who was Mr. Knight? Was it an error on the part of
whoever recorded the payment, and should it read
"Kent" instead?

The contract between Rysbrack and Stanhope's
sister, Lady Fane stated ". . . in consideration of the
sum of six hundred & seventy pounds, that the said
Michll. Rysbanck shall erect a monument for the late
Earl Stanhope in Westminster according to the
designe made by Mr. Kent & finish the same in a
year and a quarter. The said Michll. Rysbanck shall
bear all expenses for erecting the said Monument,
except for the iron rail." This contract is signed by
Rysbrack, and witnessed by William Kent.

In the account-book it is noted that Rysbrack received
a total of £684. 3. for the monument between April
17th, 1731, and May 16th, 1733.

[1] Vertue Note-books, III, *Walpole Society*, 1934, page 141.
[2] *Ibid.*, page 50.
[3] Information from Rupert Gunnis, 1965.

# JOHN MICHAEL RYSBRACK (*1694–1770*)

*Figure 53 (below):* The monuments to Sir Isaac Newton and James, 1st Earl Stanhope, against the west side of the nave screen, Westminster Abbey, before the 19th century reconstruction of the screen by Edward Blore.
Plate to *The history of the Abbey Church of St. Peter's Westminster, its Antiquities and Monuments*, Volume 2, published by R. Ackermann, 1812.

*Figure 54 (right):* The monument to James, 1st Earl Stanhope (c. 1674–1721), against the nave screen, Westminster Abbey.
Photograph: *Warburg Institute.*

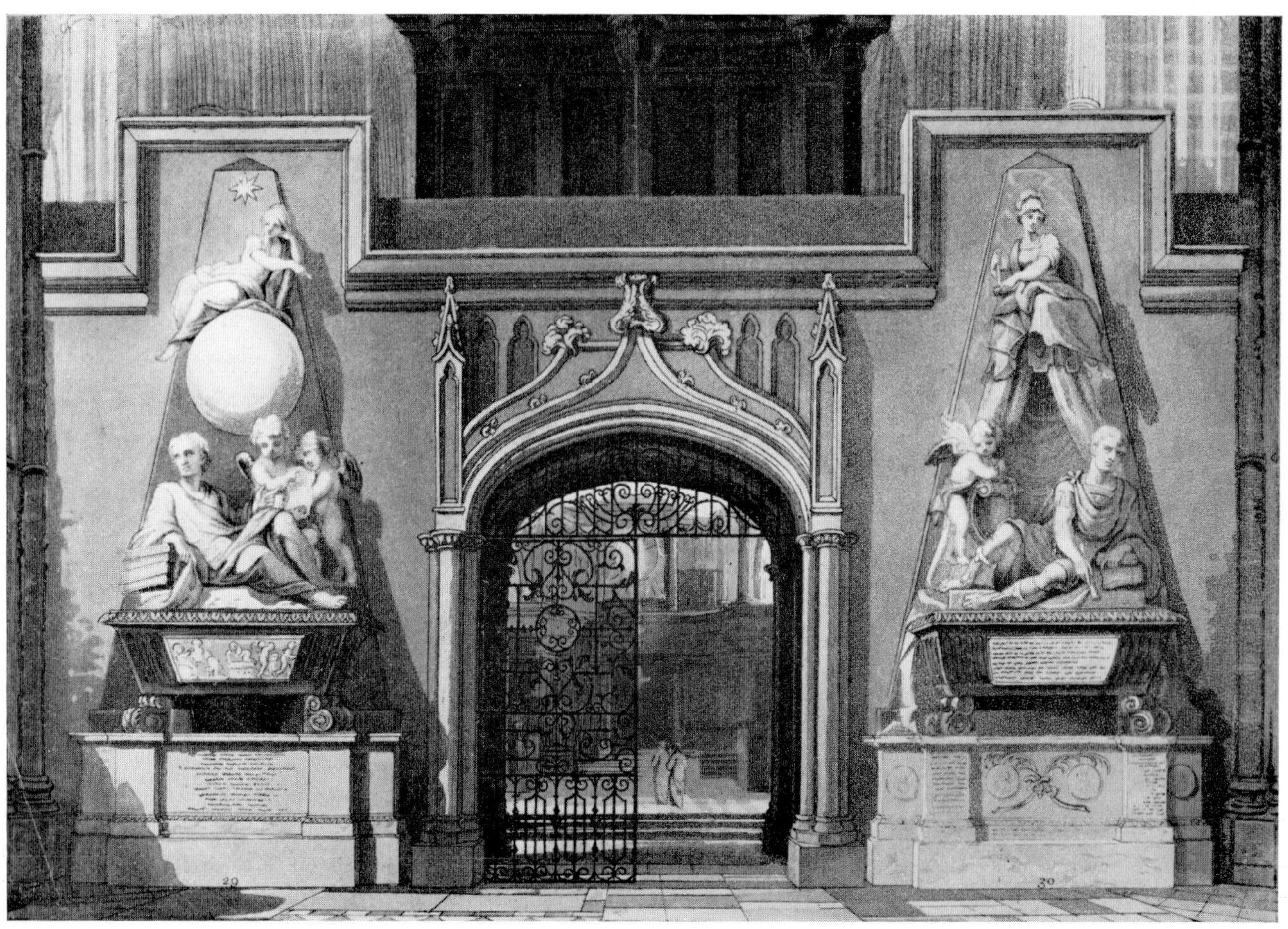

**Fig. 53**

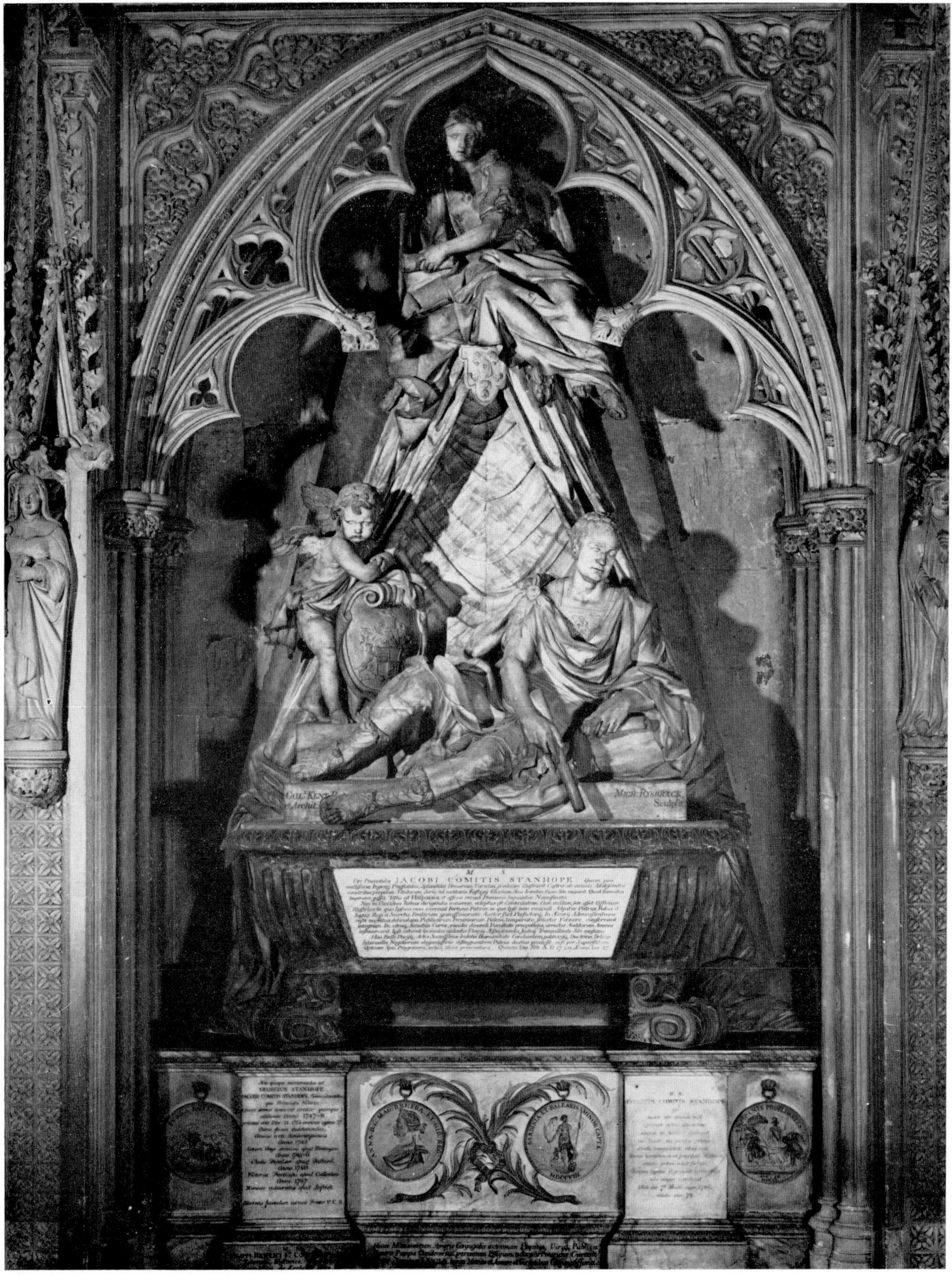



Fig. 54

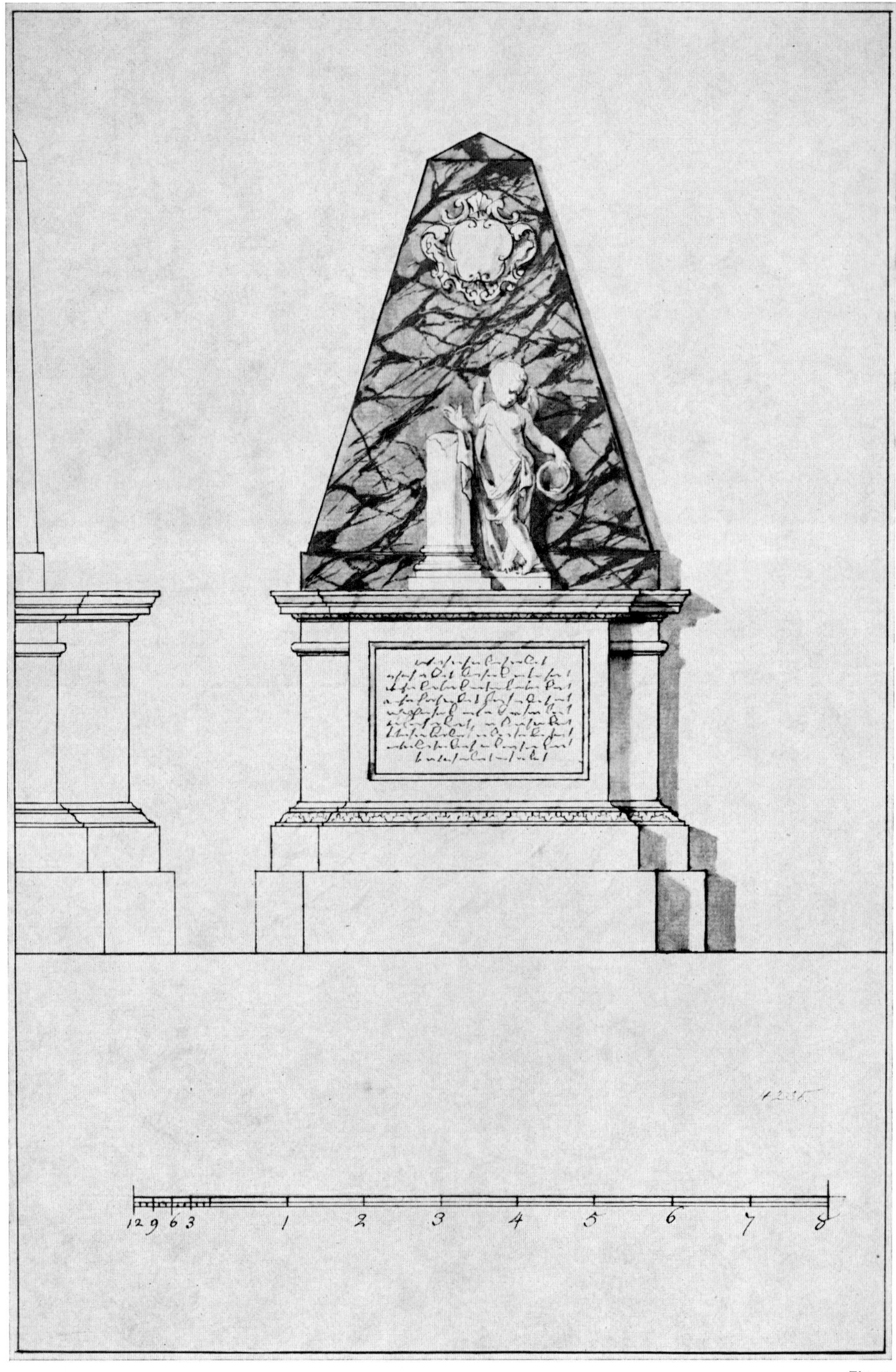



Fig. 55

# JOHN MICHAEL RYSBRACK (*1694–1770*)

*Figure 55 (left):*   Design, with a profile, for the monument to the Rev. Thomas Busby (died 1725), Addington, Buckinghamshire.
Inscribed with a scale in feet and on the back with measurements.
Pen and ink and wash, 13¾ × 9 inches. No. 4235.

*Figure 56 (below):* Detail of the monument to the Rev. Thomas Busby (died 1725), Addington, Buckinghamshire.
Photograph: *Mr. Bruce Bailey.*

---

**55**   This drawing is one of 19 by Rysbrack which were bought from Miss Helen Oakes of Bath, on December 13th, 1864, for £10. 10s.

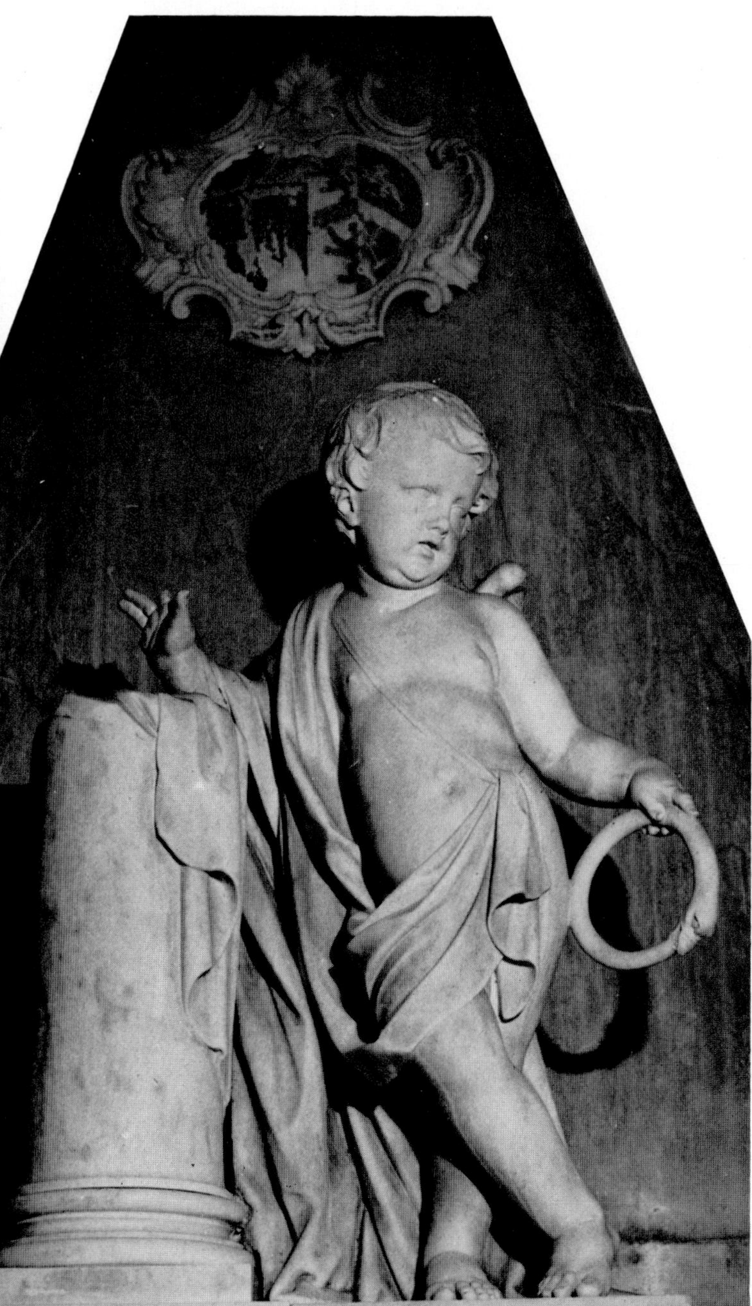

**Fig. 56**

**56**   The monument is signed and dated 1753.

"Near this Place lie the remains of the Rev^d Tho^s. Busby L.L.D. (son to Sir John Busby K^t). He was Lord of this manor, and Rector of the Parish, and one of his Majestys Justices of the Peace. He dyed April y^e 20^th 1725.

This worthy clergyman had an honest Heart, & a generous Spirit. He served his Friend with steadiness, His Country with Fidelity, and His Maker with Zeal & Reverence. Ambitious only of doing his Duty, He adminstered Impartial Justice to his Neighbours, and was ever attentive to the Care of his Parish. He married Ann, Daughter of John Limbrey of *Hoddington* in the County of *Hants.*, Esq^r who survived him twenty Years, & by a faithful care of their children left to her charge, testified the Affection She bore to her Husband. She was fervent & Sincere in her Piety to God, and expressed her Good will to All by a generous Hospitality & extensive charity, Virtues, which Prudence & Œconomy enabled Her to exert in an eminent Degree.

To the memory of so worthy a Pair, this monument was Erected by their only Issue, Ann, married to Sir Cha^s Kemeys Tynte, & Jane as yet unmarried in the Year 1753."

Rysbrack used this figure of a putto holding the snake symbolising eternity, on the monument to Harriot Bouverie at Coleshill, Berkshire (1751). His design for this memorial is also in the Museum (see fig. 14). The putto appears also on the monument to John Sympson (1752), in Canterbury Cathedral.

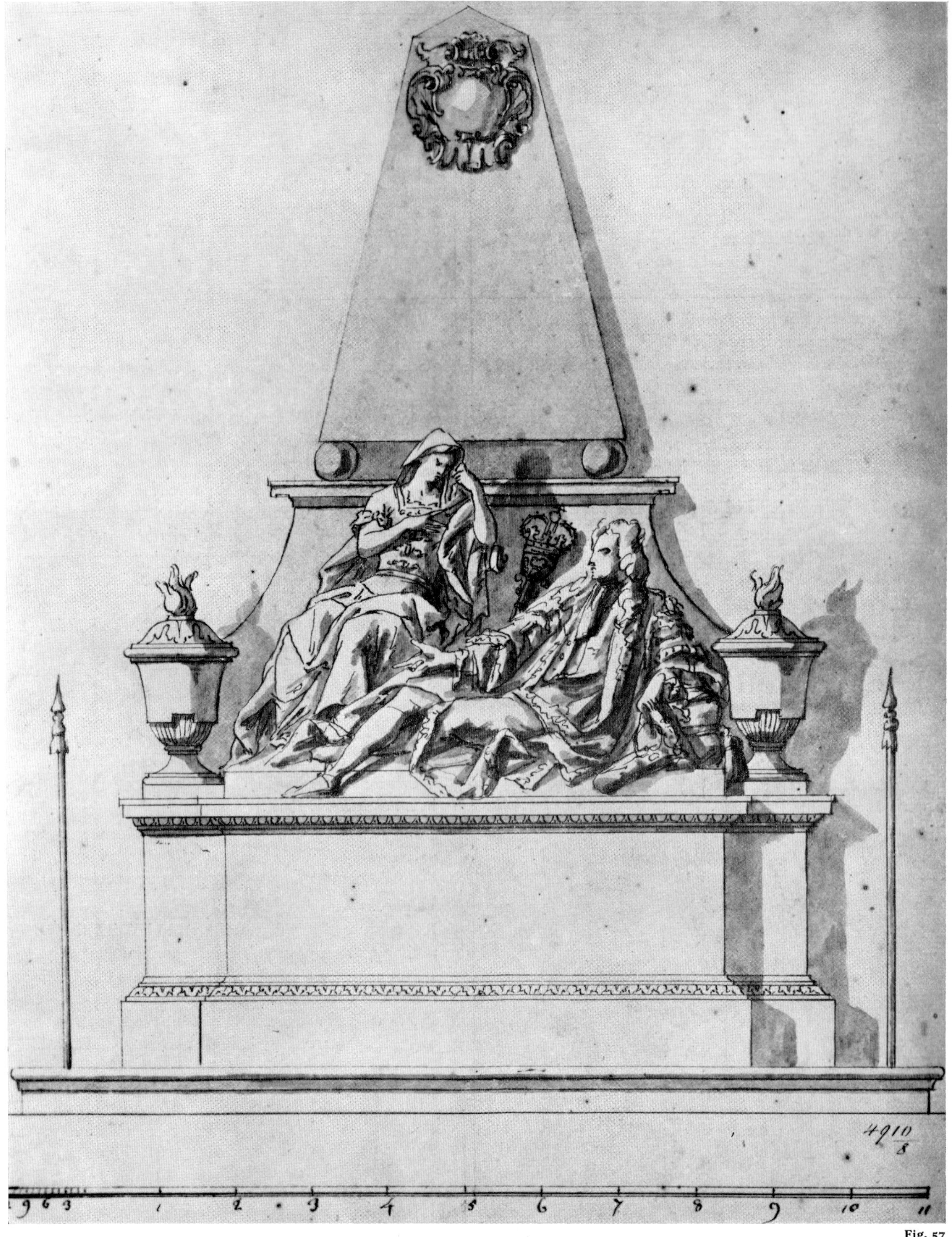


Fig. 57

# JOHN MICHAEL RYSBRACK (*1694–1770*)

*Figure 57 (left):*   Design for the monument to Peter, Lord King (1670–1734), Ockham, Surrey.
Inscribed with a scale in feet.
Pen and ink and wash, size of sheet $14\frac{1}{4} \times 9\frac{3}{8}$ inches. No. 4910.8.

*Figure 58 (below):*  Detail of the monument to Peter, Lord King (1670–1734), Ockham, Surrey.
Photograph: *National Monuments Record.*

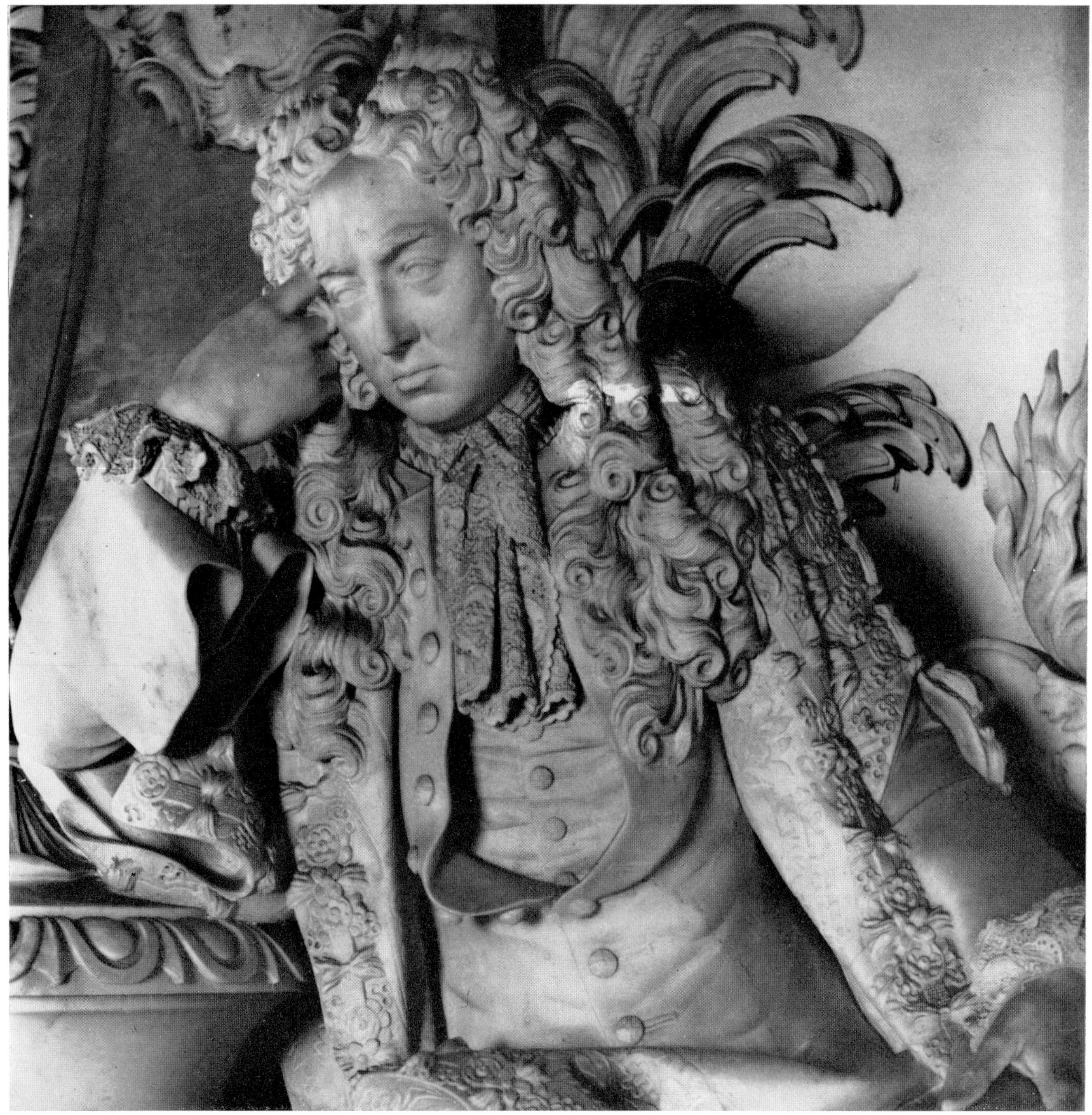

Fig. 58

**57** This drawing was one of 60 "by Rysbrack" bought from Mr. B. Quaritch on January 25th, 1867, for £1. 5s.

**58** The mausoleum (1735) in which this monument stands in Ockham church was, perhaps, designed by Nicholas Hawksmoor.[1]

The catalogue of Rysbrack's sale of April 18th, 1767, records as Lot 18 "Two models of monuments in wood, one for Lord King and his Lady, the figures in burnt clay, the other in wax."

Lettered on the urn "Depositum Petri Domini King, Baronis De Ockham".

On the plinth:
"He was born in the City of Exeter, of worthy and substantial parents, but with a Genius superior to his Birth. By his Industry, Prudence, Learning and Virtue, he raised himself to the highest Character and Reputation, and to the highest Posts and Dignities.

He applied himself to his Studies in the Middle Temple; and, to an exact and complete knowledge in all parts and history of the Law, added the most extensive Learning, Theological and Civil.

He was chosen a Member of the House of Commons in the year 1699; Recorder of the City of London in the year 1708; made Chief Justice of the Common Pleas in 1714, on the Accession of King George I. Created Lord King, Baron of Ockham, and raised to the post and dignity of *Lord High-Chancellor* of Great Britain, 1725; under the Laborious Fatigues of which weighty place sinking into a paralytic Disease, he resigned it November 19, 1733. And dyed July 22, 1734, aged 65. A Friend to true Religion and Liberty.

He married Anne, daughter of Richard Seys, of Boverton in Glamorganshire, Esquire; with whom he lived to the day of his Death in perfect Love and Happiness; and left issue four sons, *John*, now Lord King; *Peter, William* and *Thomas*; and two daughters, *Elizabeth* and *Anne*."

[1] Kerry Downes, *English Baroque Architecture*, 1966.

# JOHN MICHAEL RYSBRACK (*1694–1770*)

*Figure 59 (p.92):* Design for the monument to Nicholas Rowe (died 1718), for the south transept, Westminster Abbey, London. c. 1740.
Pen and ink and wash, $13\frac{1}{8} \times 9\frac{1}{8}$ inches. No. E.441–1946.

*Figure 60 (p.93):* Monument to Nicholas Rowe (died 1718), now in the triforium, Westminster Abbey, London. c. 1740.
Photograph: *Warburg Institute.*

---

**60**   The monument is signed *M. Rysbrack Invt et Fect.*

"To the Memory of *Nicholas Rowe Esq.* who died in *1718* Aged *45*, And of *Charlotte* his only Daughter the Wife of *Henry Fane Esq.* who, Inheriting her Fathers Spirit, and Amiable in her own Innocence & Beauty, died in ye 22d. year of her Age, *1739*.

> *Thy Reliques,* Rowe, *to this sad Shrine we trust,*
> *And near thy* Shakespeare *place thy honour'd Bust,*
> *Oh next him skill'd to draw the tender Tear,*
> *For never Heart felt Passion more sincere:*
> *To noble Sentiment to fire the Brave.*
> *For never* Briton *more disdain'd a Slave,*
> *Peace to thy gentle Shade, and endless Rest,*
> *Blest in thy Genius, in thy Love too blest:*
> *And blest, that timely from Our Scene remov'd*
> *Thy Soul enjoys that Liberty it lov'd.*
>
> *To those, so mourn'd in Death, so lov'd in Life,*
> *The childless Parent & the widow'd Wife*
> *With tears inscribed this monumental Stone,*
> *That holds their Ashes & expects her own.*"

The monument to Charlotte and Henry Fane's daughter, Charlotte St. Quintin who died in 1762 is at Harpham, Yorkshire. It was carved by Joseph Wilton, R.A., and his design is in the Victoria and Albert Museum, Department of Prints and Drawings, E.501–1964.

A terracotta maquette of the seated figure of Rowe's widow, as executed on the monument, was Lot 56 at Christie's sale of June 18th, 1968, where it fetched £5,000. The model, signed and dated *1740*, is 1 ft. 6 in. high, and is illustrated as fig. 1 on page 446 of *Country Life,* August 22nd, 1968.

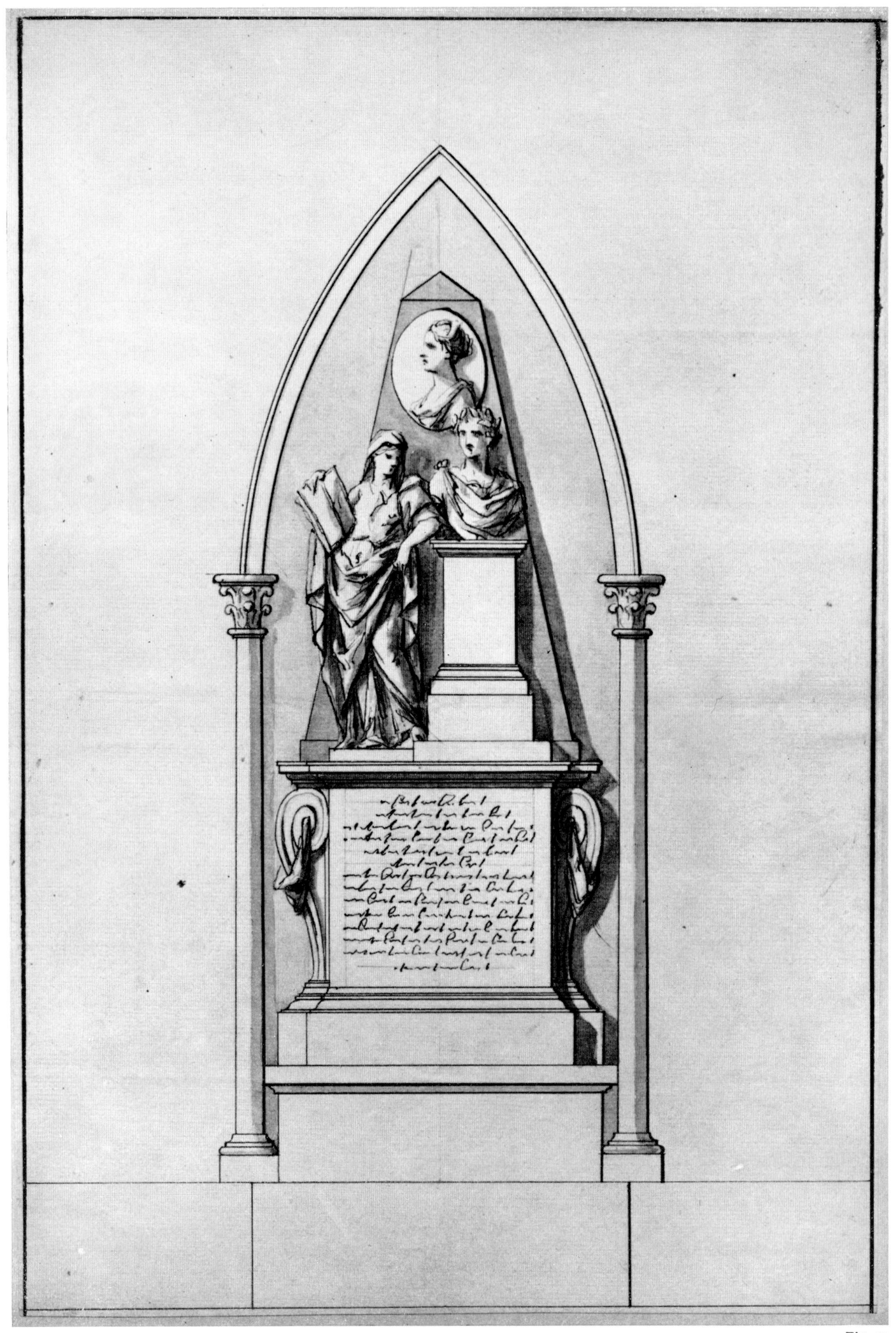

Fig. 59

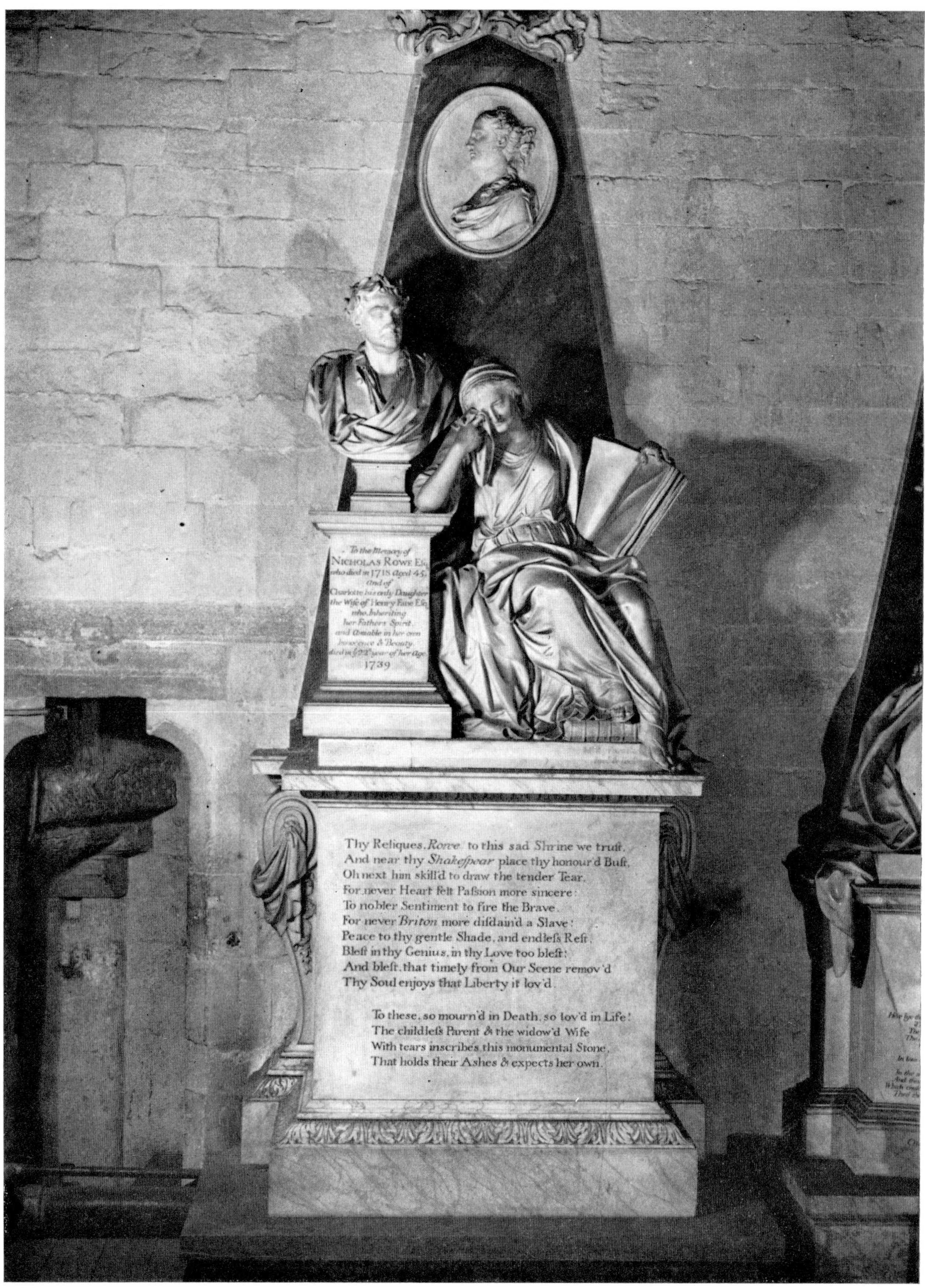
To the Memory of
NICHOLAS ROWE Esq.
who died in 1718 Aged 45,
And of
Charlotte his only Daughter
the Wife of Henry Fane Esq.
who Inheriting
her Fathers Spirit,
and Amiable in her own
Innocence & Beauty
died in ye 22d year of her Age,
1739

Thy Reliques, Rowe. to this sad Shrine we trust,
And near thy Shakespear place thy honour'd Bust.
Oh next him skill'd to draw the tender Tear,
For never Heart felt Passion more sincere:
To nobler Sentiment to fire the Brave,
For never Briton more disdain'd a Slave!
Peace to thy gentle Shade, and endless Rest,
Blest in thy Genius, in thy Love too blest:
And blest, that timely from Our Scene remov'd
Thy Soul enjoys that Liberty it lov'd.

To these, so mourn'd in Death, so lov'd in Life!
The childless Parent & the widow'd Wife
With tears inscribes this monumental Stone,
That holds their Ashes & expects her own.

Fig. 60

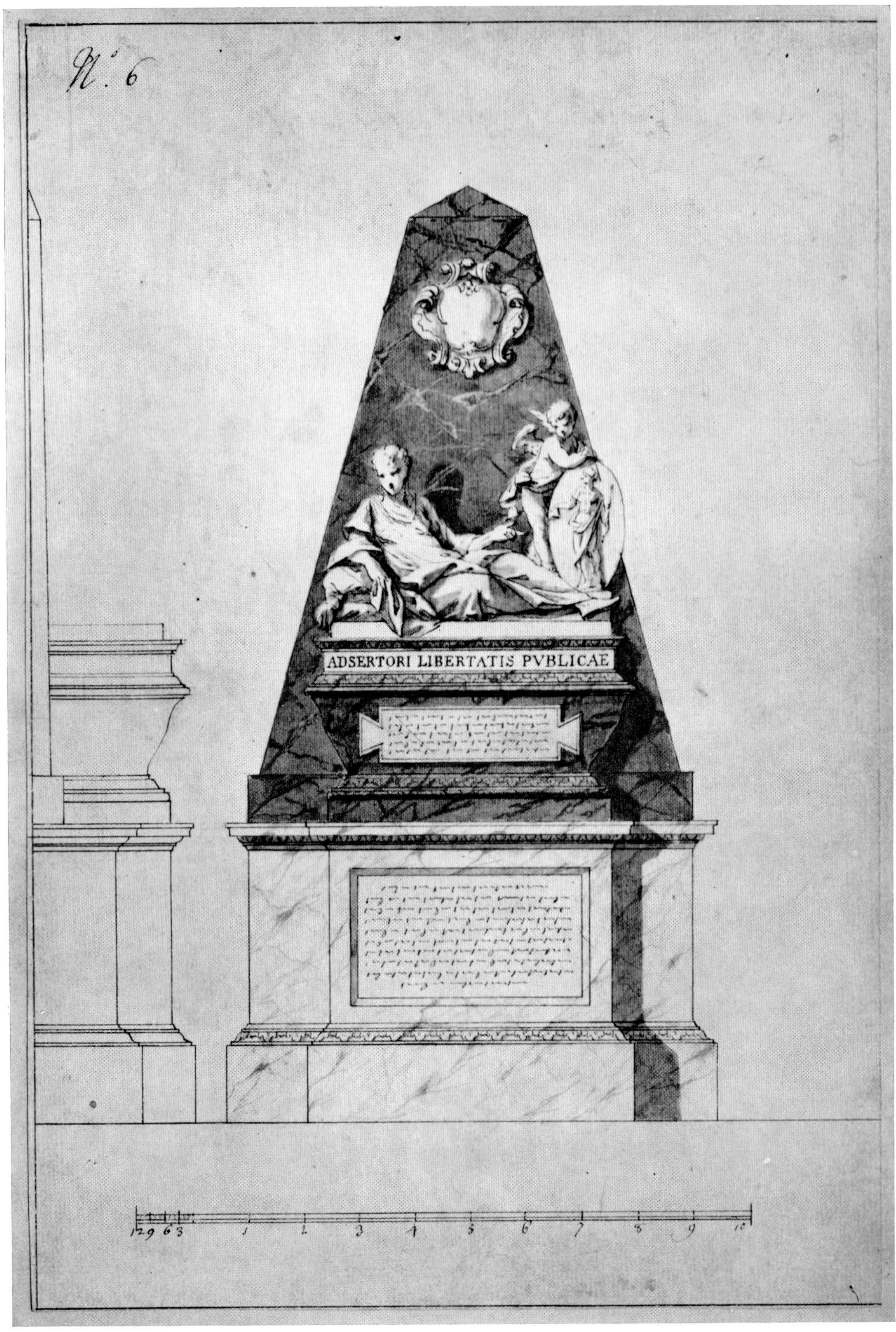


94

Fig. 61

# JOHN MICHAEL RYSBRACK (*1694–1770*)

*Figure 61 (left):*   Design for the monument to Sir Watkin Williams Wynn (1692–1749), Ruabon, Denbighshire.
Pen and ink and wash, $13\frac{7}{8} \times 9\frac{1}{2}$ inches. No. E.426–1946.

*Figure 62 (below):* Monument to Sir Watkin Williams Wynn (died 1749), Ruabon, Denbighshire.
Photograph: *National Monuments Record.*

---

**61**   Inscribed on the back *This is the Drawing approved of By his Grace the Duke of Beaufort, and Doctor King. The Height 16 ft. 2 in., Width 8 ft. 10 in., Projection 2 ft. 10 in.* Numbered *6*, and with a scale in feet.

In the City Art Gallery and Museum, at Plymouth, is an unrecorded Rysbrack design among the Cottonian Collection, which is an alternative version for Sir Watkin's monument; it is numbered *4*.

Among the Wynnstay Papers in the National Library of Wales, at Aberystwyth, are a number of references to the agreement between Lady Williams Wynn and Rysbrack for Sir Watkin's monument; they date from 1750. In 1751 Lady Williams Wynn chose Design No. 6 which the sculptor estimated to cost £485:

| | |
|---|---|
| Value of the marble | £176 |
| Statue | £150 |
| Boy and medal | £50 |
| Ornaments | £33 |
| Masonry | £28 |
| Polishing | £48 |

Rysbrack undertook to finish the monument within two years.

Charles Noel, 4th Duke of Beaufort, was one of Sir Watkin Williams Wynn's fellow trustees under the will of Dr. Radcliffe, who in March, 1745, asked Rysbrack to make a statue of Radcliffe for the Library in Oxford.[1]

Lot 30 at Rysbrack's sale of 20 April 1765 was a bust of Dr. King of Oxford, possibly William King, D.C.L. (1685–1763), Principal of St. Mary Hall.

**62**   The monument is signed and dated *M. Rysbrack Sculpt 1754.*

[1] M. I. Webb, *op. cit.*, page 168.

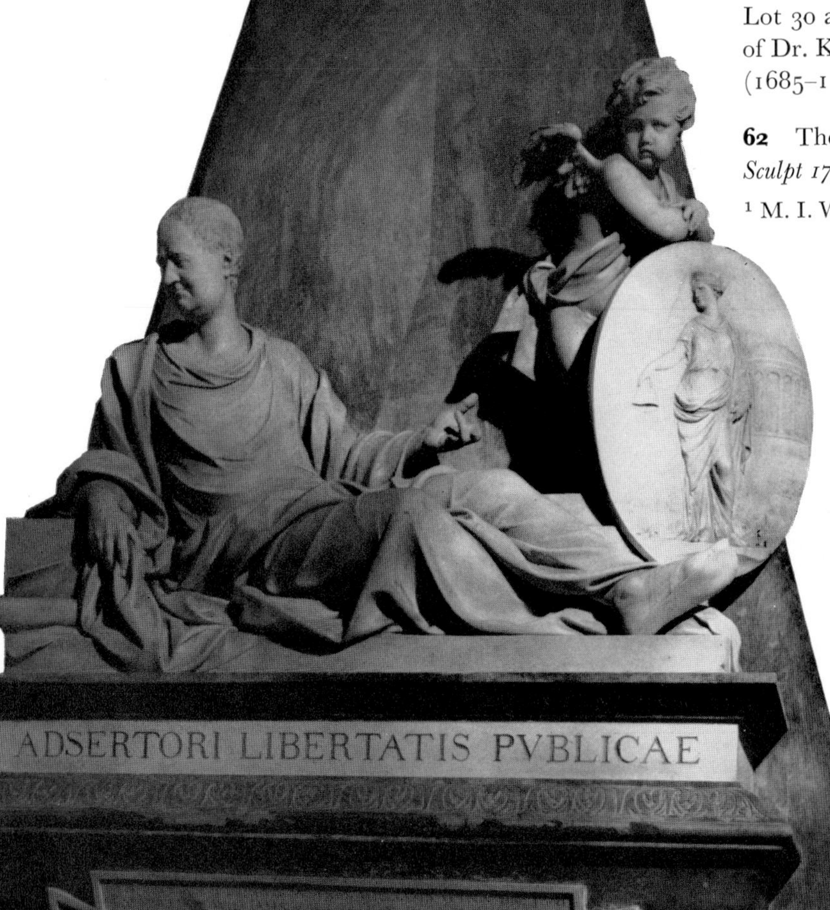


**Fig. 62**

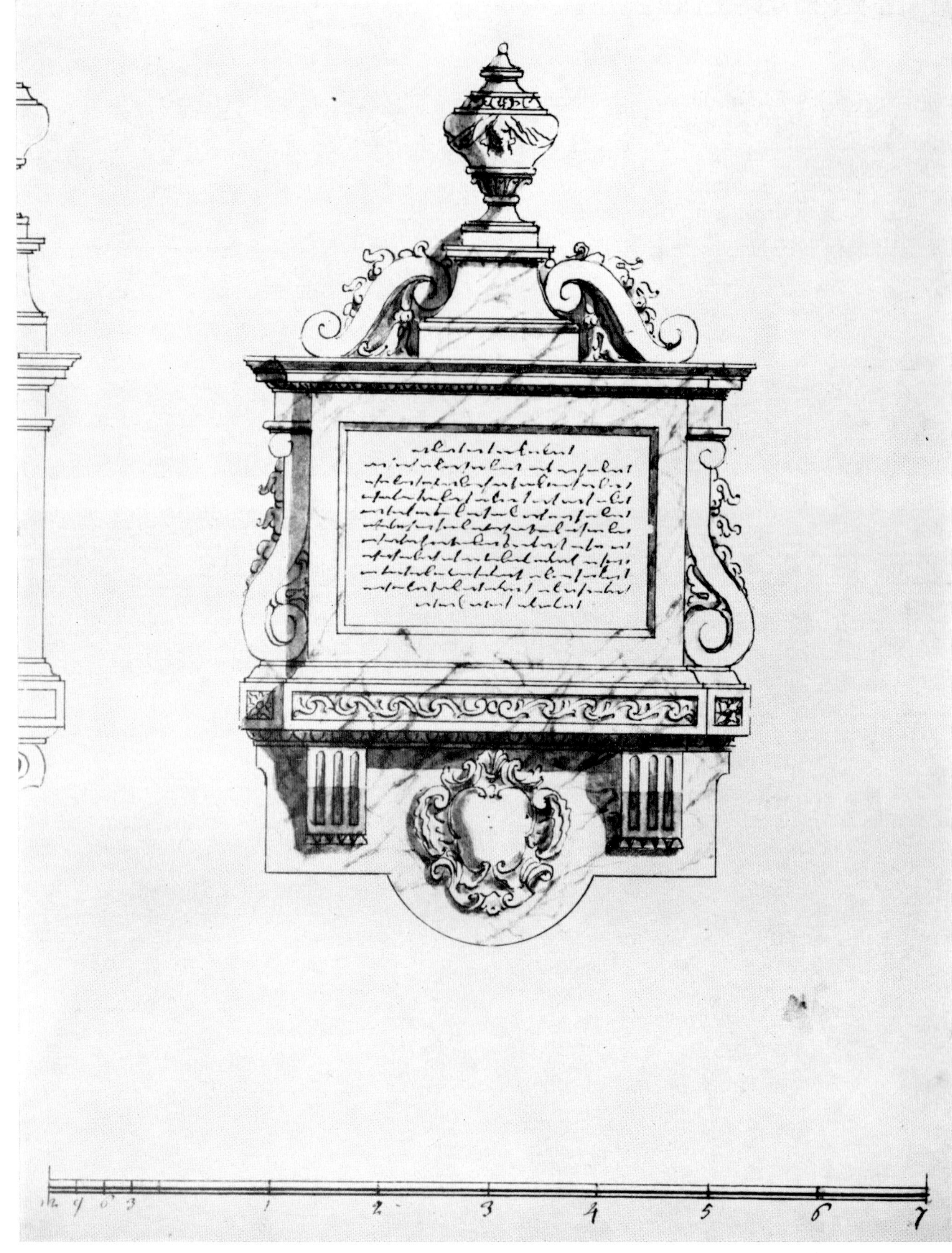



Fig.63

*Figure 63 (left):*   Design for the monument to Charlotte (died 1726) and Mary Pochin (died 1732), Barkby, Leicestershire: 1747.
Pen and ink and wash, size of sheet 15 × 10⅞ inches. No. 4230.

*Figure 64 (below):* Monument to Charlotte (died 1726) and Mary Pochin (died 1732), Barkby, Leicestershire.
Photograph: *Mr. Bruce Bailey.*

---

**63**   This drawing was one of 19 by Rysbrack which were bought from Miss Helen Oakes of Bath, on December 13th, 1864, for £10. 10s.

Inscribed with a scale in feet, and on the back is written *May 14th. 1747. This is the Model referred to in an Agreement bearing even Date herewith between me and Michael Rysbrack excepting the Arms are to be Double. Tho. Pochin. Witness John Hood.*

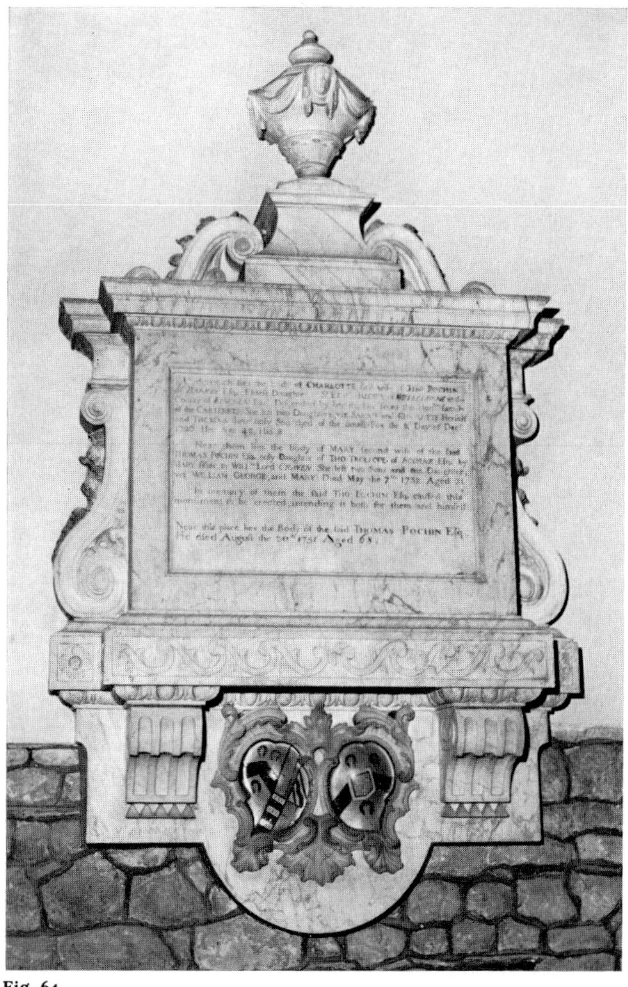

Fig. 64

**64**   The monument is signed *M^L Rysbrack Fecit.*

"Underneath lies the body of Charlotte first wife of Tho Pochin of *Barkby* Esq, Eldest Daughter of S^r Edw^d Hussey of *Wellbourne* in the County of *Lincoln* Bar^t, Descended by her mother from the Hon^ble family of the Carterets. She left two Daughters, viz. Sarah and Charlotte. Herself and Thomas their only Son died of the Small-pox the 2^d Day of Dec^r 1726. Her Age 42, His 8.

Near them lies the body of Mary second wife of the said Thomas Pochin Esq, only Daughter of Tho Trollope of *Bourne* Esq. by Mary sister to Will^m Lord *Craven*. She left two Sons and one Daughter, viz. William, George, and Mary. Died May the 7^th 1732, Aged 31.

In memory of them the said Tho: Pochin Esq. caused this monument to be erected, intending it both for them and himself.

Near this place lies the Body of the said Thomas Pochin Esq, He died August the 30^th 1751 Aged 68."

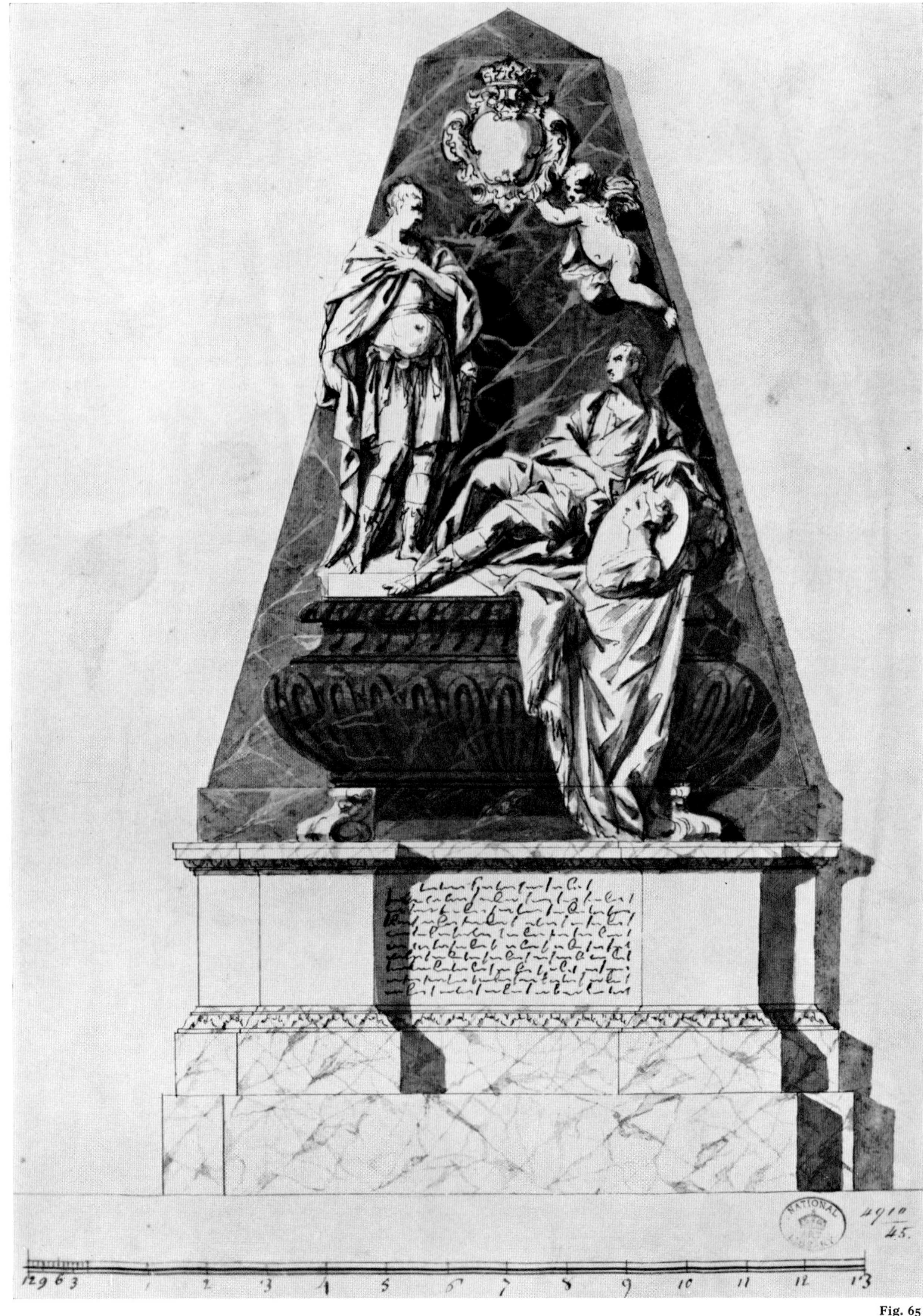



**Fig. 65**

# JOHN MICHAEL RYSBRACK (*1694–1770*)

*Figure 65 (left):* Design for the monument to the 2nd and 3rd Dukes of Beaufort, at Badminton, Gloucestershire.
Inscribed with a scale in feet.
Pen and ink and wash, size of sheet $14 \times 9\frac{7}{8}$ inches. No. 4910.45.

*Figure 66 (below):* Monument to the 2nd and 3rd Dukes of Beaufort, at Badminton, Gloucestershire.
Photograph: *National Monuments Record.*

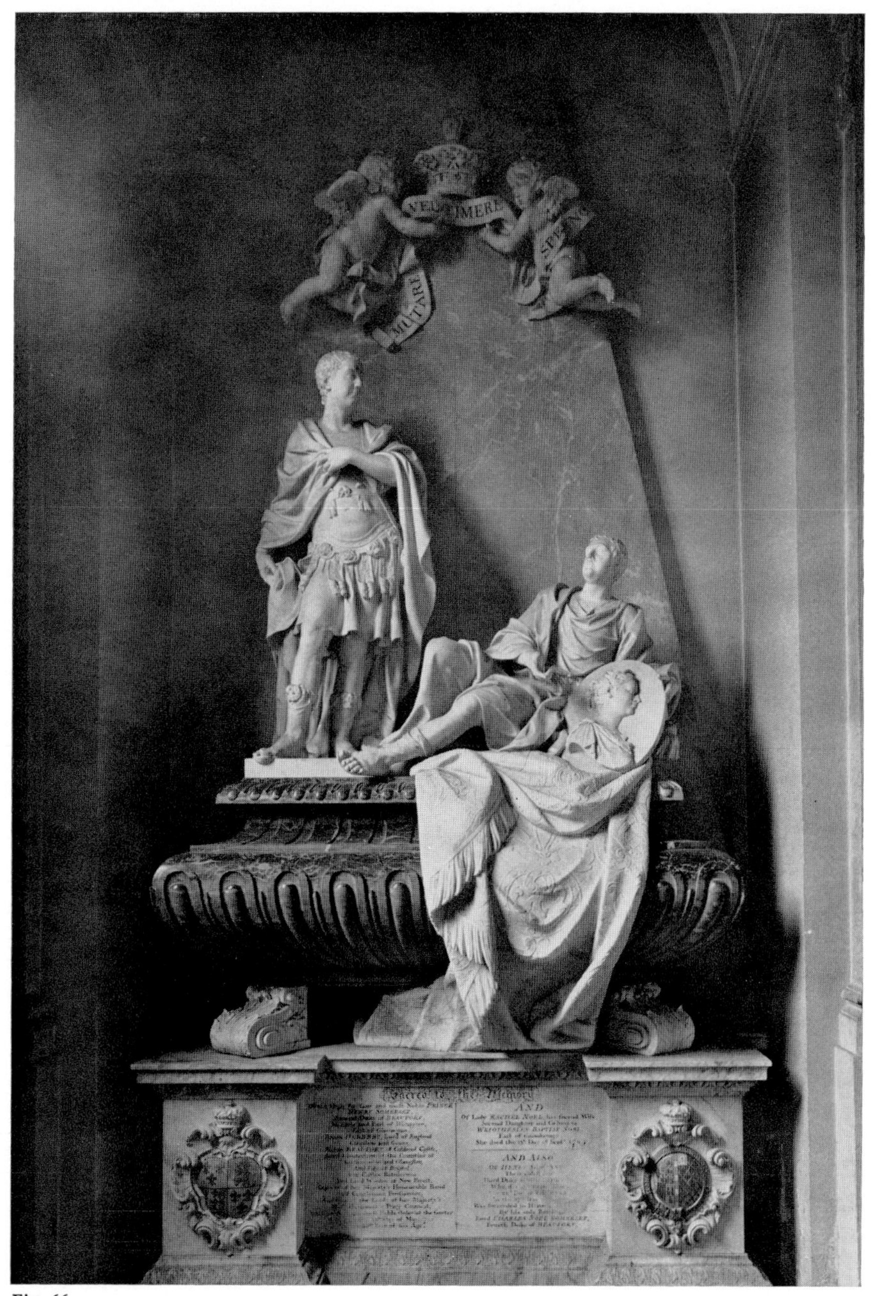

**Fig. 66**

**65**  This drawing was one of 60 "by Rysbrack" bought from Mr. B. Quaritch, on January 25th, 1867, for £1. 5s.

**66**  The monument is signed, and dated 1754. It would seem, however, that it was not taken to Badminton Church and assembled there until several years later, because in a letter to the Duchess of Beaufort, dated April 14th, 1766, Rysbrack wrote:

"According to Your Orders, received by a Gentleman who has been twice with me, I send the number of the Boxes, which are as follow. For the Monument of His Grace the late Duke of Beaufort [Charles, 4th Duke, died 28th October, 1756]: the Number of Boxes are Nine. And the remaining for the Monument of Duke Henry the Number is Four, (all the other boxes of that Monument are at Badminton) one Box contains the Laying figure of the Father of Duke Henry, holding the Medal of his Dutchess, one contains the Die's of the Pedestal with the two Coats of Arms, another contains part of the Pyramid & the last the Inscription table, which boxes will make a Load for a Waggon. I beg Your Grace will be so good as to conclude upon the Inscription for the Monument, that it may be finished as speedily as possible. Because I am not well, and if I should Die, I know [*sic*] what will become of the Monument. Therefore I hope your Grace will please to have the Boxes taken away with all convenient Expedition. I conclude with wishing you all health and Happiness. . ." (information, Rupert Gunnis). (See Ida M. Roper, *The Monumental Effigies of Gloucestershire*, 1931, pages 463–5.)

"Sacred to the Memory of the High, Puissant and most Noble Prince Henry Somerset Second Duke of Beaufort Marquis and Earl of Worcester, Earl of Glamorgan Baron Herbert, Lord of Ragland Chepstow and Gower, Baron Beaufort of Caldecot Castle, Lord Lieutenant of the Counties of Southampton and Gloucester And City of Bristol And Custos Rotulorum And Lord Warden of New Forest, Captain of her Majesty's Honourable Band of Gentlemen Pensioners, And One of the Lords of her Majesty's Most Honourable Privy Council And Knight of the most Noble Order of the Garter who died the 24th Day of May 1714 in the 30th Year of his Age. And of Lady Rachel Noel his second Wife Second daughter and Co-heir to Wriothesley-Baptist Noel Earl of Gainsborough She died the 13th Day of Sept. 1709 And also of Henry Somerset their eldest Son Third Duke of Beaufort &c. Who, dying without Issue the 24th Day of Feb. 1745–6 in the 37th year of his Age Was succeeded in Honours and Estate By his only Brother Lord Charles Noel Somerset Fourth Duke of Beaufort."

# JOHN MICHAEL RYSBRACK (*1694–1770*)

*Figure 67* (*p.102*): The chimney-piece design and the relief of Charity, formerly at Teddesley Hall, Staffordshire, and now in the Victoria and Albert Museum, Department of Architecture and Sculpture.
Inscribed *No: (6) The Height 4 feet 9 in. Width 5.8. Projection 1.1.*
Pen and ink and wash, $8\frac{7}{8} \times 7\frac{3}{4}$ inches. No. E.465–1946 and A.58, 59–1953.

*Figure 68* (*p.103*): Design for the chimney-piece for the hall of Teddesley Hall, Staffordshire.
Inscribed *No: (2) The Height 5 feet 6 inch. Width 7.9. Projection 0.10½.*
Pen and ink and wash, $9 \times 9\frac{1}{2}$ inches. No. E.462–1946.

*Figure 69* (*p.103*): Chimney-piece in the hall of Teddesley Hall, Staffordshire, now demolished: c. 1760.
Photograph: *National Monuments Record*.

---

**69** The model of the relief in the Foundling Hospital was bought by Sir Edward Littleton of Teddesley Hall in Staffordshire. During the first half of 1756 Sir Edward wrote to Rysbrack asking for a suitable chimney-piece to support the relief. On July 31st Rysbrack replied:

"I really did not remember that I was to have given you a Design for a Chimney Piece, but if you please to send me the dimensions of the outside of the frame to the Model of Charity, and the Width of the light of the Chimney and the Height, I will send you a drawing for it. . ."[1]

On November 18th of the same year Rysbrack wrote again to Littleton:

"According to Your Honour's desire I have made You a Drawing of a Chimney Piece Proportioned to your Room and the Model of the Basso Relievo for the Foundling Hospital. I have tried a Great Many Ways, but believe this will do, and I beg the favour that You will shew it to all your Friends. I do not think it proper to Enclose it in a Letter, because it will spoil it, but I shall send it Rolled on a Stick, in a Very little box, by Kirk and Saunder's Waggon on Monday Next, directed to Your Honour at Tedgeley Coppice. Sir, if You have a Desire that I should make the Chimney Piece I will do it with the Greatest Care, and I Believe as well as any Body, as I suppose Your Design is to have the Chimney Piece of Statuary Marble; and all the Work above the Cornice, and about the Model of the Basso Relievo, of wood. . . Sir, if You Approve of the Drawing, of which I have taken a Copy, it will be best to Bespeak the Chimney Piece in Time, and then you will be sure to have it Done well and of Good Marble."[2]

So far there had been nothing in these letters to link any of the Museum's designs by Rysbrack with chimney-pieces at Teddesley Hall, but three years later, on December 11th, 1759, Rysbrack wrote again to Sir Edward Littleton:

"I Have no time to Joake now Tho' I am in high Spirits; but very busy. And You shall see I am in the Land of the living by the Drawings I Send you by a West Chester Coach, to Morrow Morning; which are Six in number in a little Box. And with the Drawings is Enclosed a Paper Containing the Price of five of the Chimney Pieces. Marked No. 1. No. 2. No. 3. No. 4. No. 5. as on the Back of the Drawings.

No. 2 is the Drawing of a Chimney Piece with the Frize which your Honour have Seen finished at my house, and Mention in your letter. And No. 6. is a Drawing for a Chimney Piece for the Model which you have of the Basso Relievo at the Foundling Hospital, which you need not to make all of Marble, but only the Architraves (round the Light of the Chimney,) and all the rest in Wood. The Other Chimney pieces are all of Statuary Marble. . ."[3]

Among a collection of drawings by Rysbrack for monuments and chimney-pieces acquired by the Museum in 1946, were several of chimney-pieces on the backs of which Rysbrack had written numbers and dimensions. They are No. 1, E.461–1946; No. 2, E.462–1946; No. 3, E.463–1946; No. 4, E.459–1946; No. 5(?), E.460–1946; No. 6, E.465–1946; No. 7, E.464–1946. Of these, Numbers 1 and 2 are almost

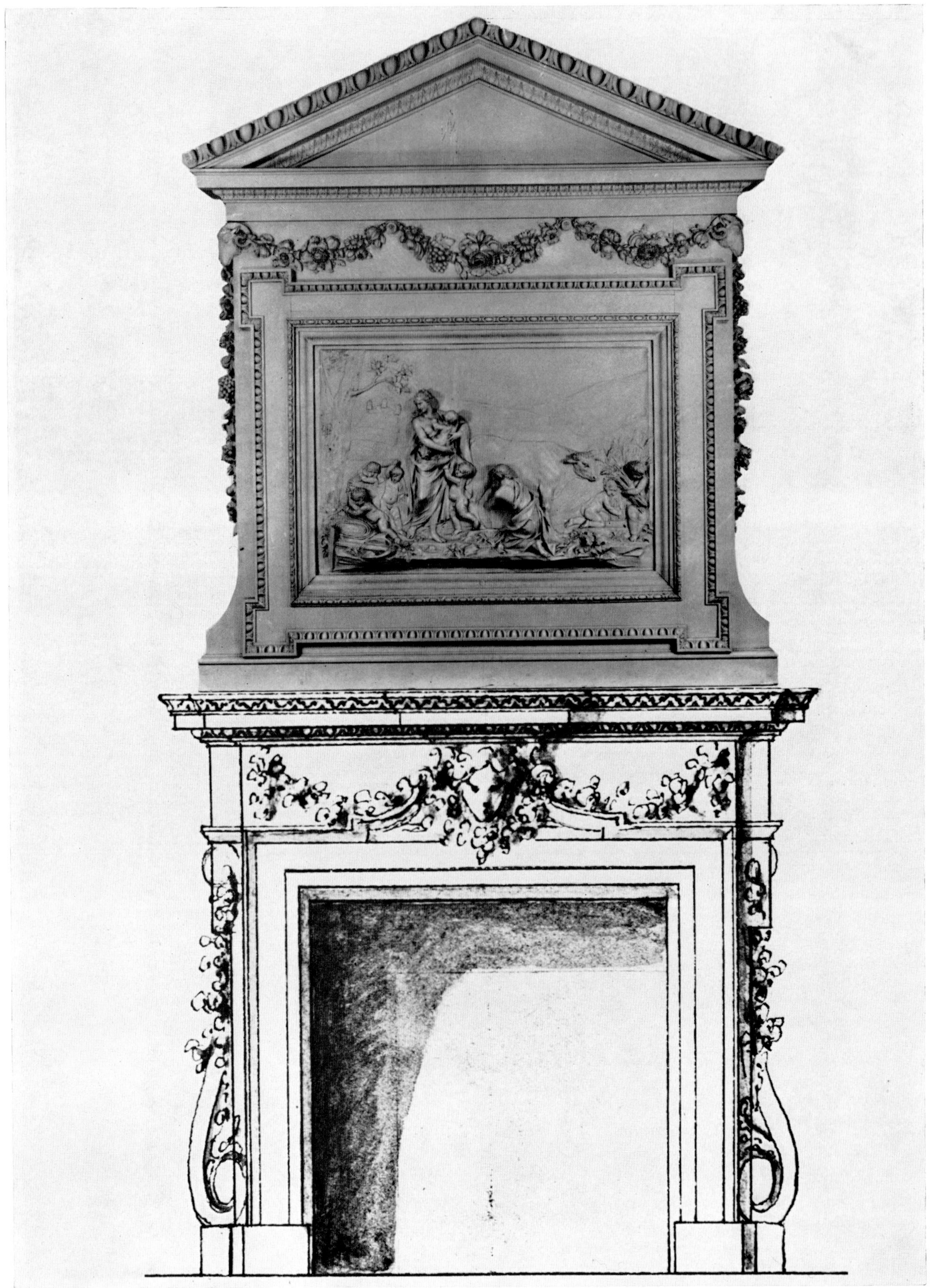

Fig. 67

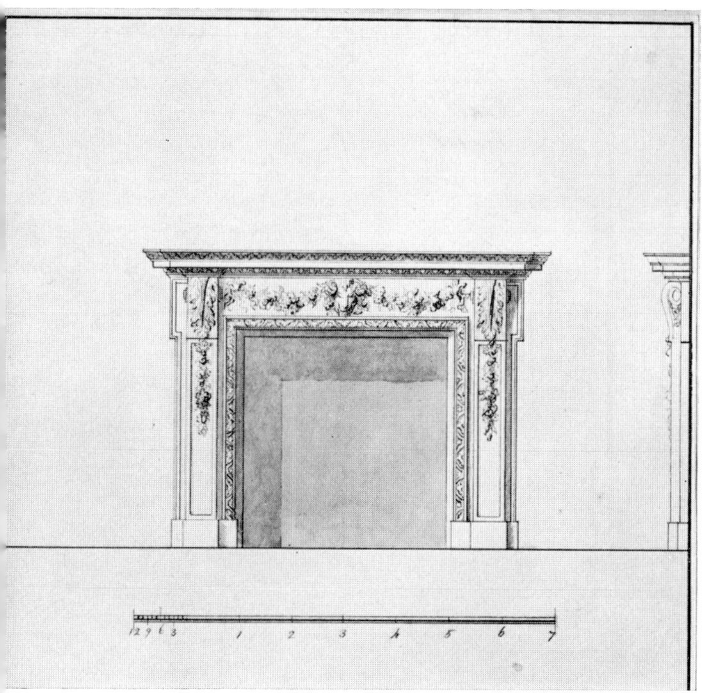



g. 68

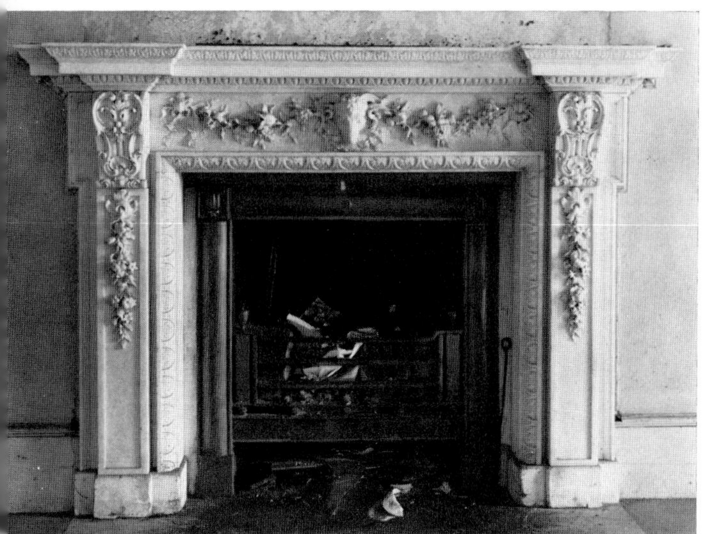

g. 69

identical designs, No. 1 with a ram's head flanked by cornucopias, while No. 2 has a ram's head with garlands. In a letter to Littleton, dated April 7th, 1761, Rysbrack refers specifically to drawing No. 1:

"Agreeable to Your desire I shall enclose you Eight Drawings of Chimneys, in a little Box, and Pack it up in the Box Marked No. 3. in which Box is the Frieze of the Chimney Piece [? *for the Foundling Hospital Relief*], the Drawings No. (7) and No. (8) are new designs which I did not send before, No. (7) is proportioned to the Brickwork of Your Best Parlour, and Mr. Macro, thinks it is the Properest for that Room, the Price of it is £200, it being a large Chimney Piece, Your Honour have the Prices of all those Drawings which I sent You last Year if You should like the Design No. (8) it must be drawn to another Scale, but I am afraid it should smoke as I told Mr. Macro. In regard to the Design No. (1) with the Rams Head and Cornucopias, it will be too much like your Other Chimney which is Done. . ."[4]

It was apparent, therefore, from the similarity of our drawings marked No. 1 and No. 2. that the Museum possesses at least seven of the eight drawings sent to Sir Edward Littleton. The eighth drawing may well be in the collection also, but as all the drawings have been cut down in size, the number 8 has probably been discarded.

Drawing No. 2 was the design for the chimney-piece in the octagonal hall of Teddesley Hall. The house was demolished in 1954, before the relationship of these drawings with the house had been discovered, so that it is not now possible to say whether there were any other Rysbrack chimney-pieces in the building.

[1] M. I. Webb, *Michael Rysbrack, Sculptor*, 1954, page 195.
[2] M. I. Webb, *op. cit.*, page 196.
[3] M. I. Webb, *op. cit.*, page 204.
[4] M. I. Webb, *op. cit.*, page 205.

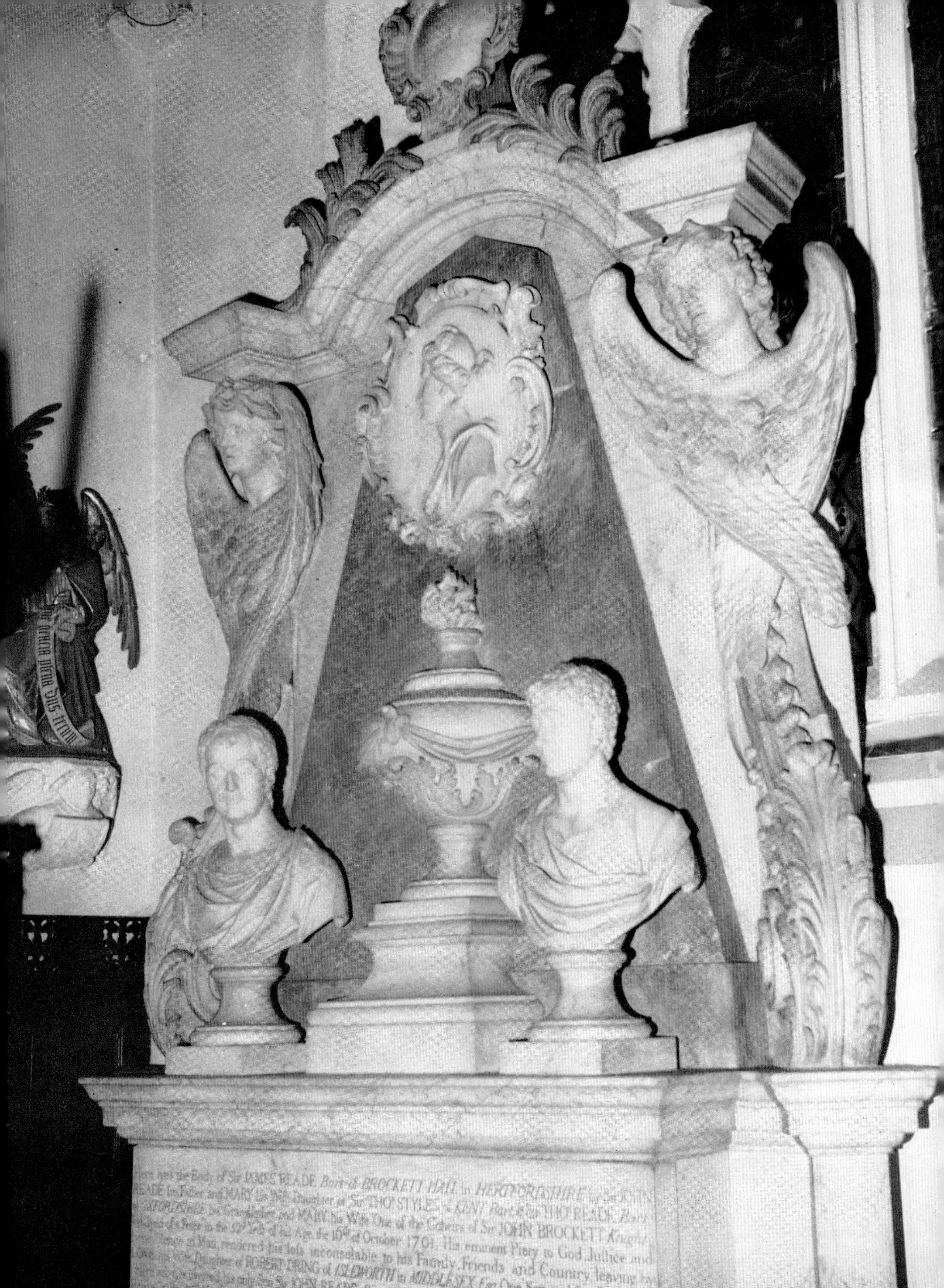

Here lyes the Body of Sir JAMES READE, Bart of BROCKETT HALL in HERTFORDSHIRE by Sir JOHN
READE his Father and MARY his Wife Daughter of Sir THO: STYLES of KENT Bart & Sir THO: READE Bart
in OXFORDSHIRE his Grandfather and MARY his Wife One of the Coheirs of Sir JOHN BROCKETT Knight
He dyed of a Fever in the 52d Year of his Age, the 16th of October 1701. His eminent Piety to God, Justice and
Benevolence to Man, rendered his loss inconsolable to his Family, Friends and Country, leaving by
LOVE his Wife Daughter of ROBERT DRING of ISLEWORTH in MIDDLESEX Esq One Son

# JOHN MICHAEL RYSBRACK (*1694–1770*)

*Figure 70 (p.106):*  Design for the monument to Sir James Reade, Bart. (died 1701), and to his son Sir John Reade, Bart. (died 1712), Hatfield, Hertfordshire.
Inscribed with a scale in feet.
Pen and ink and wash, size of sheet $13\frac{1}{2} \times 9\frac{3}{4}$ inches. No. 4910.31.

*Figure 71 (p.107):*  Design for the monument to Sir James Reade, Bart. (died 1701), and to his son Sir John Reade, Bart. (died 1712), erected in 1760, Hatfield, Hertfordshire.
Inscribed with a scale in feet, and on the back with dimensions.
Pen and ink and wash, $11\frac{1}{8} \times 9\frac{3}{8}$ inches. No. E.1183–1965.

*Figure 72 (left):*  Monument to Sir James Reade, Bart. (died 1701), and to his son Sir John Reade, Bart. (died 1712), erected in 1760, Hatfield, Hertfordshire.
Photograph: *Mr. Bruce Bailey.*

---

**70**  This drawing was one of 60 "by Rysbrack" bought from Mr. B. Quaritch on January 25th, 1867, for £1. 5s.

**71**  This drawing was bequeathed to the Museum by Rupert Gunnis, J.P.

**72**  The monument is signed and dated *Mich Rysbrack 1760.*

"Here lyes the body of Sir James Reade, Bart. of Brockett Hall, in Hertfordshire, by Sir John Reade, his father, and Mary his wife, daughter of Sir Thos. Stules, of Kent Bart. and Sir Thos. Reade, Bart. of Oxfordshire, his grandfather, and Mary his wife, one of the co-heirs of Sir John Brockett, Knight. He dyed of a fever in the 52d year of his age, the 16th of October, 1701. His eminent piety to God, justice and benevolence to man, rendered his loss inconsolable to his family, friends and country, leaving by Love his wife, daughter of Robert Dring, of Isleworth, in Middlesex Esq. one son and five daughters. Here also lyes interred his only son Sir John Reade, Bart. who dyed of the small-pox in his travells at Rome, in the 22d year of his age, the 22d Feb. 1711–12, to the irreparable loss of his family, a gentleman of great hopes, learning and parts, well versed in the liberal arts and sciences, but, above all, blessed with that natural rectitude of mind which only can render all other endowments valuable to his friends and country. By his death, the name and title became extinct in this branch of the Reades; and his five sisters becoming co-heirs to his estate, the eldest, Dorothea, married Robert Dashwood, Esq. son and heir of Sir Robert

Dashwood, Bart. of Oxfordshire; and in the present Sir James Dashwood, Bart. her son, is the only living branch of the said co-heirs; the third sister, Anne, married Robert Myddleton, Esq. of Chirk Castle, in Denbighshire; the fourth sister, Love, married Thomas Winnington, Esq. of Worcestershire, late Secretary at War; the fifth sister, Susan, dyed of a consumption in the 17th year of her age, the 24th March, 1717–18, and is also here interred, a lady much lamented for her prudence, piety and charity.

To the much revered memory of these dear relations, this monument is dedicated by their second daughter Mary Reade, who also lyes here interred by them, whose hope is full of immortality of a joyful resurrection with them to the mansions of the blessed. Amen."

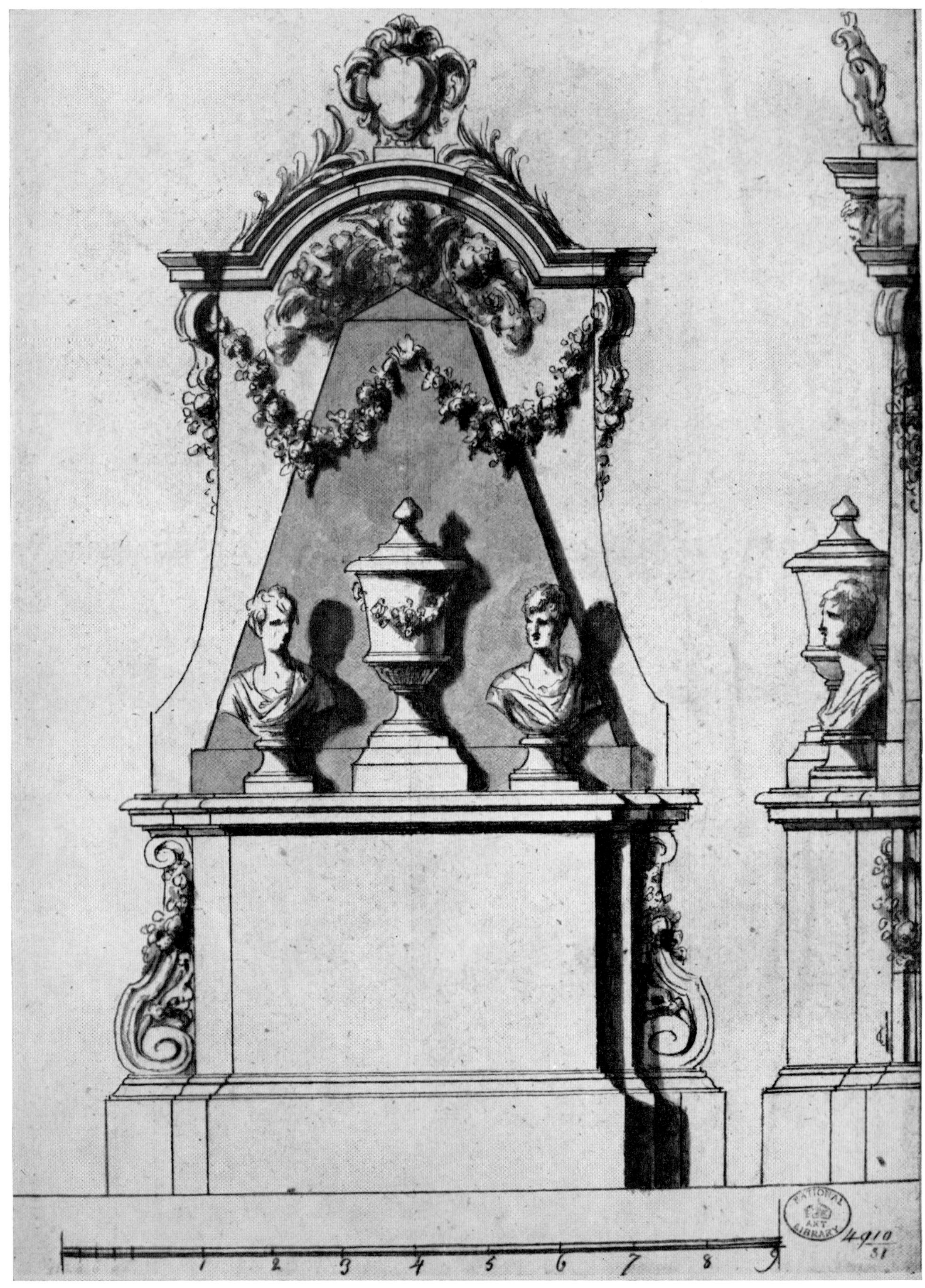



Fig. 70

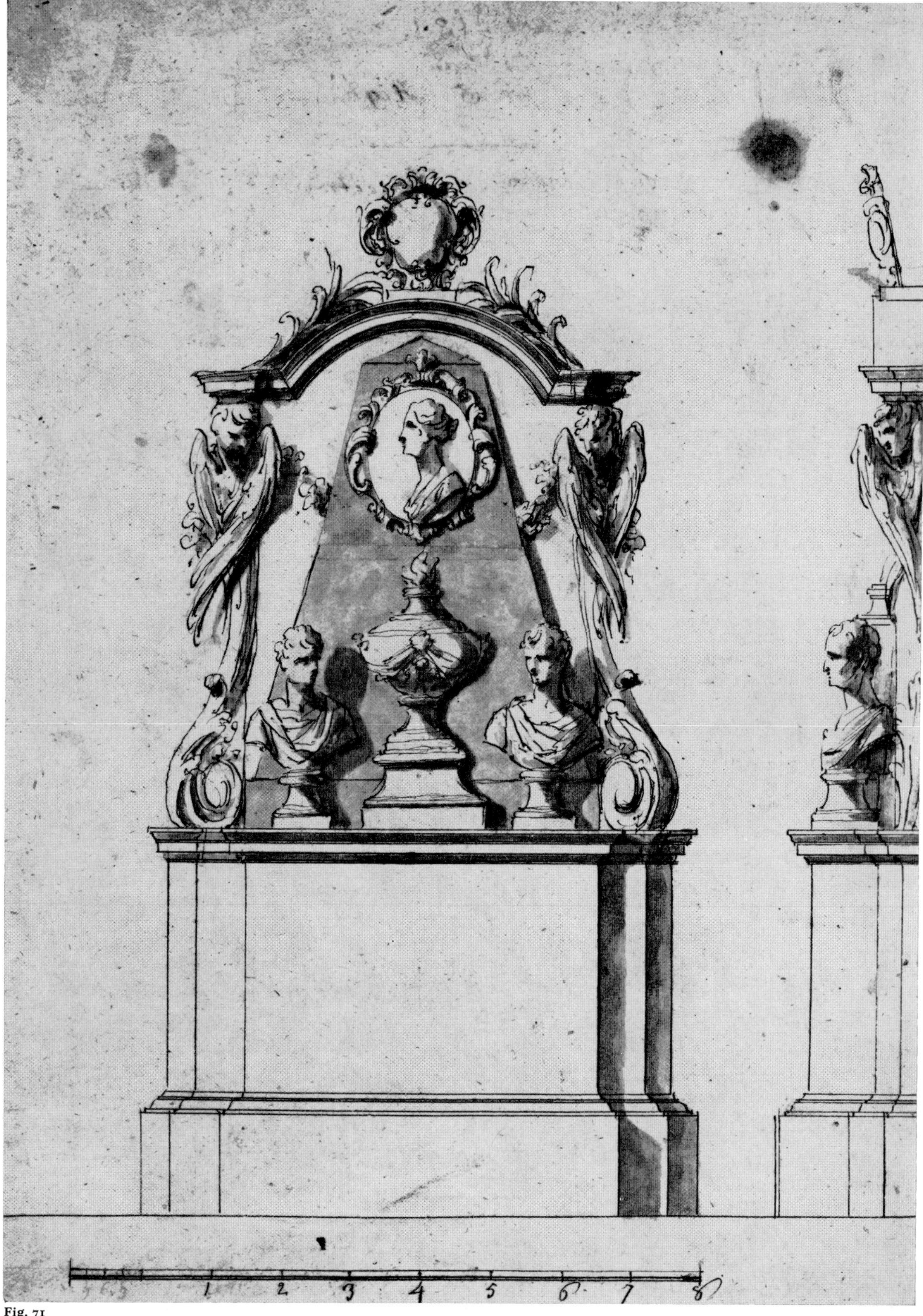

Fig. 71

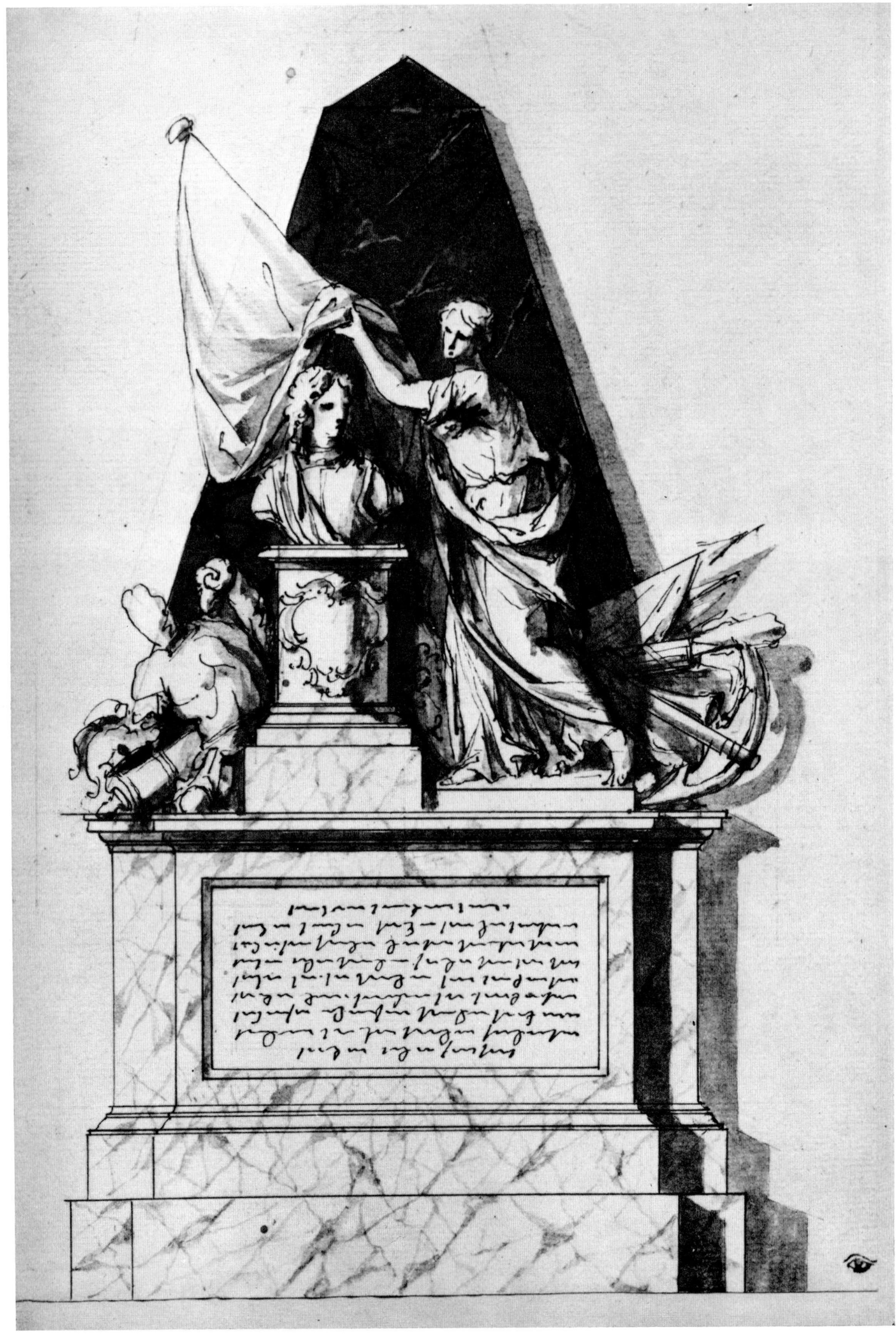

Fig. 73

# JOHN MICHAEL RYSBRACK (*1694–1770*)

*Figure 73 (left):*    Design for the monument to Admiral Vernon (died 1757), in the north transept, Westminster Abbey.
Inscribed on the back *No. (2) £650. The Height—14 ft. 4 in. 6 pts. Width—8. 3. 0.*
Pen and ink and wash, with the mark of the collection of Nathaniel Hone, R.A. $8\frac{1}{2} \times 5\frac{3}{8}$ inches. No. E.433–1946.

*Figure 74 (below):*  Monument to Admiral Vernon (died 1757), in the north transept, Westminster Abbey.
Photograph: *Warburg Institute.*

---

**74**  The monument is signed and dated *Mich Rysbrack Fecit 1763.*

"Sacred to the Memory of Edward Vernon, Admiral of the White Squadron of the British Fleet. He was the second Son of James Vernon, who was Secretary of State to King William III, and whose abilitys and Intregrety were equally conspicuous. In his youth he served under Admirals Shovell & Rook; by their Example he learned to conquer; by his own Merit he rose to command. In the War with Spain of MDCCXXXIX. he took the Fort of Porto Bellow with six Ships; a force which was thought unequal to the Attempt. For this he received the Thanks of both Houses of Parliament. He subdued Chagre, and at Carthagena conquered as far as Naval Force could carry Victory. After these services he retired, without Place or Title, from the Exercise of Publick to the Enjoyment of Private Virtue. The Testimony of a good Conscience was his Reward; the Love and Esteem of all good Men, his Glory. In Battle, though Calm, he was Active, & though Intrepid, Prudent: successful, yet not ostentatious; ascribing the Glory to God. In the Senate he was Disinterested, Vigilant, and Steady. On the xxxth. day of October MDCCLVII, he died as he had lived, the Friend of Man, the Lover of his Country, and the Father of the Poor; aged LXXIII. As a Memorial of his own Gratitude and the Virtues of his Benefactor, this Monument was erected by his Nephew, *Francis*, Lord Orwell, in the year 1763."

Another design by Rysbrack, priced at £625, may be an alternative for this monument (see fig. 42).

The sculptor's terracotta model for the figure of Victory as executed, is in the Department of Architecture and Sculpture, No. A. 1–1969.

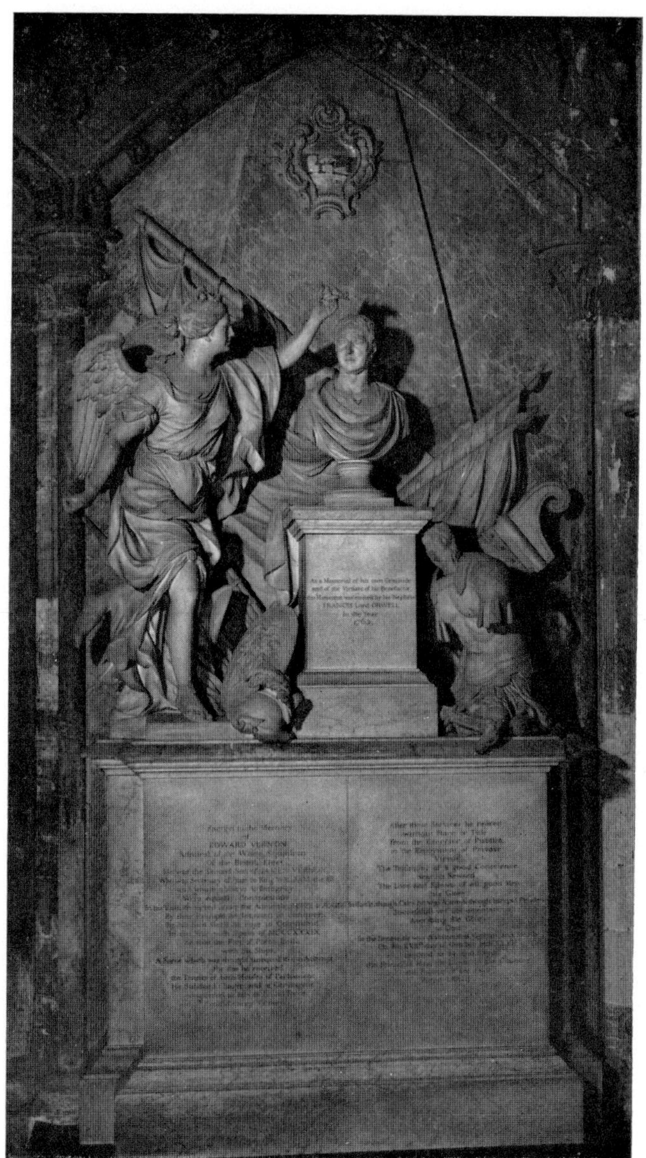

**Fig. 74**

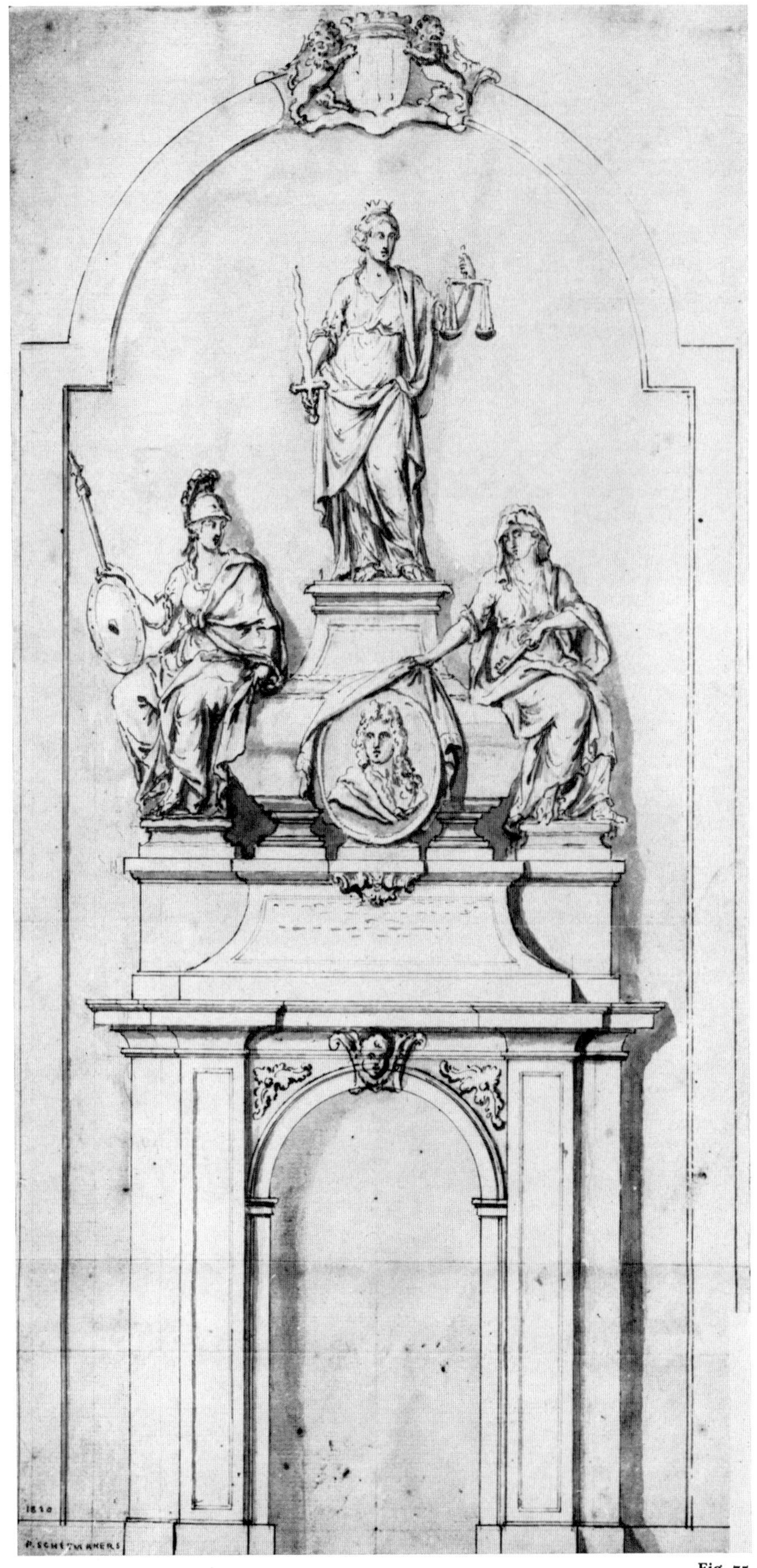

Fig. 75

# PETER SCHEEMAKERS (*1691–1781*)

*Figure 75 (left):*    Design for the monument to John, Lord Somers (1651–1716), at North Mimms, Hertfordshire.
Pen and ink and wash, size of sheet 16⅞ × 8¼ inches. No. D.1060–1887.

*Figure 76 (below):* Monument to John, Lord Somers (1651–1716), at North Mimms, Hertfordshire.
Photograph: *Mr. Bruce Bailey.*

**75**   This drawing was bought with 38 other miscellaneous drawings from Mr. E. Parsons, of Brompton Road, on August 15th, 1887, for £5. 9. 0d.

**76**   John Somers was born in Worcester, and studied law. He eventually became M.P. for his native town, and held office as the Solicitor-General from 1688 until 1692, when he was appointed Attorney-General. The following year he became Lord Keeper of the Great Seal and Speaker of the House of Lords until 1697 when he was created a Baron. From that year he was Lord Chancellor, but was dismissed from office in 1700 by William III. He was then impeached by the House of Commons but the charge was not successful. Back in favour, once again, in 1708 Somers was Lord President of the Council until 1710.

He lived at Brookmans Park, Hertfordshire, and died on April 26th, 1716. The monument in North Mimms Church was erected by his sister "Dame Elizabeth Jeckyll".

The large marble door, an integral part of the design, leads into the vestry.

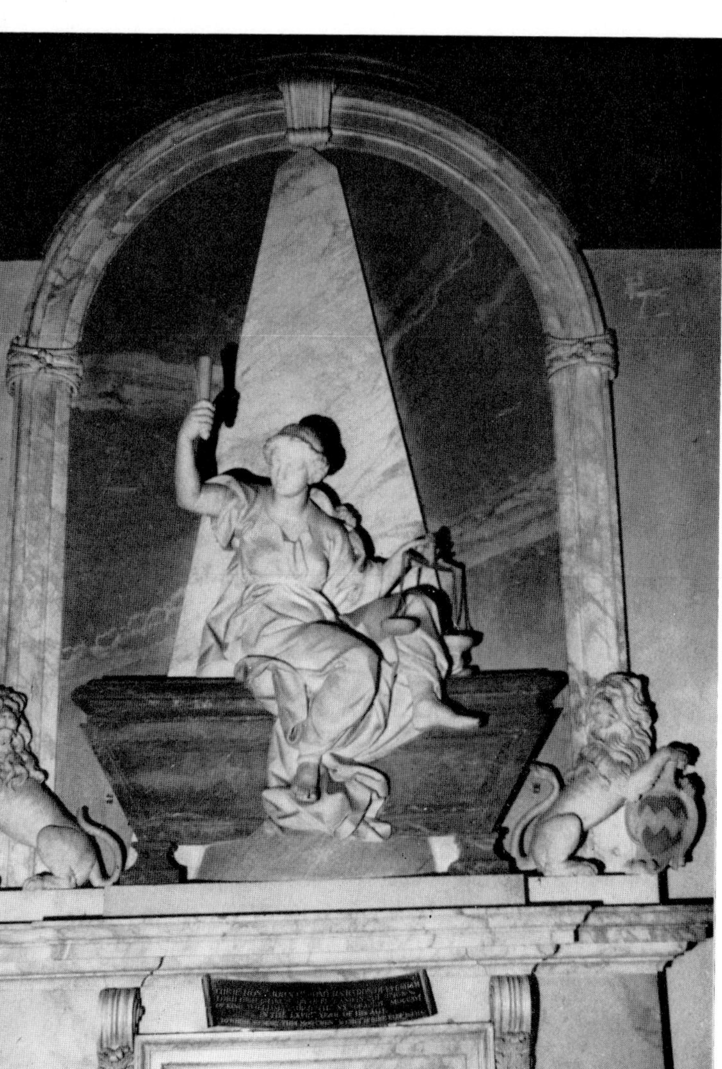

Fig. 76

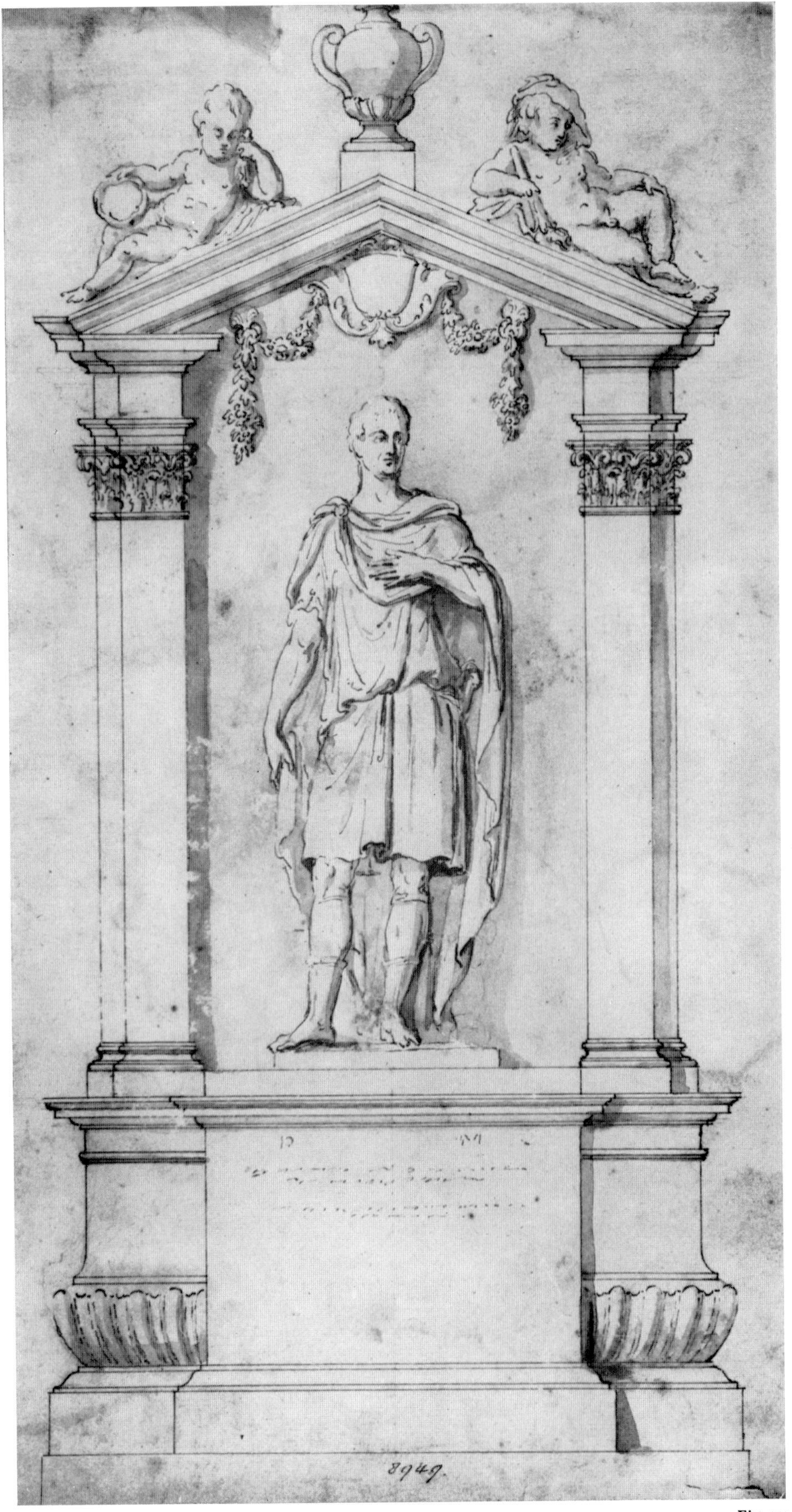


D        M

# PETER SCHEEMAKERS (*1691–1781*)

*Figure 77 (left):*  Design for the monument to Sir Samuel Ongley (died 1726), at Old Warden, Bedfordshire.
Pen and ink and wash, size of sheet 15 × 7⅞ inches. No. 8949.

*Figure 78 (below):*  Monument to Sir Samuel Ongley (died 1726), at Old Warden, Bedfordshire.
This was the joint work of Scheemakers and Laurent Delvaux.
Photograph: *Mr. Bruce Bailey.*

---

**77**  This drawing was bought from Mr. E. Parsons, of Brompton Road, on February 1st, 1883, for 3 shillings.

**78**  The monument is signed *P. Chiemaker en L. Delvaux Inventor et Fecit.*

Sir Samuel Ongley, who died on August 25th, 1726, aged 80, was a Linen Draper of Cornhill, in London. He was also a Director of the South Sea Company, and was knighted in 1713, when he presented an address from the Company to Queen Anne at Kensington Palace. Ongley was Member of Parliament for Maidstone, Kent, from 1713–15, and "was very Rich, said 10000 li. p' ann. 5 to be sure."
(*Pedigrees of the Knights* by Peter Le Neve, published by the Harleian Society, 1873, page 508.)

Robert Henley (later Henley-Ongley), his nephew, was created Baron Ongley, of Old Warden, in the peerage of Ireland, in 1776.

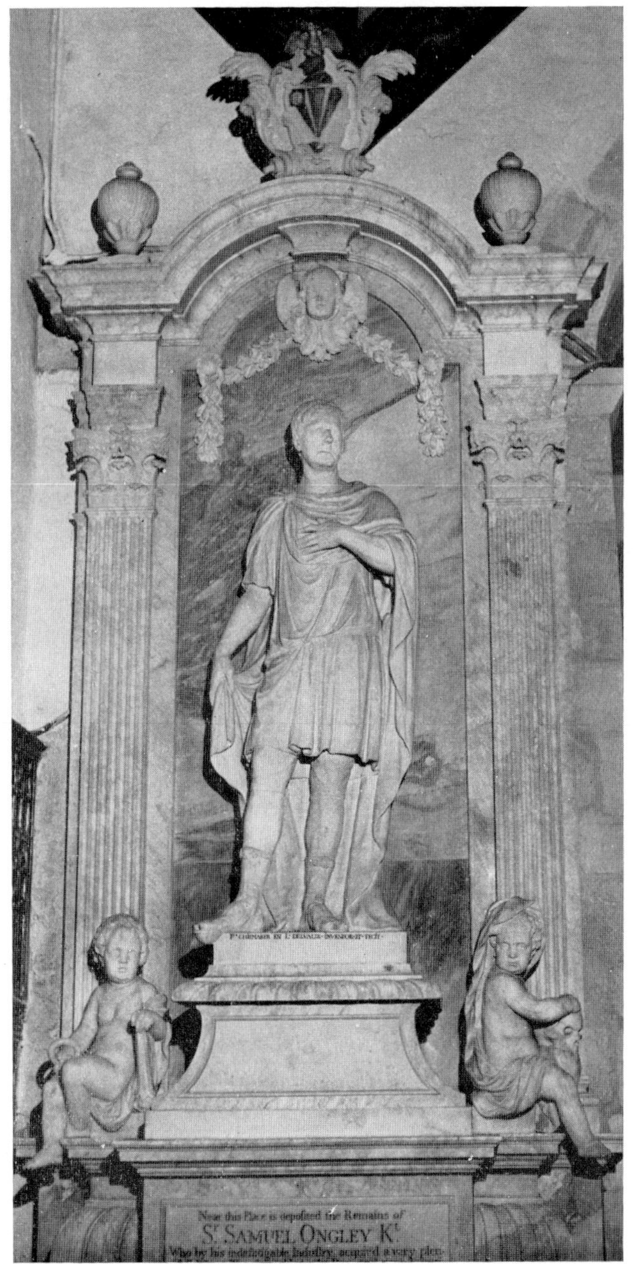


Fig. 78

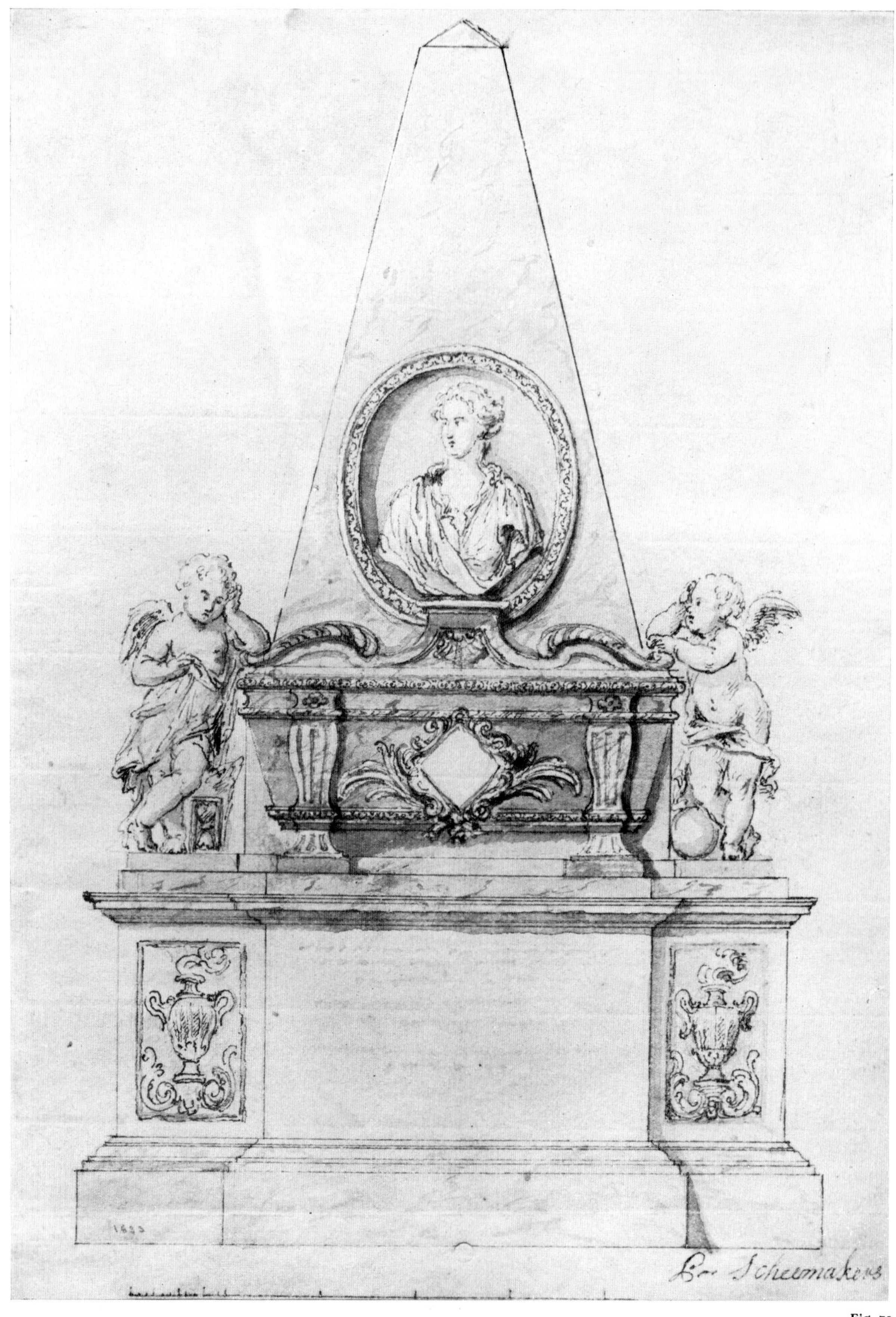





Fig. 79

# PETER SCHEEMAKERS *(1691–1781)*

*Figure 79 (left):*  Design for the monument to Ann Colleton (died 1741), in the church of All Hallows-by-the-Tower, London.
Signed *P Scheemakers*. Inscribed with a scale in feet.
Pen and ink and wash, size of sheet 12 × 8¾ inches. No. D.1035–1887.

*Figure 80 (below):*  Monument to Ann Colleton (died 1741), in the church of All Hallows-by-the-Tower, London. The monument was destroyed when the church was reduced to a shell in 1941, during the Second World War, and only a few fragments of it now remain in the rebuilt church.
Photograph: *National Monuments Record.*

**79**  Bought from Mr. E. Parsons, of Brompton Road; see fig. 75.

**80**  "In a vault near this place belonging to the Family of the Richardson's and now closed up Is Interred the Body of Ann Colleton of Stratford Langthorne in Essex, youngest Daughter of Sr. Peter Colleton of St. James's Baronet who dyed the 5th. of July 1741. At whose Desire and Cost this Monument was Erected by her Executor in Memory of Her, and the Family of the Richardson's particularly Robert Richardson, Katherine his Second Wife Eldest Daughter of Sr. Peter Colleton & the four Children John, John, Leslie and Elizabeth, Also two Children of her Brother Sr. John Colleton Baronet: Elizabeth & Katherine Hannah.

Gifts & Charitys given to this Church From Robert Richardson the Elder in 1685 The whole large Altar with the Pillars Carvings Guildings Inscriptions &c. And by Ann Colleton in 1741 Twenty Pounds to the Charity Children of the Parish & Ten Pounds to the Poor of the Parish not Pensioners."

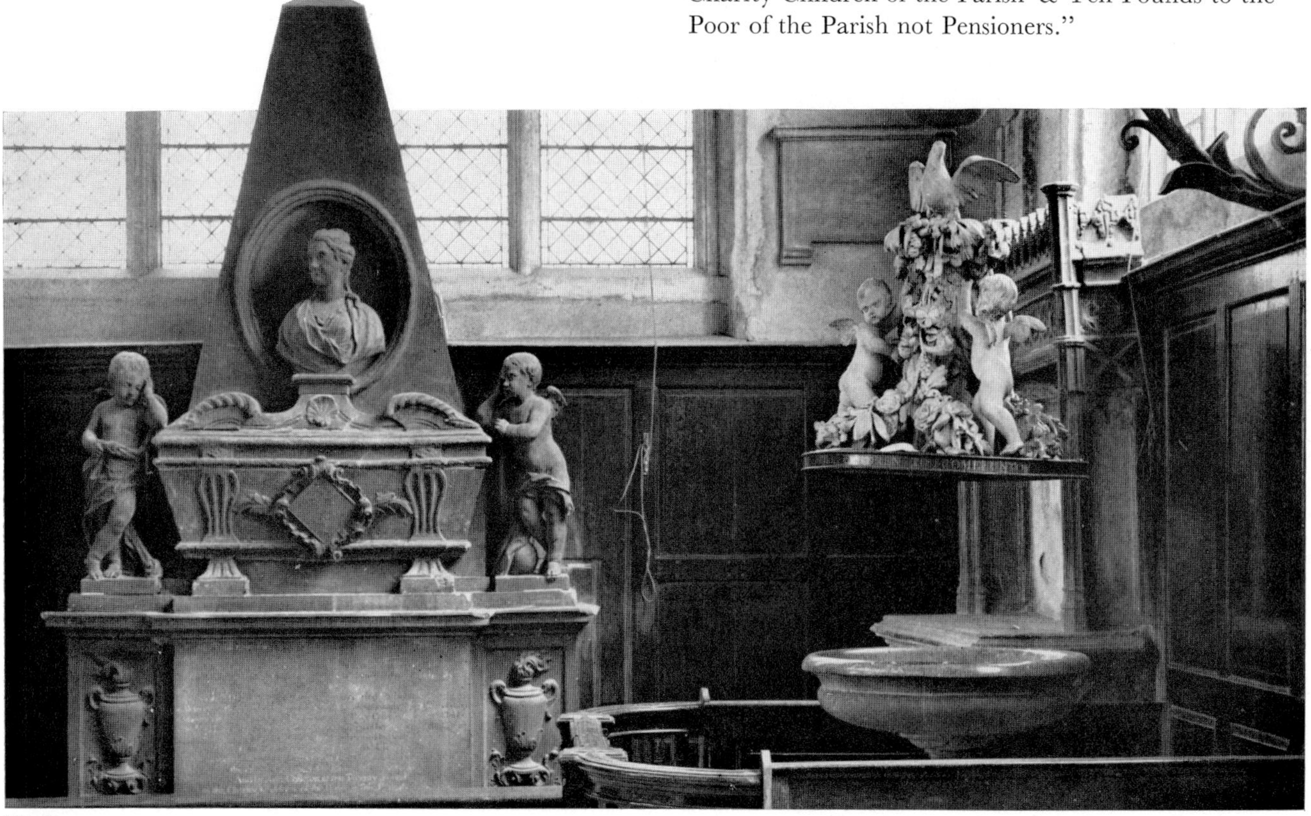

Fig. 80

# PETER SCHEEMAKERS (*1691–1781*)

*Figure 81 (right):* Design for the monument to Lord Aubrey Beauclerk (died 1740), in the North Transept, Westminster Abbey, London.
Pen and ink and wash, 11 × 5⅜ inches. D.1058–1887.

*Figure 82 (below):* Monument to Lord Aubrey Beauclerk (died 1740), in the North Transept, Westminster Abbey, London.
Photograph: *Warburg Institute.*

---

**81**  Bought from Mr. E. Parsons, of Brompton Road; see fig. 75.

**82**  The monument is signed *P. Scheemakers Ft.*

*"While Britain boasts her Empire o'er the Deep,*
*This Marble shall compell the Brave to weep;*
*As Men, as Britons, & as Soldiers, mourn—*
*'Tis Dauntless, Loyal, Virtuous Beauclerk's Urn.*
*Sweet were his Manners, as his Soul was great,*
*And ripe his Worth, tho' immature his Fate.*
*Each tender Grace yt. Joy and Love inspires,*
*Living, he mingled with his Martial Fires:*
*Dying, he bid* Britannia's *Thunder roar,*
*And* Spain *still felt him when he breath'd no more.*

The *Lord* Aubrey Beauclerk was the youngest Son of Charles, Duke of St. Alban's, by *Diana,* Daughter of Aubrey de Vere, Earl of Oxford. He went early to Sea, and was made a Commander in 1731. In 1740, he was sent upon that Memorable Expedition to Carthagena, under the Command of Admiral Vernon, in his Majesty's Ship the Prince Frederick, which with three others was ordered to Cannonade the Castle of *Boca-Chica.* One of these being obliged to quit her Station, the Prince Frederick was exposed not only to the Fire from the Castle, but to that of Fort St. Joseph, and to two Ships that guarded the Mouth of the Harbour, which he Sustained for many Hours that Day, and part of the next, with uncommon Intrepidity. As he was giving his Commands upon Deck, both his Legs were Shot off, but such was his Magnanimity, yt. he would not Suffer his Wounds to be drest, till he had communicated his Orders to his first Lieutenant, wch. were, "To Fight his Ship to the last Extremity." Soon after this he gave some Directions about his private Affairs, & then resigned his Soul, wth. the Dignity of a Hero and a Christian. Thus he was taken off in the 31st. year of his Age, an illustrious Commander, of Superior Fortitude & Clemency: Amiable in his Person, Steady in his Affections, & equall'd by few in the Social & Domestick Virtues of Politeness,

Modesty, Candour, and Benevolence. He marry'd the Widow of Coll. Frs. Alexander, a Daughter of Sr. Henry Newton, Kt. Envoy Extraordinary to the Court of Florence, & the Republick of Genoa, & Judge of the High Court of Admiralty, &c."

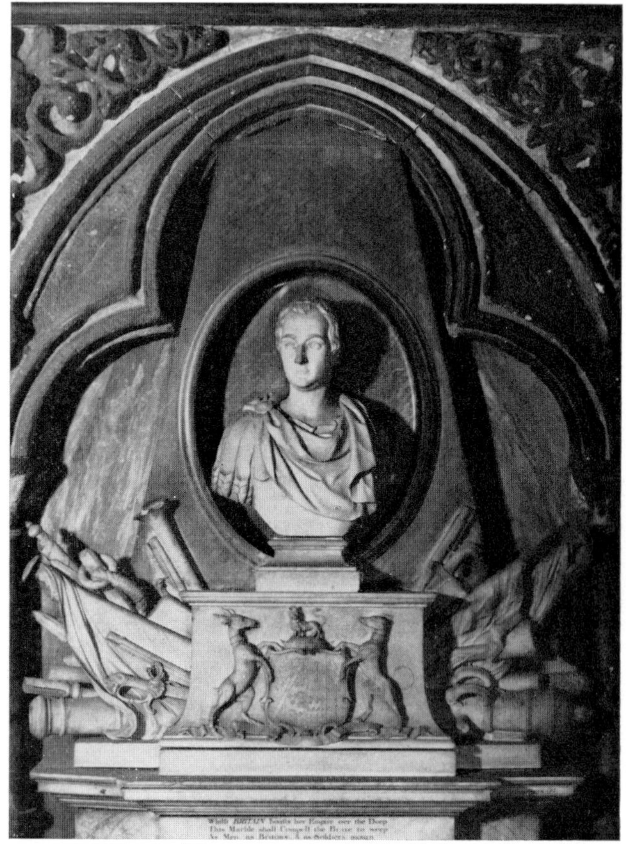

**Fig. 82**

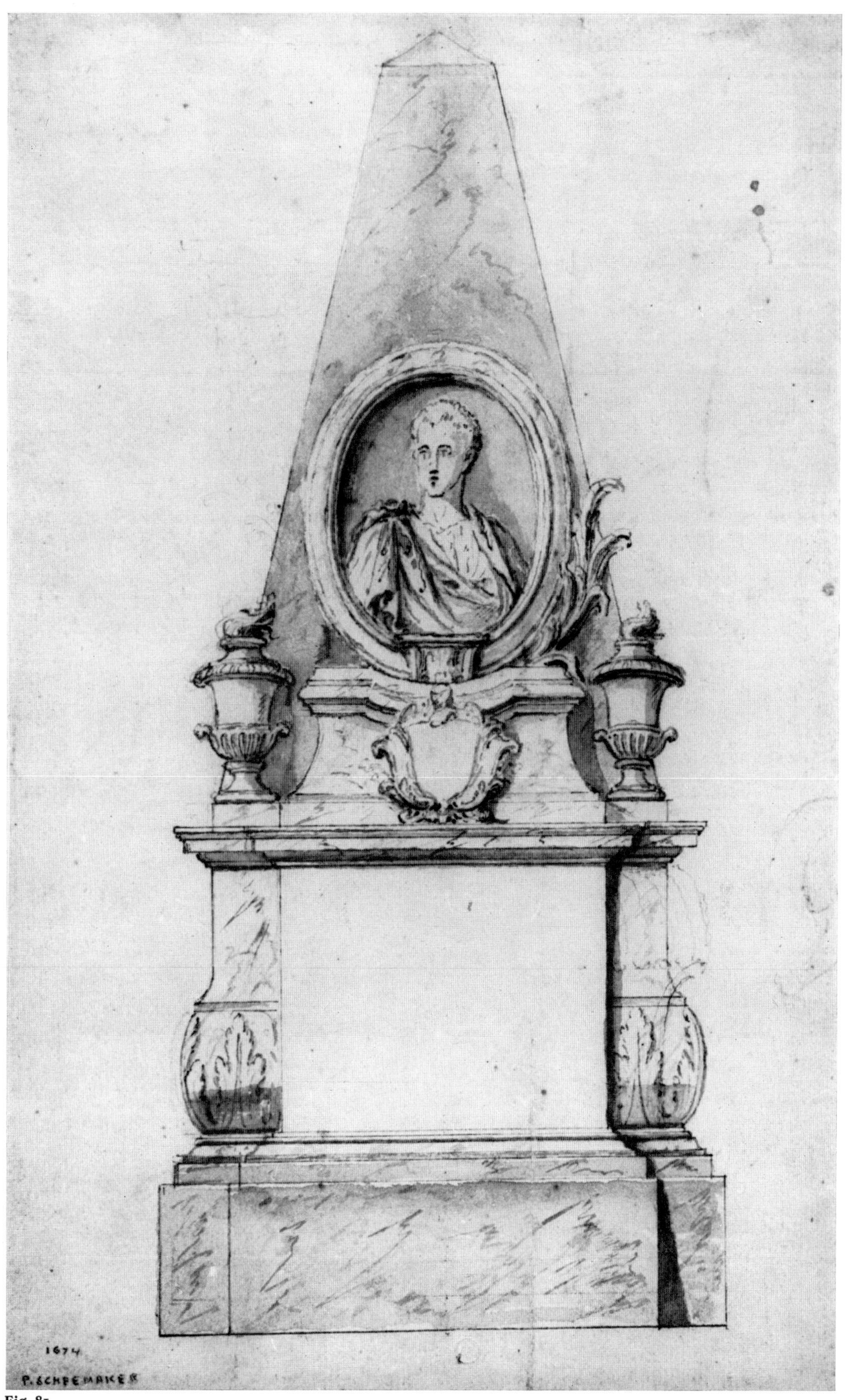



**Fig. 81**

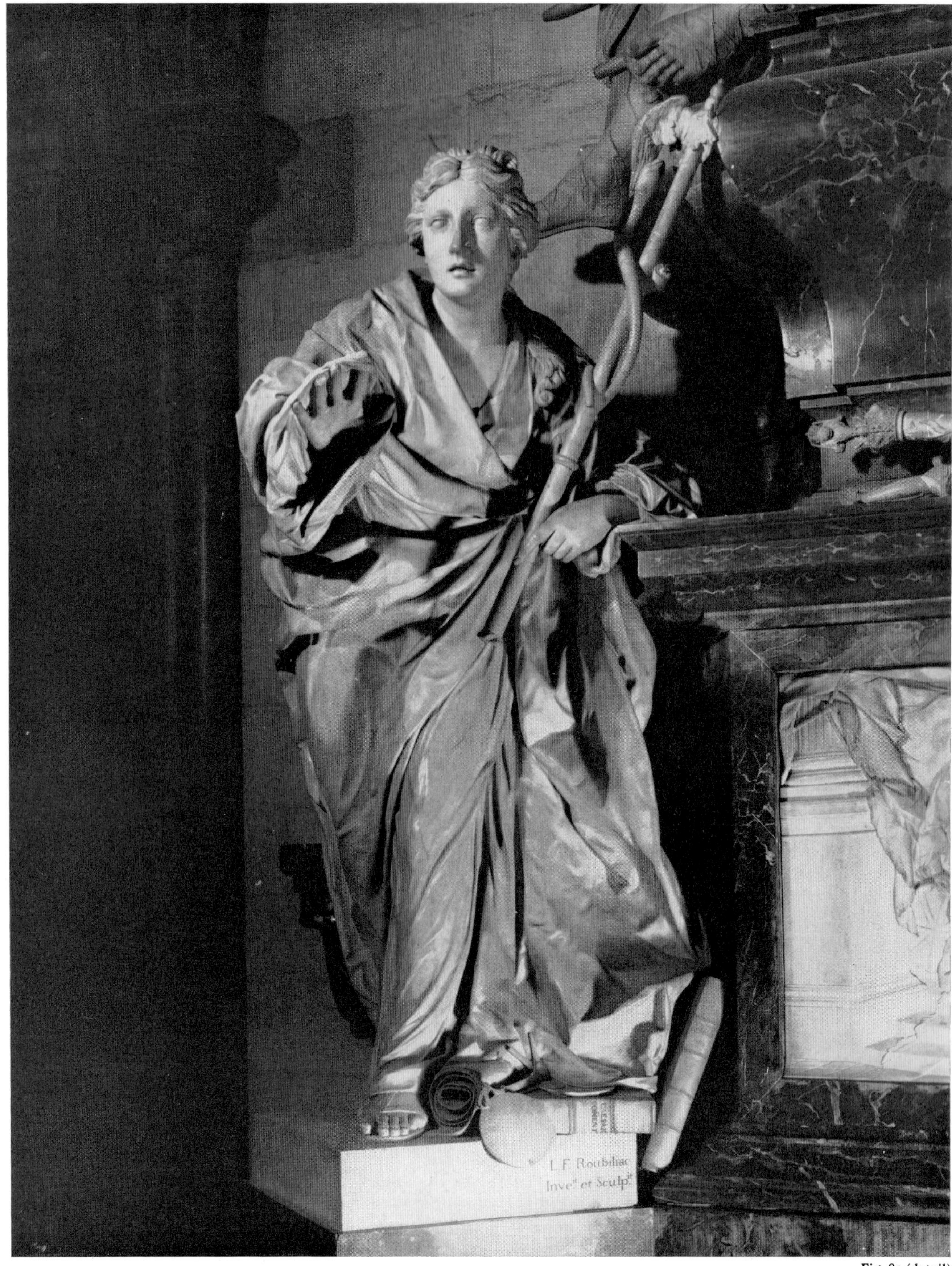



Fig. 84 (detail)

*Figure 83 (p.120):* Design for the monument to John Campbell, 2nd Duke of Argyll and
Greenwich, K.G., K.T. (died 1743), Westminster Abbey.
Signed *L. F. Roubiliac Inv^{it}*.
Pen and ink, black and white chalks, 28½ × 17 inches. No. 8381.

*Figure 84 (p.121):* The monument to John Campbell, 2nd Duke of Argyll and Greenwich,
K.G., K.T. (died 1743), in the south transept, Westminster Abbey.
(*Left*) Detail, the figure of Eloquence.
Photographs: *Warburg Institute*.

---

**83** At the sale of Joseph Nollekens's collection by
Evans on December 4th, 1823, Lot 252 was the
original design for the Duke of Argyll's monument,
together with a MS. reference to the agreement which
was signed by the sculptor and the Duchess of
Argyll on May 25th, 1745. The design was bought
from Mr. E. Parsons, of Brompton Road, on April 8th,
1878, for £3. 3s., and I think that this competent
drawing is signed by Roubiliac as the designer only;
he does not, as might be expected, state that he drew
it. Referring to Roubiliac's design for the tympanum
of the pediment of the Mansion House, Mr. William T.
Whitley (*Times Literary Supplement*, August 17th, 1922,
page 533) wrote that Roubiliac "was not happy with
the pencil; and it is stated that he declined to submit
a drawing of his design to the committee as the other
artists did. 'Give me some clay,' said Roubiliac,
'and shut me up in a room, and I will show you what
I can do.'" It seems possible that the Argyll drawing
was produced by a more competent artist at
Roubiliac's request specially for submission to the
Duchess of Argyll.

On page 5 of *A descriptive list of original drawings,
engravings, autograph letters, and portraits illustrating the
Catalogues of the Society of Artists of Great Britain* [1760–
1791] *in the possession of Edward Jupp*, 1871, which is in
the Victoria and Albert Museum Library, is an entry
which must refer to the drawing which was once in
Nollekens's possession—

Drawing: the original Design for the Monument of the
Duke of Argyle and Greenwich, which Drawing
accompanied the contract for the Monument. Signed
"L. F. Roubiliac invt." On the back of the Drawing
is the following memorandum:—

25th May, 1748.—This case contains the drawing
design'd for the late Duke of Argyle and Greenwich's

Monument, and is referr'd to in the Articles signed
by her Grace the Duchess of Argyle and me this day.

Louis François Roubiliac.

Witness: William Smith.
William Bates.

The drawing has been mounted on card since its
arrival in the Museum in 1878, so that at the moment
it is impossible to know whether the inscription remains
on the back.

The date, 1748, given by Jupp, must either be a
misreading of the handwriting, or a printer's error.
The terracotta model in the Museum is dated 1745,
and Mrs. Esdaile's supposition (*Louis François Roubiliac*,
page 62) that the Duchess and Roubiliac signed their
agreement in 1748, less than one year before the
unveiling of the finished monument on May 18th,
1749, was mistaken.

Michael Rysbrack also prepared designs for this
monument; two of his drawings for it are in the Art
Gallery and Museum (Cottonian Collection) at
Plymouth. The drawings which are not numbered
by that Museum, are described (probably by Cotton,
died 1784) on their backs as designs for the Argyll
monument. One which incorporates a ducal coronet
is inscribed by Rysbrack with the measurements which
show that it was to be a large work nearly twenty feet
high and just over twelve feet wide. The other drawing
has no ducal attributes, but they both incorporate
military trophies and Time holding an hour-glass.

Roubiliac's terracotta model dated 1745 is in
the Victoria and Albert Museum, Department of
Architecture and Sculpture, No. 21–1888, and is
fig. 11 of "Some eighteenth-century designs for monuments in Westminster Abbey" by John Physick,
*Victoria and Albert Museum Bulletin*, January, 1967.

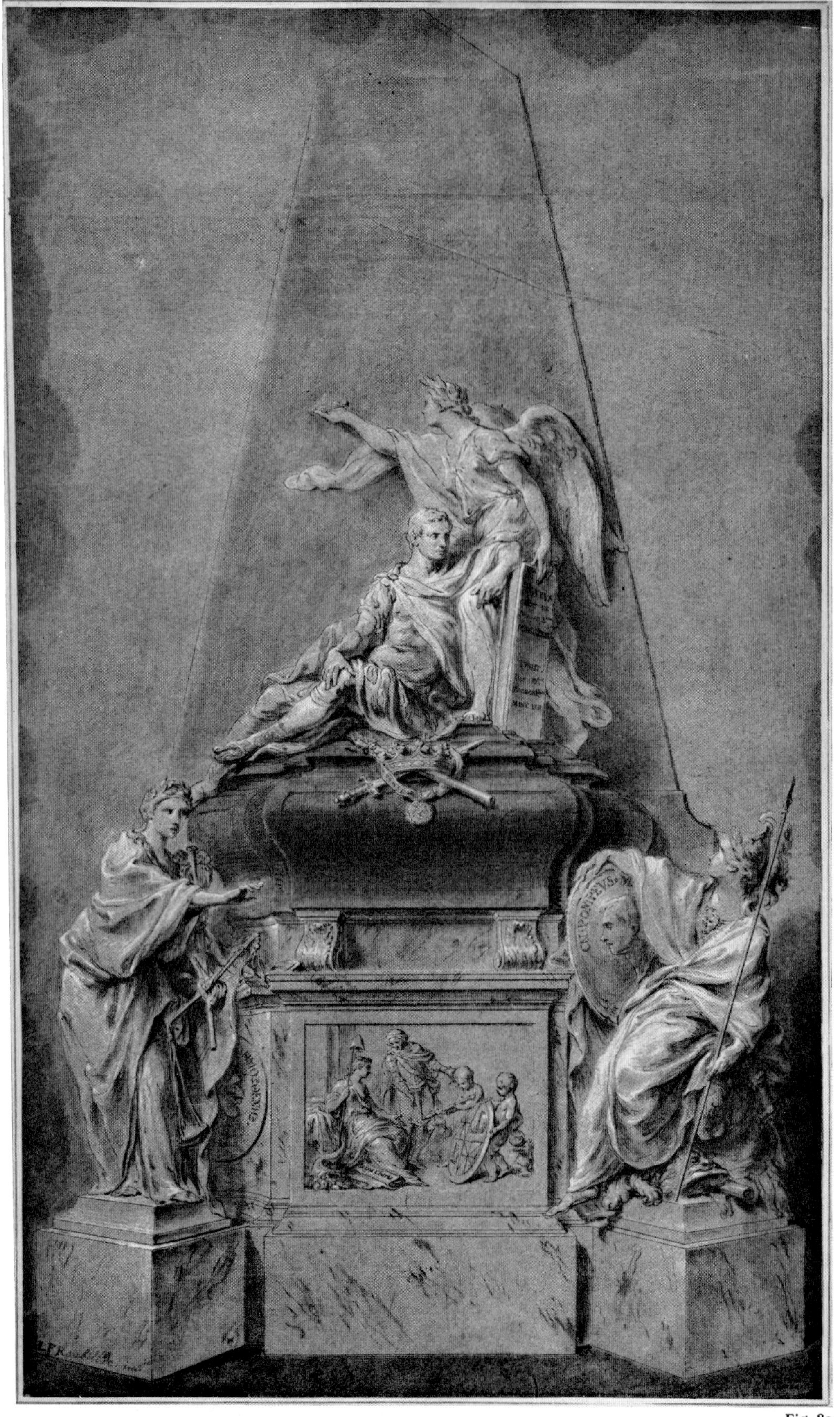



Fig. 83

Fig. 84 ▶

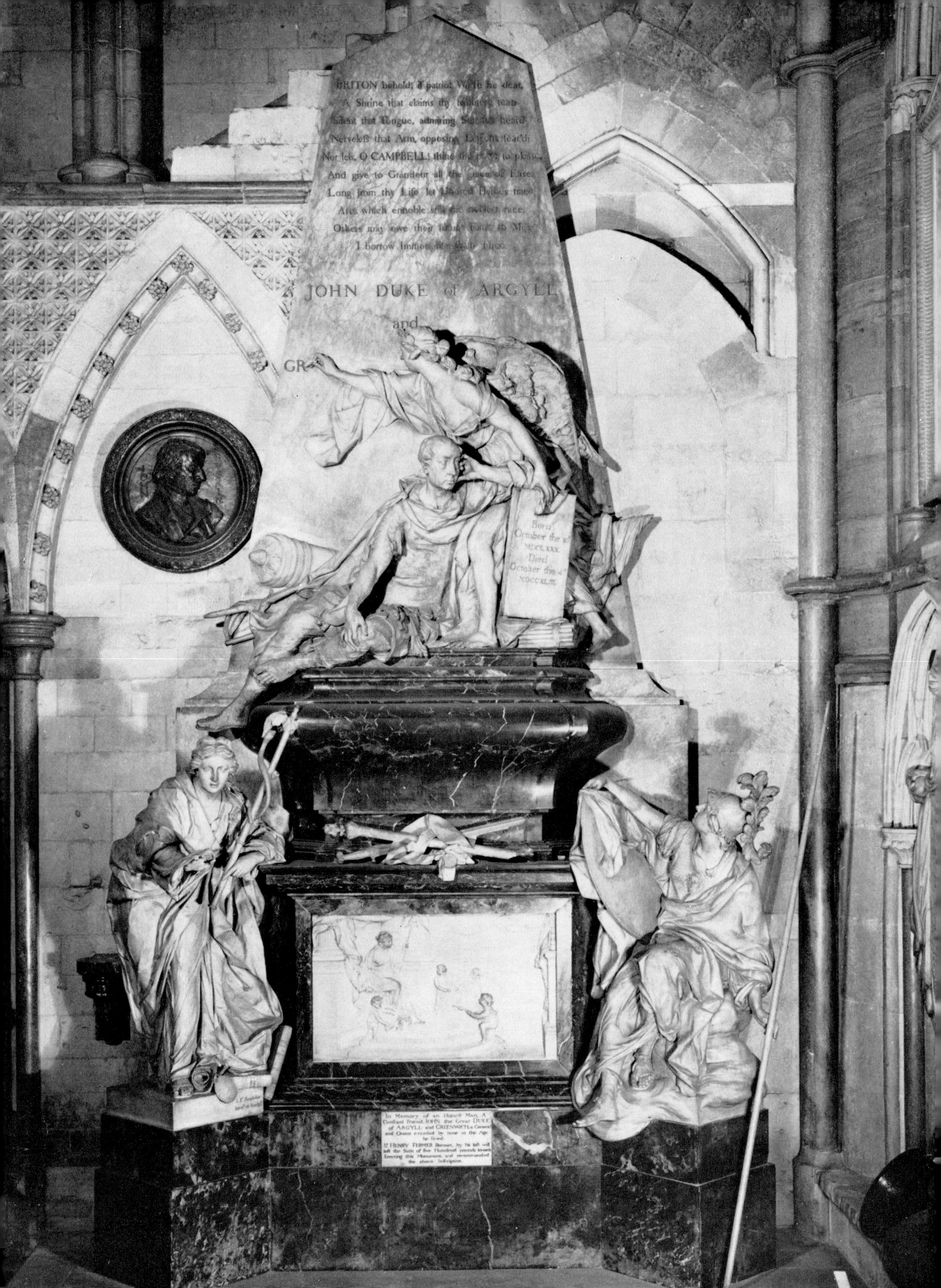


BRITON behold, if patriot Worth be dear,
A Shrine that claims thy tributary tear.
Silent that Tongue, admiring Senates heard,
Nerveless that Arm, opposing Legions fear'd;
Nor less, O CAMPBELL! thine the power to please,
And give to Grandeur all the ease.
Long from thy Life let kindred Heroes trace
Arts which ennoble still the noblest race.
Others may owe their future fame to Me,
I borrow Immortality from Thee.

JOHN DUKE of ARGYLL
and
GR

In Memory of an Honest Man, A
Constant Friend, JOHN the Great DUKE
of ARGYLL and GREENWICH, a General
and Orator exceeded by none in the Age
he lived.
S.r HENRY FURNESE Baronet, by his last will
left the Sum of five Hundred pounds towards
Erecting this Monument, and recommended
the above Inscription.

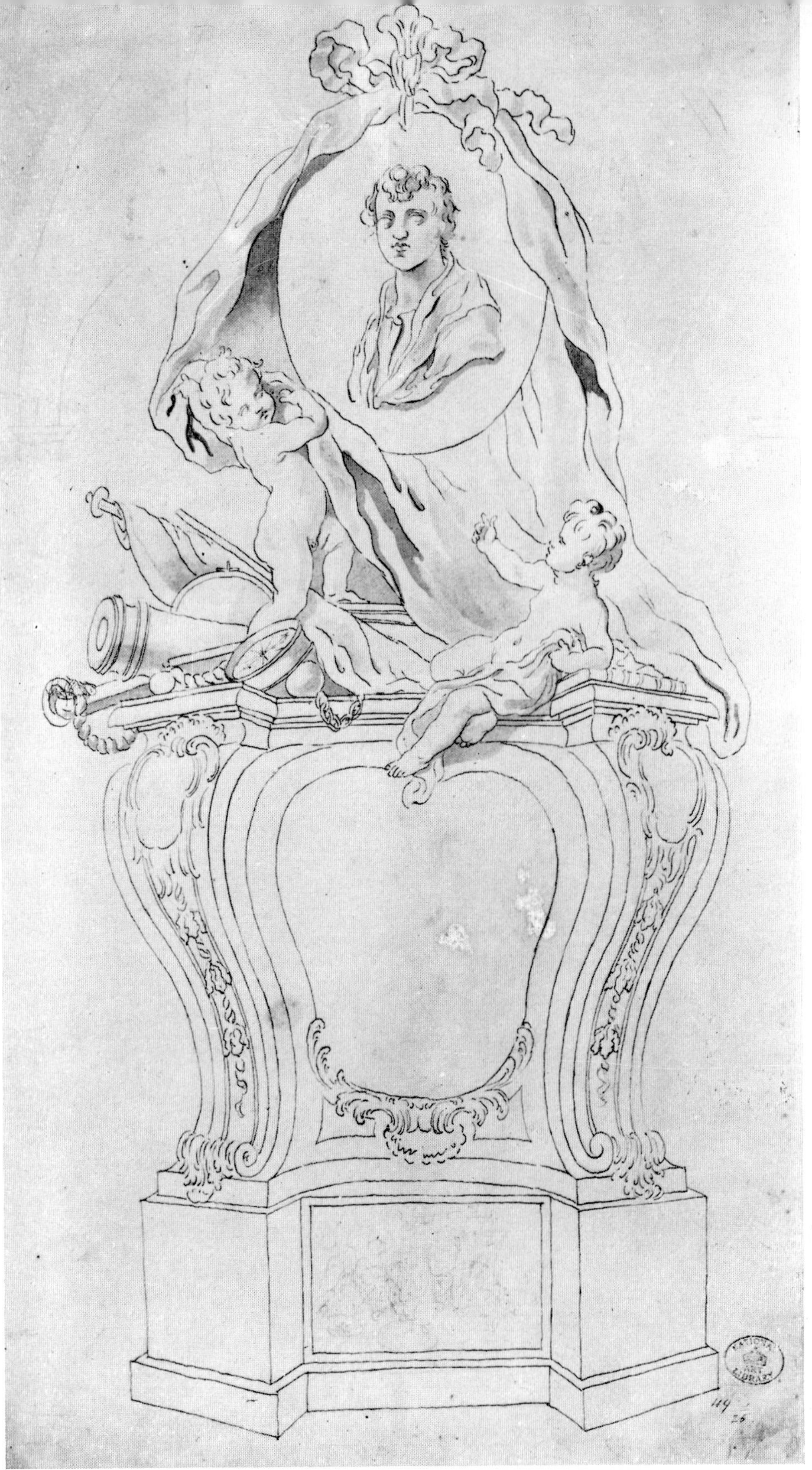

Fig. 85

**85** This drawing was one of 60 "by Rysbrack" bought from Mr. B. Quaritch on January 25th, 1867, for £1. 5. od.

**86** Philip de Sausmarez was the son of Matthew de Sausmarez, of Guernsey. He joined the Royal Navy when he was sixteen years old, and by 1746 was Captain of H.M.S. *Nottingham*, a 60 gun ship, which, unaided, captured *Mars*, a larger French vessel. "In the first Engagement of the following Year, when Admiral Anson defeated and took a Squadron of French Men of War & India Men, He had an honourable Share; and in the Second under Admiral Hawke, when the Enemy after a long & obstinate Resistance was again routed, in pursuing two ships that were making their Escape, He gloriously but unfortunately fell." De Sausmarez was buried in St. Andrew's Church, Plymouth, and the monument in Westminster Abbey was erected by his brothers and sisters. It cost £270 and Cheere was corresponding with the De Sausmarez family in the early months of 1750. (See "Henry Cheere, Sculptor and Businessman and John Cheere" by Mrs. M. I. Webb, in *The Burlington Magazine*, Volume 100, 1958, page 239.)

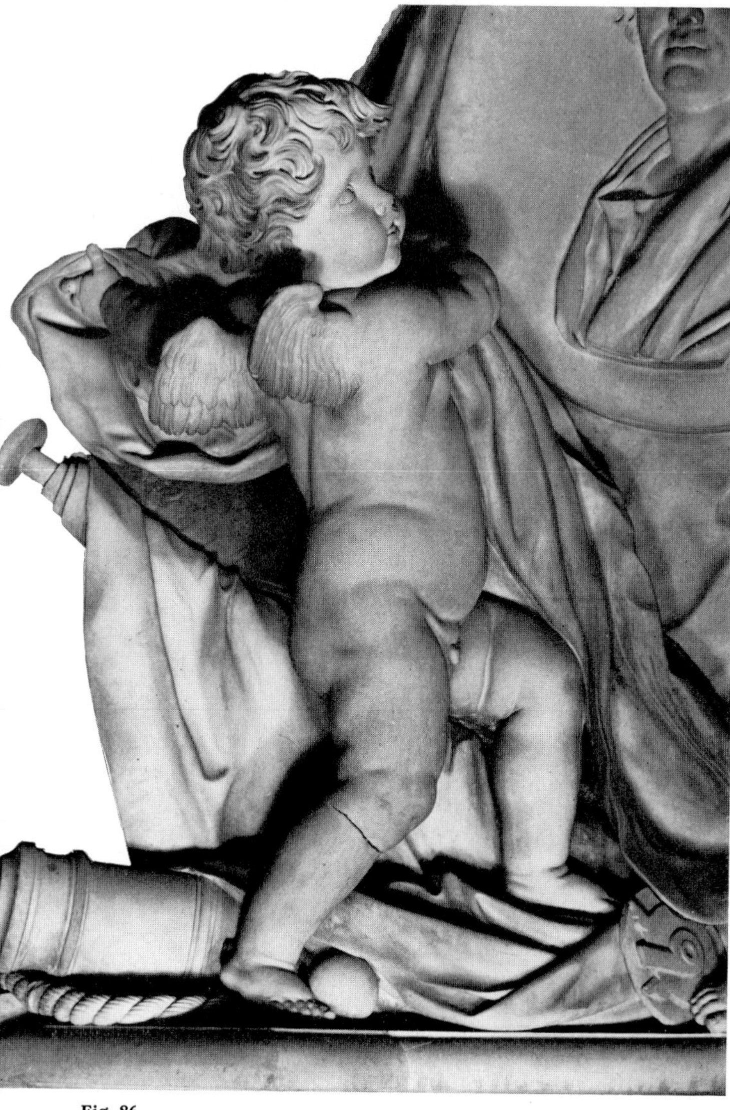

**Fig. 86**

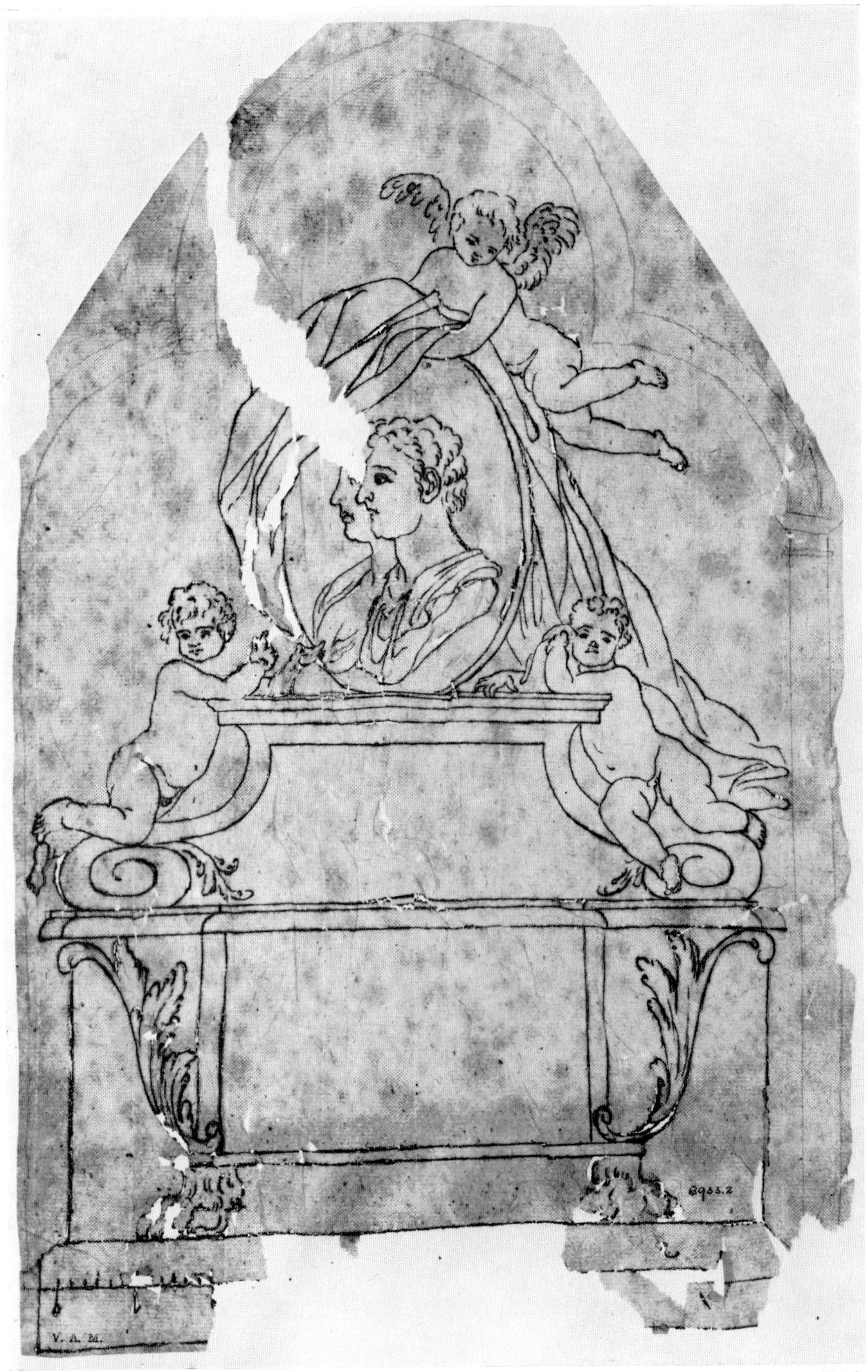



Fig. 87

# SIR HENRY CHEERE, Bart. (*1703–1781*)

*Figure 87 (left):*  Design for the monument to Sir Edmund Prideaux, Bart. (died 1728) and his wife Anne (died 1741), in the north aisle of the nave, Westminster Abbey. Pen and ink, 13¾ × 8½ inches. No. 8933.2.

*Figure 88 (below):*  Monument to Sir Edmund Prideaux, Bart. (died 1728) and his wife Anne (died 1741) in the north aisle of the nave, Westminster Abbey. Photograph: *Warburg Institute.*

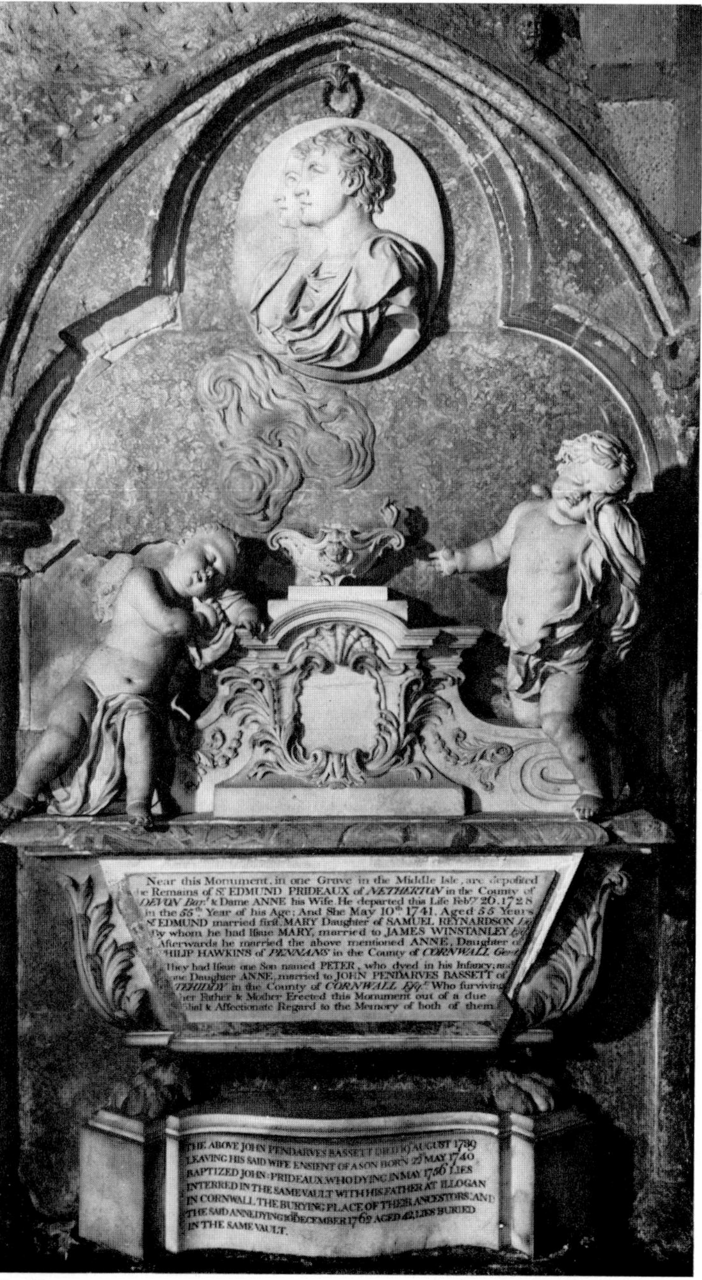

Fig. 88

**87**  This drawing was part of a miscellaneous collection of sculpture designs, numbering 738, bought from Mr. E. Parsons, of Brompton Road, on September 11th, 1882, for £25, as "apparently the work of J. Bacon".

The design was more closely followed for the monument to Thomas Swayne (died 1747) and his wife Benet (died 1748) in St. Martin's, Salisbury.

**88**  "Near this Monument, in one Grave in the Middle Ile, are deposited the Remains of Sr. Edmund Prideaux of Netherton in the County of Devon Bart. & Dame Anne his Wife. He departed this Life Febry. 26. 1728 in the 55th. Year of his Age; and She May 10th. 1741, Aged 55 Years. Sr. Edmund married first, Mary, Daughter of Samuel Reynardson Esqr. By whom he had Issue Mary, married to James Winstanley Esqr. Afterwards he married the above mentioned Anne, Daughter of Philip Hawkins of Pennans in the County of Cornwall Gent.

They had Issue one Son named Peter, who dyed in his Infancy; and one Daughter Anne, married to John Pendarves Bassett of Tehiddy in the County of Cornwall Esqr.: Who surviving her Father & Mother Erected this Monument out of a due filial & Affectionate Regard to the Memory of both of them."

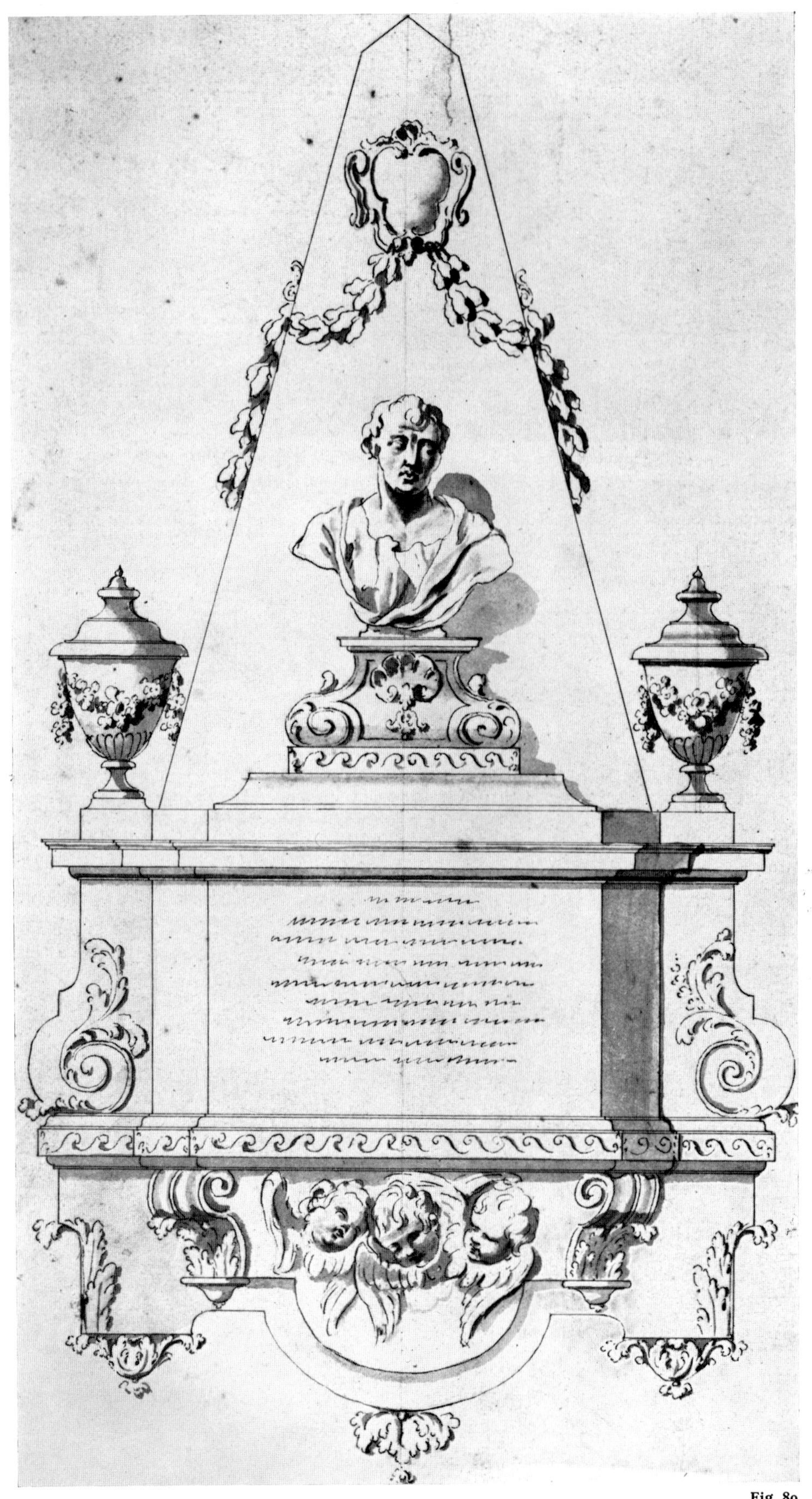



Fig. 89

# SIR HENRY CHEERE, Bart. (*1703–1781*)

*Figure 89 (left):*  Design for the monument to David Polhill (c. 1675–1754), at Otford, Kent. Pen and ink and wash, 13 × 7¼ inches. No. 4910.41.

*Figure 90 (below):*  Monument to David Polhill (c. 1675–1754), at Otford, Kent. Photograph: *Mr. Bruce Bailey.*

---

**89**  This drawing was one of 60 "by Rysbrack" bought from Mr. B. Quaritch on January 25th, 1867, for £1. 5. od.

**90**  This monument is almost identical with that in memory of George, 2nd Baron Carpenter (died 1749), at Owlesbury, Hampshire, the design for which is also in the Victoria and Albert Museum, Department of Prints and Drawings, No. 4910.2.

"Near this Place are deposited the Remains of David Polhill of Cheapstead in this County Esqr. Son of Thomas Polhill of Otford Esqr. by Elizabeth Daughter of Henry Ireton by Bridgett, Daughter of Oliver Cromwell. He was ever active and steady, in promoting the true Interest of his Sovereign; and defending the just Liberties of the Subject, both Civil and Religious: with which laudable view, he generously hazarded his own Safety: by being one of the Kentish Petitioners, in the Reign of King William the Third.
His Humanity to his Dependants, Generosity to his Relations, Tenderness, and Affection to his Family, Steadiness, and Sincerity to his Friends: Added to a most Benevolent Temper, Merited, and gained him, a very general Approbation, and Esteem.

He died (Member of Parliament for the City of Rochester and Keeper of the Records in the Tower of London) January the 15th. 1754, in the Eightieth year of his Age. He married three wives. The First was Elizabeth, Daughter of Thomas Trevor of Glynd in the County of Sussex Esqr. The Second Gertrude, Sister to the Most Noble Thomas Holles Duke of Newcastle, both these died without Issue. The Third was Elizabeth Daughter of John Borrett of Shoreham in this County Esqr. by whom he had Issue four Sons, and one Daughter. His Widow, and surviving Children, Charles and Elizabeth, have erected this Monument to his Memory."

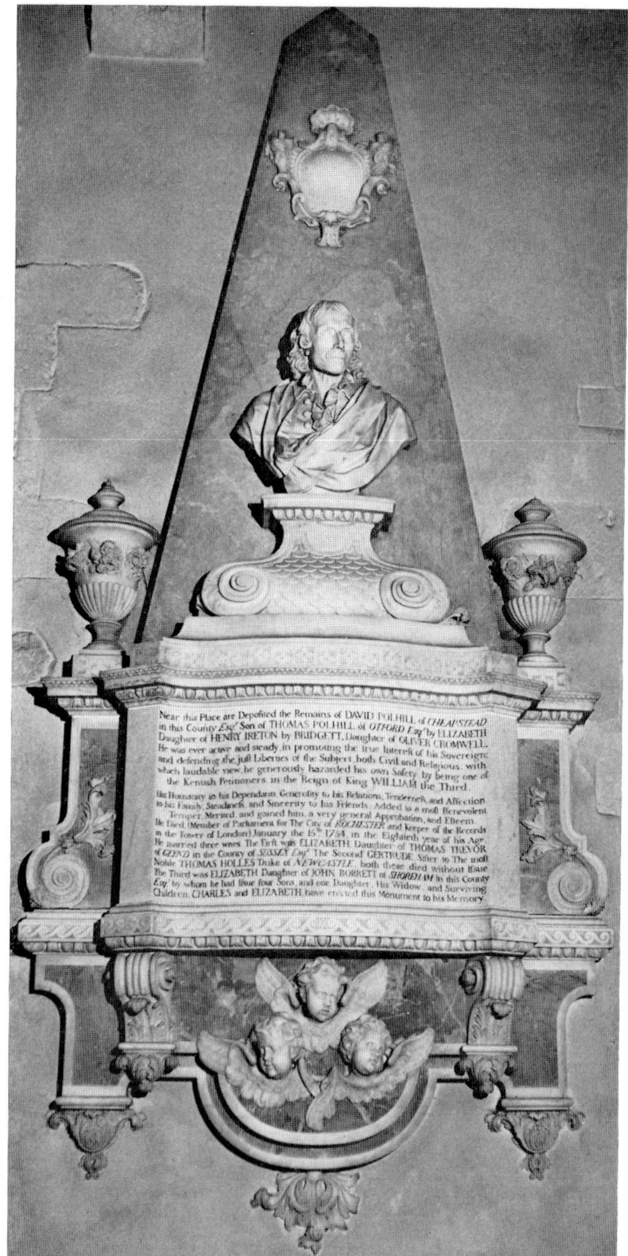

Fig. 90

*Figure 91 (below):* Design for a chimney-piece, with a central relief of children skating, flanked by carvings of a bear, on the left, and a beaver, on the right.
Pen and ink and water-colour, $5\frac{1}{2} \times 6\frac{1}{2}$ inches. No. D.715(13)–1887.

*Figure 92 (p.129):* Chimney-piece in the Dining Room, at Picton Castle, Pembrokeshire, which incorporates the carving of children skating, a bear and a beaver.
Photograph: *National Monuments Record.*

*Figure 93 (p.129):* Design for a chimney-piece. The carved panel of two children as a shepherd and shepherdess, appears on a chimney-piece at Biddick Hall, Durham, formerly at Lambton Castle (Christopher Hussey, *Country Life*, May 5th, 1966), and also on a chimney-piece in a ground-floor room at 43 Parliament Street, Westminster.
Pen and ink and water-colour, $5\frac{3}{8} \times 6\frac{1}{8}$ inches. No. D.715(23)–1887.

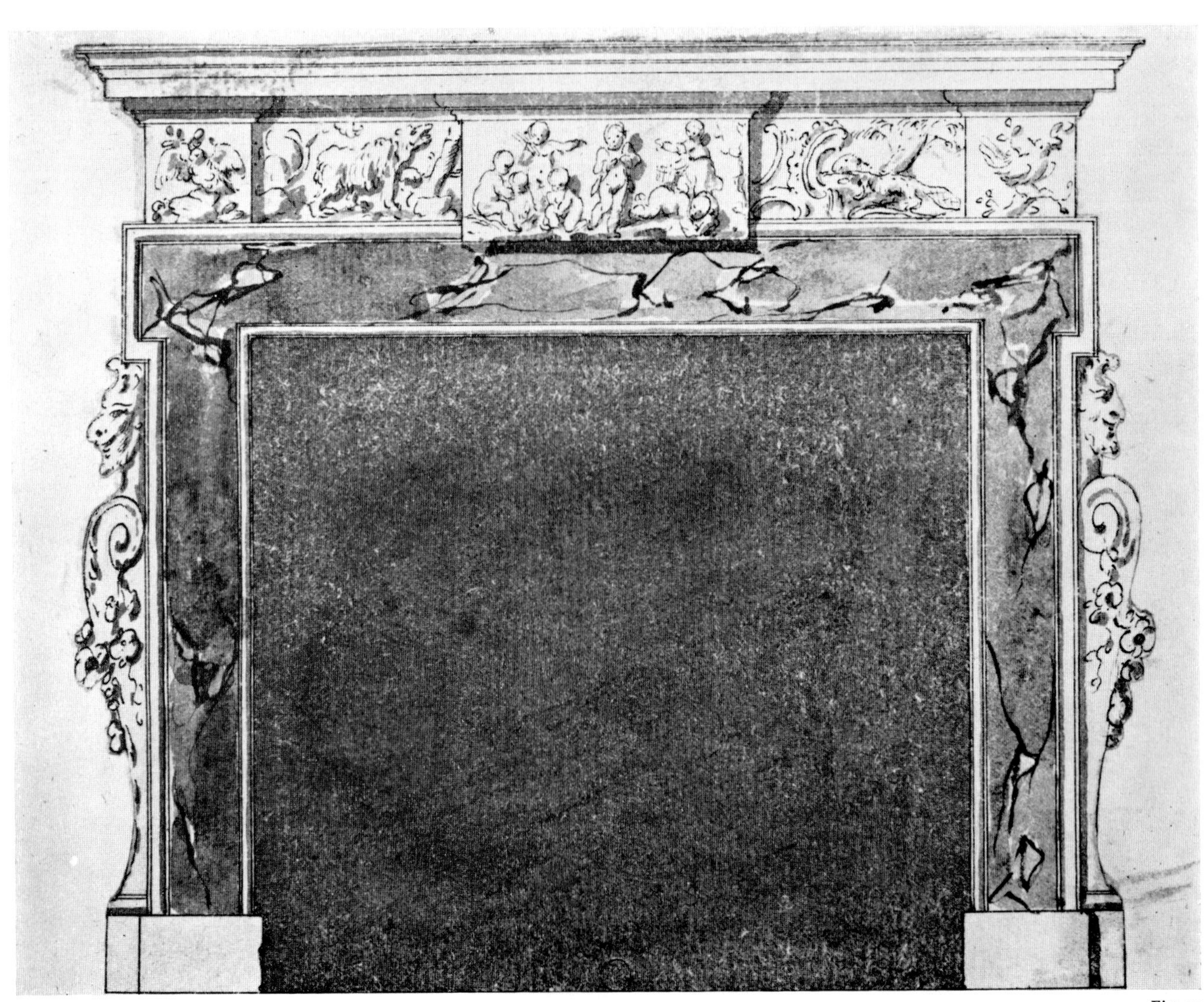

Fig. 91

**91** This drawing was one of 28 designs by Sir Henry Cheere, bought from Mr. E. Parsons, of Brompton Road, on July 13th, 1887, as "Modern, or late 18th century, French?", for £4. 10. od.

**93** This drawing was bought from Mr. E. Parsons, of Brompton Road; see fig. 91.

(See Mark Girouard, 'English Art and the Rococo', *Country Life*; I, 'Coffee at Slaughter's', January 13th, II, 'Hogarth and his friends', January 27th, and III, 'The two worlds of St. Martin's Lane', February 3rd, 1966.)

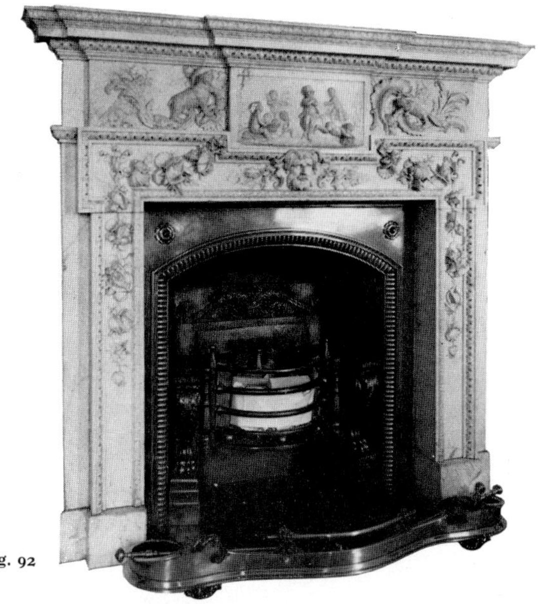

Fig. 92

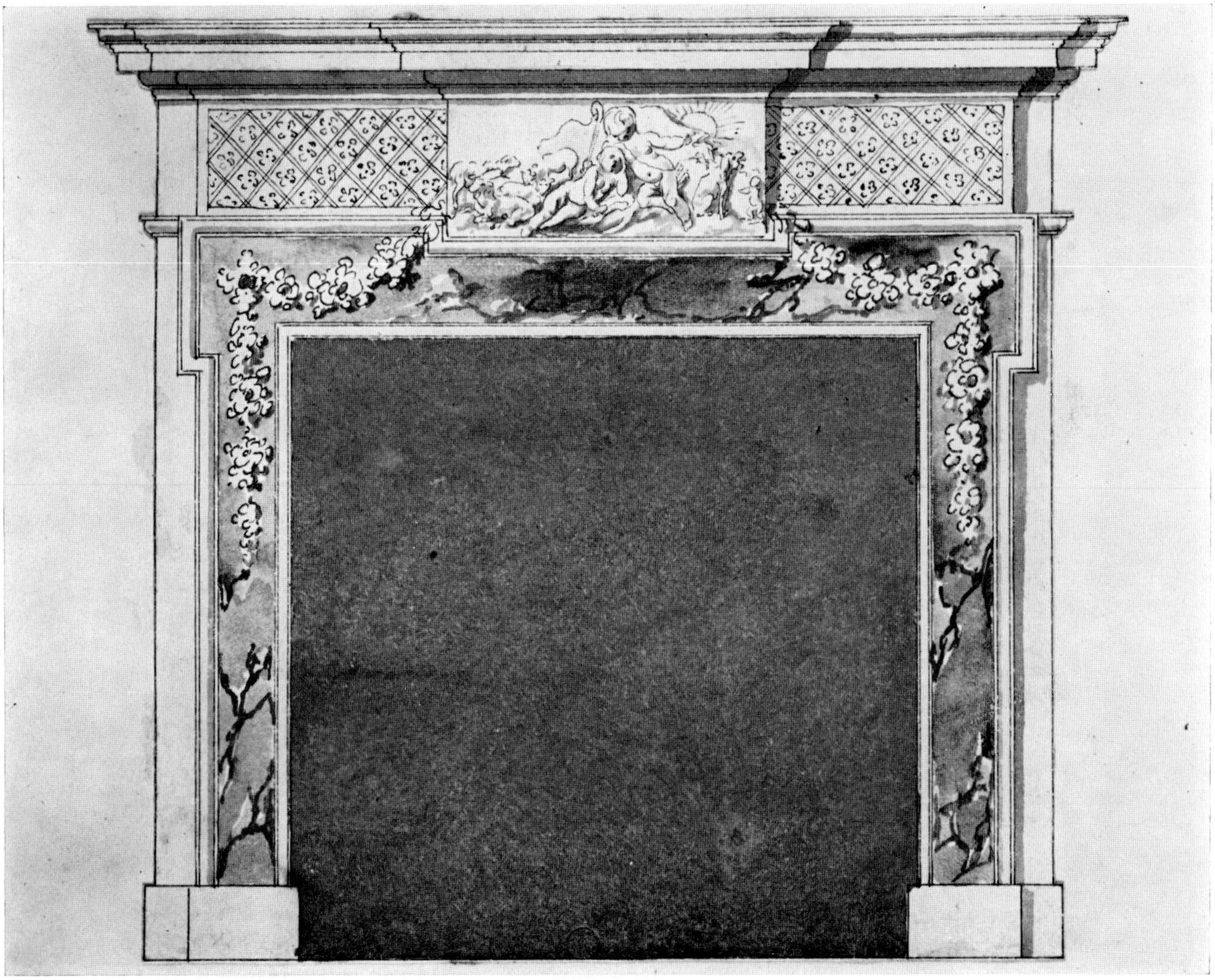

Fig. 93

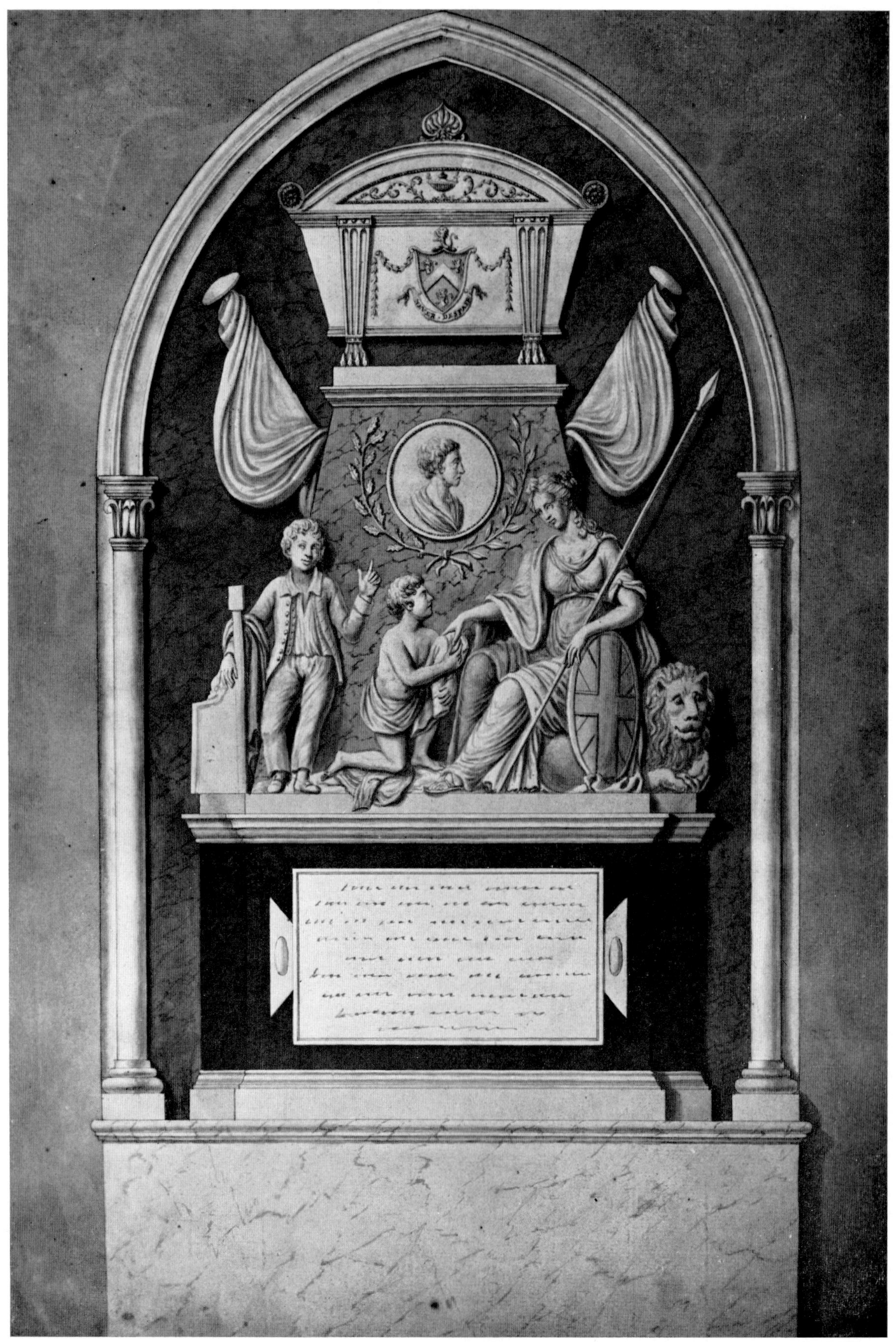

Fig. 94

# JOHN FRANCIS MOORE (*died 1809*)



**94** An alternative design, also in the Victoria and Albert Museum, Department of Prints and Drawings, is No. 4910.20. Both designs were bought, with 58 others, as "by Rysbrack" from Mr. B. Quaritch on January 25th, 1867, for £1. 5. od.

**95** Hanway was a City merchant, traveller and philanthropist, and was one of the founders of the Marine Society and gave them their first training-ship. Much of his energies were devoted also to improving the conditions of outcast women and children, and he was one of those who assisted in the founding of the Foundling Hospital, London. Today, however, he is probably best remembered as being the first Londoner to carry an umbrella. All his activities are reflected in Moore's design for his monument, which was considerably modified in execution.

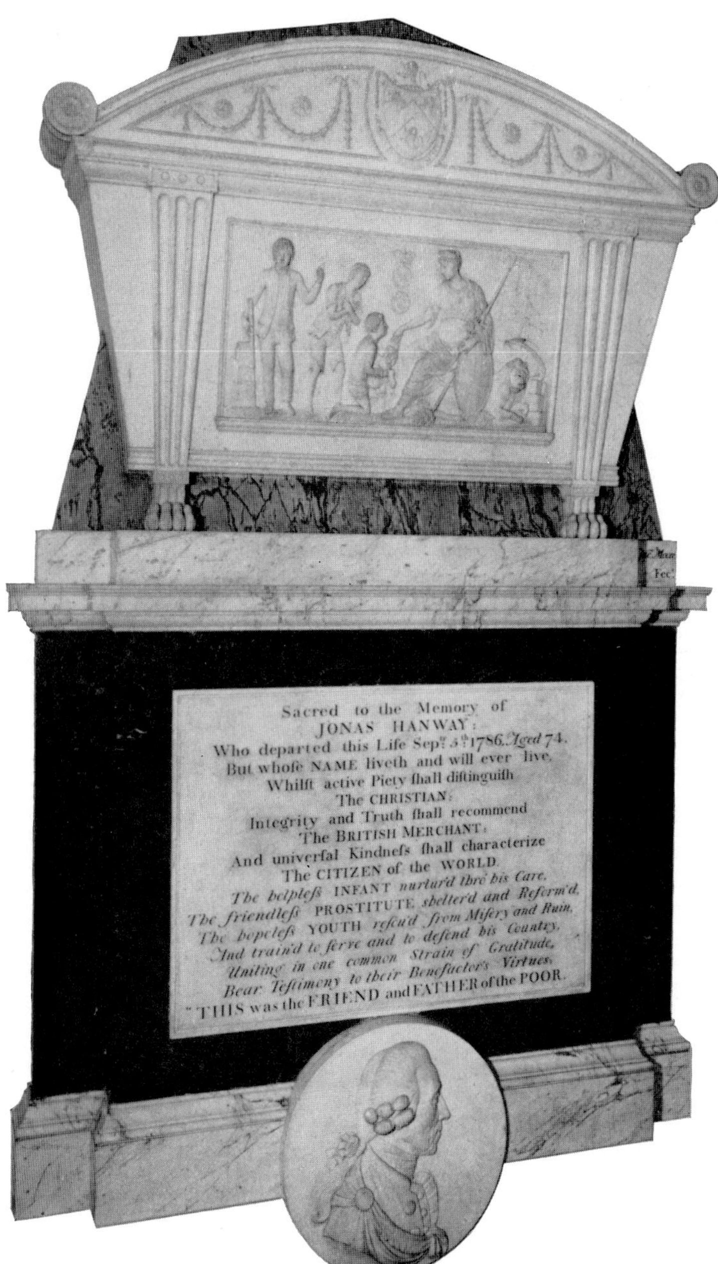


**Fig. 95**

# JOHN FRANCIS MOORE *(died 1809)*

*Figure 96 (right):* Design for the monument to Edward, 1st Baron Hawke, K.B. (died 1781), at North Stoneham, Hampshire.
Inscribed *H. 13. 6 by 7. 4.*
Pen and ink and water-colour, $16\frac{1}{2} \times 10\frac{5}{8}$ inches. No. 4910.4.

*Figure 97 (below):* Monument to Edward, 1st Baron Hawke, K.B. (died 1781), at North Stoneham, Hampshire.
Photograph: *National Monuments Record.*

---

**96** Another design for this monument in the Victoria and Albert Museum, Department of Prints and Drawings, is No. 4910.5. Both drawings were bought, with 58 others as "by Rysbrack", from Mr. B. Quaritch, on January 25th, 1867, for £1. 5. 0d.

**97** "D.O.M. This Monument is Sacred to the Memory of Edward Hawke Lord Hawke, Baron of Towton in the County of York, Knight of the Bath, Admiral and Commander in Chief of the Fleet. Vice Admiral of Great Britain, &c. who died October the 17th 1781 Aged 76. The Bravery of his Soul was equal to the Dangers he encountered: The Cautious Intrepidity of his Deliberations superior even to the Conquests he Obtained. The Annals of his Life compose a Period of Naval Glory unparralleld [*sic*] in later Times. For wherever he Sailed Victory attended him.

A Prince unsollicited conferred on him Dignities which he Disdained to ask. This Monument is also Sacred to the Memory of Catherine Lady Hawke, his Wife, the Beauty of whose Person was Excelled only By the accomplished Elegance of her Mind. She died October the 27th 1756, Aged 36. In the Conjugal Parental and Social Duties of Private Life They were equalled by few, excelled by none."

In 1783 the *Universal Magazine* stated that the monument had been unveiled on 29 August, and that the relief of "the last battle he [Lord Hawke] fought in the Royal George against Conflans, is done after the original picture painted by [Dominic] Serres, in white marble, truly delicate and beautiful".

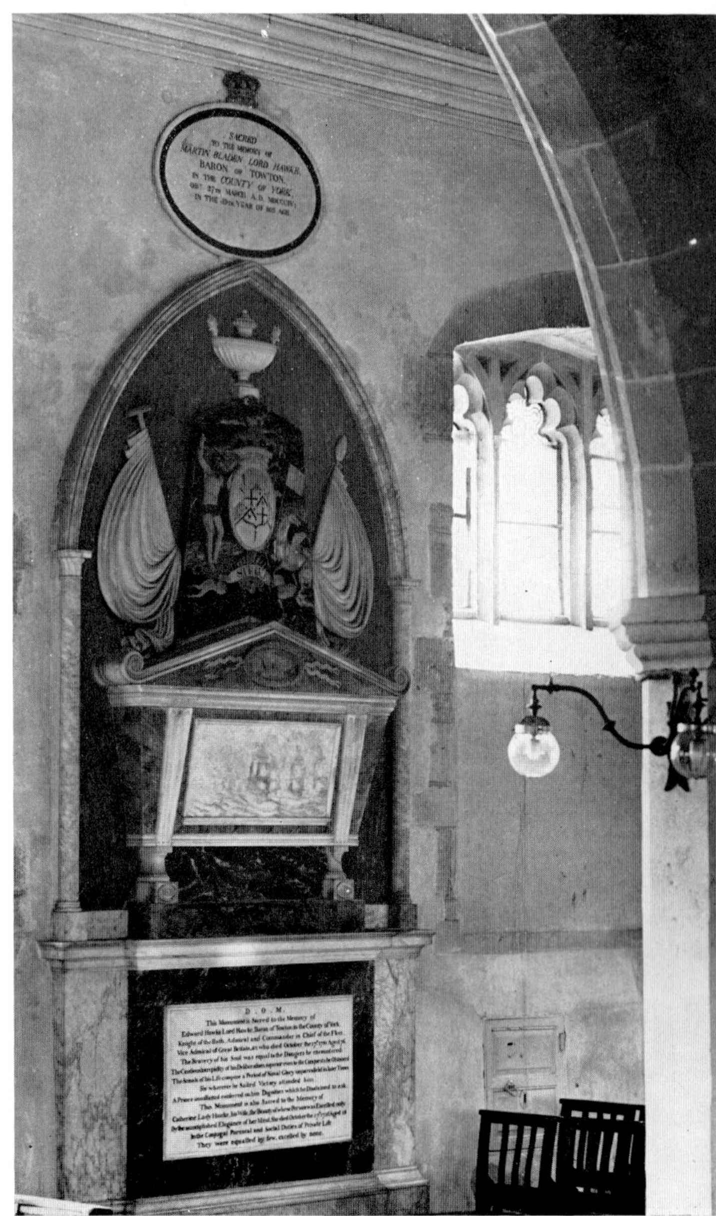

Fig. 97

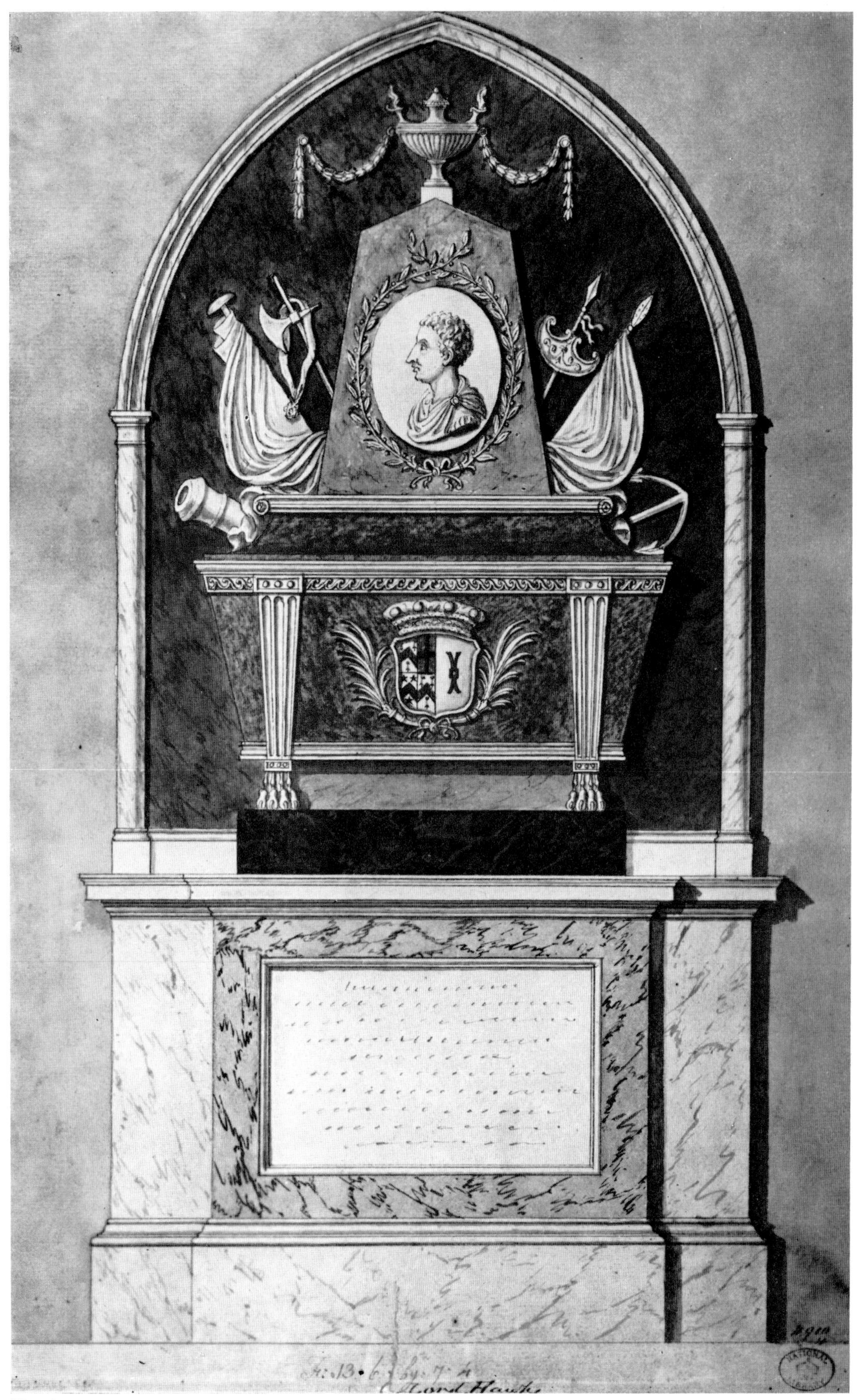



**Fig. 96**

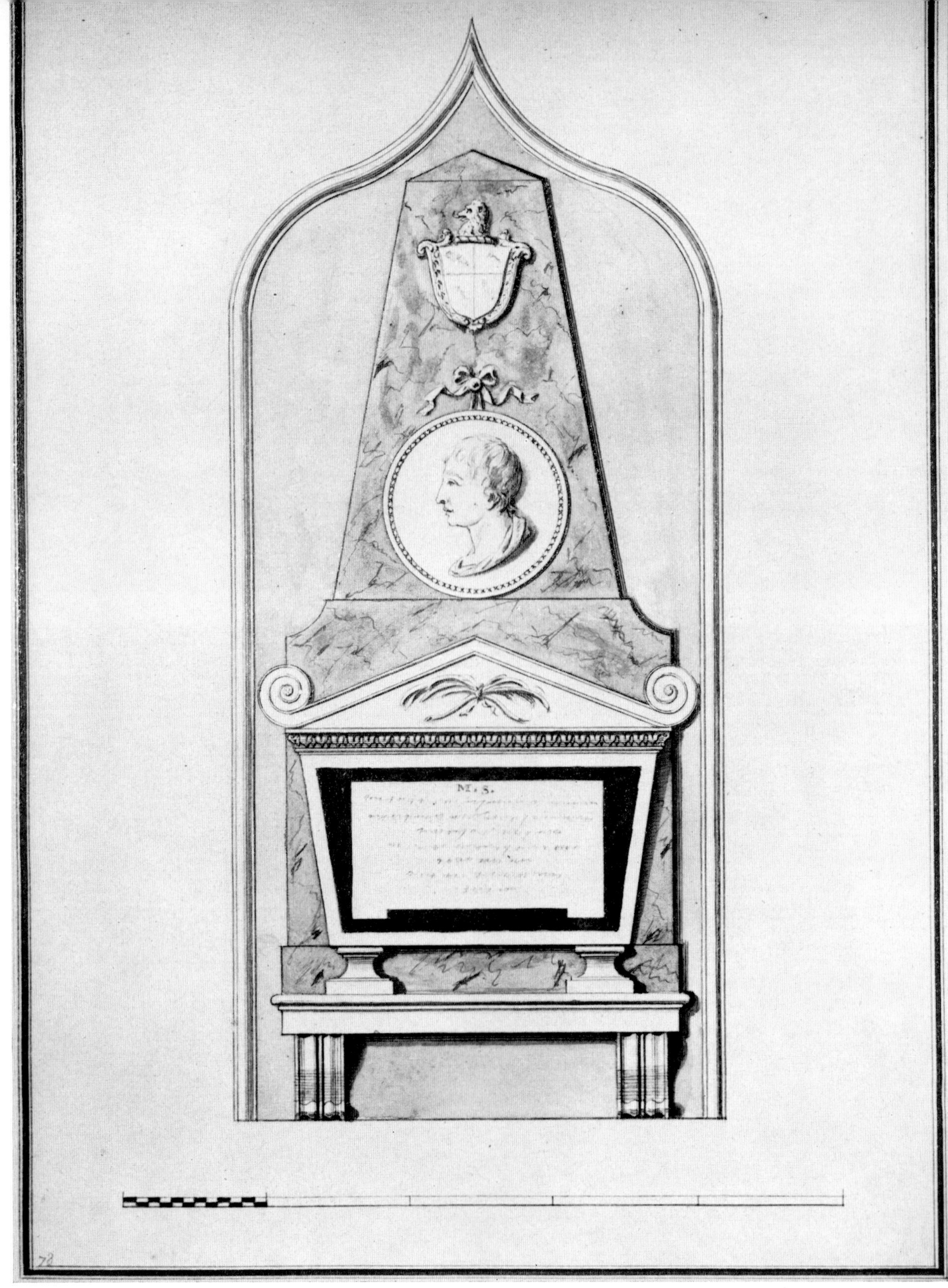

134

**98**   This drawing was one of 25 designs by Thomas Scheemakers bought from Mr. E. Parsons, of Brompton Road, on June 10th, 1878, for £2.

**99**   The monument was designed by James ("Athenian") Stuart, for the church at Preston-on-Stour, which had been rebuilt in a Gothic style by Edward Woodward (died 1766), for James West of Alscot, Warwickshire (H. M. Colvin, *A Biographical Dictionary of English Architects 1660–1840.* 1954, page 697).

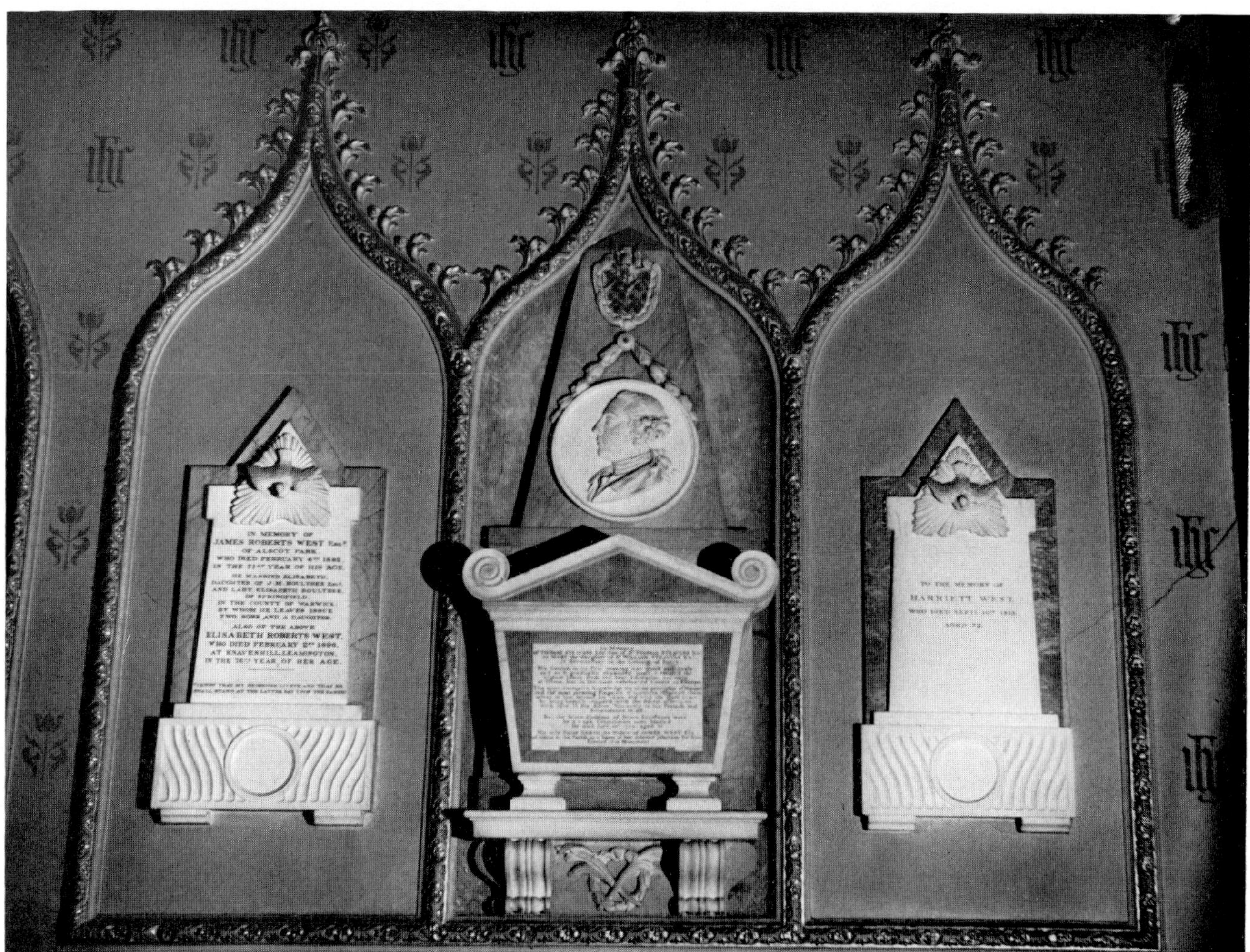

**Fig. 99**

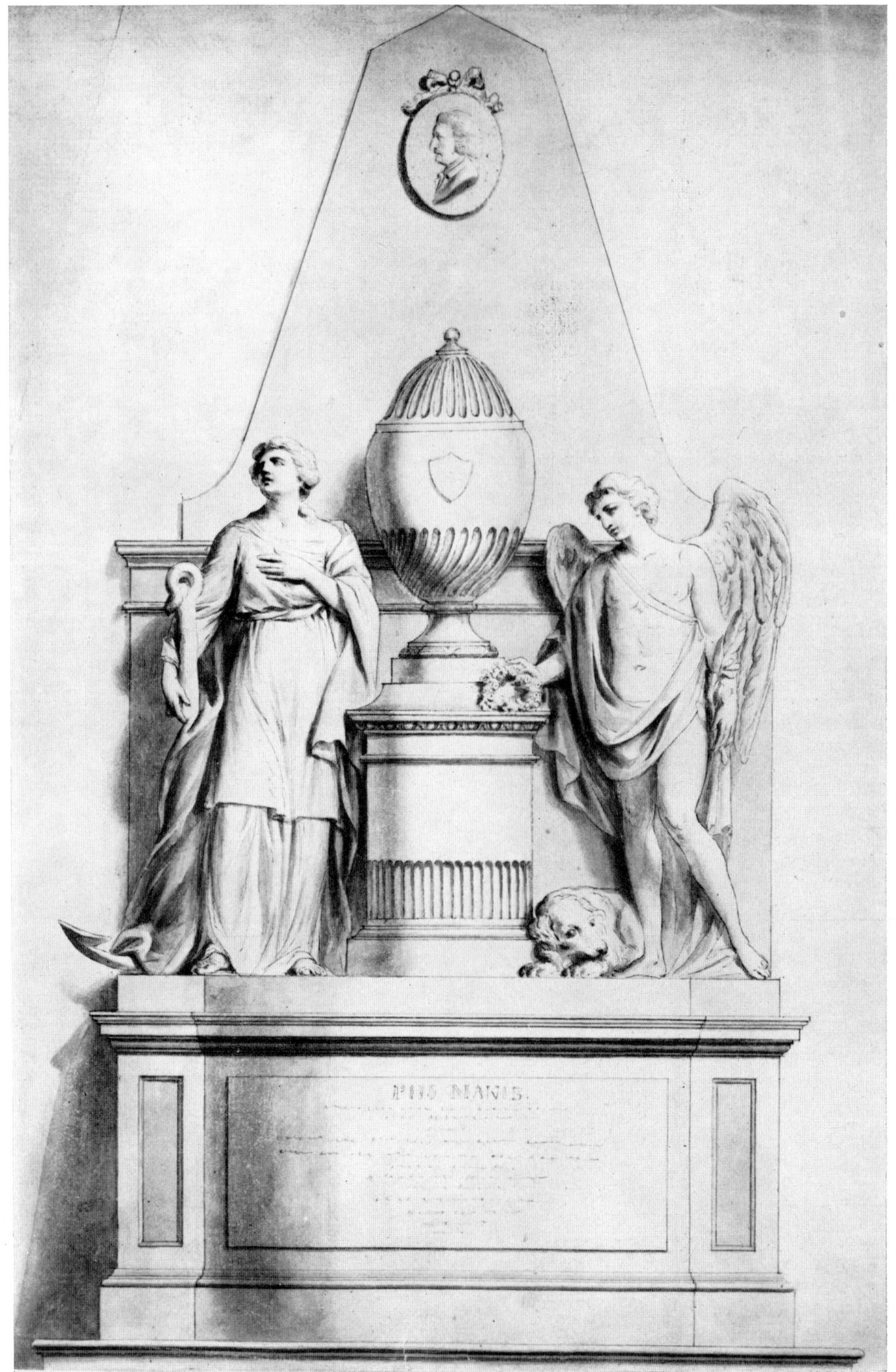



Fig. 100

# JOSEPH WILTON, R.A. *(1722–1803)*

*Figure 100 (left):*   Design for the monument to Elizabeth Bacon, and her brother, Peter
Standly, at Linton, Cambridgeshire.
Pen and ink and wash, $16\frac{5}{8} \times 10\frac{1}{8}$ inches. No. E.504–1964.

*Figure 101 (below):* Monument to Elizabeth Bacon, and her brother Peter Standly, dated 1782,
at Linton, Cambridgeshire.
Photograph: *Mr. Bruce Bailey.*

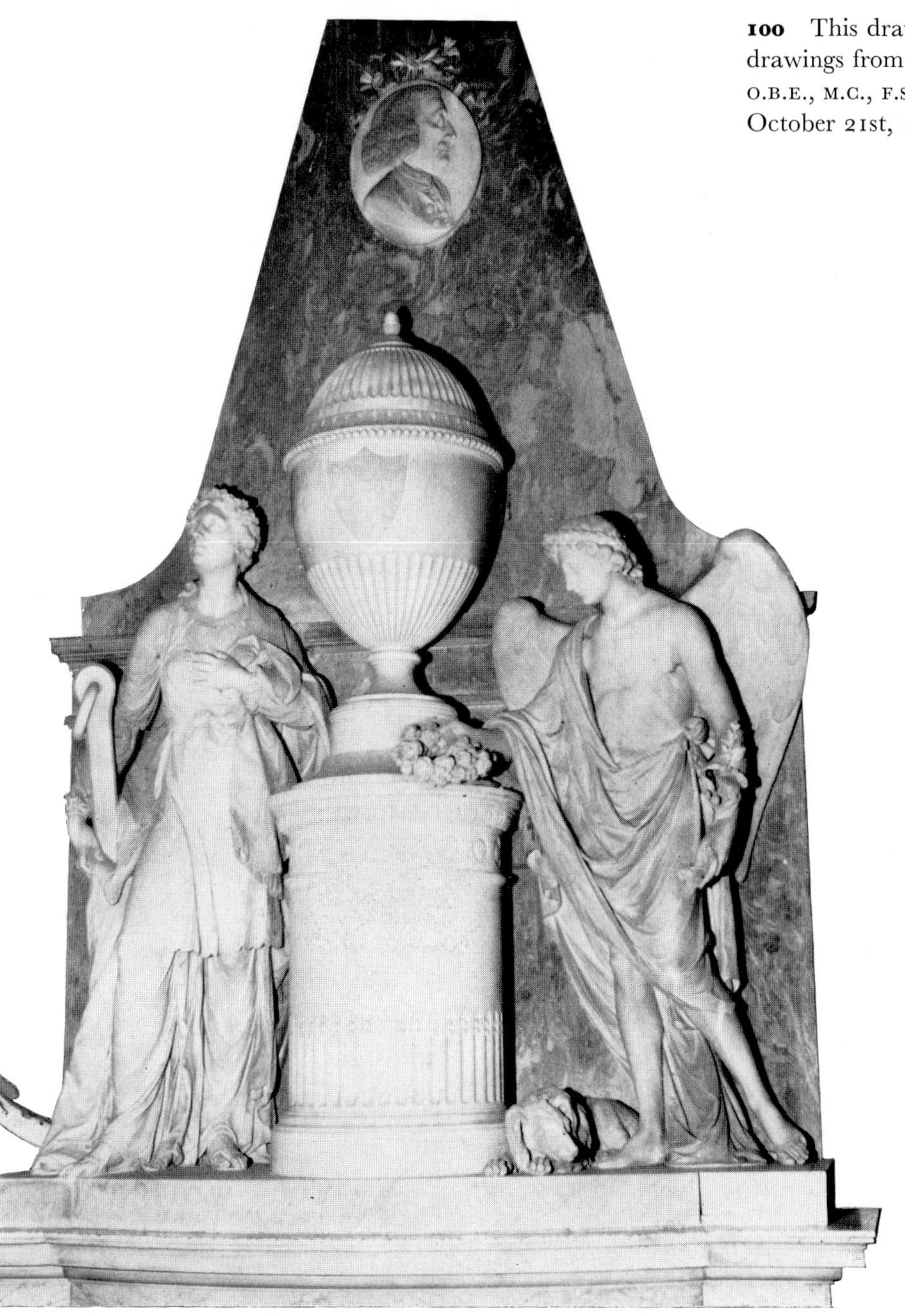

**100**   This drawing was part of Lot 196 at the sale of drawings from the collection of Sir Bruce Ingram, O.B.E., M.C., F.S.A., held at Messrs. Sotheby's, on October 21st, 1964.

Fig. 101

# JOSEPH WILTON, R.A. *(1722–1803)*

*Figure 102 (right):* Design for the monument to John Tillotson, D.D. (1630–1694), Archbishop of
Canterbury, at Sowerby, Yorkshire.
Pen and ink and wash, $12\frac{1}{4} \times 6\frac{1}{2}$ inches. No. E.1184–1965.

*Figure 103 (below):* Monument to John Tillotson, D.D. (1630–1694), Archbishop of Canterbury,
erected in 1796, at Sowerby, Yorkshire.
Photograph: *Mr. Bruce Bailey.*

**102**  This drawing was part of Lot 196 at the sale of drawings from the collection of Sir Bruce Ingram, O.B.E., M.C., F.S.A., held at Messrs. Sotheby's, on October 21st, 1964. It was later acquired by Rupert Gunnis, J.P., by whom it was bequeathed to the Museum.

**103**  Archbishop Tillotson was born at Sowerby, and this monument to his memory was erected in the church to the order of George Stansfeld. Wilton's model is in Field House, Sowerby, and is dated 1796.

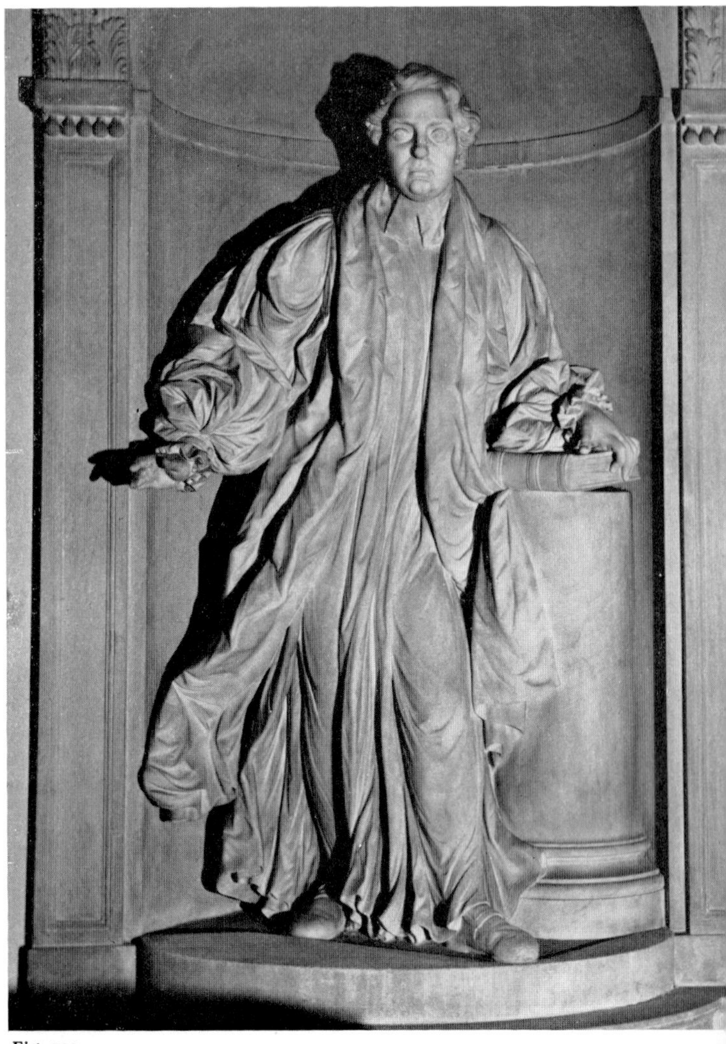

Fig. 103

138

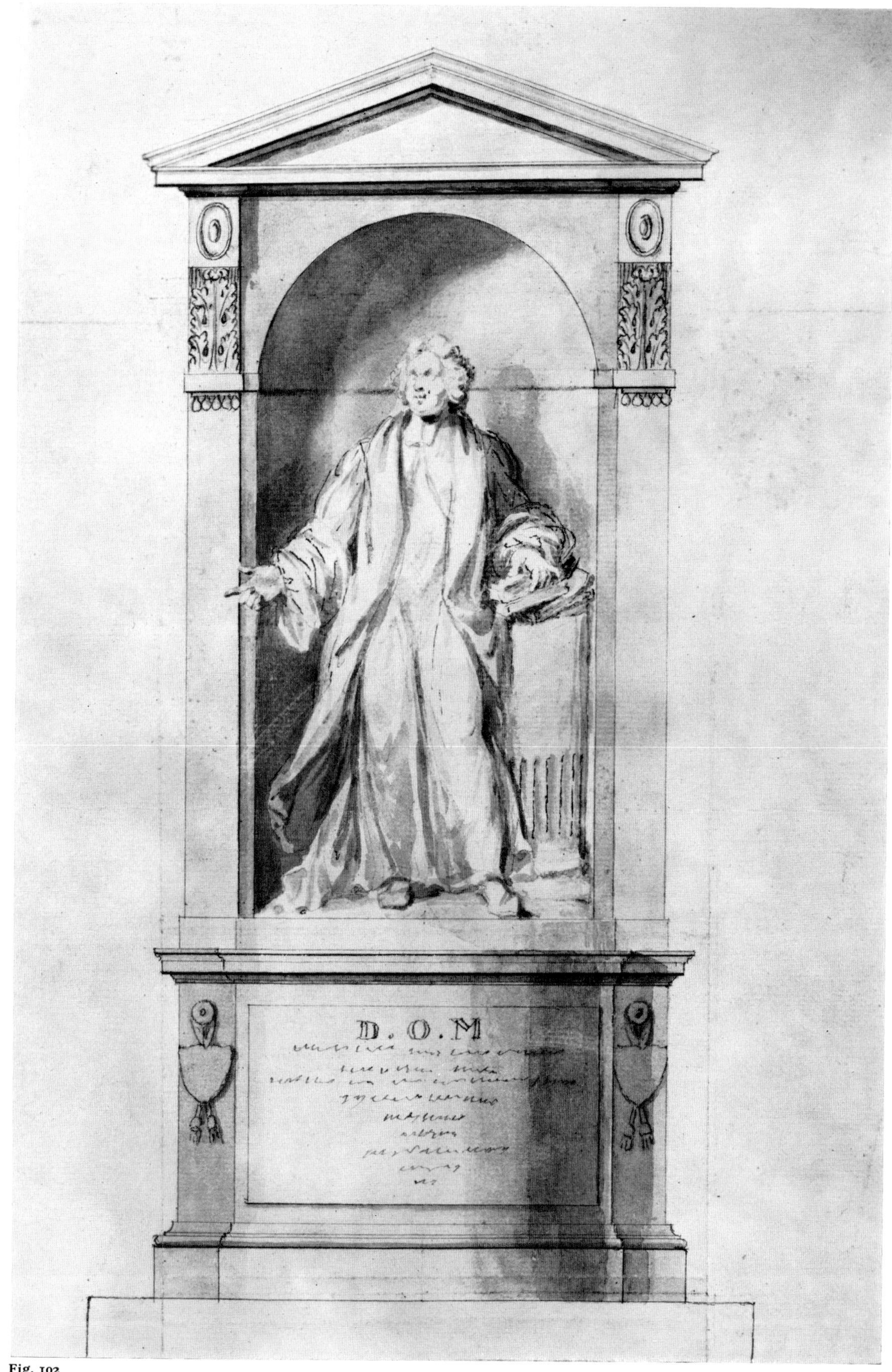



Fig. 102

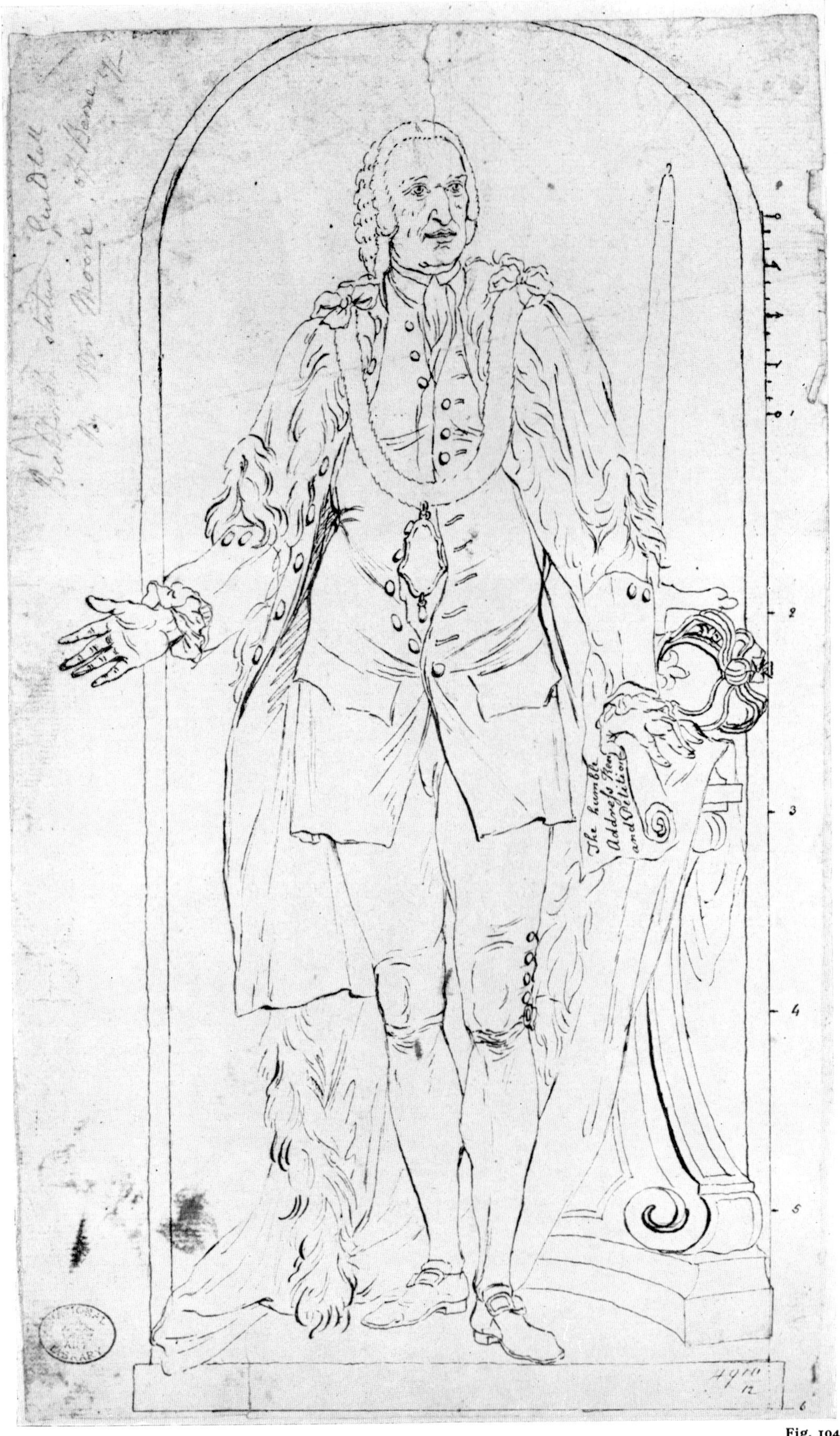



Fig. 104

# NATHANIEL SMITH (*c. 1741–died after 1800*)

*Figure 104 (left):*  Design for the proposed statue of Alderman William Beckford, at Guildhall, London.
Inscribed *Beckford's statue guildhall By Mr Moore of Berners St.*, and with a scale in feet.
Pen and ink, $11\frac{7}{8} \times 6\frac{5}{8}$ inches. No. 4910.12.

*Figure 105 (below):*  Model in terracotta, in the Department of Architecture and Sculpture, of the proposed statue of Alderman William Beckford, at Guildhall, London.
Signed and dated *1770*. No. A.48–1928.

---

**104**  This drawing was one of 60 "by Rysbrack" bought from Mr. B. Quaritch, on January 25th, 1867, for £1. 5. od.

**105**  The model was given to the Museum by Dr. W. L. Hildburgh, F.S.A. The statue by the father of Nollekens's biographer, J. T. Smith, was not executed, that in Guildhall was the work of John Francis Moore, and is dated 1772.

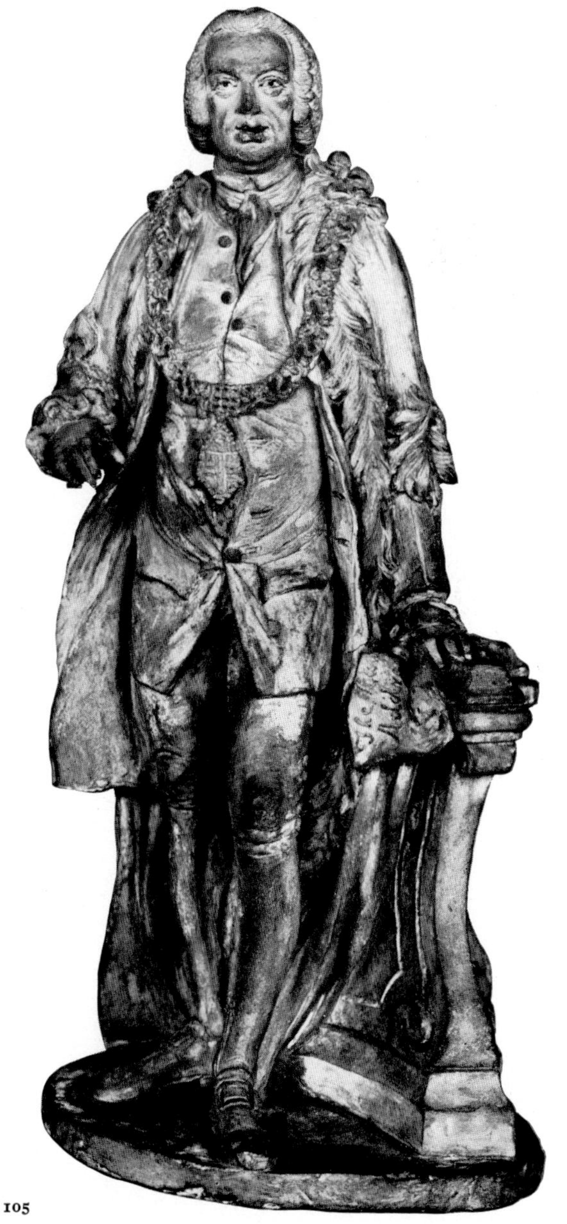

Fig. 105

# ROBERT ADAM (*1728–1792*)

*Figure 106* (*right*): Design for the monument to Robert Child, of Osterley Park (died 1782), in Heston Church, Middlesex.
Pen and ink and wash, $8\frac{1}{2} \times 3\frac{3}{4}$ inches. No. E.973–1965.

# PETER MATHIAS VAN GELDER (*1739–1809*)

*Figure 107* (*below*): Monument to Robert Child, of Osterley Park (died 1782), in Heston Church, Middlesex.
Photograph: *National Monuments Record*.

**106**  The drawing was bequeathed to the Museum by Rupert Gunnis, J.P.

**107**  Robert Child's daughter and heiress, Sarah Ann, was the first wife of John, 10th Earl of Westmorland. Their eldest daughter Sophia married George Villiers, 5th Earl of Jersey at Gretna Green on May 23rd, 1804.

Lady Jersey inherited Osterley Park from her maternal grandfather.

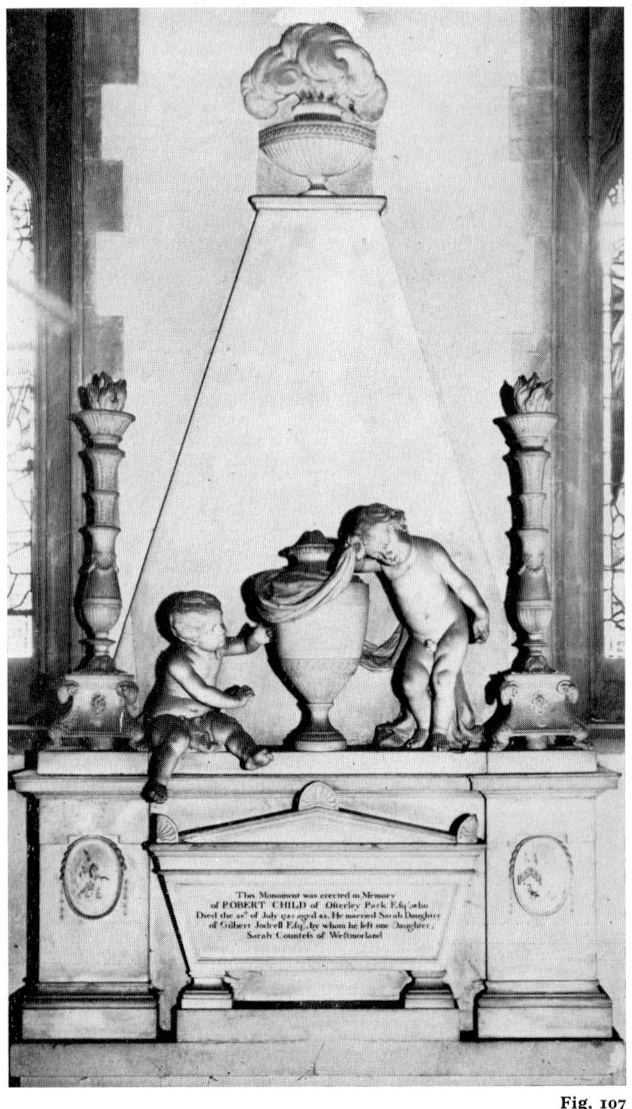


Fig. 107

142

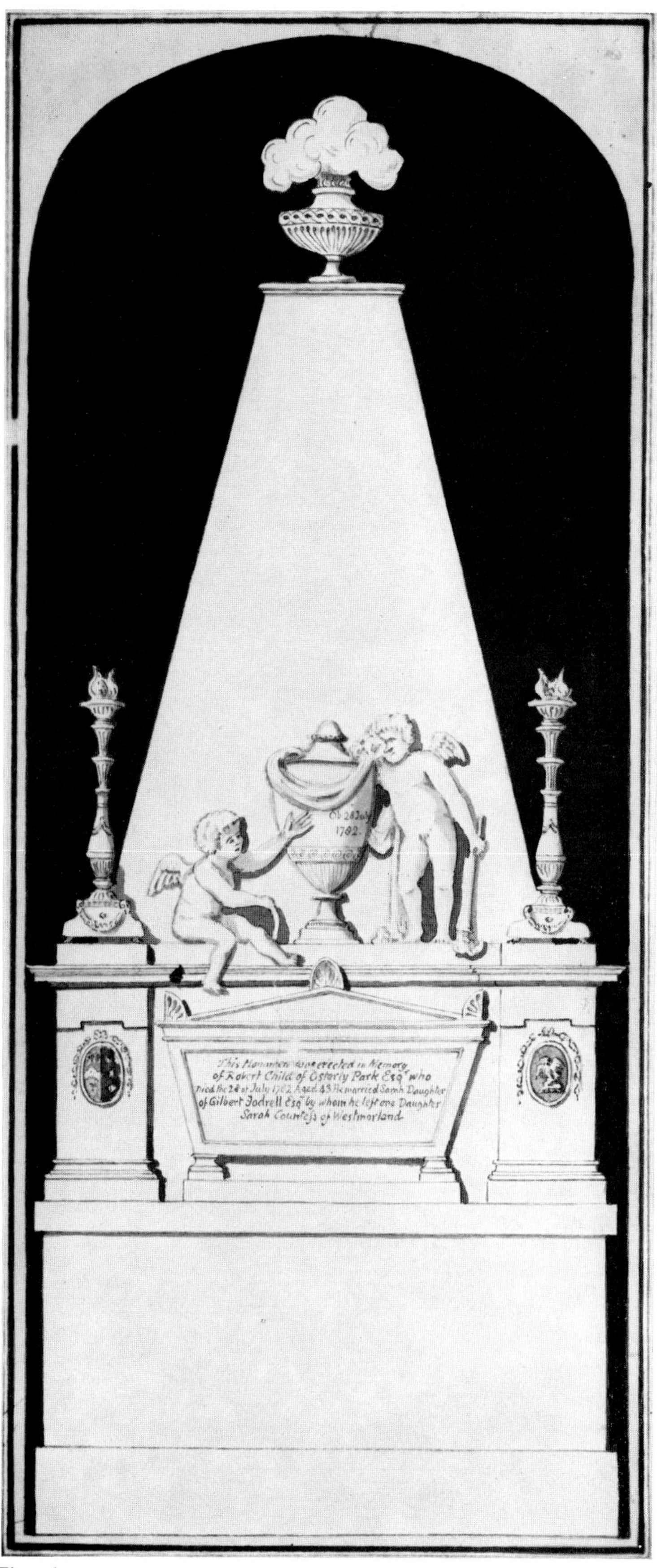

Fig. 106

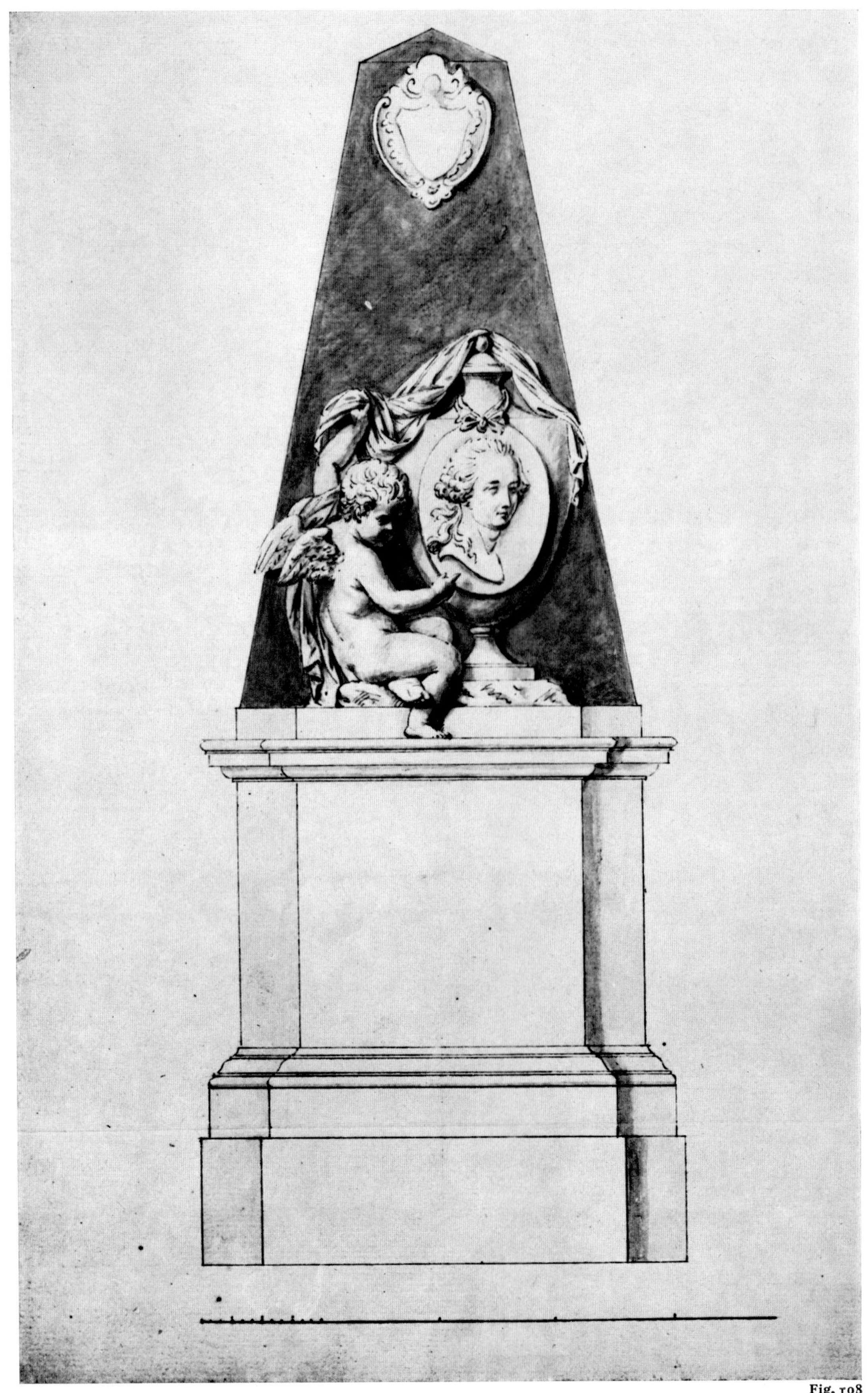

Fig. 108

# JOSEPH NOLLEKENS, R.A. *(1737–1823)*

*Figure 108 (left):*  Design for the monument to Sir Robert Cunliffe, Bart. (1719–1778), Bruera, Cheshire.
Pen and ink and wash, size of sheet $12\frac{5}{8} \times 7\frac{7}{8}$ inches. No. E.4354–1920.

*Figure 109 (below):* Detail of the monument to Sir Robert Cunliffe, Bart. (1719–1778), Bruera, Cheshire.
Photograph: *National Monuments Record.*

**108**  This drawing was formerly in the collection of Fairfax Murray, and was bought as part of Lot 157, at the sale of Messrs. Sotheby's held in December, 1920, for £7.

**109**  Robert Cunliffe, by special remainder, succeeded his brother as second Baronet in 1767. He was Sheriff of Nottingham in 1776, and is buried in the Cunliffe vault beneath the south chapel of Bruera church.

"Erected by conjugal gratitude to the memory of Sir Robert Cunliffe, of Saighton, bart. who departed this life in the year 1778, aged 58 years. He married, from sincere affection and disinterested esteem, Mary, daughter of Ichabod Wright, of Nottingham, esq. who, with one son and three daughter, survived him, regretting their loss, but resigned to the will of God. For pious and humane through the whole course of life he so discharged the connubial, social, and parental duties, as truly to deserve this comprehensive character, He was a Good Man."

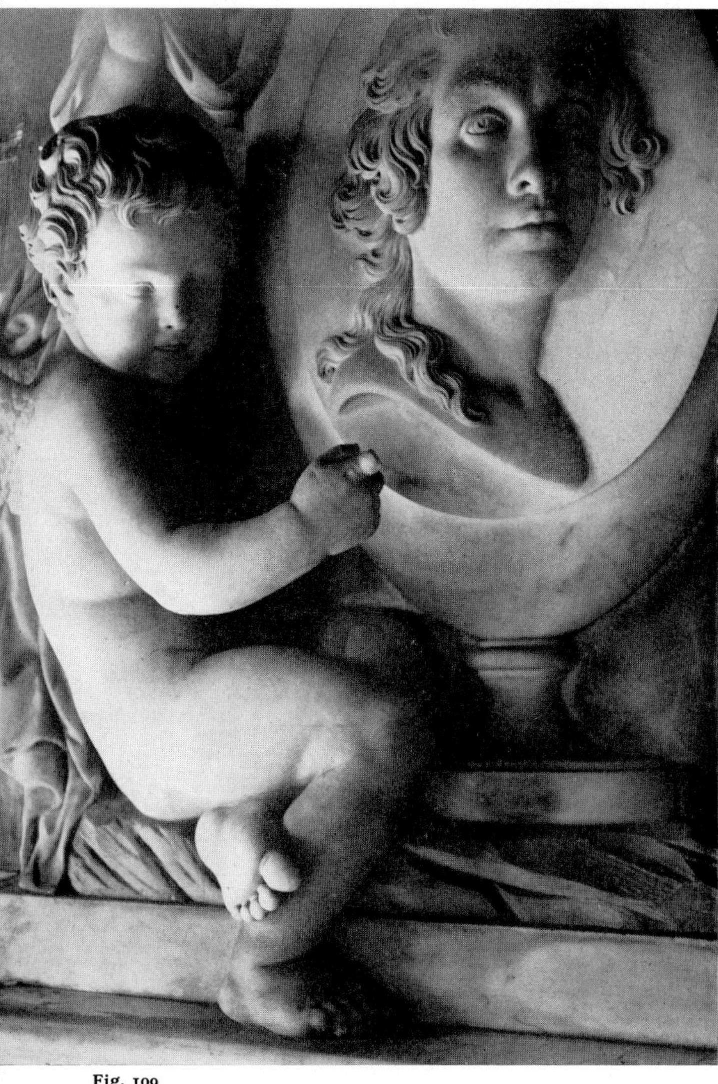

**Fig. 109**

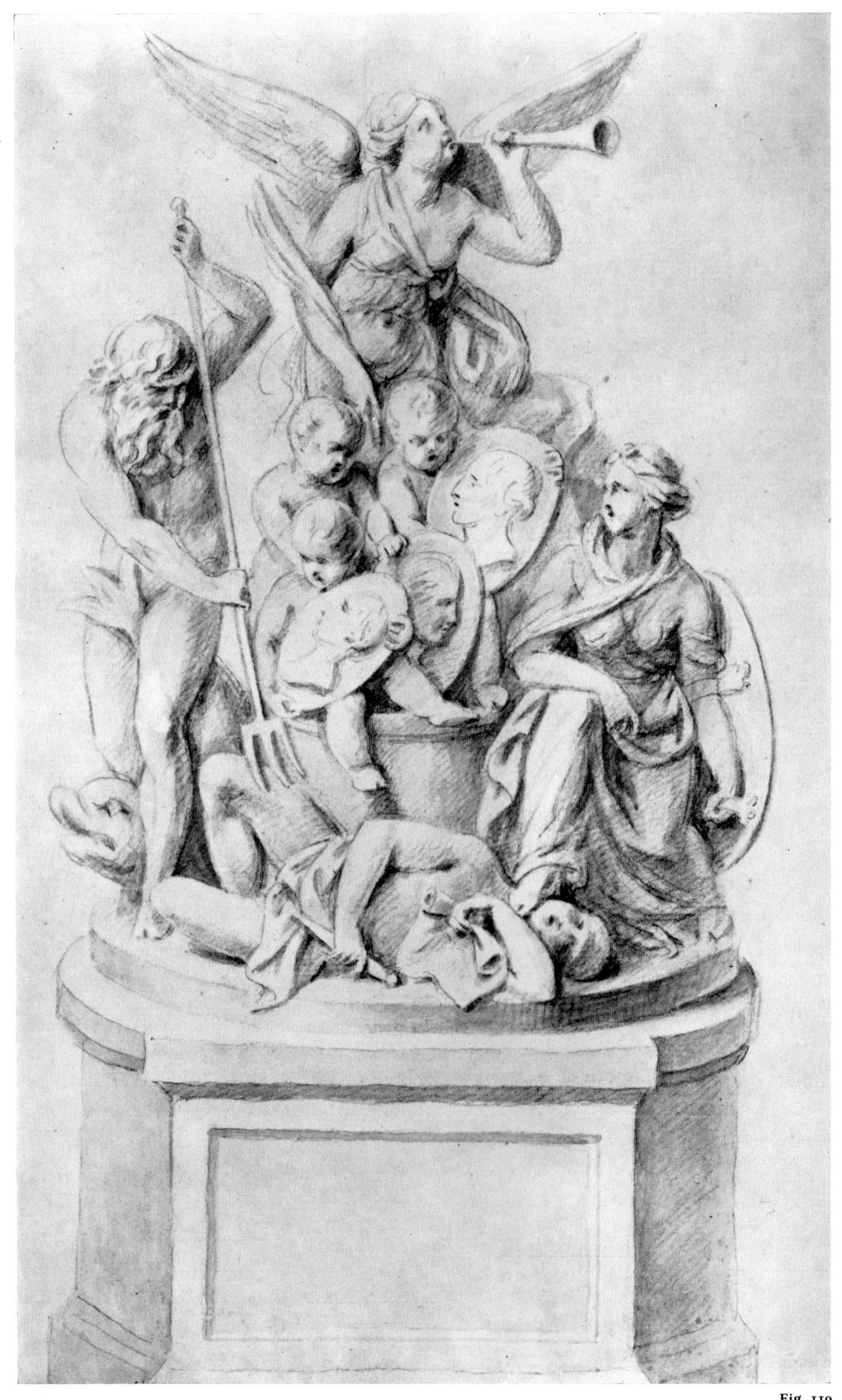



Fig. 110

*Figure 110 (left):*    Design for the monument to Captains Bayne, Blair and Lord Robert
Manners, R.N. (died 1782), Westminster Abbey.
Pencil and wash, size of sheet 12¾ × 7¾ inches. No. E.4379–1920.

*Figure 111 (below):* Monument to Captains Bayne, Blair and Lord Robert Manners, R.N.
(died 1782), in the north transept, Westminster Abbey.
Photograph: *Warburg Institute.*

**110**   This drawing was formerly in the collection of Fairfax Murray; see fig. 108.

**111**   The three naval captains had been killed during Lord Rodney's engagements with the French in 1782. The monument in the Abbey was erected to their memory by George III and Parliament, for £4,000. Farington recorded in his diary, July 25th, 1793:

"Nollekens offered a design during the administration of Lord North for a monument to be erected to the three Captains killed on the 12th of April, fighting under Lord Rodney, which he estimated at £4,500. Dance, during the administration of Lord Shelburne (after consulting Banks, R.A.), estimated the design at £3,500. The monument was not determined on till the administration of Mr. Pitt, when with some alterations, at an estimate given in by Bacon and Wilton, Nollekens's design was adopted at £4,000."

The monument was not executed according to the design illustrated, but Nollekens used this again, for the competition for the monument to two more naval captains, Harvey and Hutt, killed under Lord Howe at Brest in 1794. He was not successful, however, as the commission was awarded to John Bacon the Younger. This competition drawing, which is in the Victoria and Albert Museum, Department of Prints and Drawings, E.4375–1920, was probably that which was exhibited at the Royal Academy in 1805 as No. 711.

"*Nollekens,* if not the best, one of the best statuaries of the time, the publick will be glad to hear, has his hands full. The parliamentary monument for Lord Robert Manners, and Capt. Blair, and Blair [*sic*]—with a colossal figure of Ocean on one side—Britannia on the other.

The three portraits, on as many medallions appended to a most beautiful picture of victory, with naval emblems, wreaths, &c." (from an undated and unidentified press-cutting in the Victoria and Albert Museum Library).

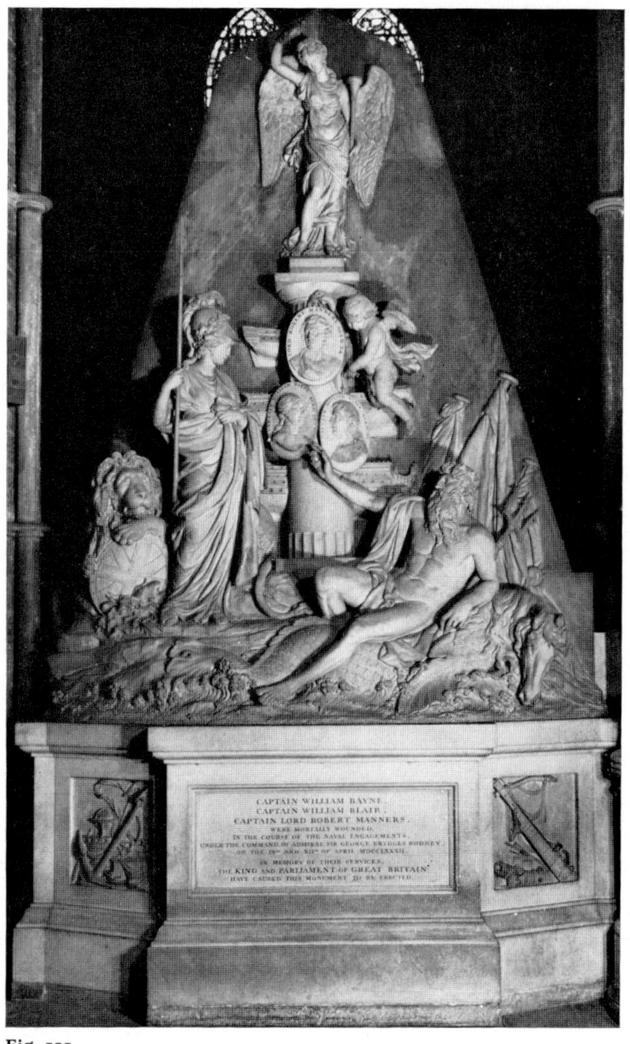


Fig. 111

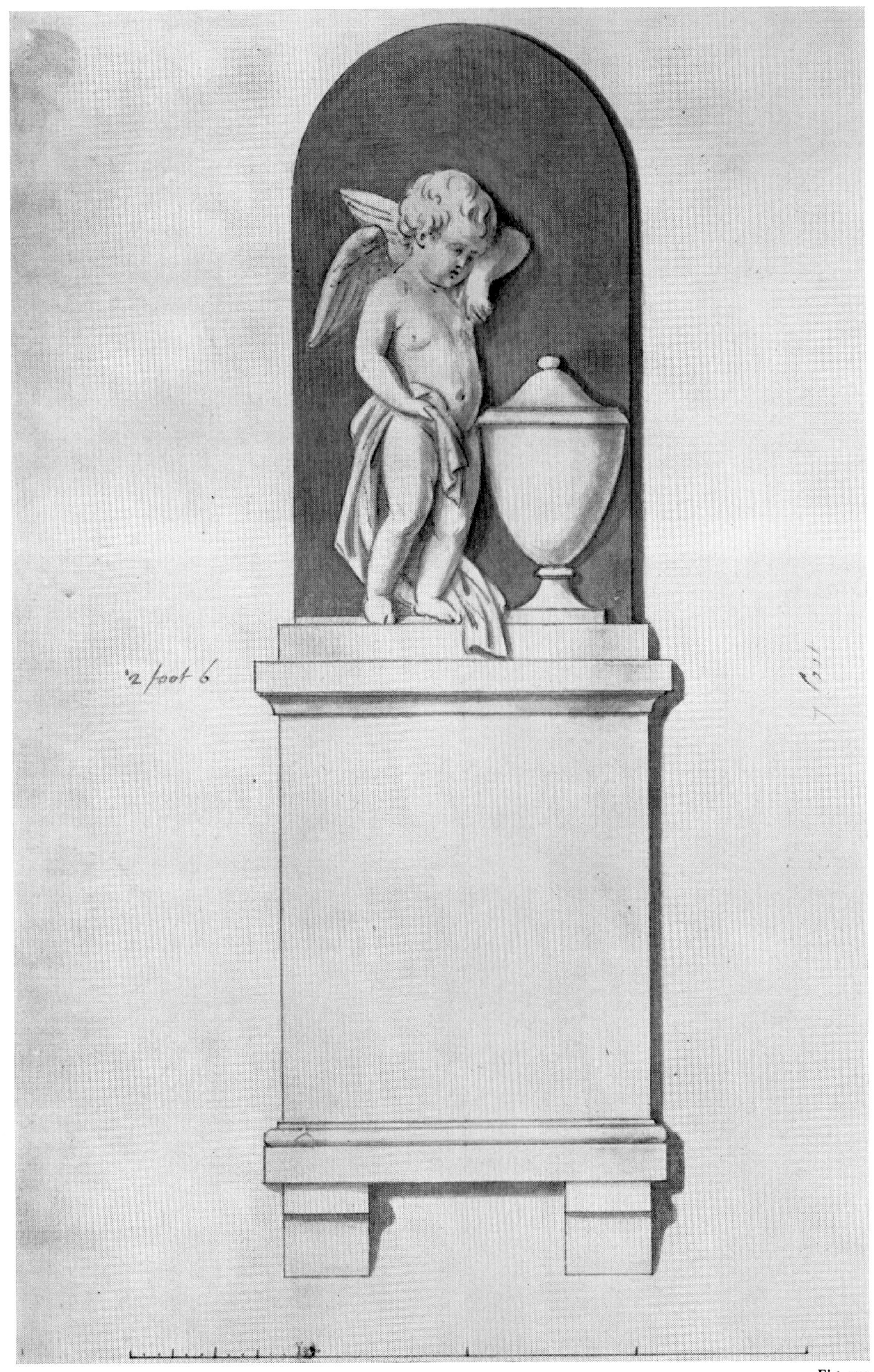




Fig. 112

# JOSEPH NOLLEKENS, R.A. *(1737–1823)*

*Figure 112 (left):*   Design for the monument to Mary Irby (died 1792), Whiston, Northampton-shire.
Pen and ink and wash, size of sheet 11 × 7½ inches. No. E.4361–1920.

*Figure 113 (below):* Monument to Mary Irby (died 1792), Whiston, Northamptonshire.
Photograph: *Mr. Bruce Bailey.*

---

**112**   This drawing was formerly in the collection of Fairfax Murray; see fig. 108. Another design, more closely related to the finished monument, is in Sir John Soane's Museum.

**113**   "Sacred to the Memory of Mary, the beloved Wife of the Hon. William Henry Irby, *youngest Daughter and Coheiress of Rowland Blackman, Esq. of the Island of* Antigua: of whom it may with strictest Truth be said that none of her Sex in any Station of Life, Supported with more uniform Consistence, The severable amiable and important Characters, Of a dutiful & attentive Daughter; Of a kind & benevolent Friend; Of a prudent & affectionate Wife; Of a tender & indulgent Mother; And (which was the Source of all her Virtues) Of a sincere & well-informed Christian.

She was, prematurely for all, except herself, Taken from this World, to the Enjoyment of endless Felicity On the 30th of July, 1792: Æt. 48."

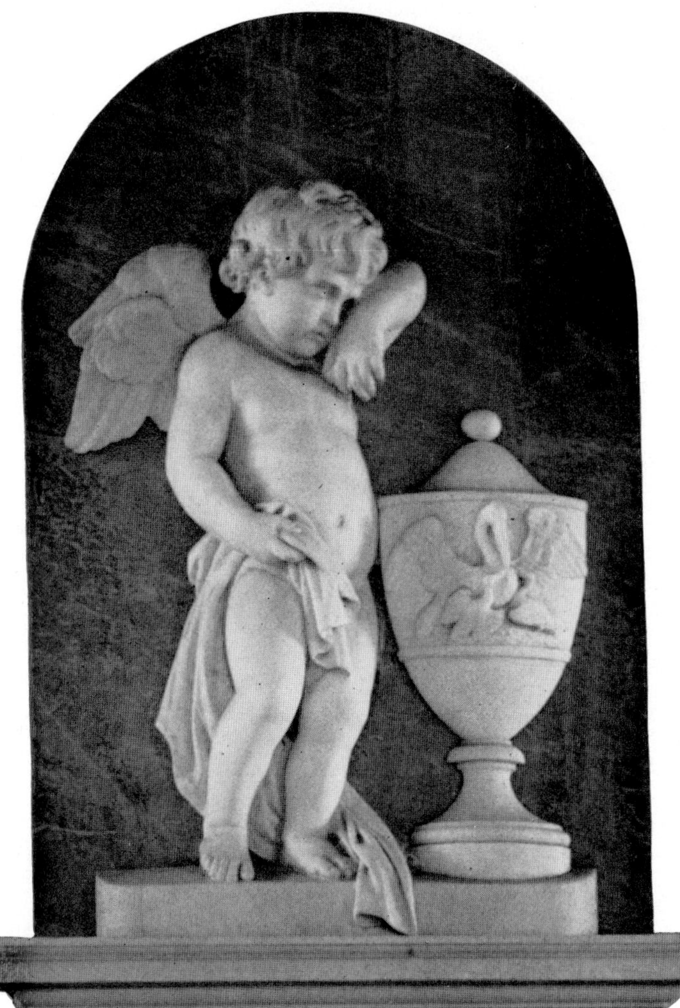

Fig. 113

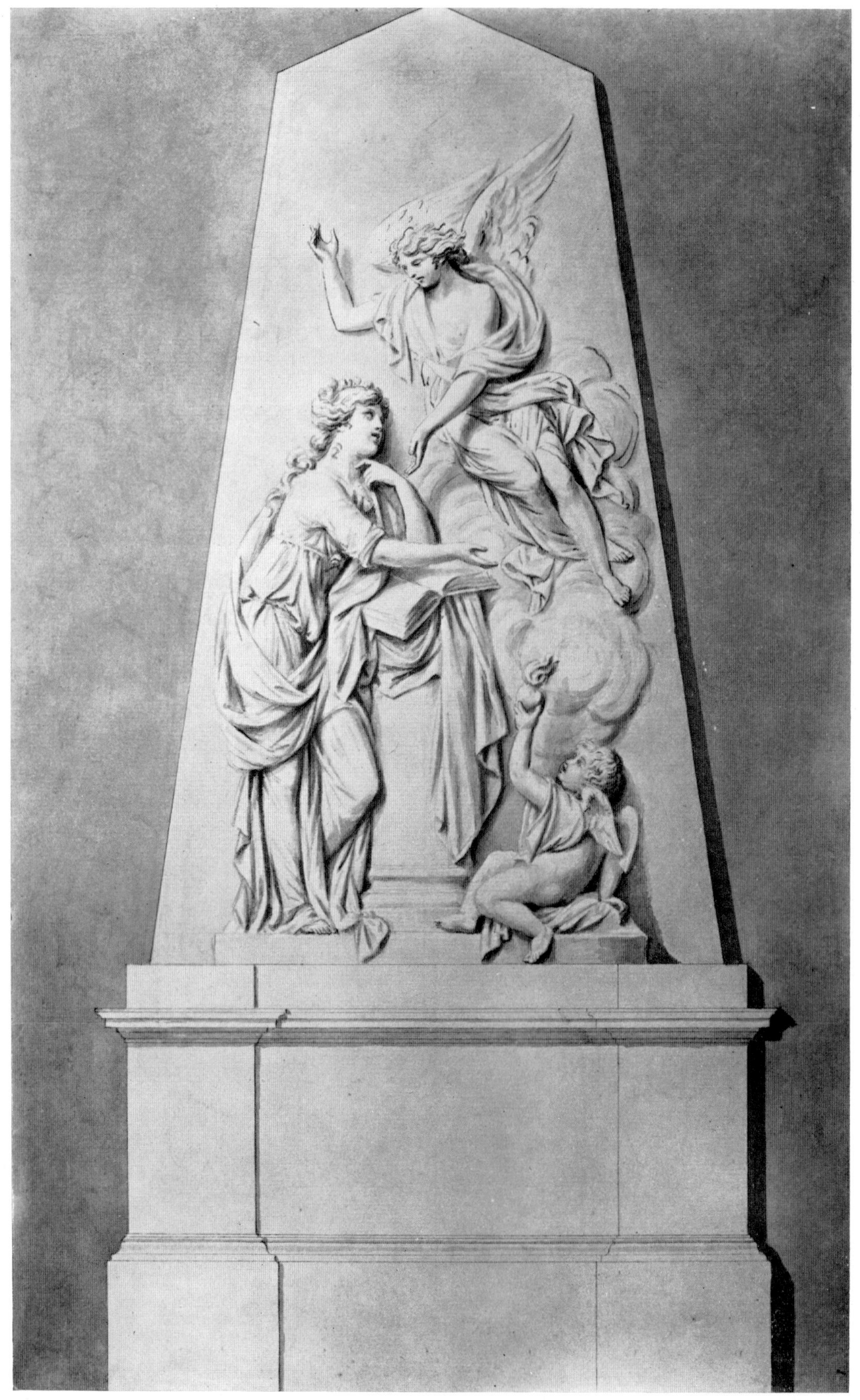

Fig. 114

# JOSEPH NOLLEKENS, R.A. (*1737–1823*)

*Figure 114 (left):*  Design for the monument to Jane (1753–1800), first wife of Thomas Coke, of
Holkham (later Earl of Leicester), at Tittleshall, Norfolk.
Pen and ink and wash, size of sheet $14\frac{1}{4} \times 8\frac{5}{8}$ inches. No. E.4358–1920.

*Figure 115 (below):*  Monument to Jane (1753–1800), first wife of Thomas Coke, of Holkham
(later Earl of Leicester), at Tittleshall, Norfolk.
Photograph: *National Monuments Record.*

---

**114**   This drawing was formerly in the collection of
Fairfax Murray; see fig. 108.

**115**   Mrs. Coke was the sister of James Dutton,
1st Baron Sherborne. She married Thomas Coke, on
October 25th, 1775, and they had three daughters.
When he was 83 years old, in 1837, Coke was
created Earl of Leicester; he died in 1842.

J. T. Smith in his biography *Nollekens and his Times*
states that the monument cost about £2,000, and that
all the figures were the work of L. Alexander Goblet,
assistant and principal carver to Nollekens.

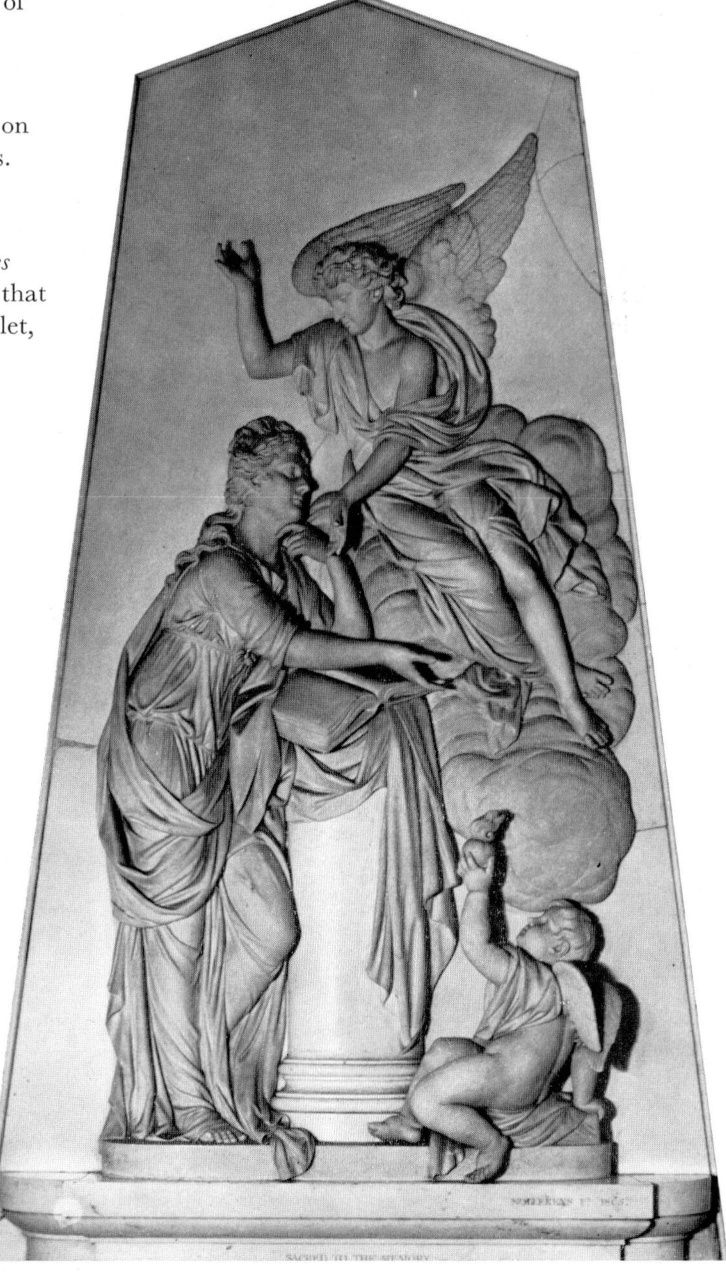

Fig. 115

# JOSEPH NOLLEKENS, R.A. *(1737–1823)*

*Figure 116 (right):*  Design for the monument to John, 3rd Duke of Dorset, K.G. (1745–1799), at Withyham, Sussex.
Pencil, $9\frac{7}{8} \times 6\frac{3}{4}$ inches. No. E.4378–1920.

*Figure 117 (below):*  Monument to John, 3rd Duke of Dorset, K.G. (1745–1799), at Withyham, Sussex.
Photograph: *National Monuments Record.*

---

**116**  This drawing was formerly in the collection of Fairfax Murray; see fig. 108.
Another drawing in the Victoria and Albert Museum, Department of Prints and Drawings, shows the complete design of the monument, E.4400–1920.

**117**  No. 1024 in the Royal Academy Exhibition of 1801 was a sepulchral bas-relief to the memory of the "late Duke of Dorset". One of the drawings by Nollekens in the Douce Bequest to the Ashmolean Museum, Oxford, is made on the back of the following bill:

---

Joseph Nollekens Esq<sup>re</sup>
    to George Gahagan

| | £ | s. | d. |
|---|---|---|---|
| 18. September, 1802. To cutting on four Busts 120 letters at 5 Shillings per [hundred] | 0 | 6 | 0 |
| To cutting two Mottos for the Duke of Dorset's Arms, 46 letters | 0 | 2 | 0 |
| Also, To cutting and painting for the Duke of Dorset's Monument an Epitaph containing 500 letters at 8 shillings p Hund | 2 | 0 | 0 |
| | 2 | 8 | 0 |

---

Gahagan was mentioned in Nollekens's will, "and to George Gahagan, another of my said workmen, twenty pounds . . . " which is quoted by J. T. Smith.

"John Frederick, Duke and Earl of *Dorset*, Earl of *Middlesex*, Baron of *Buckhurst* and Baron of *Cranfield*; Knight of the Most Noble Order of the Garter; Lord Lieutenant and Custos Rotulorum of the County of *Kent* and City of *Canterbury*; Vice-Admiral of the Coasts of the said County, and Steward of *Stratford* upon *Avon*. He was Ambassador to the Court of *France*, and Steward of His Majesty's Household. He died in the Year 1799, the 19<sup>th</sup> Day of July in the fifty fifth Year of His Age: and was buried near this Place.

To whose Memory this is offered, with the utmost Gratitude, Affection, and Honor, by his Widow Arabella Diana."

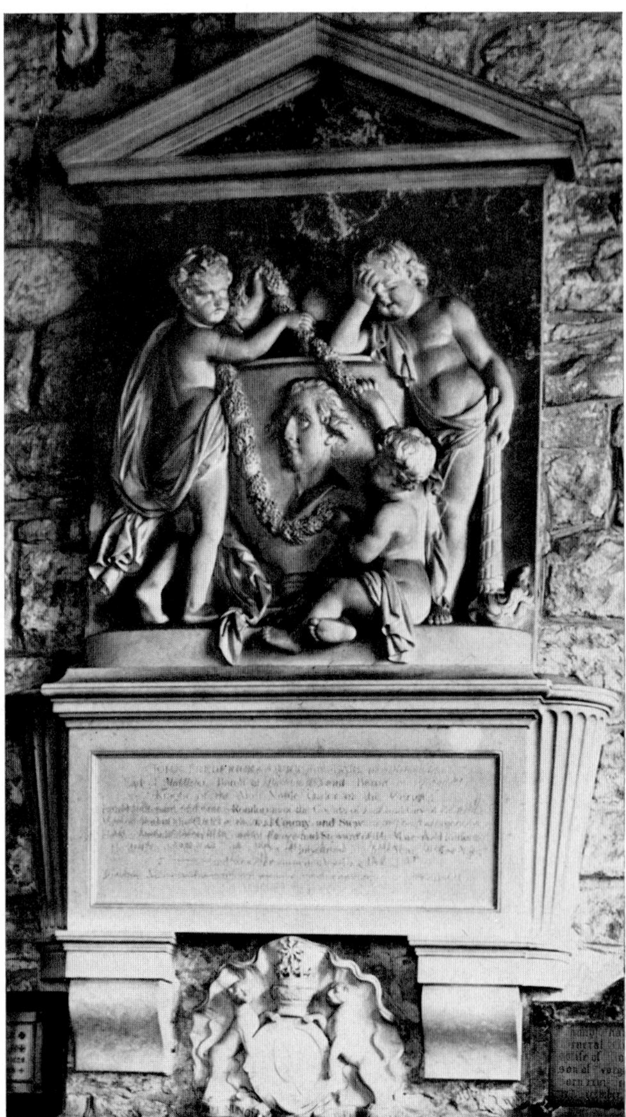

Fig. 117

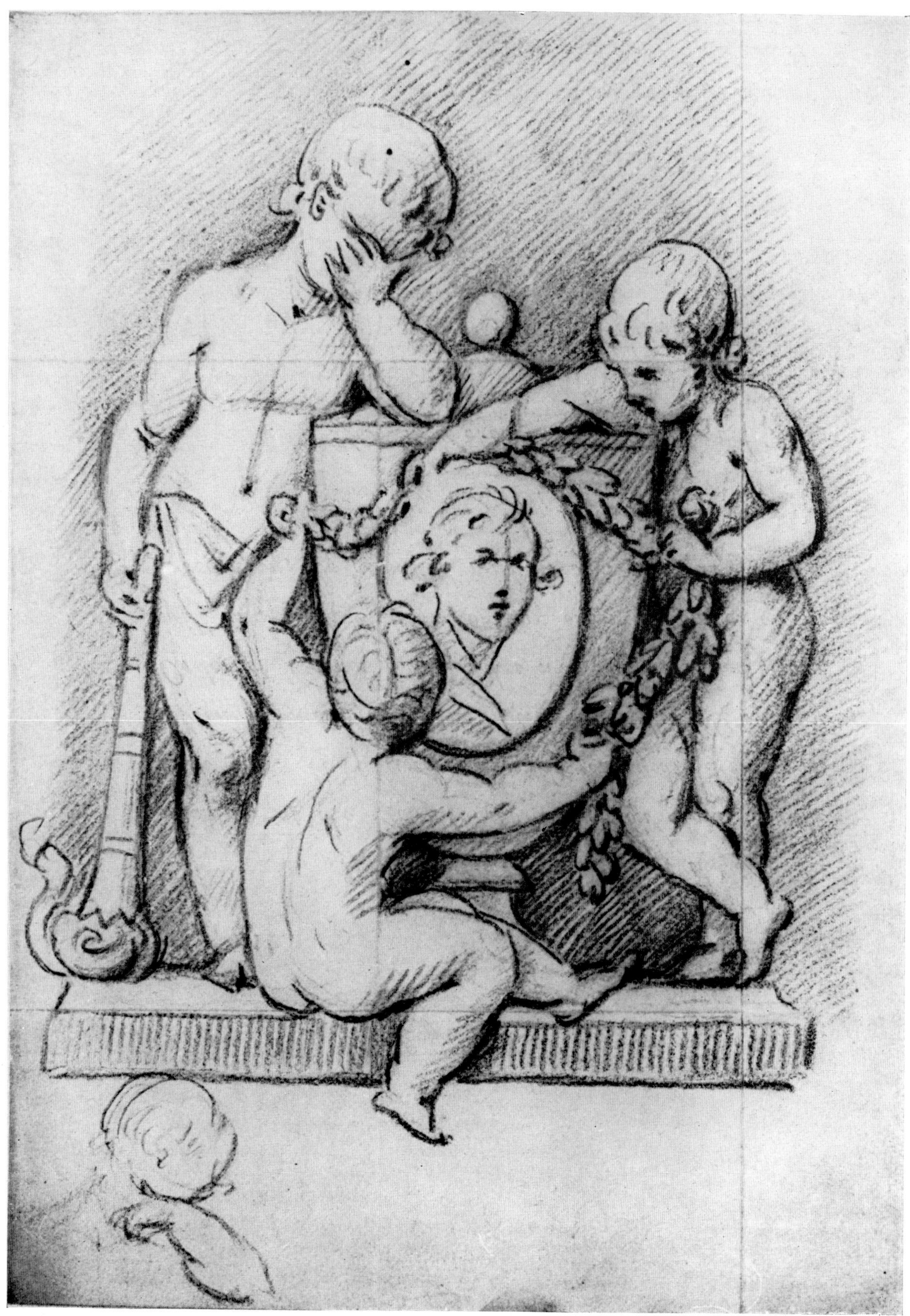

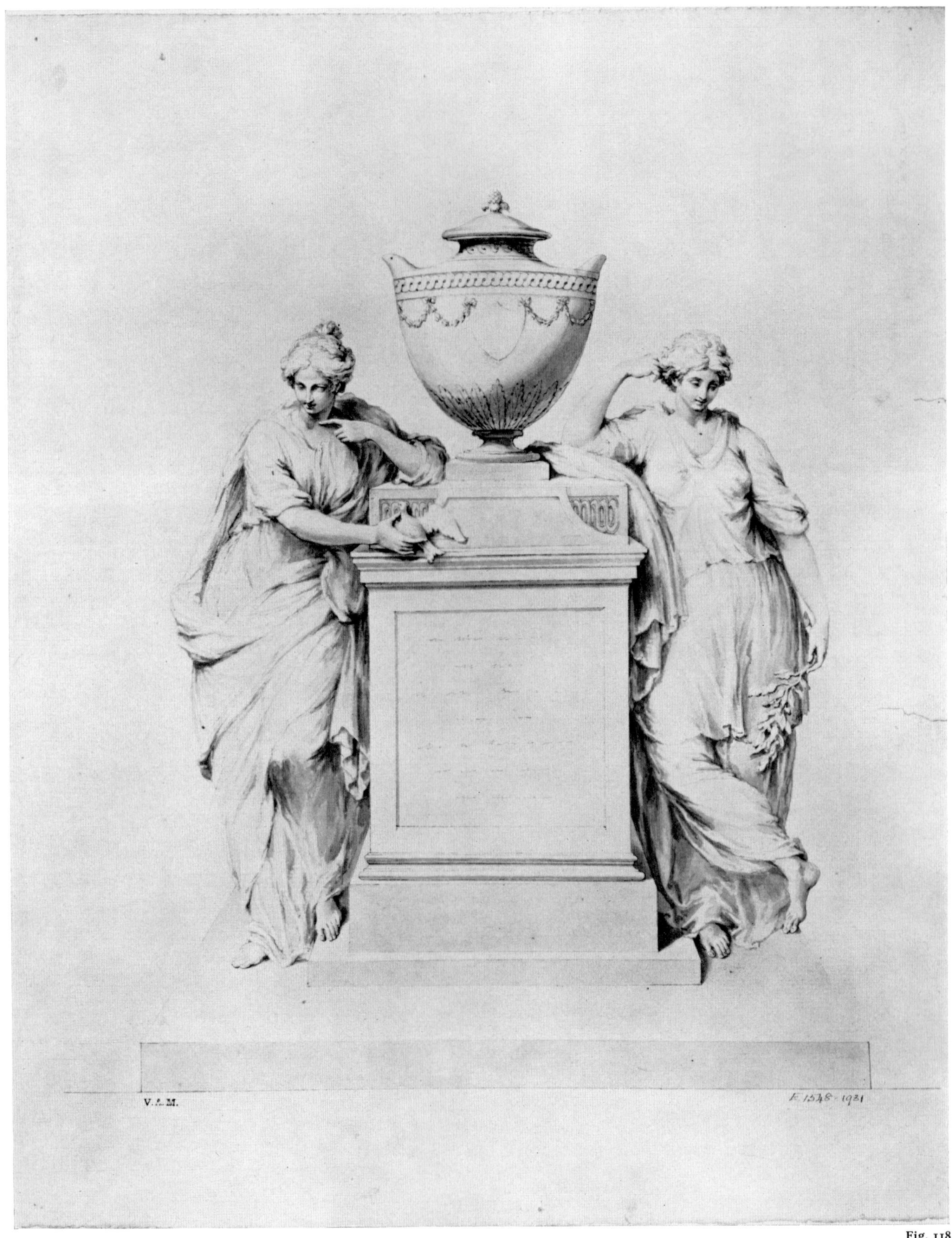





Fig. 118

# JOHN BACON, R.A. *(1740–1799)*

*Figure 118 (left):*   Design for the monument to Ann Whytell (died 1788), in Westminster Abbey. Pen and ink and wash, $10\frac{3}{8} \times 10\frac{1}{8}$ inches. No. E.1548–1931.

*Figure 119 (below):*   Monument to Ann Whytell (died 1788), in the north aisle of the nave, Westminster Abbey.
Photograph: *Warburg Institute.*

---

**118**  This drawing was one of 54 by John Bacon, R.A., and John Bacon the Younger, bought, on June 25th, 1931, from Miss Annie Bacon.

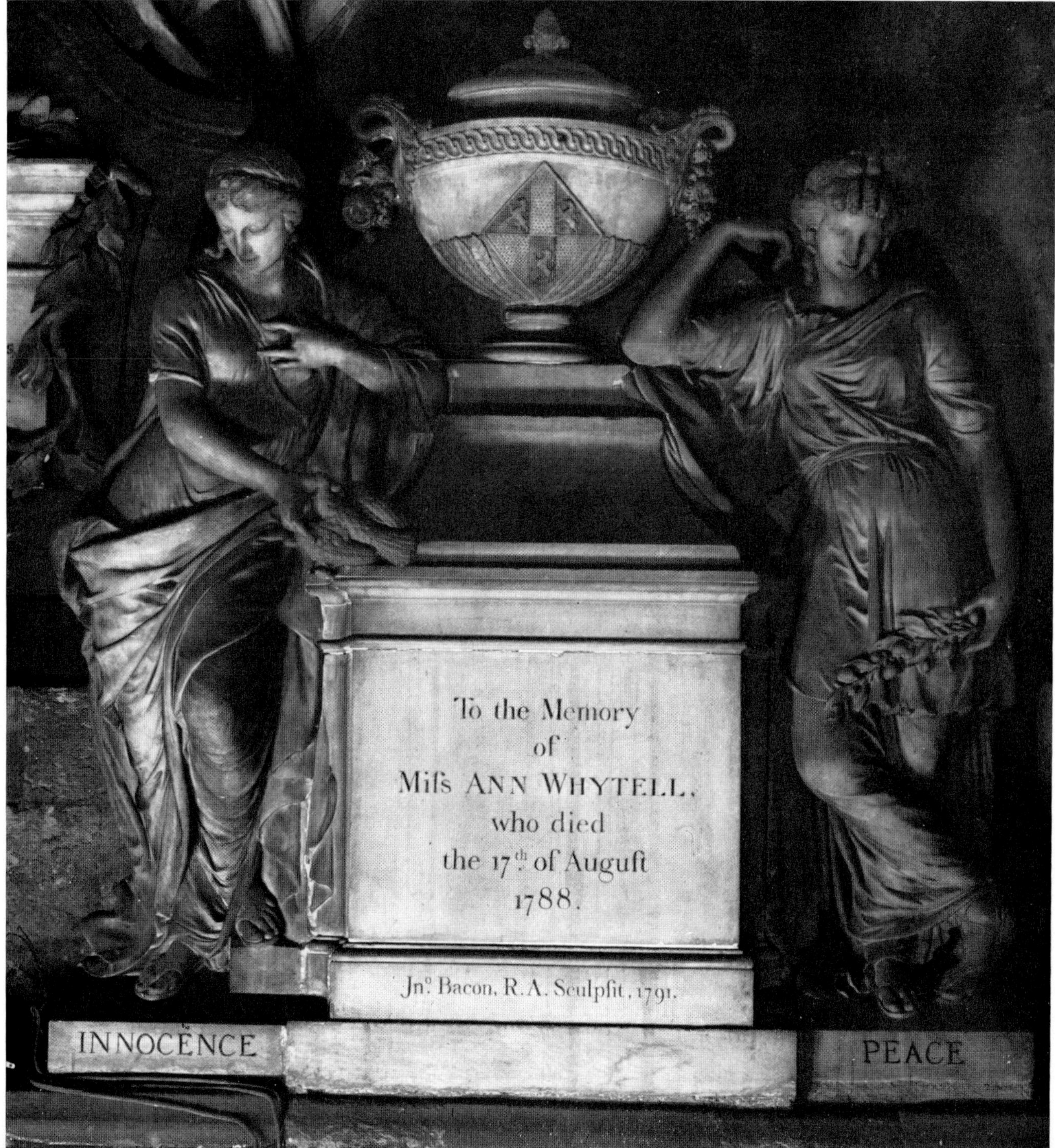


Fig. 119

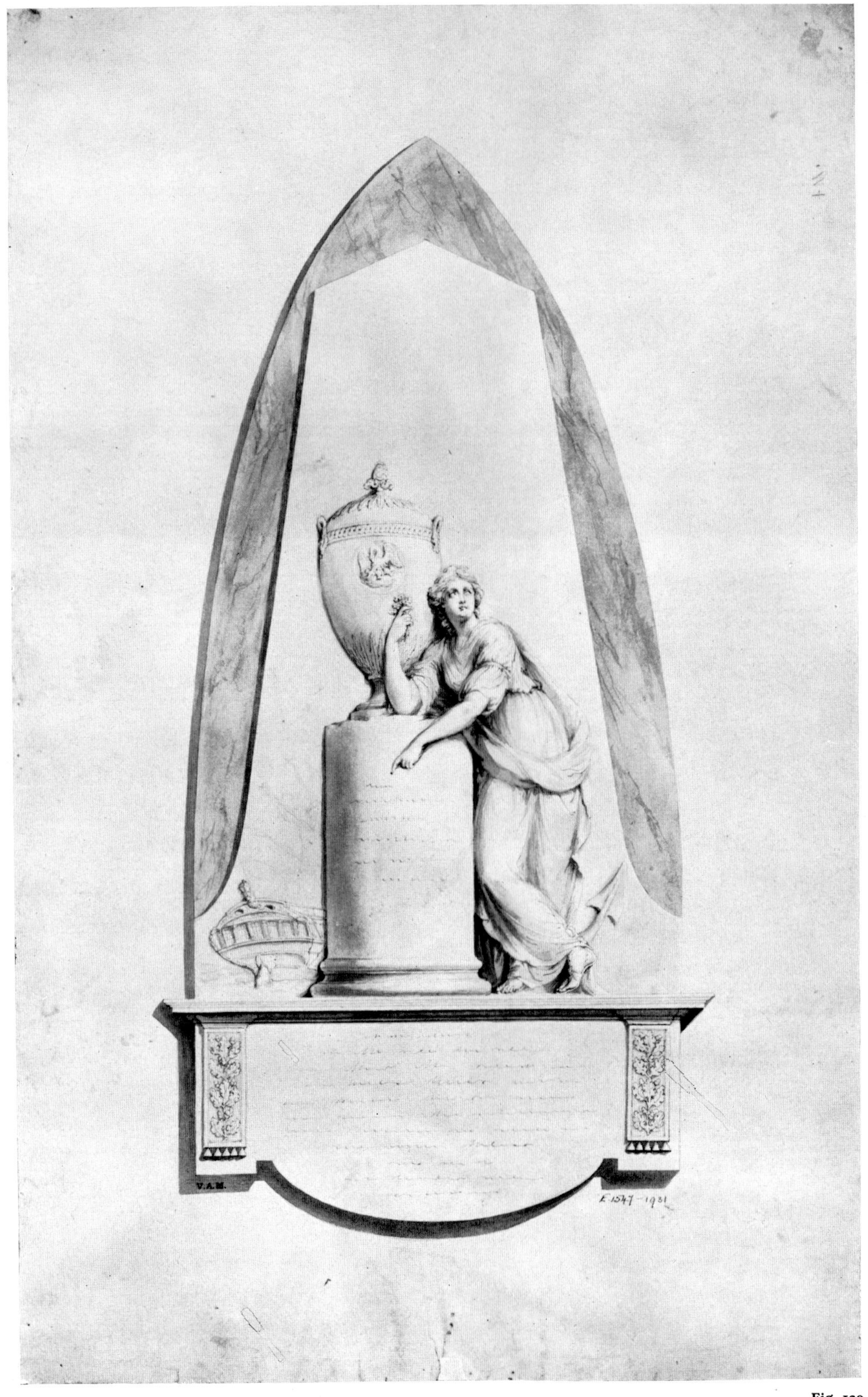

Fig. 120

# JOHN BACON, R.A. *(1740–1799)*

*Figure 120 (left):*   Design for the monument to Captain Josias Rogers, R.N. (died 1795),
Lymington, Hampshire.
Pen and ink and wash, $14\frac{3}{4} \times 7\frac{5}{8}$ inches. No. E.1547–1931.

*Figure 121 (below):* Monument to Captain Josias Rogers, R.N. (died 1795), Lymington, Hampshire.
Photograph: *Mr. Bruce Bailey.*

---

**120**   This drawing was bought from Miss Annie Bacon; see fig. 118.

**121**   The monument is signed and dated *J. Bacon, R.A. Sculptor: London, 1797.*

Captain Rogers was in command of H.M.S. *Quebec* and "during the *American* War, braved every Danger, and suffered all the severities of Wounds and Imprisonments. In the Campaign of 1794, he commanded the Naval Battalions at the Reduction of all the *French* Islands in the *West Indies*; where his Services were great to his country, and honorable to his own Character. In his Exertions to save Grenada he died of the Yellow Fever, on the 24th of April, 1795, aged 40. The Council of Grenada decreed a Monument in Honor of his Public Services: And in Remembrance of his Private Virtues his Widow soothed her Sorrows by inscribing this Tablet to his Memory.

By the same dreadful Disorder, on the 15th of May, 1794 (after having distinguish'd himself in the Dangers & Fatigues of the Campaign) fell at Guadeloupe in his 26th Year, James Rogers, his Brother, and First Lieutenant of the same Ship, Whose generous and manly Principles were admired by All who knew him.

On the 9th of the same Month, at the Age of 19, the Promise of Virtue and Talents, in Josias Rogers, his Nephew and also Lieut$^t$ of the Quebec, died in *Martinique* by the same Fatality."

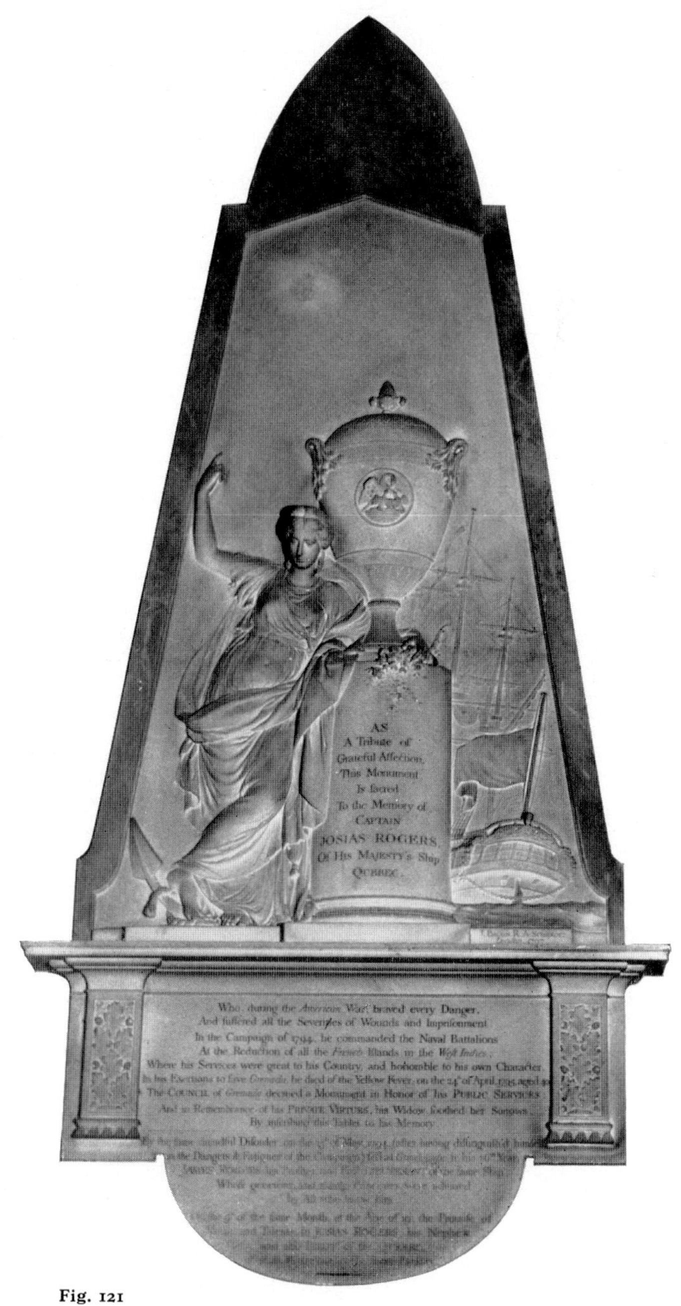

Fig. 121

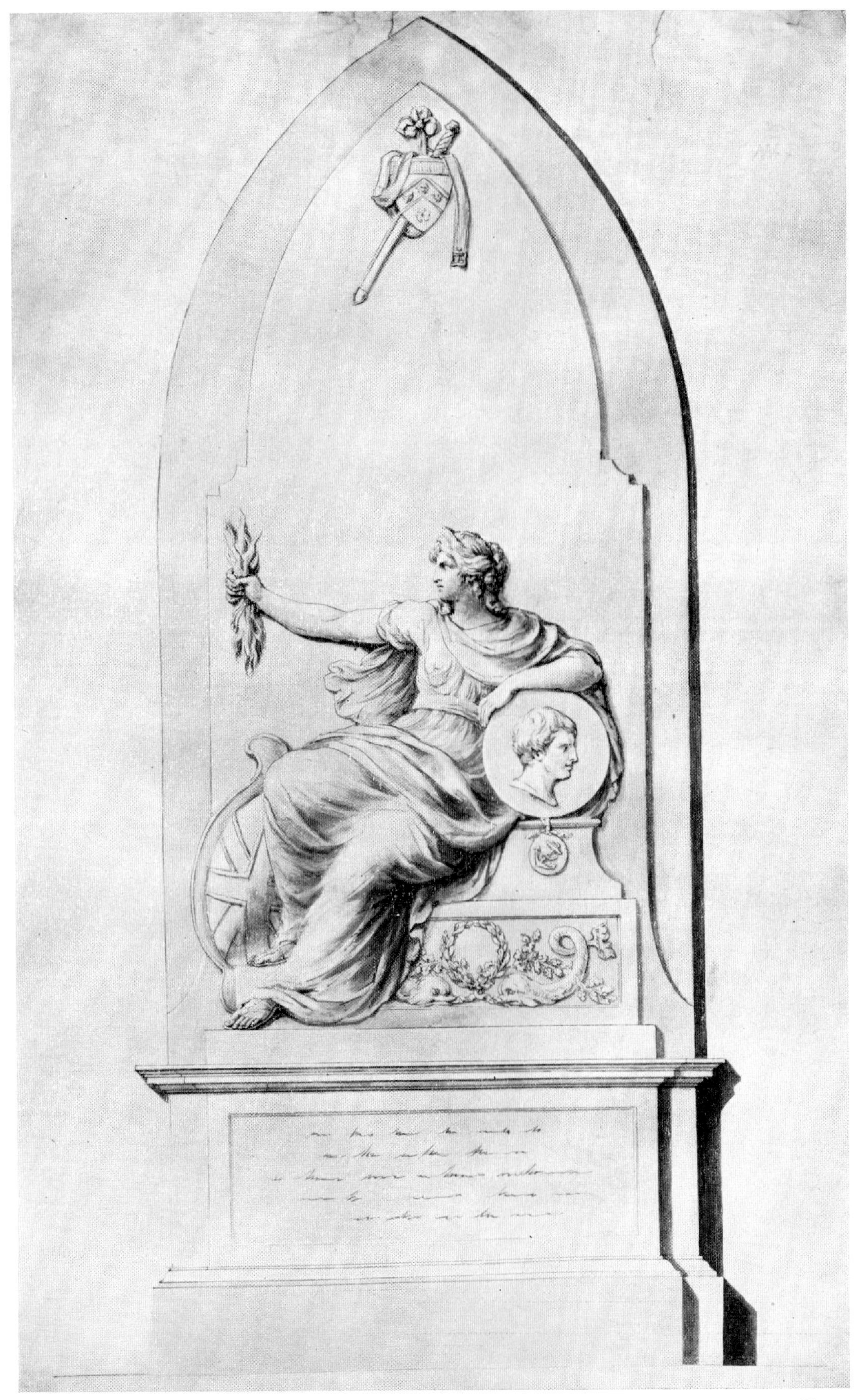

Fig. 122

# JOHN BACON, R.A. (*1740–1799*)

*Figure 122 (left):*  Design for the monument to Admiral Sir George Pocock, K.B. (died 1792), Westminster Abbey, London.
Pen and ink and wash, $18\frac{5}{8} \times 10\frac{3}{8}$ inches. No. E.1534–1931.

*Figure 123 (below):* Monument to Admiral Sir George Pocock, K.B. (died 1792), in the chapel of St. John the Evangelist, Westminster Abbey.
Photograph: *National Monuments Record.*

**122**  This drawing was bought from Miss Annie Bacon; see fig. 118.

**123**  A model by Bacon of the seated figure of Britannia, with a relief of a naval engagement on the pedestal, is in the possession of Mr. F. J. B. Watson, C.V.O., F.S.A., and was exhibited at the exhibition

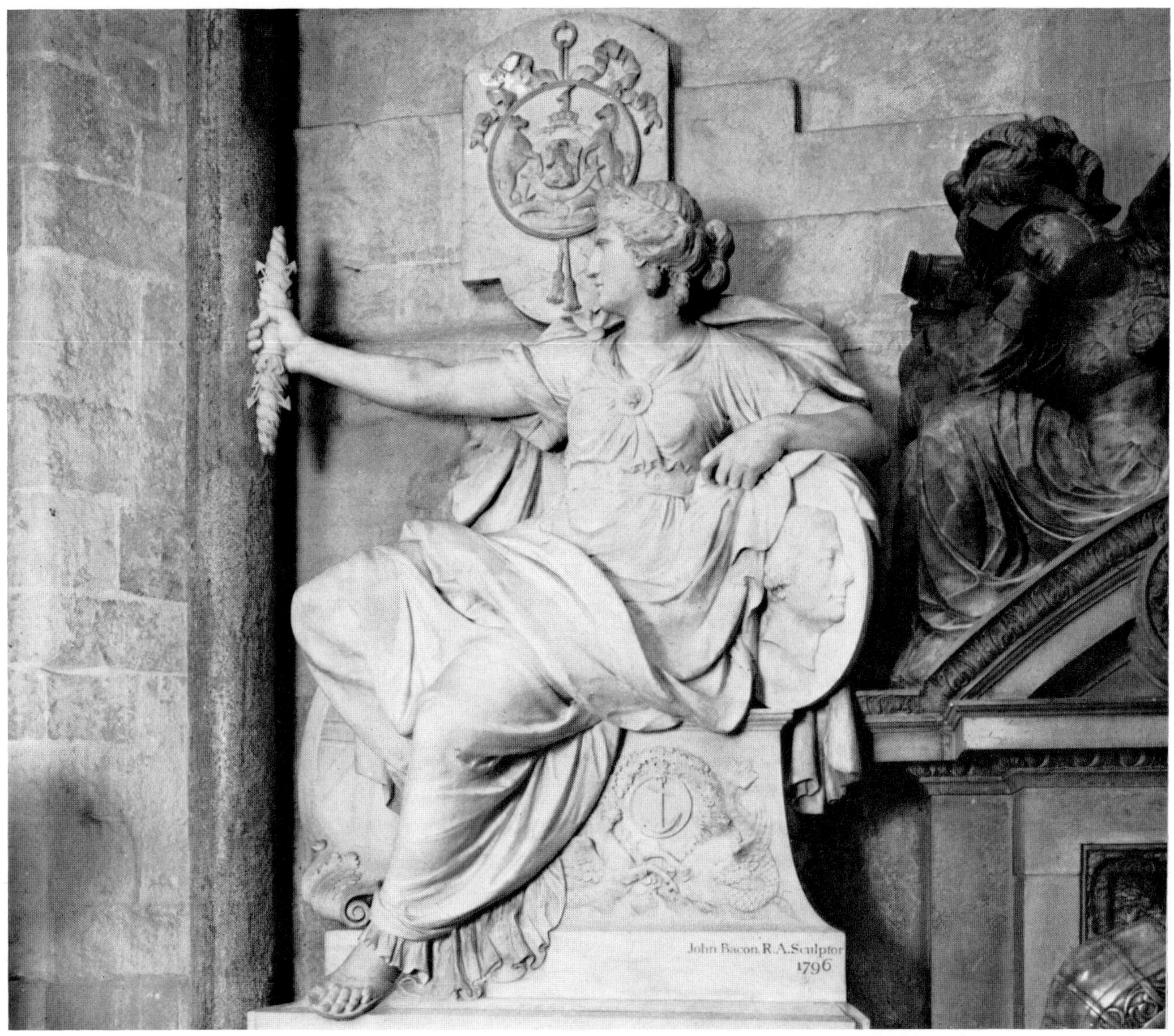

Fig. 123

Designs for English Sculpture, 1680–1860', held at the Victoria and Albert Museum, November 1966 to January 1967.

An undated, unidentified press-cutting in the Museum Library records, "The monument to the memory of the late Sir George Pocock, K.B. in Westminster Abbey was opened a few days since. The design is as follows: *Britannia* is embracing with her left arm a medallion of the Admiral, and in her right hand she holds a thunderbolt, doubtless in conformity to the figurative mode of expressing the force of British maritime power, by calling it the British Thunder. The monument is from the chisel of Bacon. It is erected at the expence of his son, George Pocock, Esq. and the inscription, which does great justice to the Admiral's character, is from the pen of the Rev. Dr. Jones, Archdeacon of Hereford."

The epitaph states, "Sacred to the Memory of Sir George Pocock, K.B., who entered early into the Naval Service of his Country, under The Auspices of his Uncle Lord Torrington; and who, emulating his great Example, rose with high Reputation to the Rank of Admiral of the Blue. His Abilities as an Officer stood confessed by his Conduct upon a variety of Occasions; but his Gallantry and Intrepid Spirit was more fully displayed by the Distinguished Part he bore at the taking of Gheriah, and in leading the Attack at the Reduction of Chandernagore; and afterwards, when, with an inferior Force, he defeated the French Fleet under M. D'Achè, in three general Engagements; shewing what British Valour can achieve, aided by professional Skill and Experience. Indefatigably active and persevering in his own Duty, he enforced a strict Observance of it in Others; at the same time with so much Mildness, with such condescending Manners, as to gain the Love and Esteem of All who served under him; whose Merits he was not more quick in discerning, or more ready to reward, than he was ever backward in acknowledging his Own. Returning from his successful Career in the East, he was appointed to command the Fleet upon the Expedition against the Havannah, by his united Efforts in the Conquest of which, he added fresh Laurels to his own Brow, and a valuable Possession to this Kingdom. Upon his retiring from Public Employment, he spent the remainder of his life in a State of dignified Ease and Splendour. Hospitable and generous to his Friends, and exhibiting a striking Picture of Christian Benevolence, by his Countenance and Support of Public Charities, and by his Liberalities to the Poor, a Life so honourable to himself, and so endeared to his Friends and his Family, was happily extended to the Age of 86; when he resigned it with the same tranquil and serene Mind, which peculiarly marked and adorned the whole Course of it. He left by Sophia, his Wife, Daughter of George Thomas Drake, Esqre. and who was first married to Commodore Dent, a Son and a Daughter; George Pocock, Esqre who caused this Monument to be erected; and Sophia, married to John Earl Poulett."

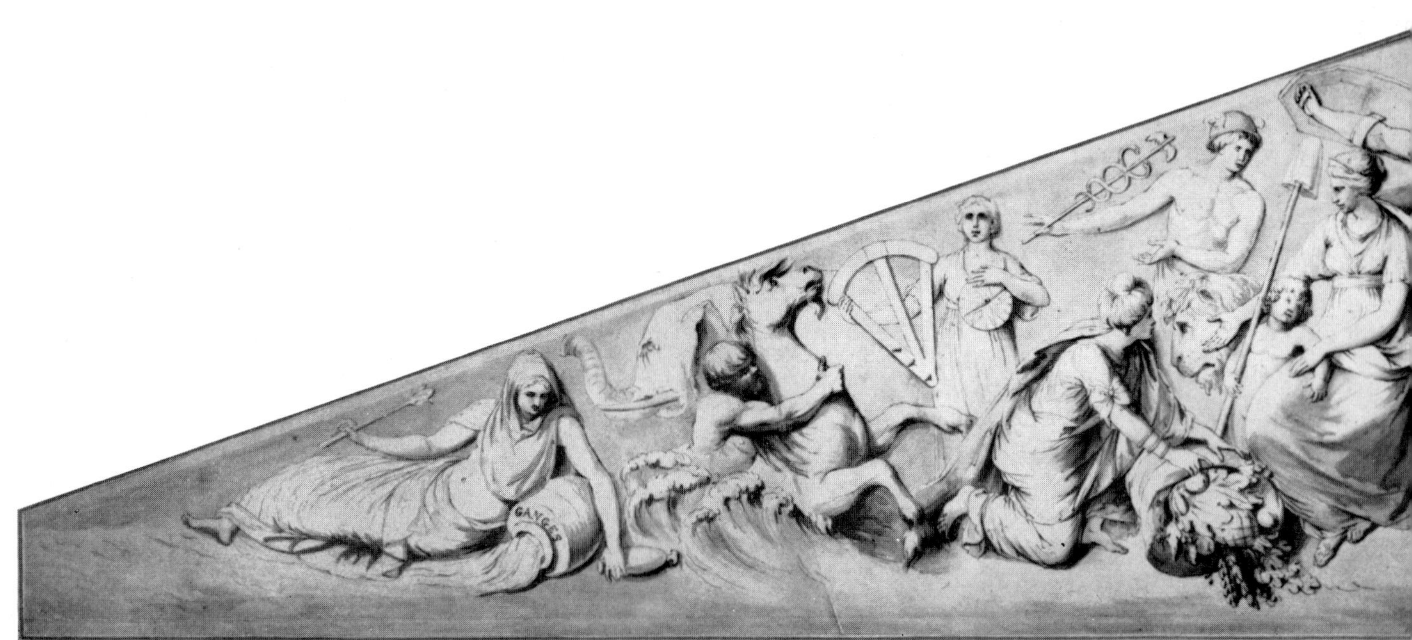

# JOHN BACON, R.A. *(1740–1799)*

*Figure 124 (below):* Design for the sculpture in the tympanum of the pediment of East India House, London.
Pen and ink and wash, $9\frac{1}{8} \times 46\frac{5}{8}$ inches. No. D.1953–1889.

**124**  This drawing was bought from Mr. E. Parsons, of Brompton Road, on November 15th, 1889, for £2. 2. od.

East India House was being rebuilt by the Surveyor to the East India Company, Richard Jupp, although at first the Company had doubts as to whether he was equal to the task. His design for the exterior was exhibited at the Royal Academy in 1798, and many of his drawings for the building are in the Victoria and Albert Museum, Department of Prints and Drawings.

John Bacon, R.A. designed the group of figures in the tympanum of the pediment, representing George III, dressed in Roman costume, defending commerce in the East. Bacon, however, died in 1799 before the completion of the work, which was taken over by his son John Bacon the Younger; altogether it cost £2,342 (Ann Cox-Johnson [Ann Saunders], *John Bacon R.A.*, 1961, page 42, note 9).

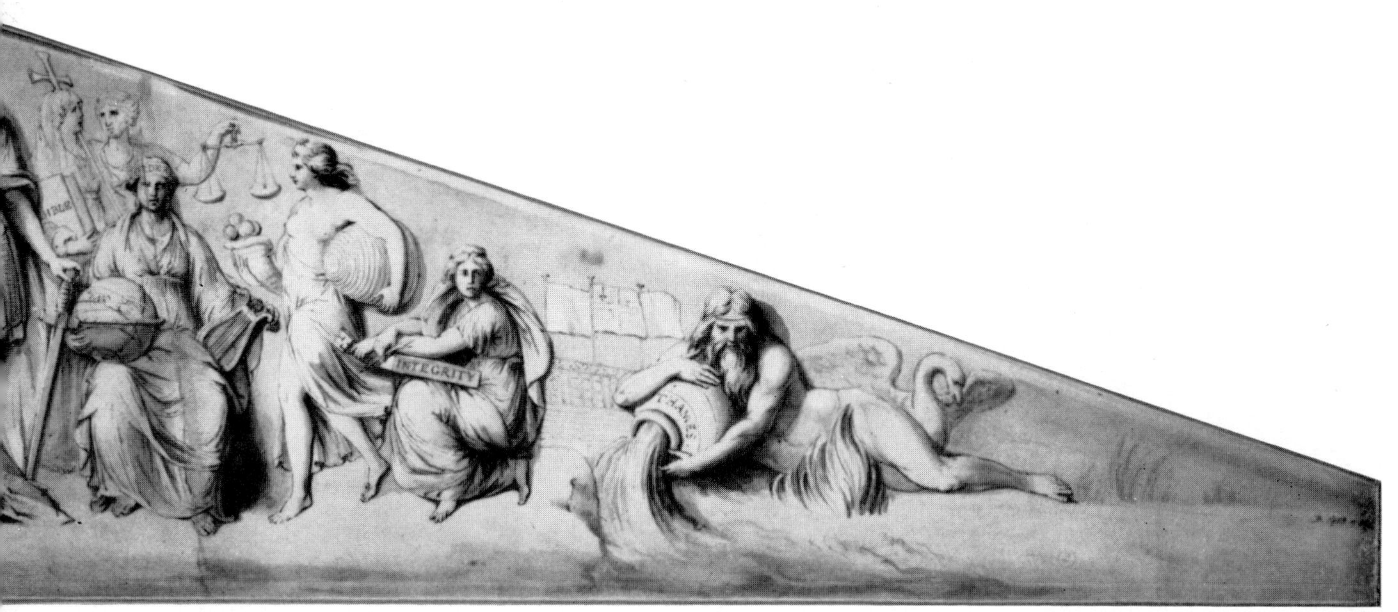


Fig. 124

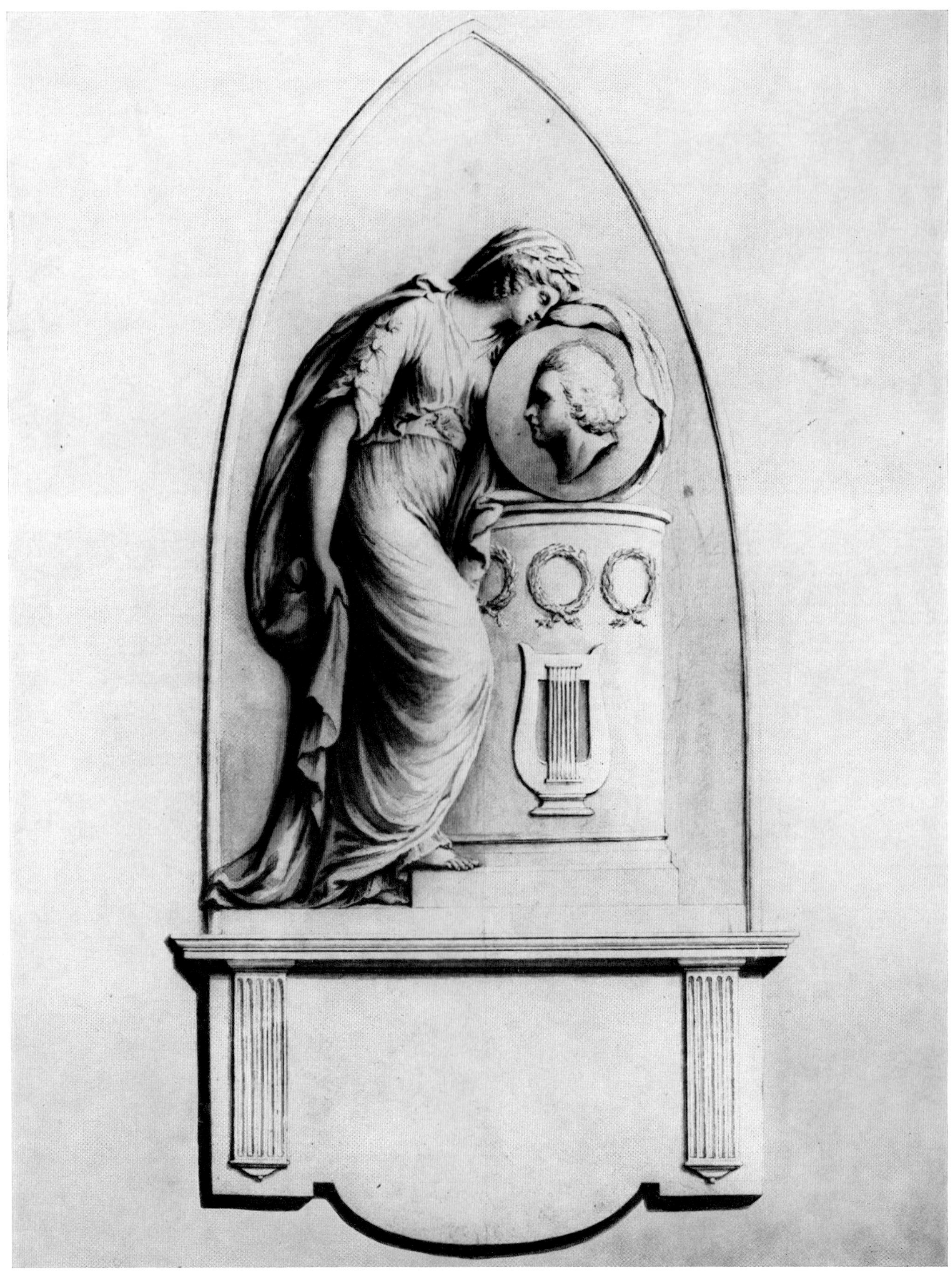

Fig. 125

# JOHN BACON, R.A. *(1740–1799)*

*Figure 125 (left):*  Design for the monument to William Mason (died 1797), in the south transept, Westminster Abbey.
Pen and ink and wash, $13\frac{5}{8} \times 6\frac{1}{4}$ inches. No. E.1529–1931.

*Figure 126 (below):*  Monument to William Mason (died 1797), in the south transept, Westminster Abbey. 1799.
Photograph: *Warburg Institute.*
The monument is signed and dated *J. Bacon, R.A. Sculp$^r$ 1799.*

---

**125**  This drawing was bought from Miss Annie Bacon; see fig. 118.

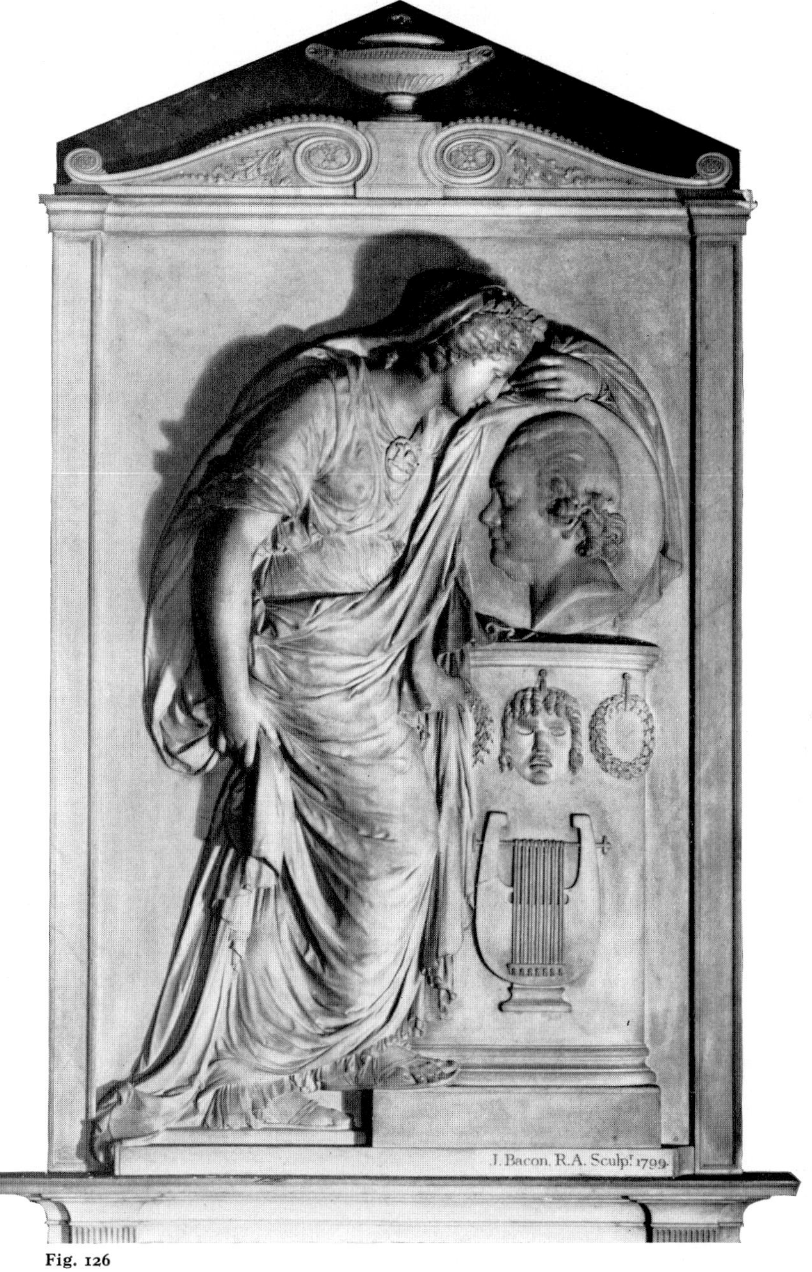

Fig. 126

# JAMES PAINE the Younger (*1745–1829*)

*Figure 127 (below):* Design for the memorial to Admiral Lord Nelson, proposed for St. Paul's Cathedral, London, with an elevation of the interior of the Cathedral. Signed *J. Paine Archt* and inscribed *The Apotheosis of Lord Nelson a Monumental Sketch.*
Pen and ink and wash, $11\frac{3}{8} \times 14\frac{1}{4}$ inches. No. 8520.10.

**127** This drawing was bought from Mr. R. Jackson, on December 19th, 1879, for 7s. 6d. Another drawing for the same monument by Paine, inscribed *As viewed from the Quire* was bought from the same dealer on July 18th, 1883, for 10 shillings; it is in the Victoria and Albert Museum, Department of Prints and Drawings, No. 9142.

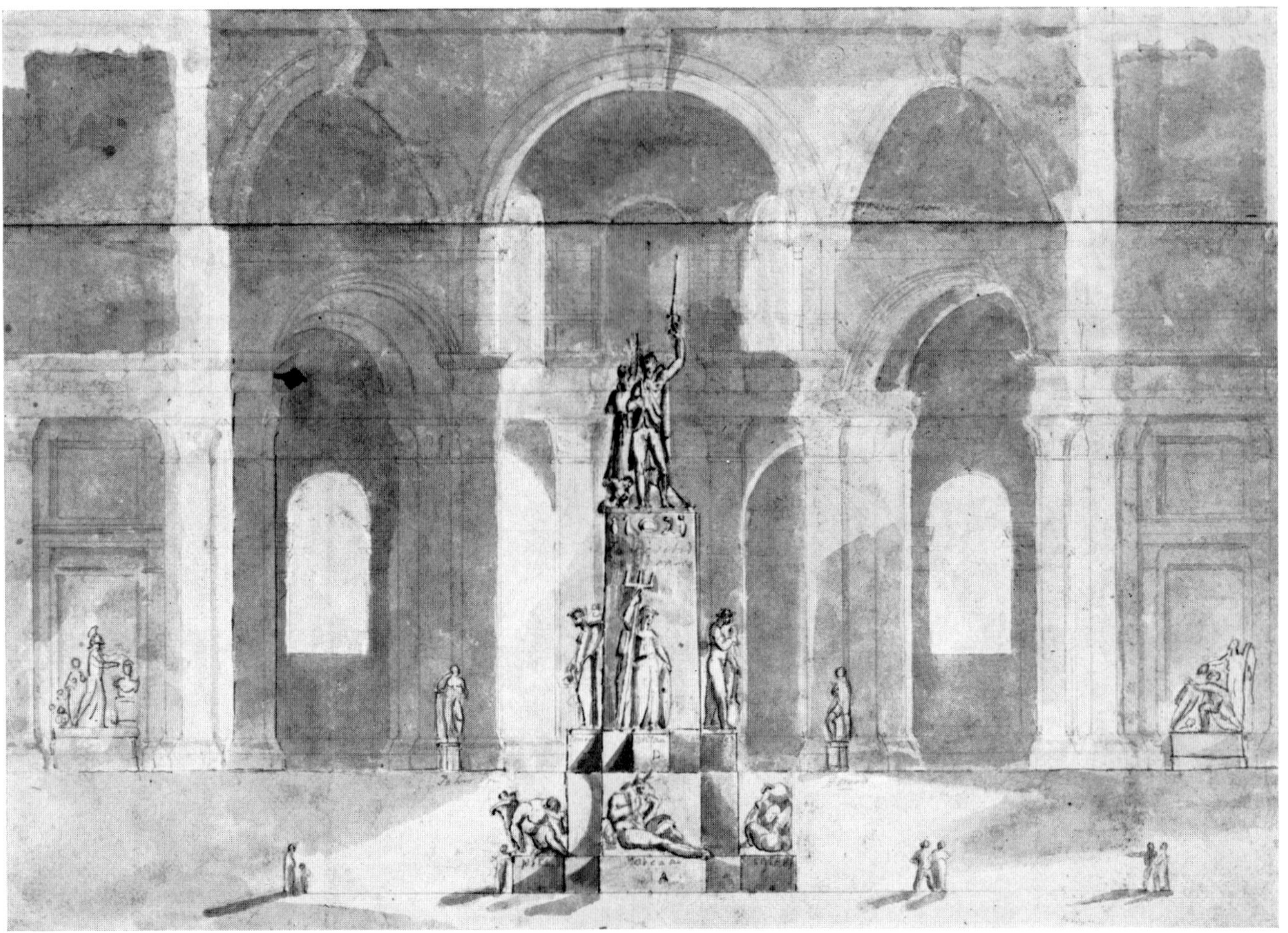

**Fig. 127**

164

## THOMAS STOTHARD, R.A. *(1755–1834)*

*Figure 128 (p.166):* Design for the monument to Charles James Fox (died 1806), in Westminster Abbey.
Pen and ink and wash, $10\frac{7}{8} \times 7\frac{1}{2}$ inches. No. 7344.

**128** The drawing was transferred from the Art Museum on March 26th, 1870.

The monument, now at the west end of the north aisle of the nave, was the work of Sir Richard Westmacott, R.A.

## JOHN FLAXMAN, R.A. *(1755–1826)*

*Figure 129 (p.167):* Design for a statue of Britannia with a lion, intended to stand in Greenwich Park, near the Observatory, as a memorial to the naval victories over the French: 1799.
Inscribed *Britannia by Divine Providence Triumphant* and *Colossal Statue 230 feet high propos'd to be erected on the summit of Greenwich*, and with a scale in feet.
Pencil, pen and ink, $7\frac{1}{2} \times 6$ inches. No. E.950–1965.

**129** This drawing was bequeathed to the Museum by Rupert Gunnis, J.P., and was engraved as the frontispiece by William Blake to Flaxman's *Letter to the Committee* (etc.), 1799.

Flaxman used a very similar design for his monument to Lord North (2nd Earl of Guilford, K.G.) who died in 1792. The model for this is in University College, London (see Margaret Whinney & Rupert Gunnis, *The Collection of Models by John Flaxman*, 1967, No. 28). The first payment was made in November, 1799, and the monument was erected in Wroxton church, Oxfordshire, during March, 1805 (Edward Croft-Murray, "An Account Book of John Flaxman, R.A.", *Walpole Society*, Volume 28, 1940, pages 65, 66).

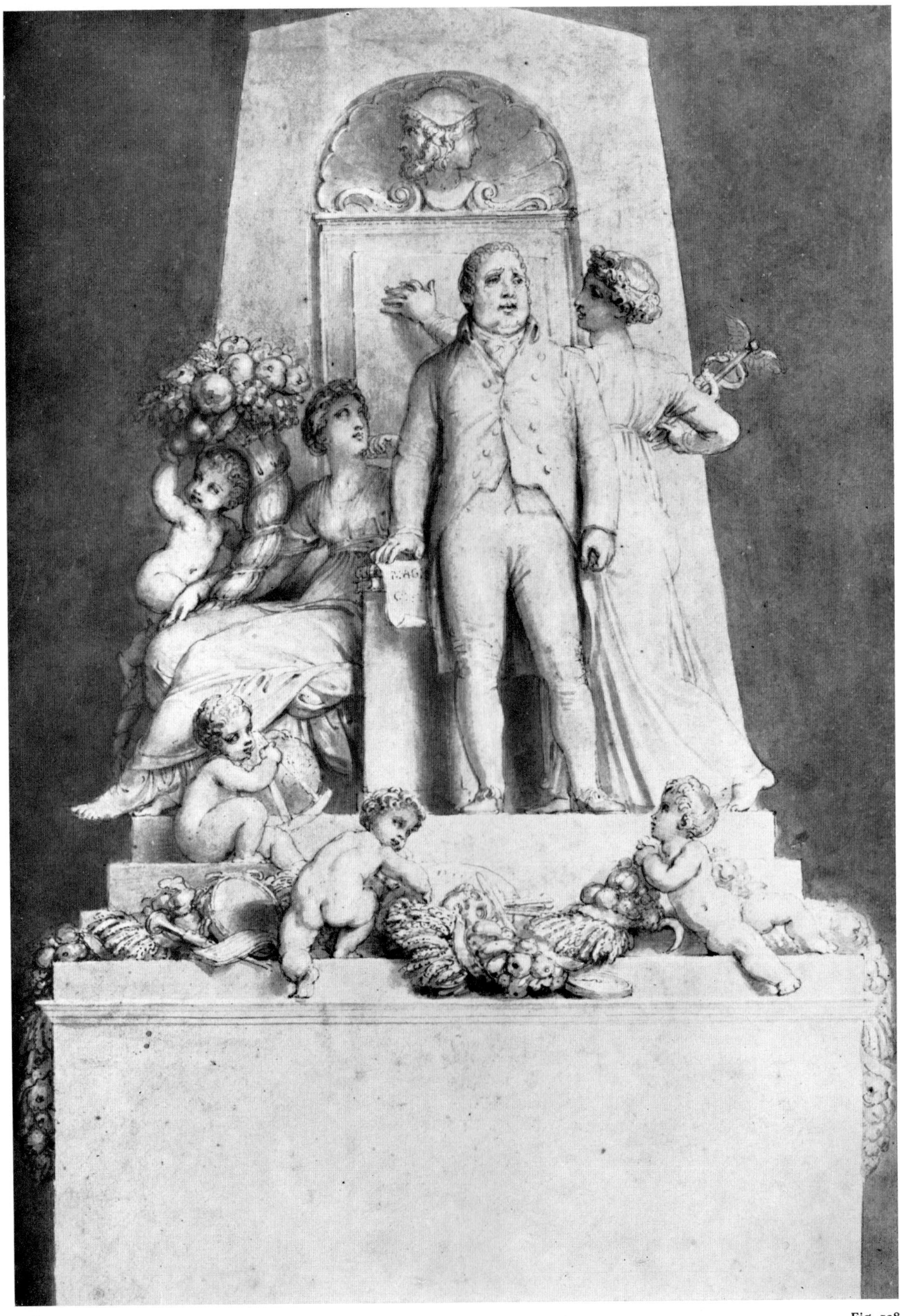

Fig. 128

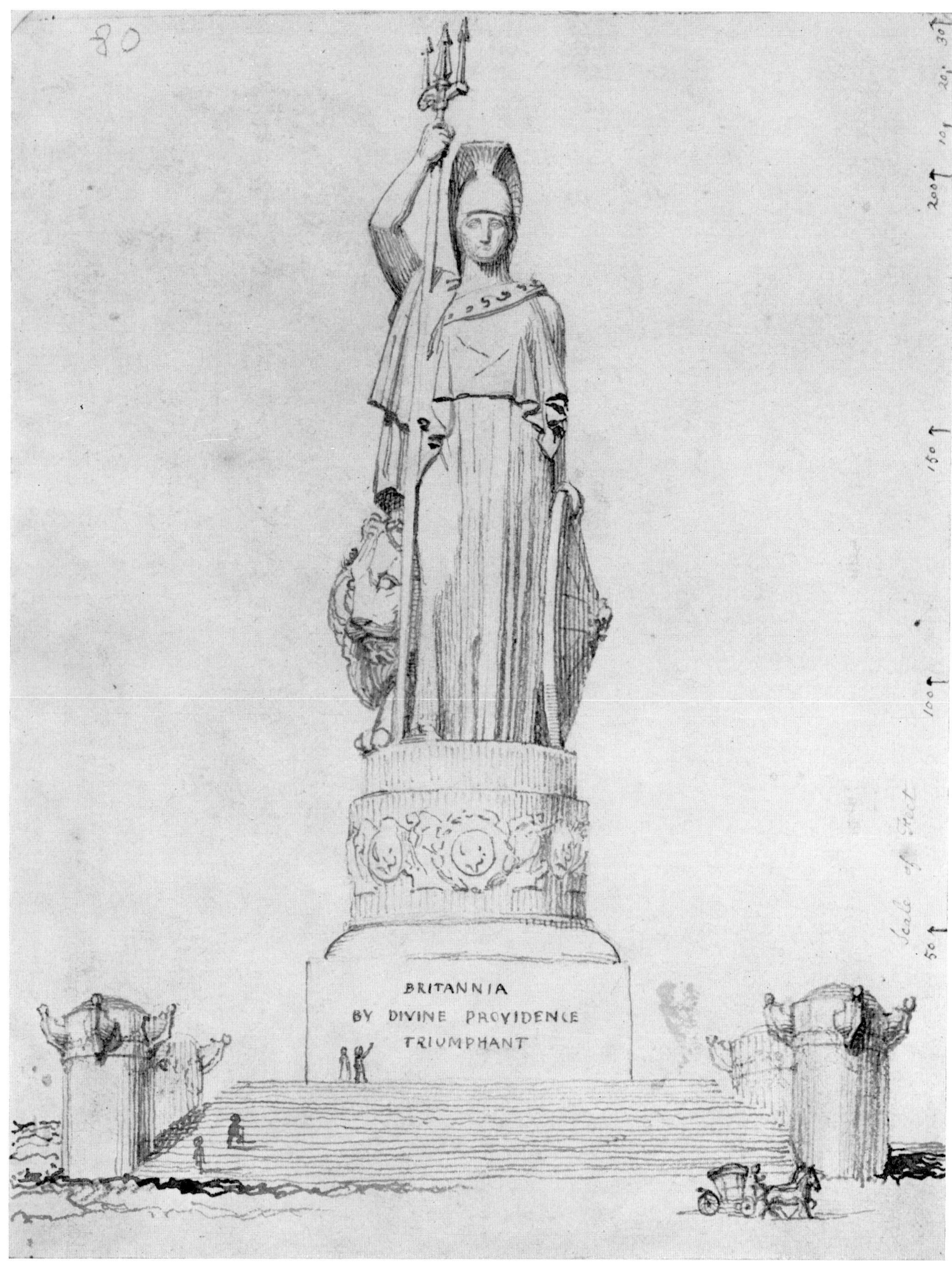

BRITANNIA
BY DIVINE PROVIDENCE
TRIUMPHANT

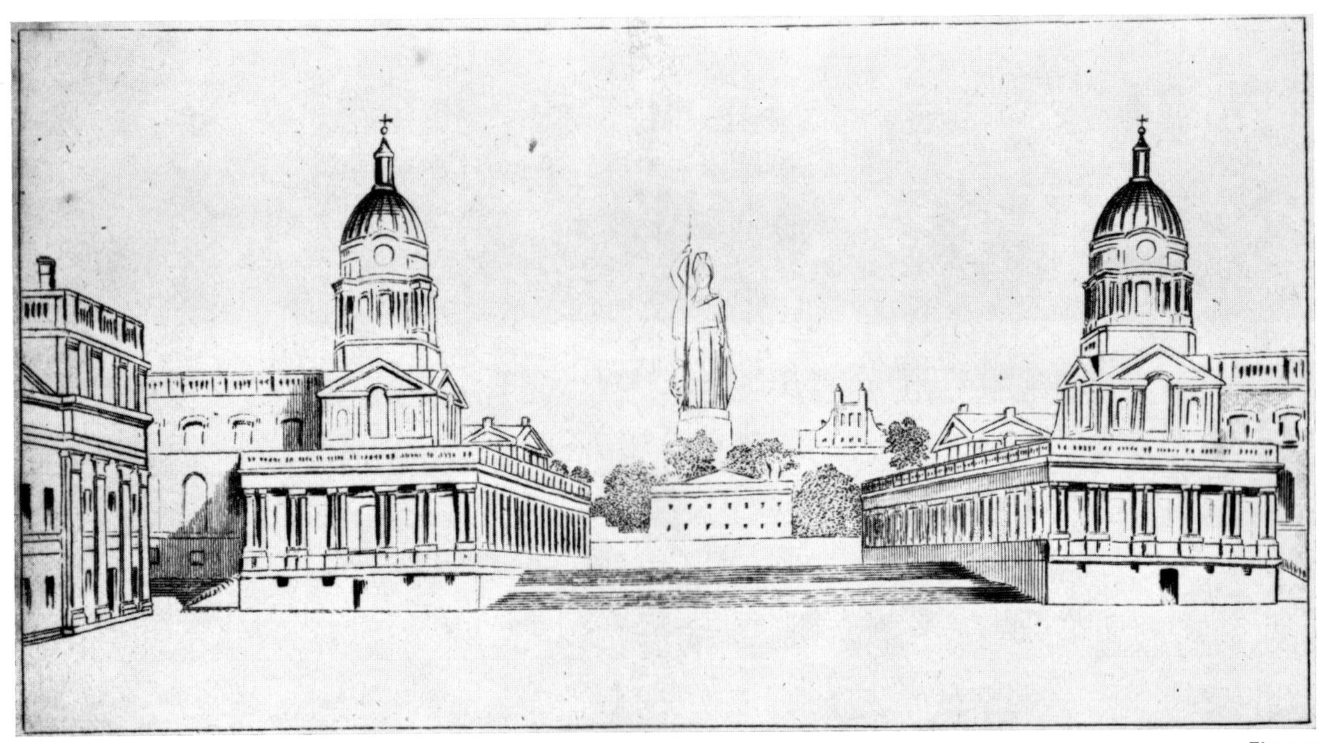

Fig. 130

# WILLIAM BLAKE (*1757–1827*)

*Figure 130 (left)*:    View of Greenwich, with the proposed statue of Britannia in Greenwich Park, near the Observatory. Plate in Flaxman's *Letter to the Committee* (etc.), given to Charles Townley by the author, and now in the Victoria and Albert Museum Library.

---

**130**   Flaxman gave his reason for choosing a statue as the form of the proposed monument in his *Letter to the Committee for raising the Naval Pillar or Monument under the Patronage of his Royal Highness the Duke of Clarence*, in December 1799, and also why he thought it should be placed on Greenwich Hill:

"The summit of Greenwich Hill appears to be the best situation for the Naval Monument, from the following considerations: the gradation of scenery from the Thames, rising with the fine architecture and porticos of this great Naval Hospital of the country, continued with the high ground and woods, and connected by the Observatory, with such a finish would afford a sublimity of prospect not to be equalled in any other place. Besides, its vicinity to and visibility in the high parts of London and its environs, to the south and east it would most likely be seen as far as the sea. It is also to be remembered, that the port of the Metropolis is the great port of the whole Kingdom; that the Kent Road is the ingress to London from Europe, Asia and Africa; and that, as Greenwich Hill is the place from whence the longitude is taken, the Monument would, like the first Milestone in the city of Rome, be the point from which the world would be measured."

This published letter brought a protest a month later, in January, 1800, from an architect Alexander Dufour, who published his own *Letter to the Nobility composing the Committee for raising the Naval Pillar or Monument . . . in answer to the Letter of John Flaxman, sculptor, on that subject*. In this he criticised Flaxman for having tried to influence the Committee against Triumphal Arches and Pillars by bad drawings, and also because as a sculptor, Flaxman would have wished some other form for the monument.

Flaxman exhibited a sketch for a "statue of Britannia" as No. 1037 in the Royal Academy Exhibition of 1801, which is presumably the model now in the Soane Museum. He concluded his *Letter* with "acknowledgements to Mr. G. Dance for some of the observations concerning the situation of the monument, as also for

the first hint, that a Colossal Statue might be the proper subject for the monument itself."

A group of drawings in the Dan Fellows Platt Collection at the Art Museum of Princeton University, shows that Flaxman considered also the design of a giantic Triumphal Arch, surmounted by a seated Britannia, and at each of the corners of the base, four sculptured groups with naval trophies. (See Malcolm Campbell, "An alternative design for a commemorative monument by John Flaxman" in *Record of the Art Museum, Princeton University*, Volume 17, 1958, pages 65–73.)

*Figure 131 (right):*  Design for the "National Cup" in the collection of H.M. The Queen, showing the figure of St. Patrick.
Pencil and wash, $12\frac{3}{4} \times 4\frac{1}{4}$ inches. No. D.379–1886.

---

This drawing was bought with 47 other miscellaneous drawings from Mr. E. Parsons, of Brompton Road, on April 6th, 1886, for £4; and it is recorded by Flaxman in his account book which is now in Columbia University Library, New York.

The "National Cup" was designed by Flaxman for George IV and was made by the Royal goldsmiths, Rundell, Bridge and Rundell in 1824. It is decorated with figures of the three patron saints of the United Kingdom, St. George, St. Andrew and St. Patrick. The Cup was exhibited in the Exhibition of Royal Plate from Buckingham Palace and Windsor Castle (Catalogue No. 129), held at the Victoria and Albert Museum in 1954. (See E. Alfred Jones, *The Gold and Silver of Windsor Castle*, 1911, Plate LXXXVII. 1; and Shirley Bury, "The lengthening shadow of Rundell's, Part 2: The substance and growth of the Flaxman tradition", *The Connoisseur*, March, 1966, page 155.)

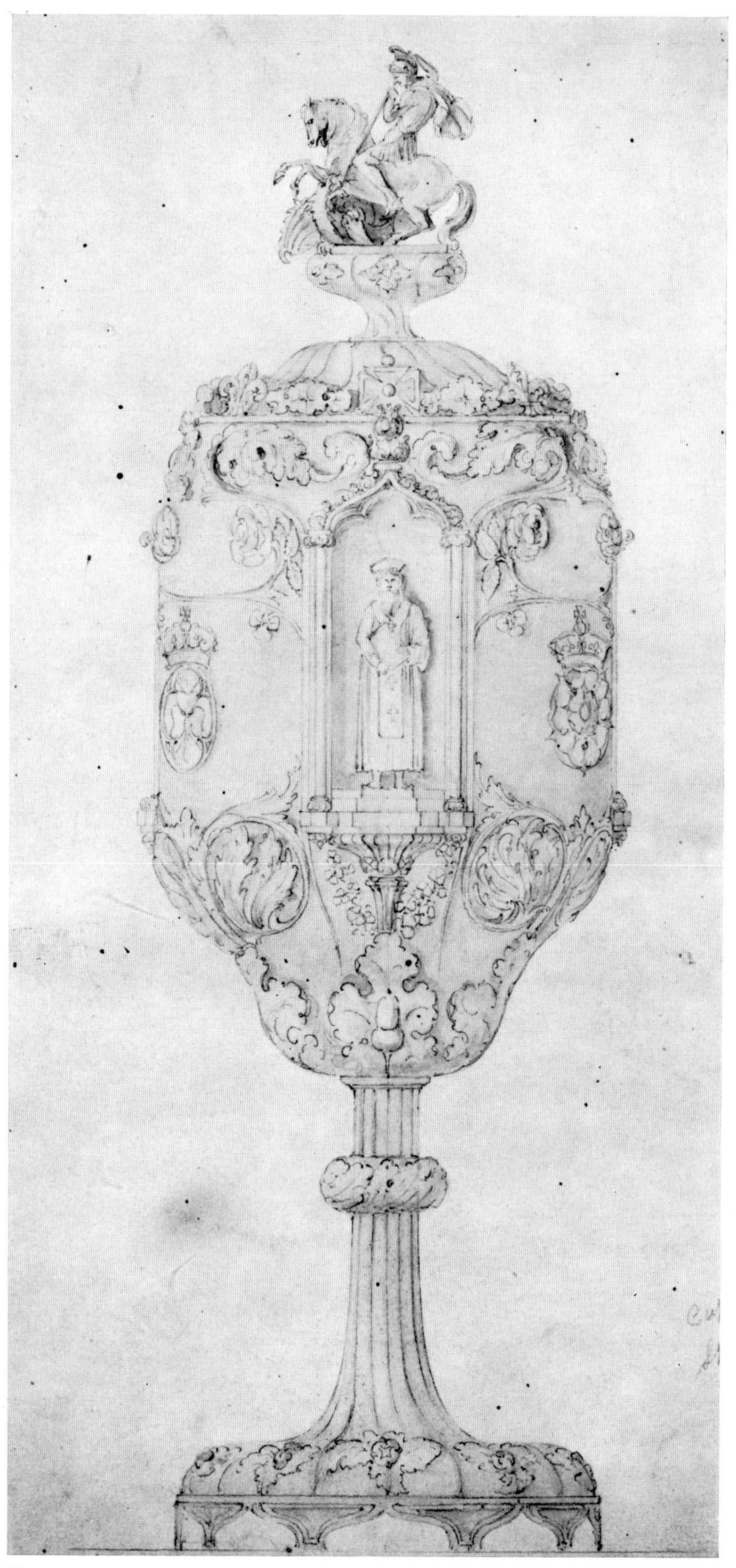

Fig. 131

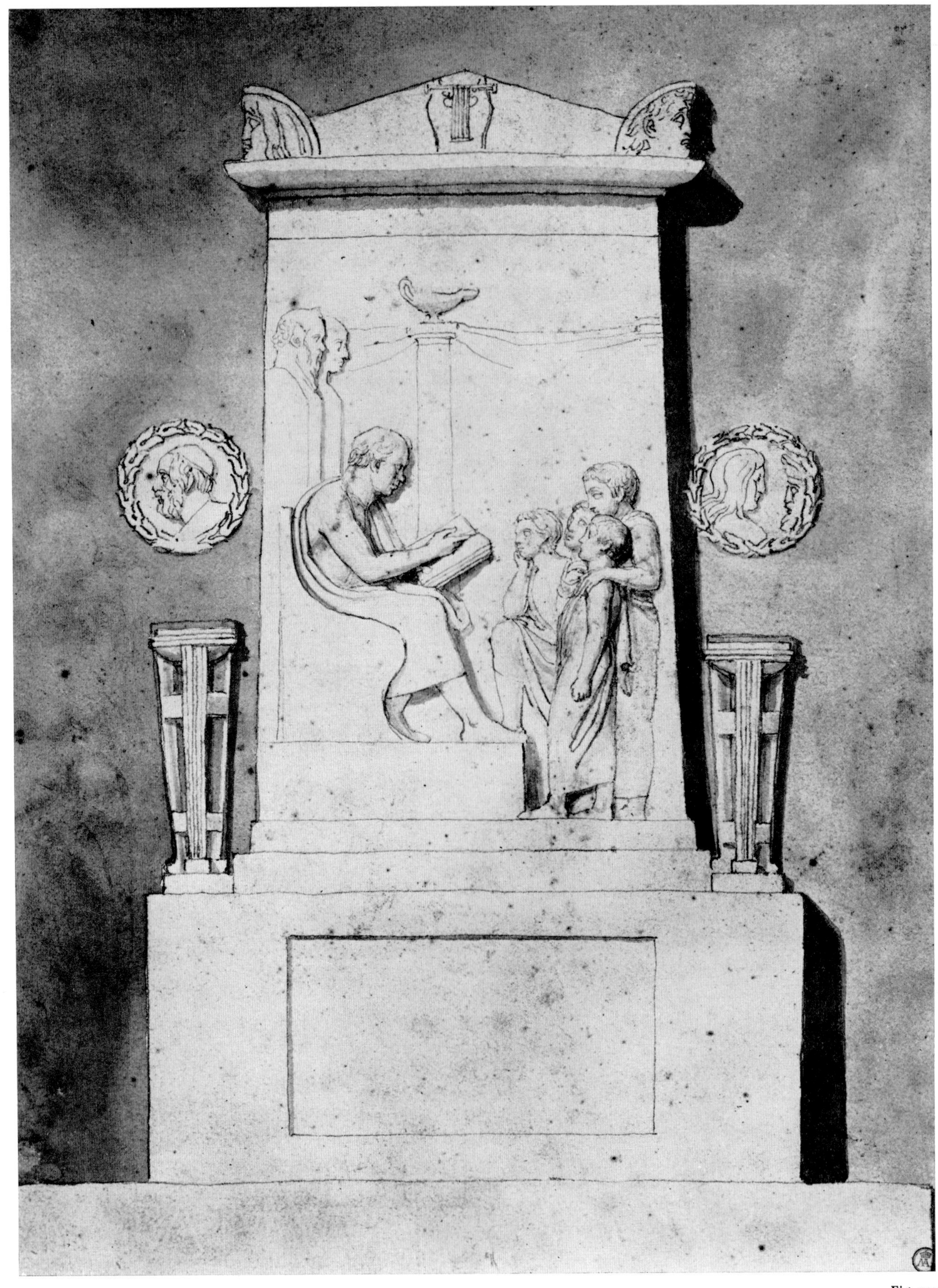

*Figure 132 (left):* Design for the monument to Dr. Joseph Warton (1722–1800), Headmaster of Winchester, in Winchester Cathedral, Hampshire.
Pen and ink and wash, $11\frac{7}{8} \times 9\frac{3}{4}$ inches. No. 7345.

*Figure 133 (below):* Monument to Dr. Joseph Warton (1722–1800), Headmaster of Winchester, in Winchester Cathedral, Hampshire.
Photograph: *National Monuments Record.*

**132**   This drawing was transferred from the Art Museum on March 26th, 1870. A related drawing for the monument is in the British Museum, No. 1888–5–3–4–5.

**133**   The account-book of John Flaxman's in the British Museum, Add. MSS. 39,784 BB, first refers to this monument on March 9th, 1801, "Robt Blake Esq^re. No. 14 Essex Street Strand for the Committee of Wickhamists Rec^d on Acc^t of 500£ for Dr. Wharton's Monument to [be] erected in Winchester Cathedral including all expence & 20£ Fees to the Church if required 166. 13. 4." The final payment of £66. 13. 4d. was made on May 30th, 1804 (Edward Croft-Murray, "An Account Book of John Flaxman, R.A.", *Walpole Society*, Volume 28, 1940, page 70).

The four boys shown are perhaps the sons of Flaxman's friends, Mr. and Mrs. Hare-Naylor. (See G. H. Blore, "Flaxman's monument to Dr. Warton", in *Winchester Cathedral Record*, 1942, page 6, and H. Clifford Smith in *Country Life*, October 12th, 1945.)

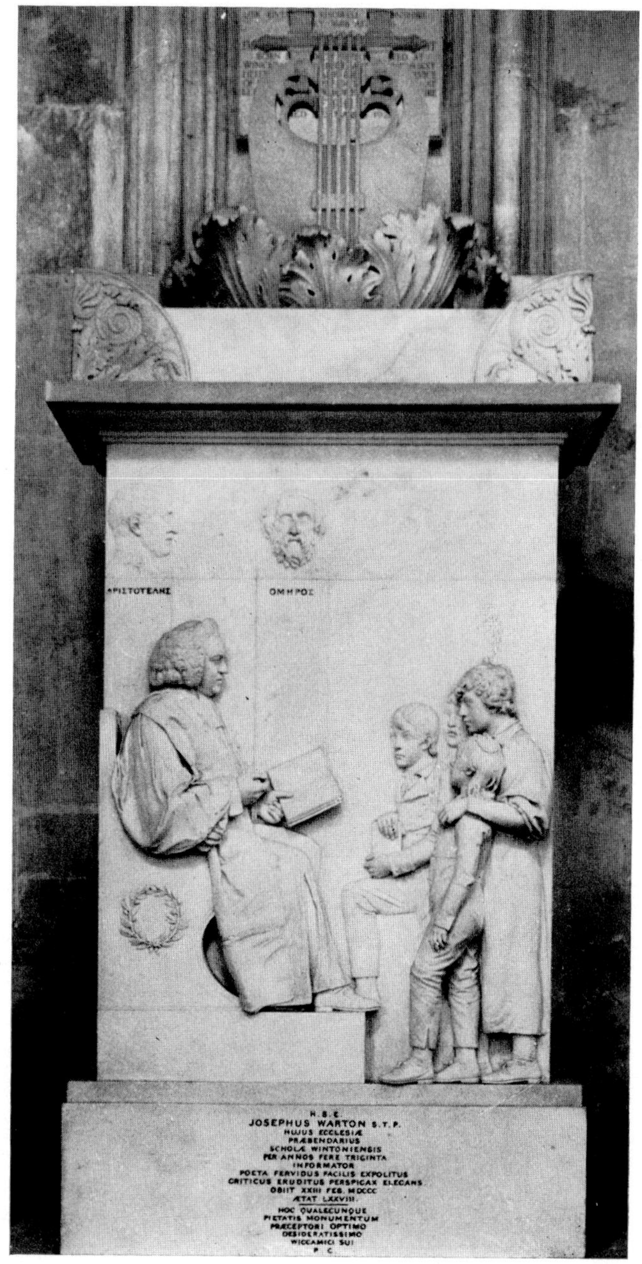


**Fig. 133**

*Figure 134 (below):* Design for the monument to General John Graves Simcoe (died 1806),
Governor of Upper Canada, in Exeter Cathedral, Devonshire.
Pen and ink and wash, $10\frac{1}{2} \times 13\frac{1}{8}$ inches. No. 8967A.

*Figure 135 (right):* Monument to General John Graves Simcoe (died 1806), Governor of Upper
Canada, in Exeter Cathedral, Devonshire.
Photograph: *Mr. Bruce Bailey.*

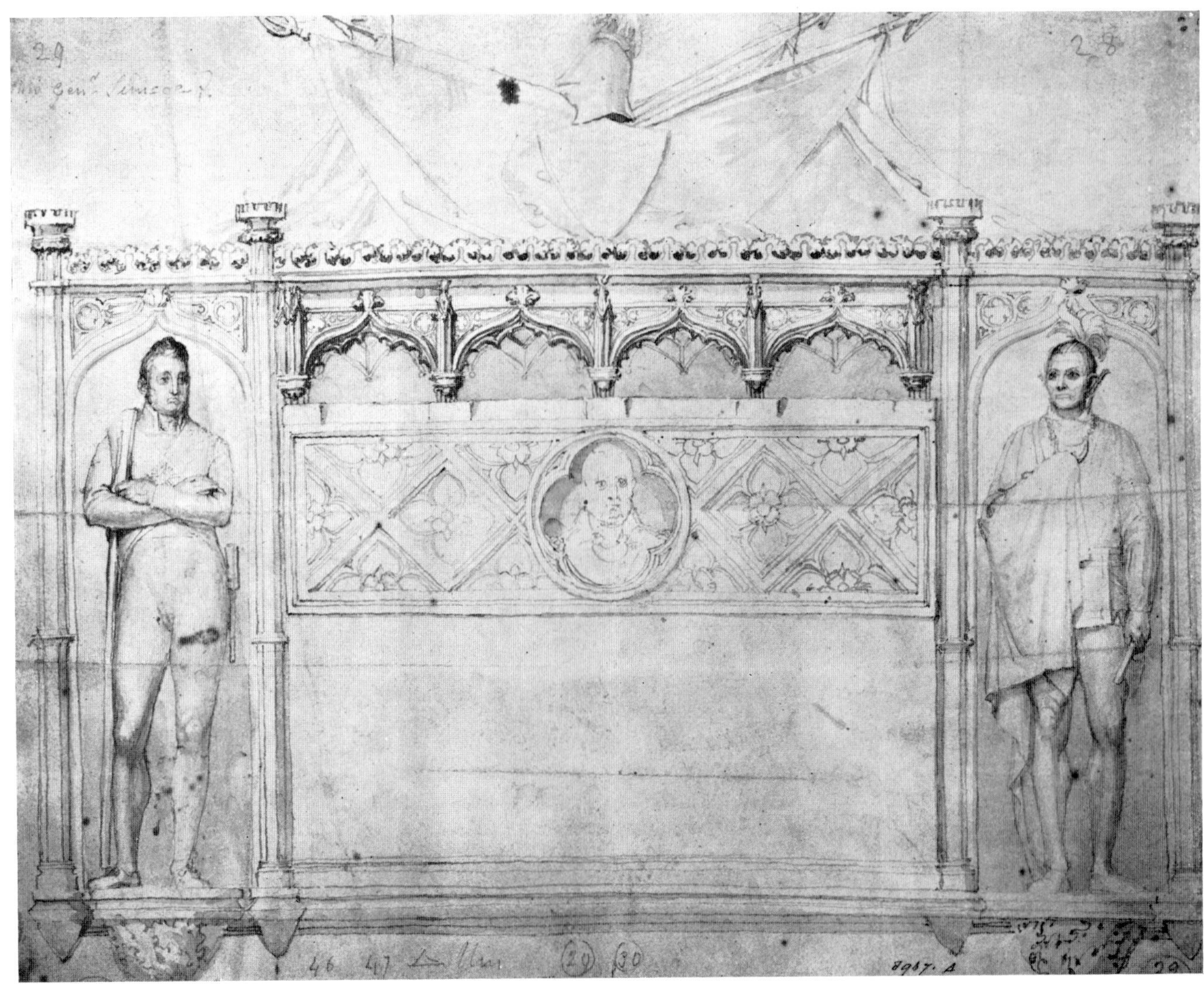

Fig. 134

**134** This drawing and 38 others by Flaxman, were bought from Mr. E. Parsons of Brompton Road, on March 19th, 1883, for £15. 12. od.

A related drawing for this monument is in the Victoria and Albert Museum, Department of Prints and Drawings, C. A. Ionides Bequest, No. 762.

**135** The monument was damaged by bombing during the Second World War. The first payment for the work was recorded in Flaxman's account-book, now in Columbia University Library, New York (Montgomery Manuscript),

"1811 May 27 John B. Cholwick Esq$^r$ Devonshire Place
Rec$^d$. 320£ on acct of 950£ for a Mon$^t$. to Gen$^l$. Simcoe to be erected in Exeter Cathdral." The final payment of £220 was made on February 27th, 1816.

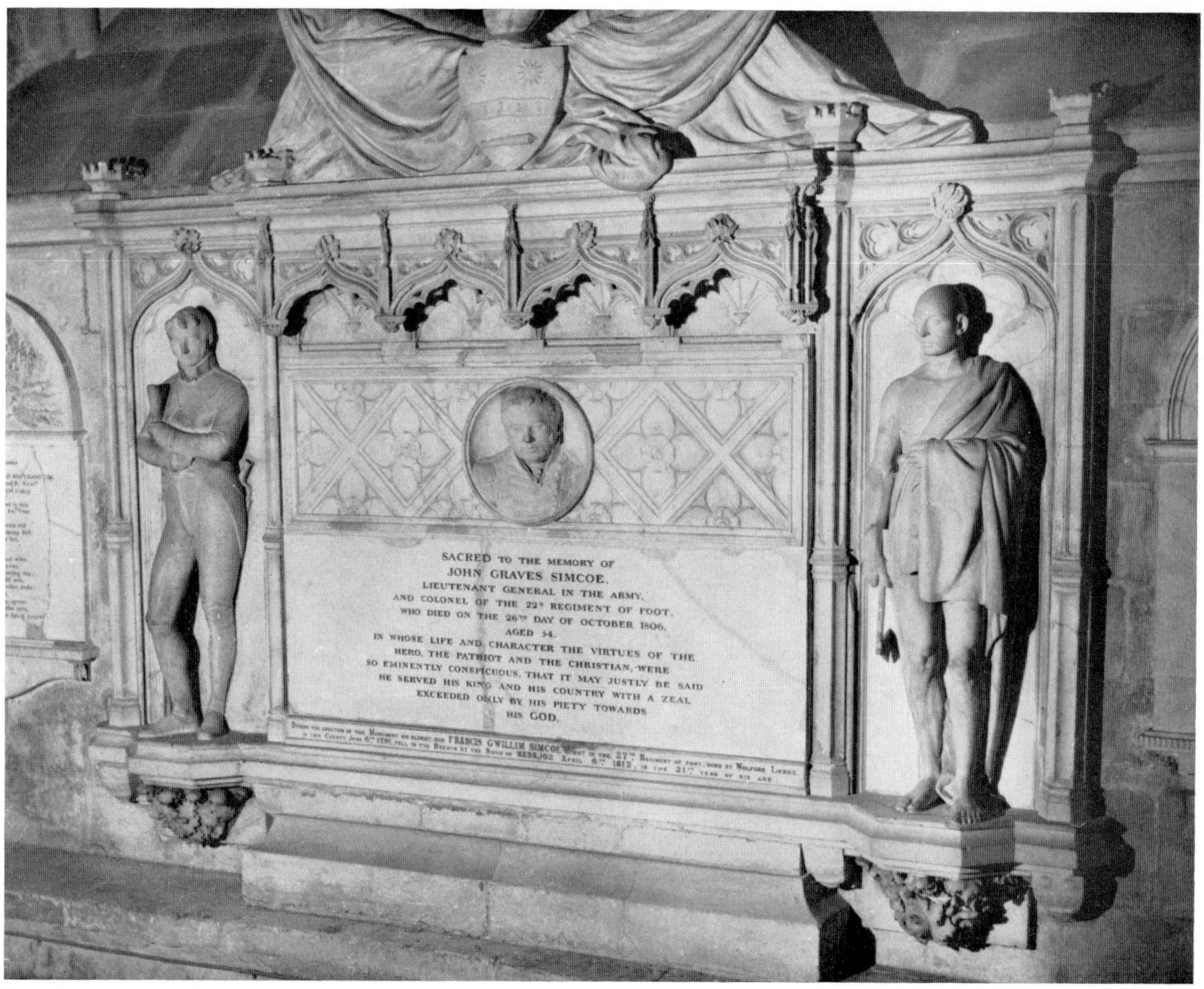


Fig. 135

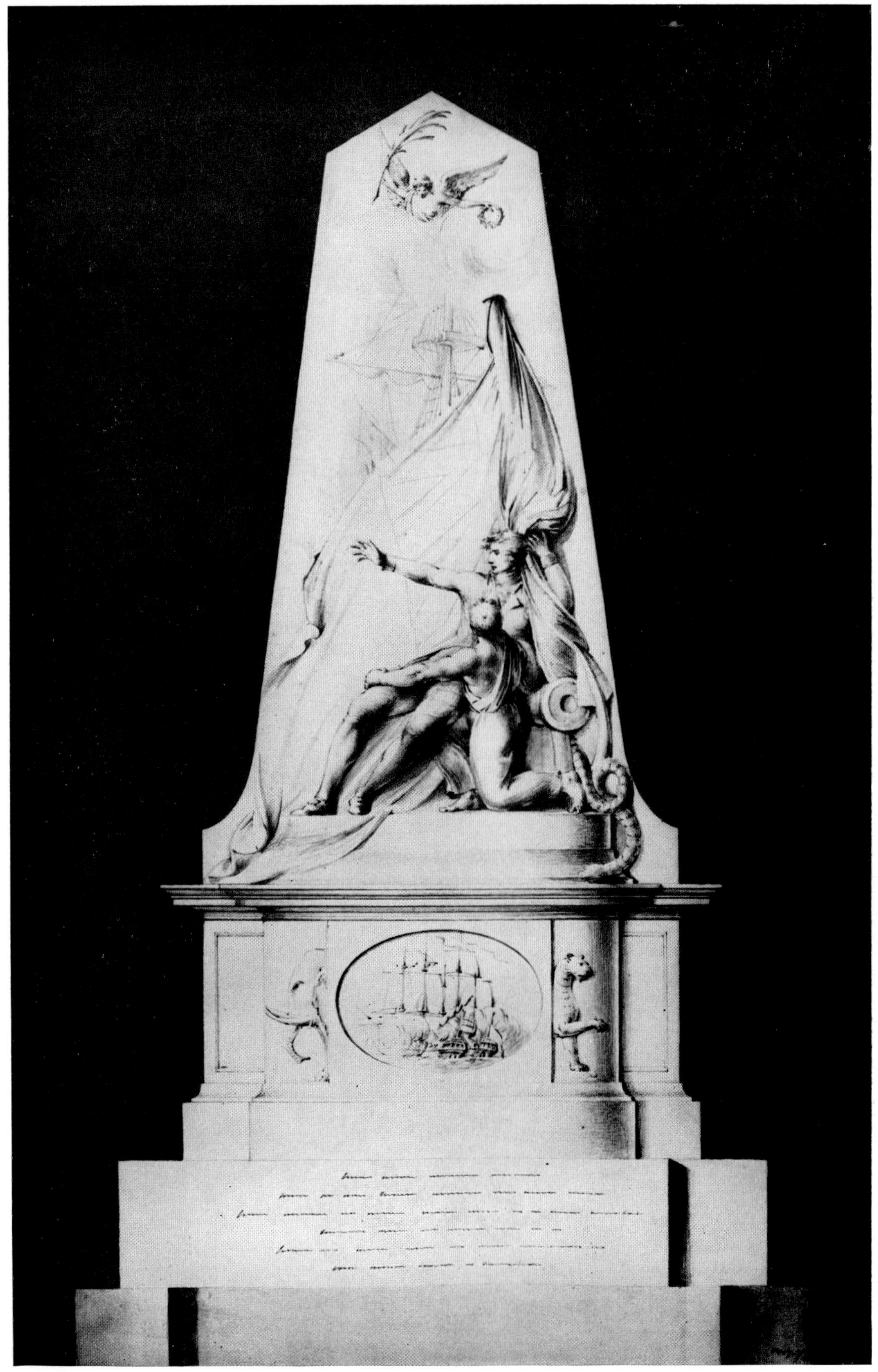



Fig. 136

# JOHN BACON the Younger (*1777–1859*)



*Figure 136 (left):*   Design for the monument to Captain Edward Cooke, R.N. (died 1799), in
Westminster Abbey.
Pen and ink and wash, size of sheet $17\frac{7}{8} \times 11\frac{5}{8}$ inches. No. 8417.7.

*Figure 137 (below):* Monument to Captain Edward Cooke, R.N. (died 1799), in the Chapel of
St. John the Evangelist, Westminster Abbey.
Photograph: *National Monuments Record.*

**136**   This drawing was bought from Mr. R. Jackson, on March 25th, 1879, for 10 shillings.

**137**   The monument is signed and dated *John Bacon junior, Sculptor. 1806.*

"Erected by the Honourable East India Company as a grateful testimony to the Valour and eminent Service of Captain Edward Cooke, Commander of his Majesty's Ship *Sybille*, who, on the 1st of March, 1799, after a long and well-contested Engagement, captured *La Forte*, a French Frigate of a very superior Force, in the Bay of Bengal: an Event not more splendid in its Achievement, than in its Result to the *British* Trade in India.

He died in consequence of the severe Wounds he received in this memorable action, on the 23rd of May, 1799, aged 27."

Bacon used the same design on the monument to Captain Percy Burrell (1779–1807), of the Sixth Regiment, Dragoon Guards, at Cuckfield, Sussex. Burrell, who was killed at Buenos Aires, is shown dying in the arms of a soldier. The drawing is in the Victoria and Albert Museum, Department of Prints and Drawings, E.1562–1931, and the monument is illustrated as fig. 6 of "History in marble" by Rupert Gunnis, *Country Life*, August 25th, 1955.

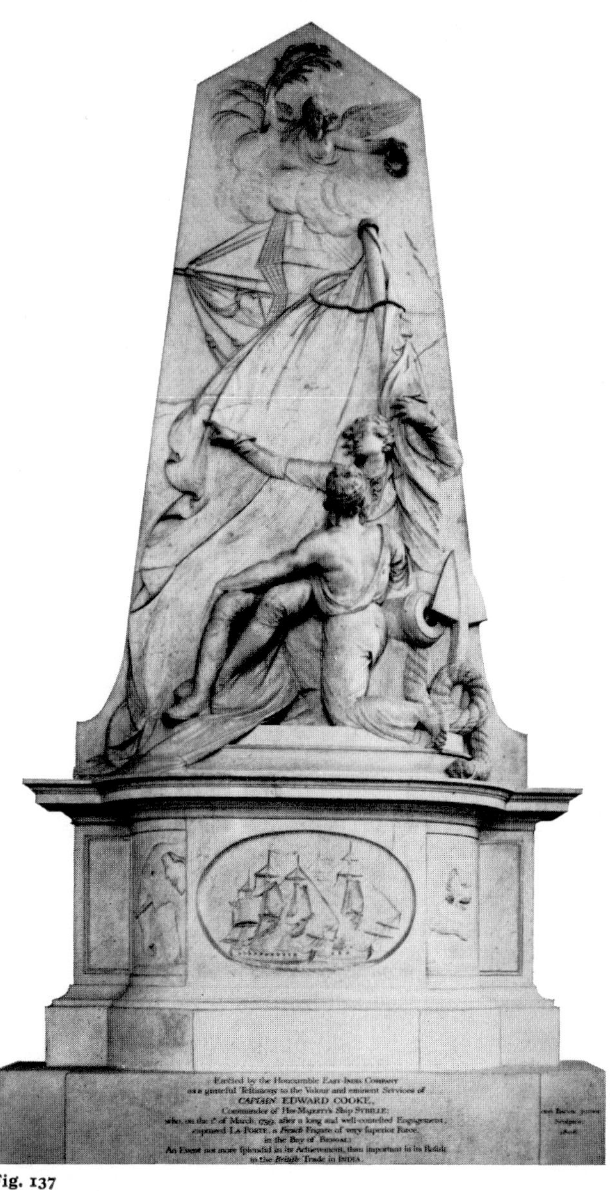

Fig. 137

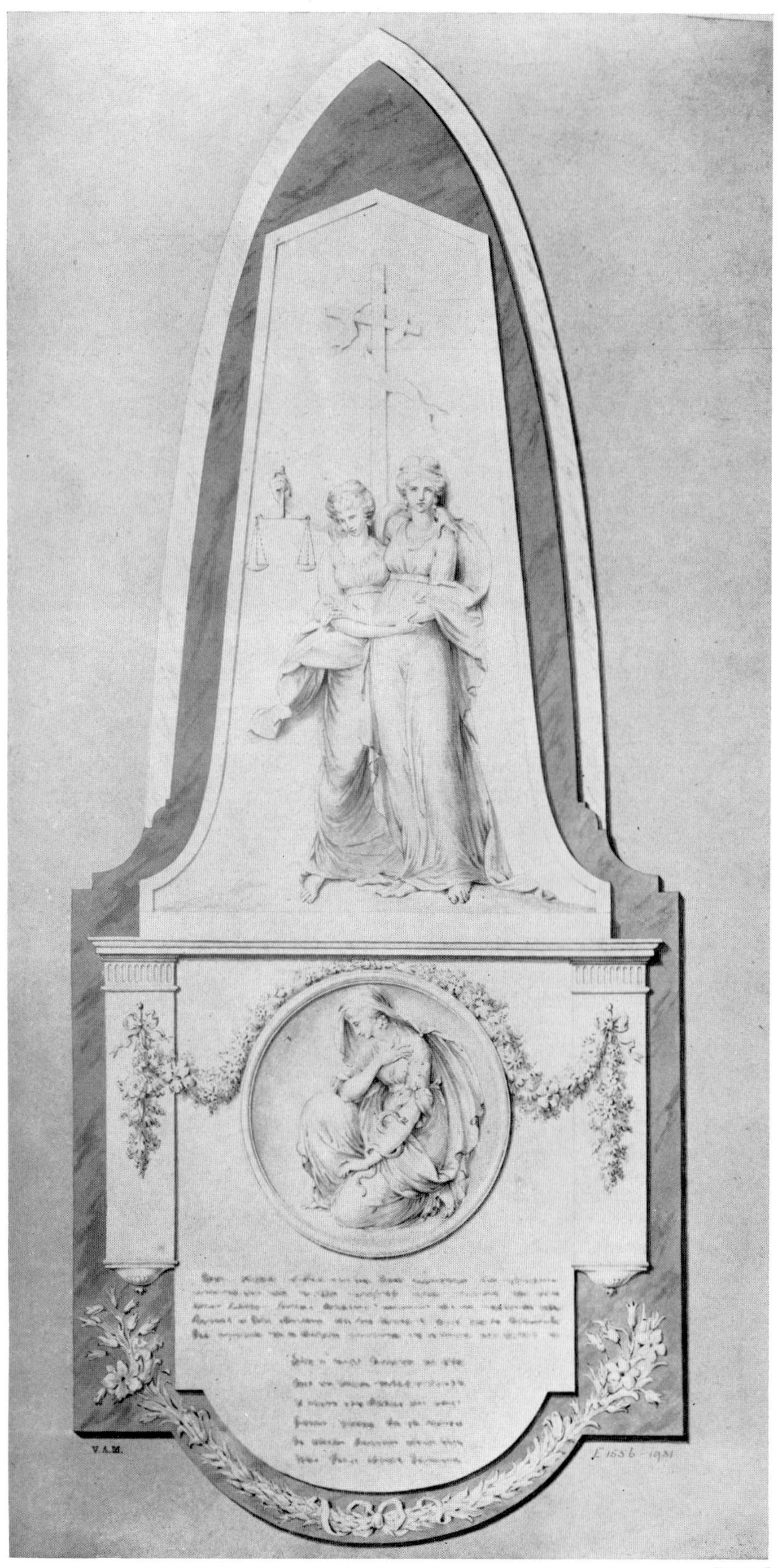



Fig. 138

# JOHN BACON the Younger *(1777–1859)*

*Figure 138 (left)*:    Design for the monument to Anna Rhodes (died 1796), St. James's Church, Hampstead Road, London.
Pen and ink and wash, 18½ × 7⅞ inches. No. E.1556–1931.

*Figure 139 (below)*: Monument to Anna Rhodes (died 1796), St. James's Church, Hampstead Road, London. Signed *J. Bacon jun^r. Sculptor.*
Photograph: *National Monuments Record.*

---

**138**  This drawing was bought from Miss Annie Bacon; see fig. 118.

**139**  The church is now derelict; the monument to Anna Rhodes has been dismantled and is now in the Victoria and Albert Museum, Department of Architecture and Sculpture.

"Erected by a Sister in Memory of her beloved Anna Cecilia Daughter of Christopher Rhodes Esq. of Chatham in the County of Kent. She departed this life June 2nd. 1796 aged 32. Her Remains were deposited in Vault of this Chapel. Distinguished by a fine Understanding and a most amiable Disposition of Heart She was the Delight of her Parents and the Admiration of all who knew her. At the age of 17 the Small-pox stripped off all the Bloom of youthful Beauty And being followed by a dreadful Nervous disorder withered those fair Prospects of earthly Happiness Which were expected from her uncommon Affection Sensibility and Tenderness. After enduring this afflictive Dispensation many years When it was difficult to say which exceeded, her Sufferings or her Submission Her Friends Concern for her Sorrows or their Admiration of her Patience She was released by Death and received into that World where there shall be no more Pain But God himself shall wipe away tears from every Eye."

This is followed by four lines of verse *Alas! how vain are feeble words to tell . . . And thro' the Gloom we see the Glory shine.*

There were two monuments by John Bacon the Younger to Anna Rhodes. That in St. James's Church, Hampstead Road, was erected by her sister. Her mother commissioned another for Whitfield's Tabernacle (destroyed during the Second World War) in Tottenham Court Road, London. A record drawing of the latter monument, made in the sculptor's studio, is now in the Victoria and Albert Museum, Department of Prints and Drawings, E.1050–1966, given by Mr. John Mallet.

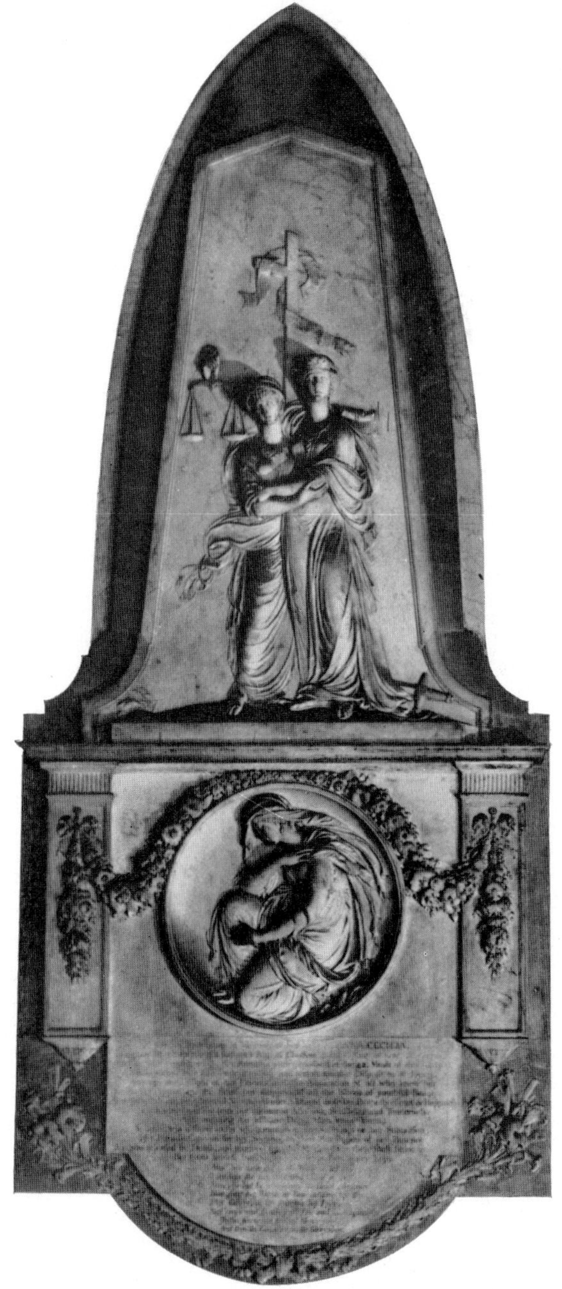

Fig. 139

*Figure 140* (*below*): Designs for decorative plaques, made while Gibson was apprenticed to Messrs.
S. & T. Franceys, of Liverpool, in 1810.
Inscribed in pencil with prices.
Pen and ink and wash, size of sheet 8 × 12¼ inches. No. D.1333–1898.

---

**140**   This drawing was one of 58 life drawings, studies after the antique, and designs for monuments, by John Gibson, bought from Mr. R. Jackson, on May 20th, 1898, for £5. 5. 0d.

Inscribed in ink on the lower part of the sheet:
"Sir We have sent you two Sketches of Comedy & Tragedy, which will cost Thirty Guineas each in Stone, as it will be the cheapest way to execute them, the head will be Twenty Guineas in Stone, if Trophys according to the Sketch you sent, we can do them for Twelve Guineas each—Packing cases to be ret. back or charged—The Sketches are Two Guineas if you keep them.

> We are
> Sir
> Your ob^t. Serv^ts.
>   S. & T. Franceys"

10th May 1810

As the designs for monuments are also early works made while Gibson was still with the Franceys, it is unlikely that, if executed, they were signed with his name; so far none has been located.

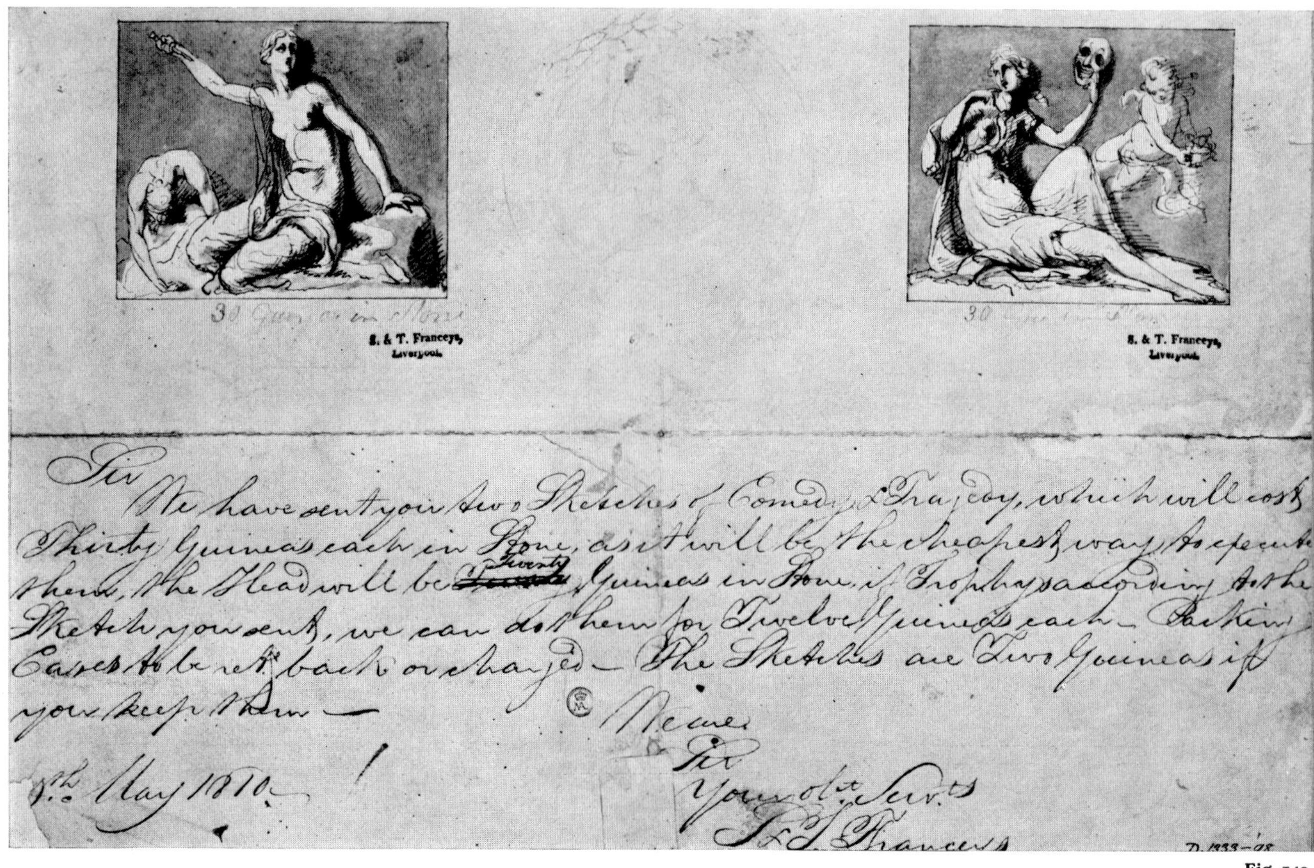


**Fig. 140**

# LEONARD WILLIAM COLLMANN (*1816–1881*)

*Figure 141 (p.182):* Design for a monument to Admiral Lord Nelson, in Trafalgar Square, London: c. 1839.
Pen and ink and water-colour, $21\frac{1}{2} \times 29\frac{3}{4}$ inches. No. 8595s.

---

**141**   This drawing was formerly in the collection of Alfred Stevens, and was one of 174 drawings and prints bought at his sale on October 27th, 1879, for £90. 15. 6d.

"Are we ever to execute any description of public monument without an exhibition of meanness, or jobbery, or incompetency?" So asked the *Art-Union* when commenting on the Nelson Monument in Trafalgar Square, and so it continued to ask on other occasions for nearly fifty years.

The proposal of a national memorial to Nelson, and also to commemorate the battle of Trafalgar, had first been put forward in about 1818, but not until 1838 was a committee formed to collect public subscriptions, and in that year a competition was held for the committee to choose a design for the monument. One hundred and fifty sculptors submitted their schemes, including William Railton, E. H. Baily, W. Woodington, William Pitts, E. G. Papworth, and George Rennie.

The first prize was given to Railton for his design, no description of which was necessary, some said, as it was only a Corinthian column. "Mortifying and dis-heartening must it be to those artists who have transmitted to the committee the results of much reflection and industry, to find their works passed carelessly by," was another comment.

Baily who received the second prize submitted a design of a figure of Nelson standing on a rock at the foot of an obelisk, and surrounded by a mythological group. George Rennie, on the other hand, put forward the suggestion that Cleopatra's Needle should be brought from Egypt. However, all the models and drawings were returned to the various artists to be revised or altered, and sent in again, if they still wished, for a new competition. This was held during the middle of 1839, and among those who entered on this occasion were Baily, Railton, Woodington, Benedetto Pistrucci, J. G. Lough, and Peter Hollins who took a leaf out of Flaxman's book and suggested a 120 feet high statue of Britannia (see fig. 129).

The *Art-Union* had, from the beginning, set itself right against Railton's column, and said that after the amount of criticism surrounding the committee's choice in the first competition, it hardly seemed likely that Railton's design would be chosen a second time—but it was. However, the money from the public was not flowing in as quickly as had been hoped, and in July, 1839, it was reported that although the fund stood at only £17,000, the site had been enclosed, and the committee intended to go ahead with the erection of the column, and with the statue of Nelson, which had been given to Baily to do. The bas-reliefs, and the four lions at the base, which J. G. Lough was to make, would not be proceeded with at that time due to the shortage of money.

By February, 1843, the column had reached its full height, and work was in hand with the casting in bronze of the foliage of the Corinthian capital. Baily finished the figure later in the year, and it was raised into position on November 3rd, 1843; critics were confounded when the whole affair did not crash to the ground.

Surrounded by a wooden fence the column stood for-lornly for a number of years. The Government asked another sculptor, a minor figure, Thomas Milnes, to prepare four lions representing Peace, War, Vigilance and Fidelity. They could not have been satisfactory as they were returned to Milnes (and are now at Saltaire, near Shipley, Yorkshire) and in the middle of 1858 authority announced that these lions were to be entrusted to the animal painter, Sir Edwin Landseer.

This announcement brought protests from sculptors, of course; "Shall we," said *The Athenaeum*, "never live to see the end of the bungling in completion of hastily-planned and half-done deeds?"

Landseer agreed to model the lions, and nothing more was heard until the mid-1860s, when Baron Maro-chetti undertook to cast the huge animals. This had been achieved by January, 1867, and the lions were unveiled to the critical public at the end of that month. Marochetti then asked for £11,000 for his work, and this led to the inevitable wrangle as to why he had been entrusted with the casting (which was not considered well done) when at least one English firm had been prepared to do it for only £6,000. Even Landseer did not escape the general censure—why had he taken so long to produce one lion (to be cast four times)? It was stated that no artist "was justified in treating a great public commission as second in importance to his private orders" nor was he "justified in unconditionally accepting such commission if he intends to allow himself to be fully employed with his usual business".

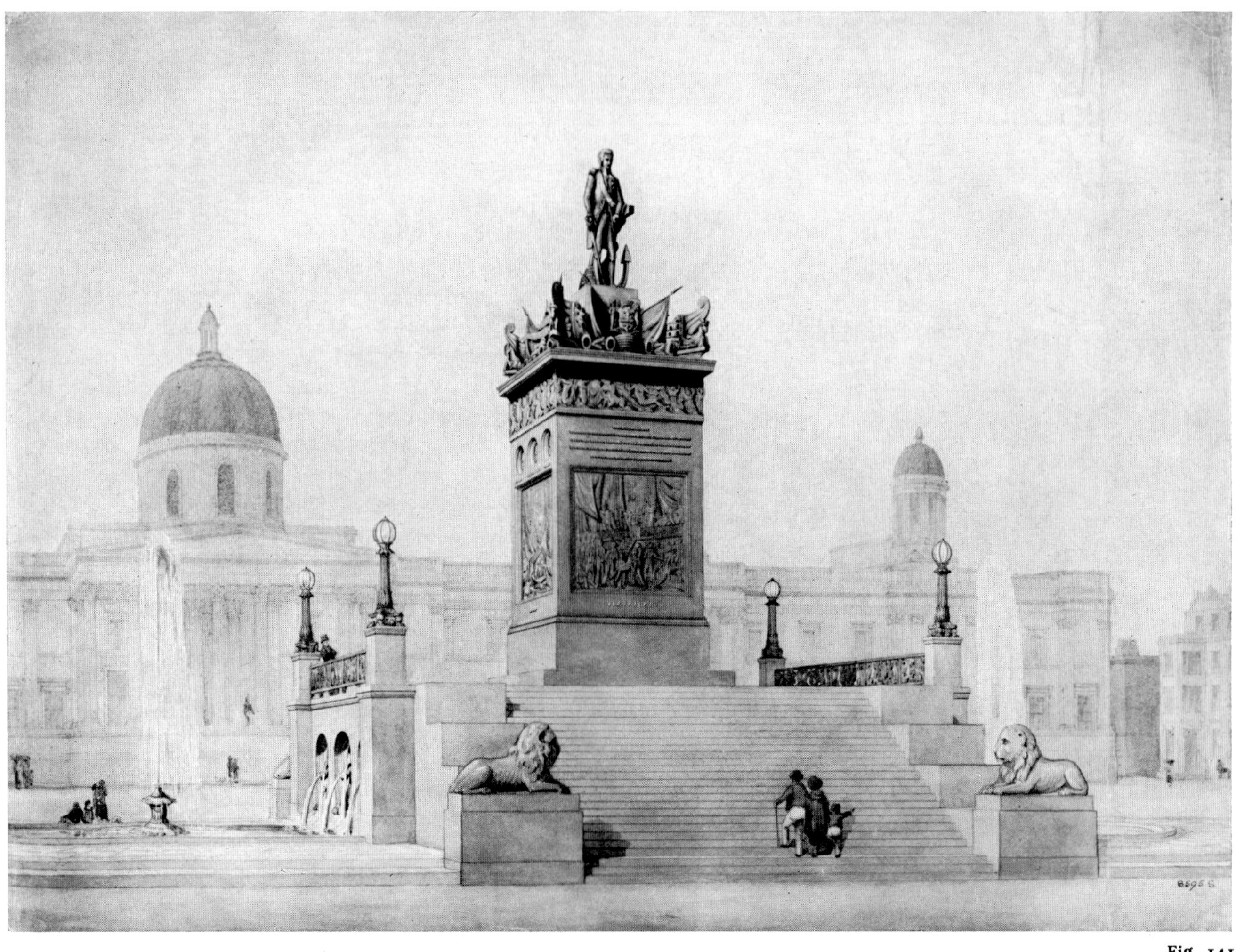



Fig. 141

# JAMES WYATT the Younger *(1808–1893)*

*Figure 142 (p.184):* The equestrian statue of the Duke of Wellington, designed by Matthew Cotes
Wyatt, for the Arch at Constitution Hill, London.
Pen and ink and wash, $18\frac{7}{8} \times 14$ inches. No. E.1896(146)–1948.

*Figure 143 (p.185):* The equestrian statue of the Duke of Wellington by Matthew Cotes Wyatt
and James Wyatt the Younger in its present position at Caesar's Camp, Aldershot, Hampshire.
Photograph: *Author.*

---

**142**   The drawing, with others by members of the
Wyatt family, was purchased from Miss Emily
P. Wyatt.

**143**   The idea of a statue to the Duke of Wellington
was suggested by the Court of Common Council, and
a committee which was formed reported in 1838 that
a sum of £14,000 had been raised for the Wellington
Military Memorial to be erected in western London.
A suitable site for this, it was suggested, would be on
the triumphal arch designed by Decimus Burton at
Hyde Park Corner. Queen Victoria gave her permission, and the Committee resolved, to the mis-
givings of the art world, that Matthew Cotes Wyatt
(1777–1862) was "eminently qualified to be entrusted
with the execution of the proposed statue". Wyatt,
assisted by his son James, worked on the project from
1838 until 1846.

Early in 1839 a wooden model was placed on top of
the arch, and led immediately to a storm of protest;
the *Art-Union* felt that the Duke of Wellington's own
feelings ought not to be forgotten for "immediately
before the hind windows of his residence stands the
statue of Achilles, erected to Arthur Wellington and
his brave companions in arms, by their countrywomen,
to the occasional embarrassment of the Duke when
visited by distinguished foreigners; and now, in order
that they may have no means of escape by turning to
the windows next Piccadilly . . . they would place
there a second statue to stare him and his guests out
of countenance".

However, after years of indecision the Government
agreed to try the completed group on the arch during
the summer of 1846. An immense carriage was made
by the army at Woolwich, and at the end of September the huge statue[1] was escorted by the military, with
bands, from Wyatt's studio in the Harrow Road down
to Hyde Park Corner, where it was winched into
position.

In spite of criticism which continued, and the Government's subsequent decision, made within a few
weeks, that the statue must come down again, it
stayed in position until 1883 when Hyde Park Corner
was laid out differently, which necessitated demolishing
Burton's arch and rebuilding it lower down Constitution
Hill. The statue was then taken by the army and
placed in its present site on a small mound near the
Garrison Church at Aldershot (John Physick, "The
Banishment of the Bronze Duke", *Country Life*, October,
1966).

---

[1] Nearly 30 feet high and, according to the *Illustrated London
News* (11 July 1846), at least eight people had been able to
dine inside the horse's body.

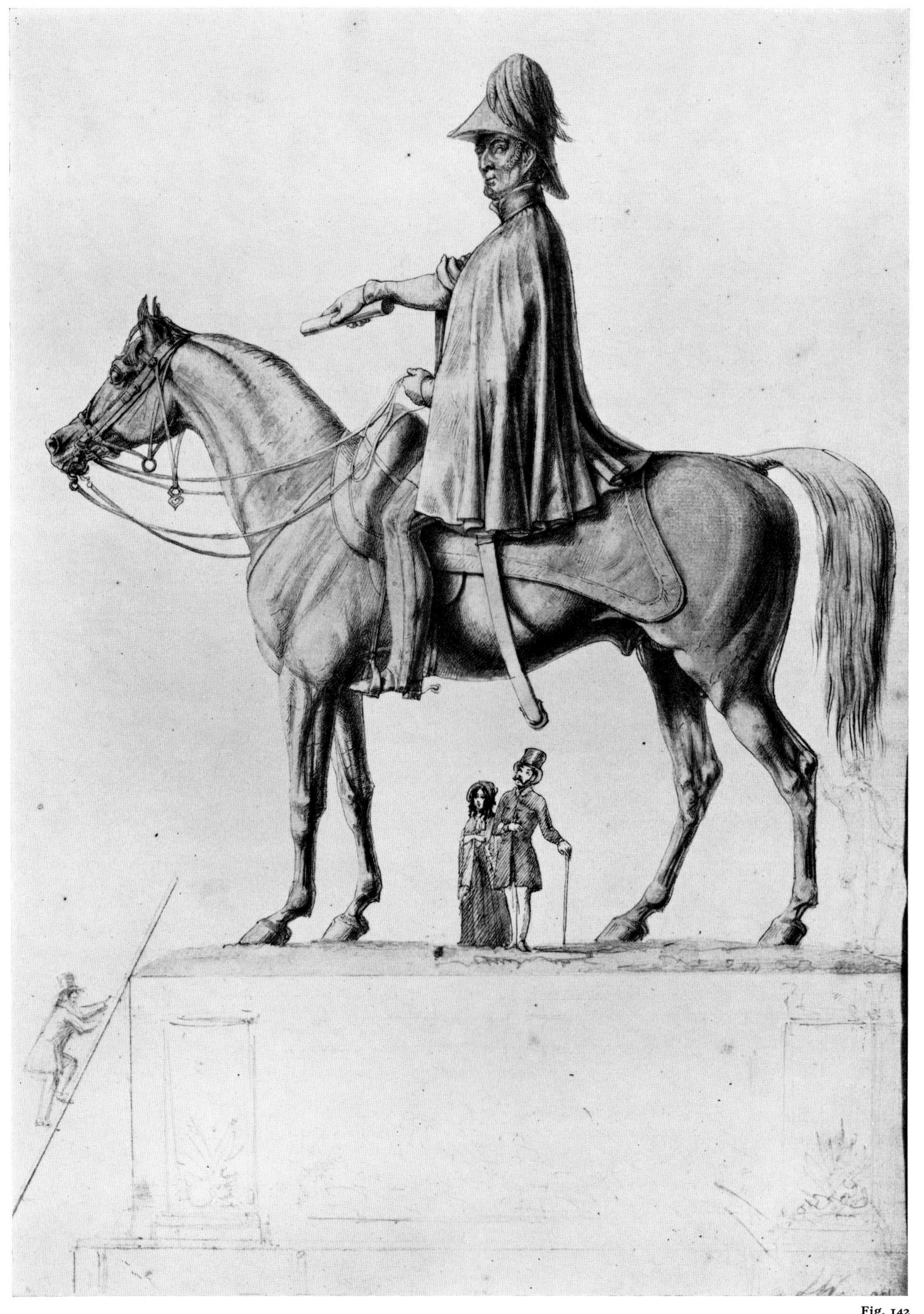

Fig. 142    Fig. 143

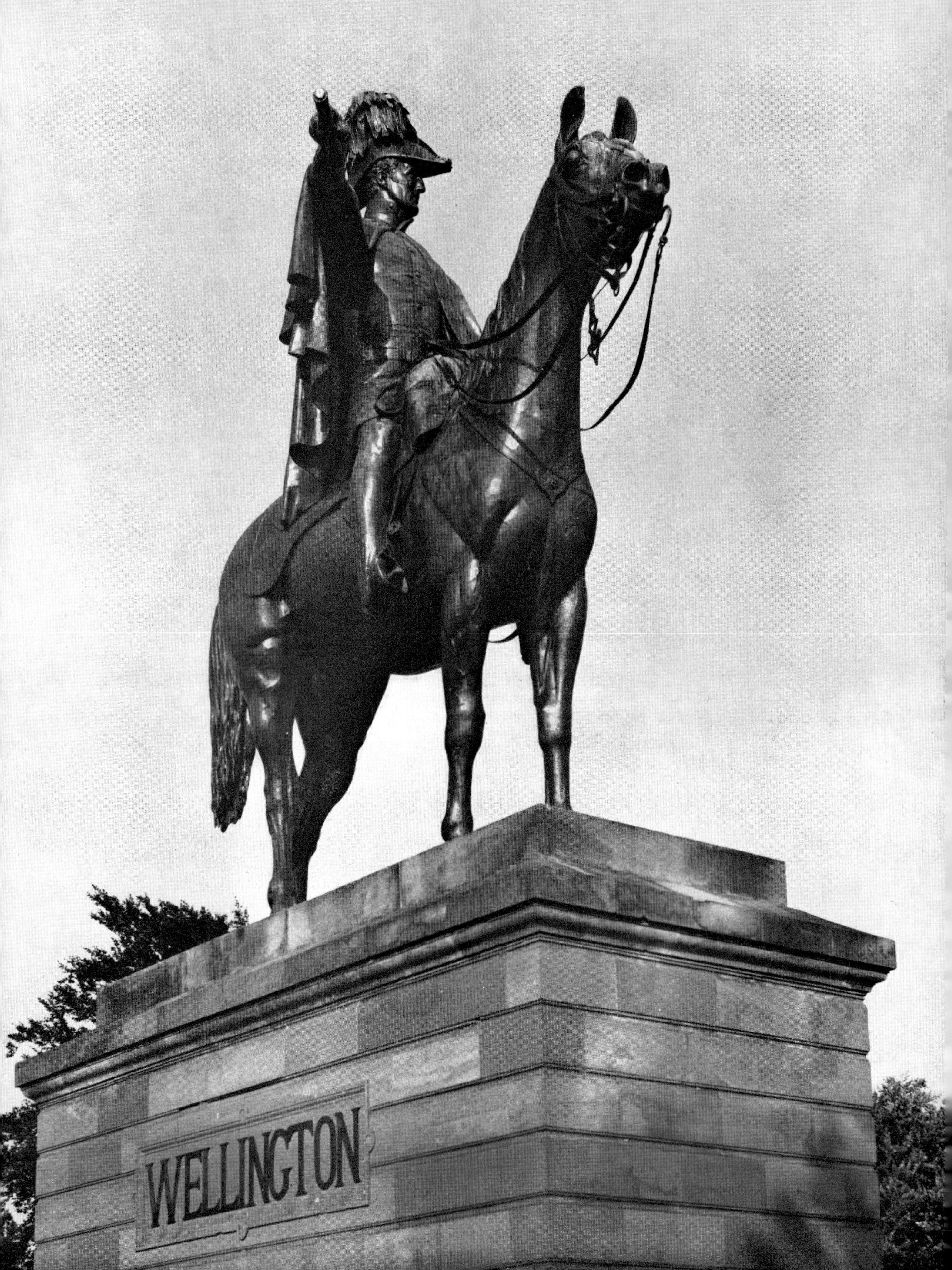
WELLINGTON

# ALFRED STEVENS (*1817–1875*)

*Figure 144* (*right*): Design for the monument to the Duke of Wellington in St. Paul's Cathedral, on the special lithographed sheet supplied for the competition in 1856.
Pen and ink, 18¾ × 25⅝ inches. No. 1119–1884.

*Figure 145* (*p.188*): The quarter-size competition model of the monument, now in the Department of Architecture and Sculpture.
Plaster and wax. 9 feet 9 inches × 3 feet 2½ inches. No. 44–1878.
Given by the Office of Works.

*Figure 146* (*p.189*): Monument to the Duke of Wellington, in St. Paul's Cathedral.
Photograph: *Royal Commission on Historical Monuments (England)*.

---

**144** This drawing was purchased in 1884 for £5. 5s.

**146** The conditions of the competition for the monument to the Duke of Wellington were announced in September 1856, and competitors had to submit a quarter-size model of their proposal by June 1st, 1857. This limitation on scale was strictly applied—John Gibson, R.A., for one, had his model rejected by the judges as it was a fraction too large. Eighty-three of these models from Europe and America were publicly exhibited in Westminster Hall during July and August, 1857. Stevens's design was placed only sixth, for which he received a premium of £100. Little more was heard for about a year, except fears that Baron Marochetti was going to execute the monument, but at last the Government announced, in spite of protests, that none of the first five premium winners had been awarded the commission: it had gone unexpectedly to Alfred Stevens, then almost unknown; and that instead of the original sum allowed of £20,000, he would have to make do with only £14,000; a most unfortunate condition to which Stevens agreed was that out of this sum he should prepare a full-size model to be placed in St. Paul's Cathedral. The reason for this appears to have been due to the fact that the announced site in the nave had been changed, and the new position was to be in the south-west chapel; the model was to be used to judge the effect of the monument in its new surroundings.

For the next few years Stevens prepared this model, but he also continued to do other work at the same time, so that the monument progressed very slowly. There was difficulty with the Dean of St. Paul's who said that he did not want a horse in the Cathedral, and refused to consider the equestrian figure of the Duke which Stevens had intended to surmount the whole structure. By 1870 the First Commissioner of Works,

after correspondence which had become progressively colder, was aghast to learn that nearly all the money had been spent, and that there was very little to show for it except a plaster model. The Commissioner, Acton Ayrton, decided therefore that Stevens was not competent to undertake such a major work, and terminated his contract. He then insisted that all the drawings, models, and such work as had been completed should be surrendered to the Government, and Stevens was threatened with legal proceedings.

Although he was championed throughout by F. C. Penrose, the architect to St. Paul's, Stevens had to give in, as the First Commissioner was firmly of the opinion that another sculptor must be found. For a while Steven's studio was sealed, and the work on the monument came to a complete standstill.

By 1871, however, certain members of the Government came to realise what a ridiculous situation had been created, as much as anything through the active dislike of Stevens by the First Commissioner of Works. The latter was still determined that a different sculptor had to be found, and proposed another competition for this purpose. In this action he was directly in opposition to the Treasury, which was sure that no other sculptor would be willing to finish a work designed and partially executed by another, and wanted Ayrton to seek competent advice before he took any further steps. This Ayrton was reluctant to do, so the Chancellor of the Exchequer finding that the "First Commissioner was averse from adopting the course suggested by the Treasury" went over Ayrton's head and asked James Fergusson if he could find a reasonable solution. Fergusson decided that Stevens should carry on with the monument, but that all the necessary financial and other business transactions should be in the hands of Leonard William Collman, who was a friend of the sculptor.

This was thought to be a very agreeable way to
end an extremely awkward situation, and assisted by
Reuben Townroe, James Gamble and Hugh Stannus,
Stevens returned to work. He died in 1875, three years
before the unveiling of the monument in St. Paul's on
April 20th, 1878, without its crowning horse and rider.

By the middle of the 1890s, due to the energy of the
President of the Royal Academy, Lord Leighton, the
monument had been moved to its present position in
the nave, which was almost that for which it had been
designed. In conditions of secrecy which caused heated
argument and bitterness when the news leaked out, a
small group of people at the suggestion of Dugald
MacColl, Keeper of the Tate Gallery, asked a young
pupil of Rodin, John Tweed, to complete the horse
and rider from Stevens's original plaster model, which
had been stored in the Cathedral crypt; and so, at
long last, at the beginning of 1912, the monument was
seen for the first time as Stevens had intended.

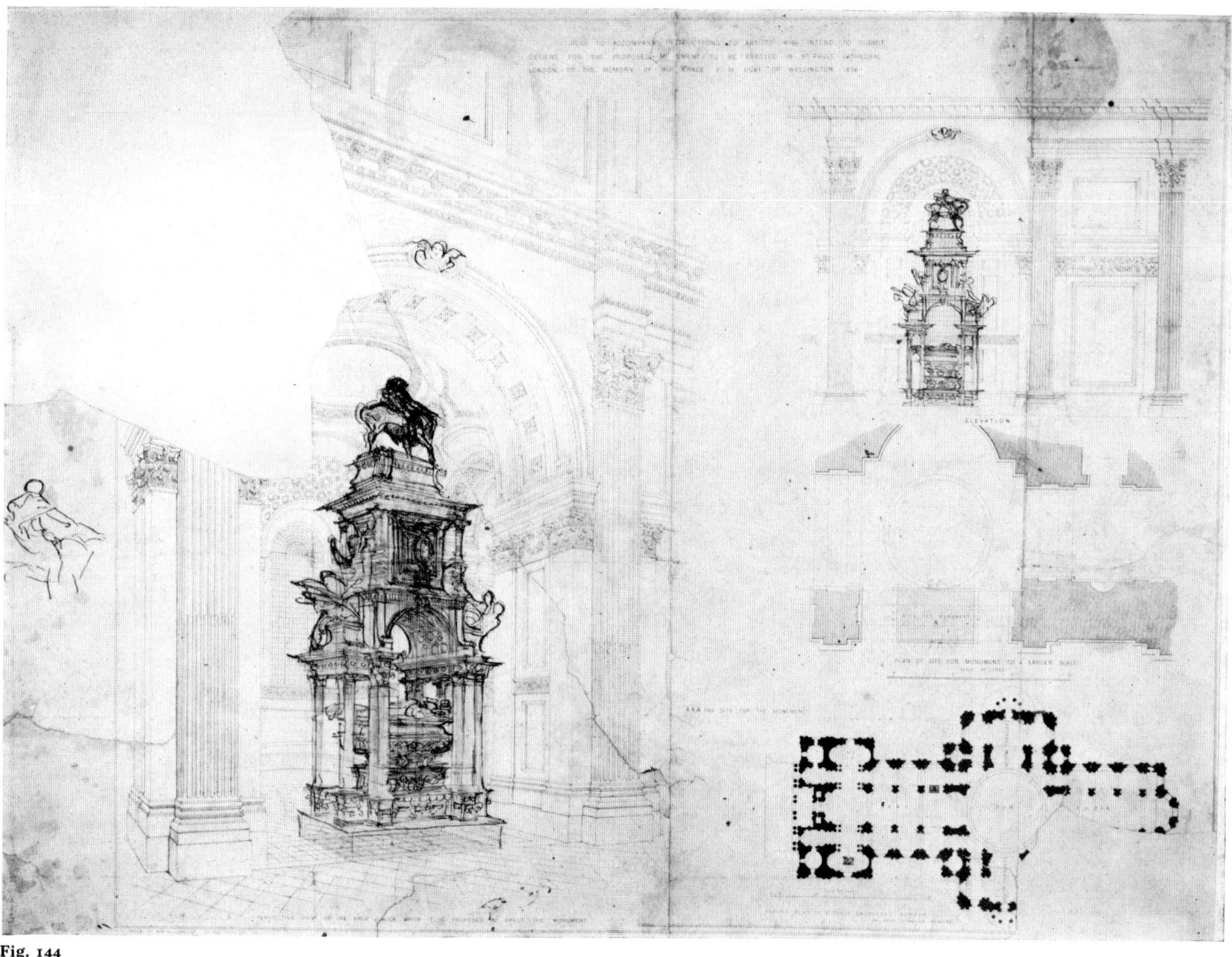

Fig. 144

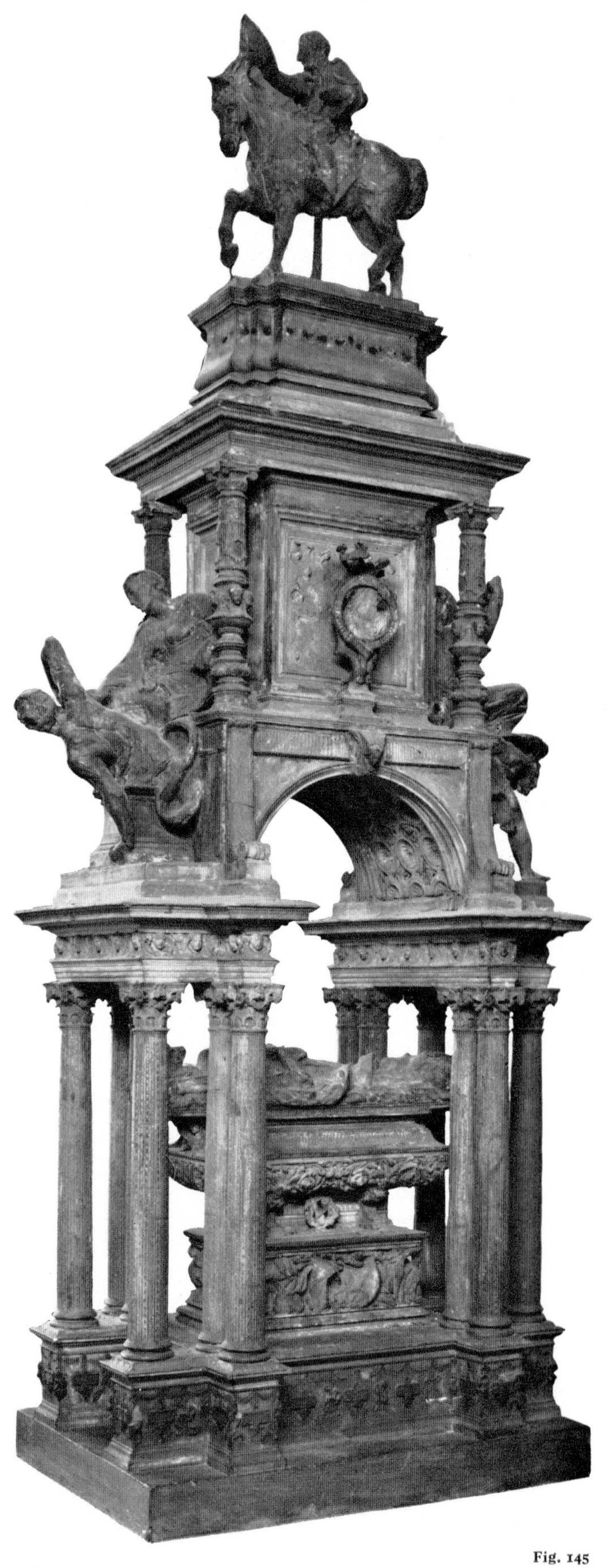



Fig. 145

Fig. 146 ▶

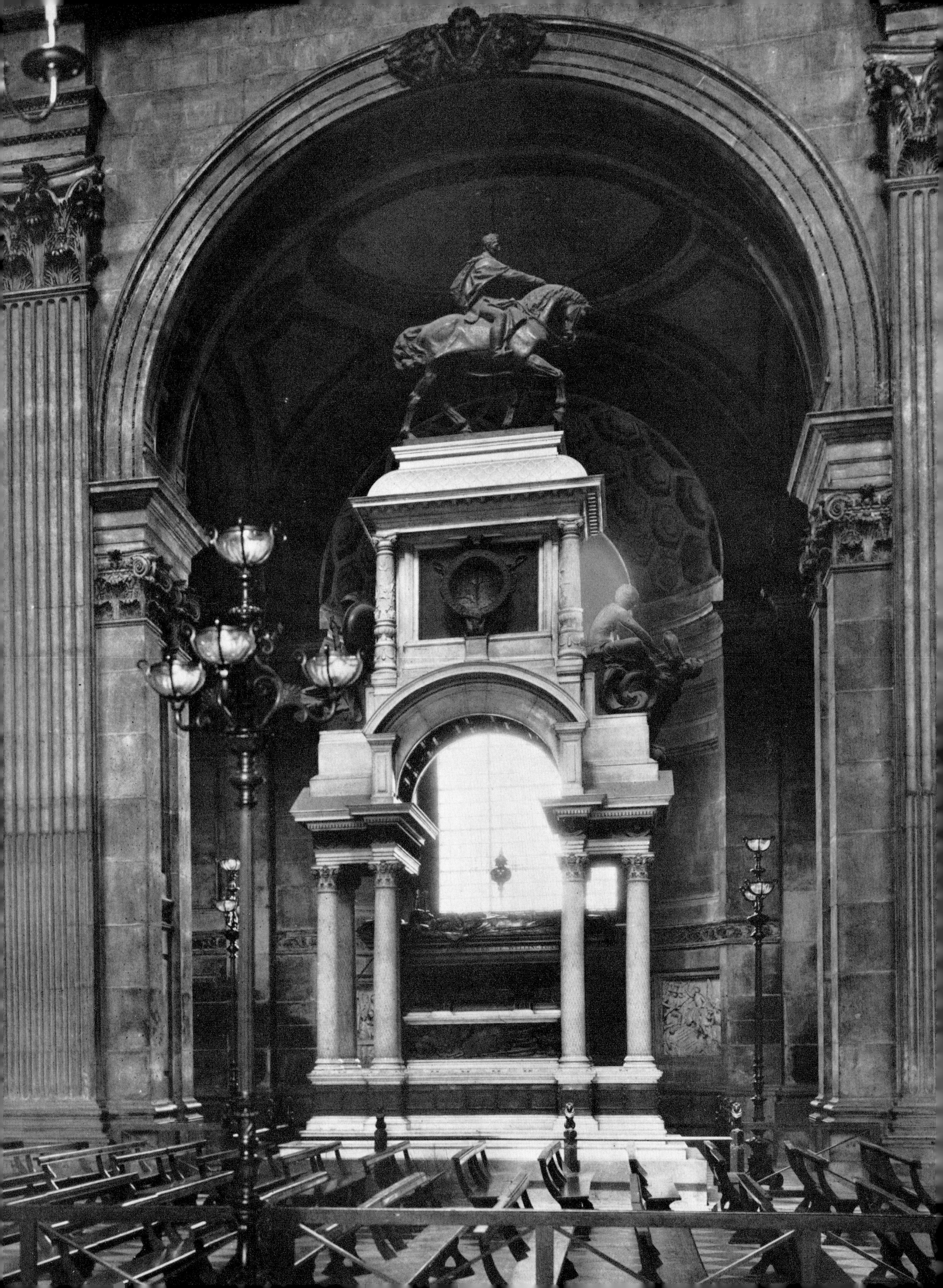

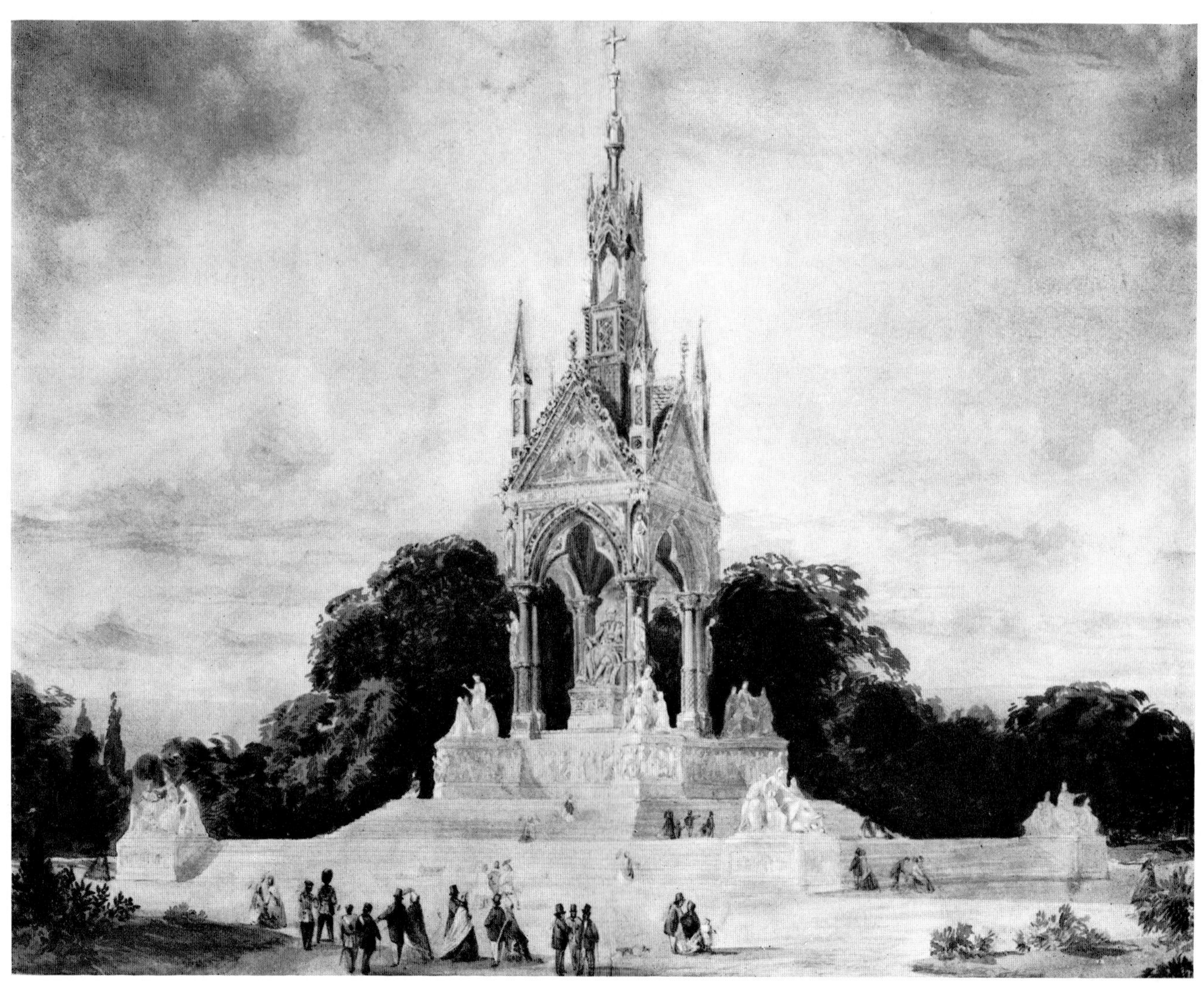

Fig. 147

# SIR GEORGE GILBERT SCOTT, R.A. *(1811–1878)*

*Figure 147 (left):*      Design for the memorial to Prince Albert in Kensington Gardens, London: 1863. Water- and body-colour, $14\frac{1}{8} \times 10\frac{1}{8}$ inches. No. E.2601–1962.

*Figure 148a (p.192):* The Albert Memorial in Kensington Gardens, London
Photograph: *National Monuments Record.*

*Figure 148b (p.193):* 'Asia', sculptured group by J. H. Foley, R.A.
Photograph: *National Monument Record.*

---

**147** This drawing was purchased in 1962 for £50. The face of the statue of the Prince Consort is a photograph which has been cut and stuck to the main sheet.

This water-colour, made before the addition of another storey to the spire, shows details in the design of the canopy, and of the statue of the Prince, which differ from those of the completed monument. Another drawing of the same design was reproduced on pages 48, 49 of the *Illustrated London News*, July, 1863.

Scott, who was knighted as a reward for designing the Albert Memorial, had a large plaster model made so that Queen Victoria could see it in three-dimensions. This model of coloured and polished plaster, with sculptured decoration by Henry Armstead, was the work of Messrs. Farmer and Brindley, of the Westminster Bridge Road, London. It was sent to the Paris Exhibition of 1867 and, on its return, exhibited at the South Kensington Museum.

**148** Prince Albert died on December 14th, 1861, and on January 14th, 1862, a public meeting, called by the Lord Mayor of London, William Cubitt, was held at the Mansion House "to consider the propriety of inviting contributions for the purpose of erecting a lasting memorial to his Royal Highness the Prince Consort, and to adopt such measures for carrying out the object as may then be decided". Subscriptions soon amounted to £35,000, and Cubitt informed Queen Victoria of the proposals and said that the nature and design of the monument would be entirely the Queen's own choice.

Queen Victoria asked the Earl of Derby, the Earl of Clarendon, Sir Charles Eastlake, P.R.A., and the Lord Mayor of London to form a committee to help her. The first proposal they considered was that of the Queen's, who wanted a tall obelisk surrounded by decorative sculpture. This was abandoned due partly to the inability to find a block of stone of sufficient size, so the Committee asked a group of architects— Sir William Tite, R.A., Sydney Smirke, R.A., G. G. Scott, R.A., Sir James Pennethorne, T. L. Donaldson, P. C. Hardwick and Sir Matthew Digby Wyatt to consider schemes and draw up a report. The recommendation of the architects was that there should be a personal memorial to Prince Albert in Kensington Gardens, at the end of Rotten Row, and on the other side of the road to Kensington there should be a memorial hall, built on the land owned by the 1851 Commissioners. The next step was that these architects should be asked to submit designs; those who did so were Scott, Pennethorne, Donaldson, Hardwick and Wyatt, and in addition C. and E. M. Barry were asked as well. The choice of the Queen, and that of the Committee, was the design by Scott, who had prudently adopted "the style of the most touching monuments ever erected in this country to a Royal Consort"—the Eleanor Crosses. Scott's design was costed, and it was found that it was nearly double the estimate, so the memorial hall was abandoned (it was subsequently built, however, due to the exertions of Sir Henry Cole), and in April 1863 Palmerston obtained a grant of £50,000 for Queen Victoria. Thus, by 1866, with public subscriptions, the money available was almost £100,000.

The original committee's function being now achieved, Queen Victoria appointed Trustees—Viscount Torrington, Sir Charles Phipps, K.C.B., Sir Alexander Spearman and William Cubitt, M.P., and also an executive committee consisting of the Hon. Charles Grey, Sir Charles Phipps, Sir Charles Eastlake, Sir Alexander Spearman, Sir Thomas Biddulph, and Doune C. Bell as secretary.

John Kelk offered to undertake the whole of the construction of the monument at only cost price, his accounts to be available for the inspection of the executive committee, who very gratefully accepted his

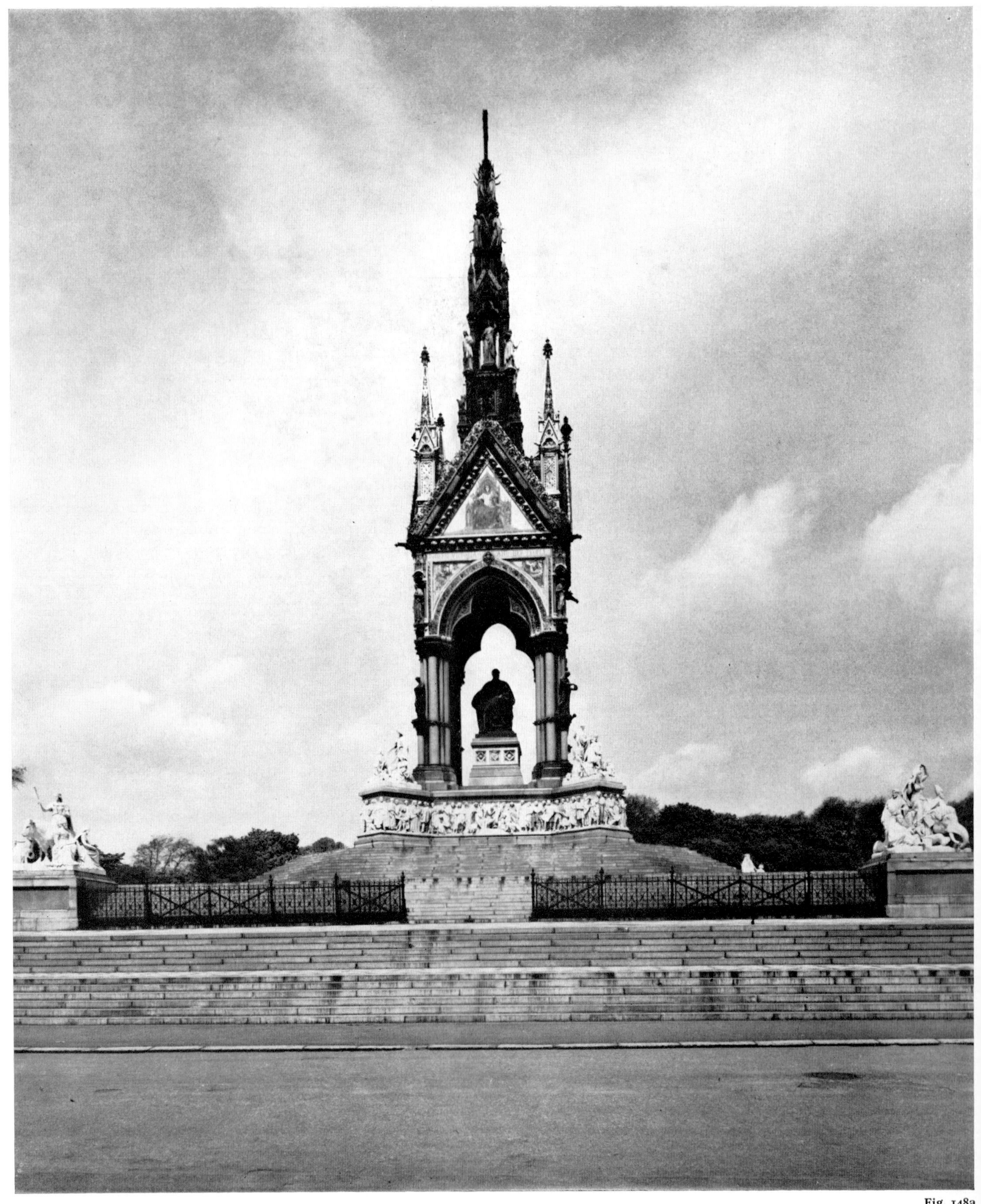

Fig. 148a

offer. Kelk was likened in contemporary publications to "the master-builder of Pharaoh".

Scott's design called for a colossal, seated figure of the Prince placed, as he wrote, "beneath a vast and magnificent shrine or tabernacle, and surrounded by works of sculpture illustrating those arts and sciences which he fostered". The glass-mosaic decoration was made by Salviati & Co., from designs by Clayton & Bell, and the sculpture which was closely to follow Scott's design was given to H. H. Armstead, J. B. Philip, J. Redfern, P. MacDowell, J. H. Foley, William Theed, John Bell, W. Calder Marshall, Henry Weekes, Thomas Thornycroft and John Lawlor. The architecture was under the superintendence of Scott, while the construction of the metalwork of the canopy, tower and spire, details such as the angels, were entrusted to the firm of F. A. Skidmore of Coventry, from whose establishment had come the choir-screens of Lichfield and Hereford Cathedrals. The monument would be the best that the artists of the period could produce.

The seated figure of Prince Albert was to be the work of the unpopular Baron Marochetti, who produced a large model which was placed in position in 1867. It would not do, so Marochetti had a second try, but he died before it was completed. At the request of Queen Victoria this model was inspected by Earl Stanhope, Henry Layard and C. T. Newton, who came to the conclusion that like Marochetti's first attempt, this also was not worthy. In May 1868, therefore, the commission was given to J. H. Foley, who in 1870 saw his model hoisted into position. It too must have been criticised, because it was taken down and not until 1874 was casting begun. In that year, however, Foley died, and it was decided that the remainder of the casting should be carried out by Prince and Co. of Southwark, under the supervision of G. F. Teniswood, F.S.A., Foley's executor. By the end of 1875 the ten-ton figure was finished and was in position when Queen Victoria in 1876 surveyed the whole creation of High Victorian architecture and sculpture.

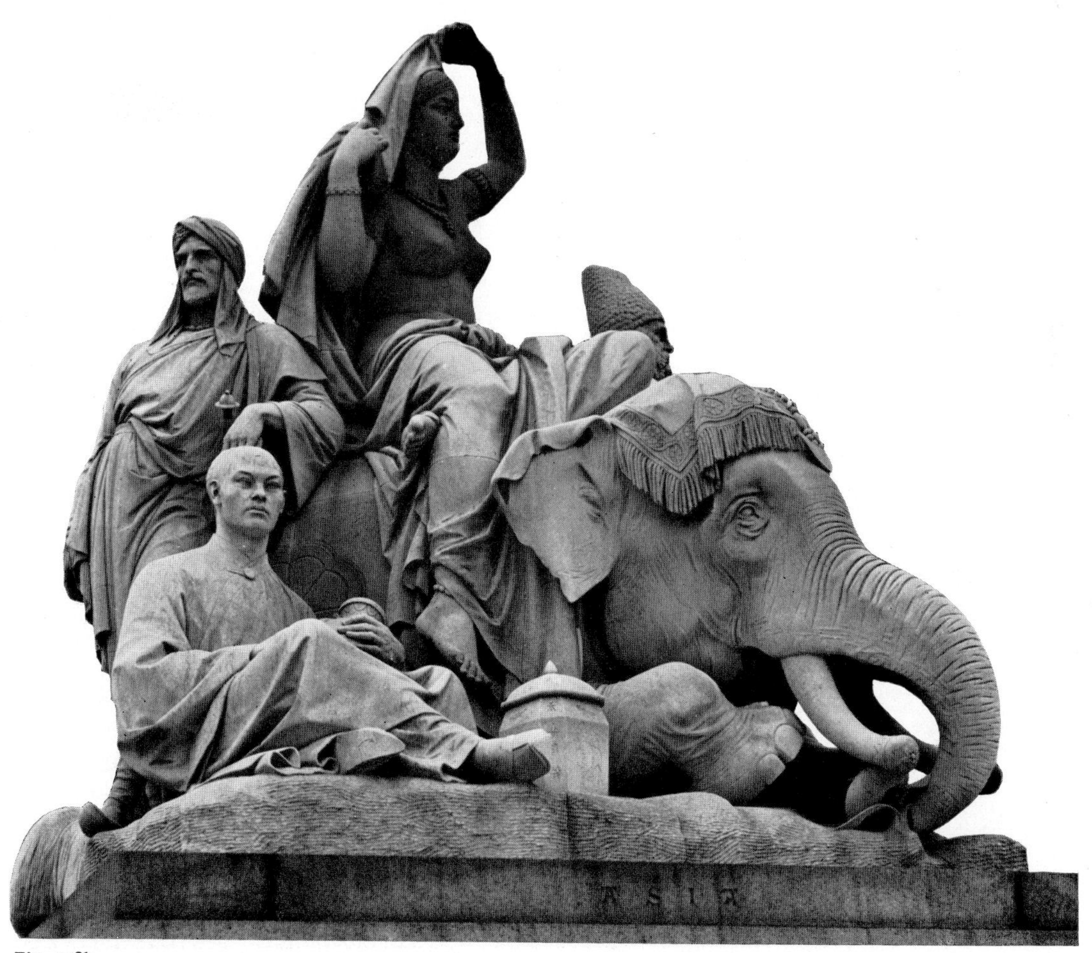


**Fig. 148b**

*Figure 149 (below):* Drawing by A. Bedborough, from a design by J. Wills, of the proposed glass-house to enclose the Albert Memorial: 1877.
Library photograph, No. 77,200.

**149** "An attractive scheme has been promulgated by Mr. John Wills, an eminent florist and horticulturist of Brompton, who is widely known as a designer and constructor of conservatories . . . His proposal is to enclose under glass the Albert Memorial in Hyde Park. He has issued lithographed plans and explanations that have given 'great satisfaction' to the Prince of Wales, and which have been submitted to the Queen. . . . there is only one objection to it—its cost. For undoubtedly, a 'winter garden' so near to the great world of London would be an acquisition of immense value; such a covering would effectually preserve from London's atmospheric influences the only one of our national monuments worthy the name, and certainly so very beautiful a design as that which has been shown to us would add greatly to the graces of the Metropolis.

The proposed structure covering the Memorial is designed for execution in iron, copper and glass. It is octagonal in plan, 200 feet in diameter, with projections on four alternate faces of the octagon 80 feet by 27 feet. The width of the central part supporting the dome is 130 feet, and the height from the ground to the springing of the dome is 145 feet. The extreme height from the ground to the top of the figure surmounting the lantern on the dome is 340 feet. The principal entrance, which is 25 feet wide, is from Kensington Gore. The archway of this entrance, richly cuspated, is carried into the gable, which is filled with elaborate Gothic tracery. The other principal faces of

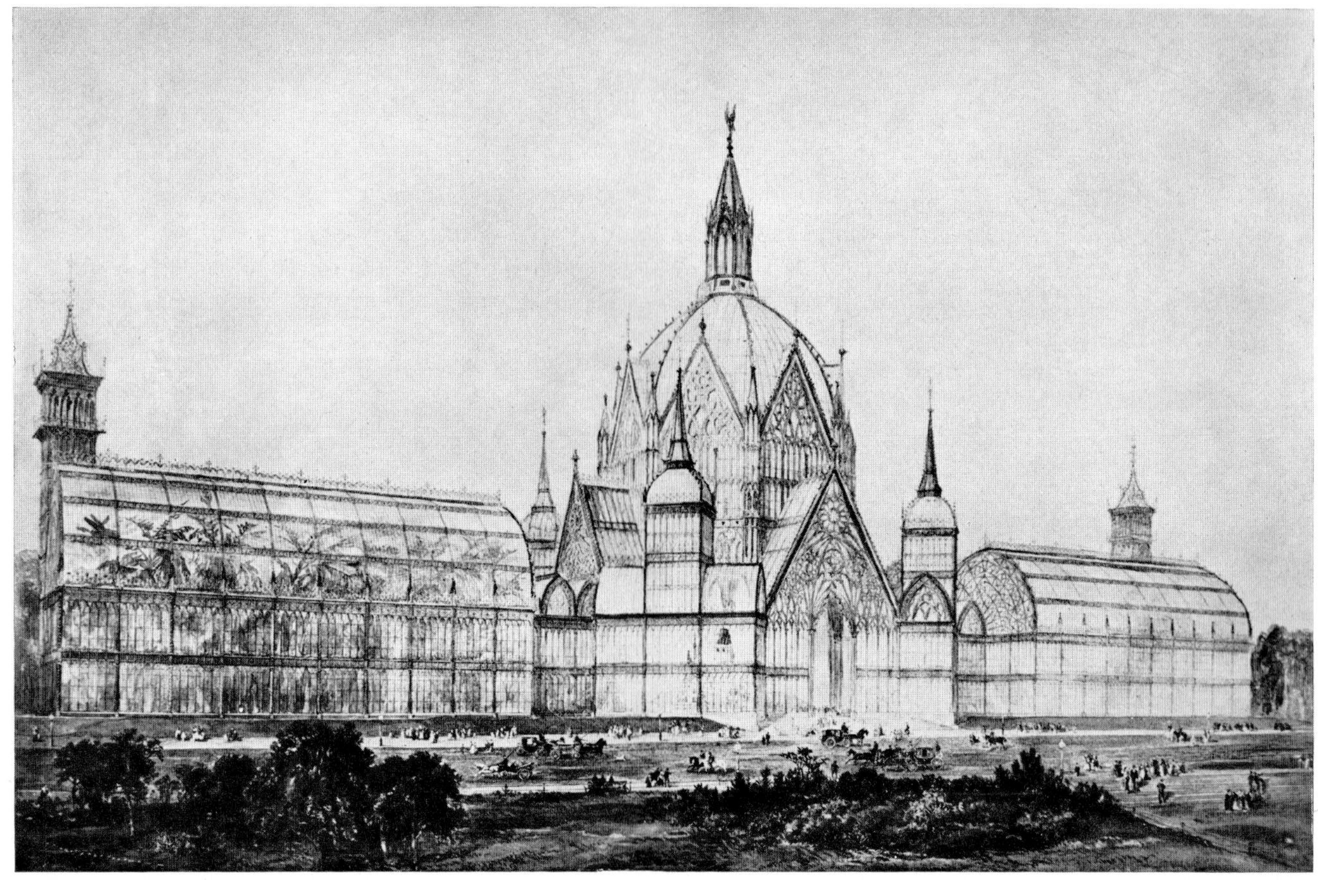

Fig. 149

the octagon are similarly treated. Clusters of columns, forming the piers at the intersecting angles of the octagon, are carried up in stages to the springing of the dome, terminating in gableted pinnacles and open traceried spires. From these piers (at the base of the dome) spring the gables which terminate the fronts of the octagon; these are filled also with cuspated Gothic tracery. East and west of the central structure, and con-

nected therewith by corridors, it is proposed to have gardens, in which shall be placed trees and plants representing the vegetable kingdoms of the four quarters of the globe.

Certainly such a scheme, well carried out, would be a public benefit unparalleled in this country; of that there is no doubt" (*Art Journal*, 1877, page 158).

# JAMES FERGUSSON, F.R.S. (*1808–1886*)

*Figure 150 (below):* Design for the Albert Memorial, exhibited at the Royal Academy in 1864. Pencil and watercolour, pen and ink, $27\frac{3}{8} \times 42\frac{7}{8}$ inches. No. D.1094–1886.

**150**   This drawing was bought from Mr. E. Parsons, of Brompton Road, on July 23rd, 1886, for £10. 10. 0d.

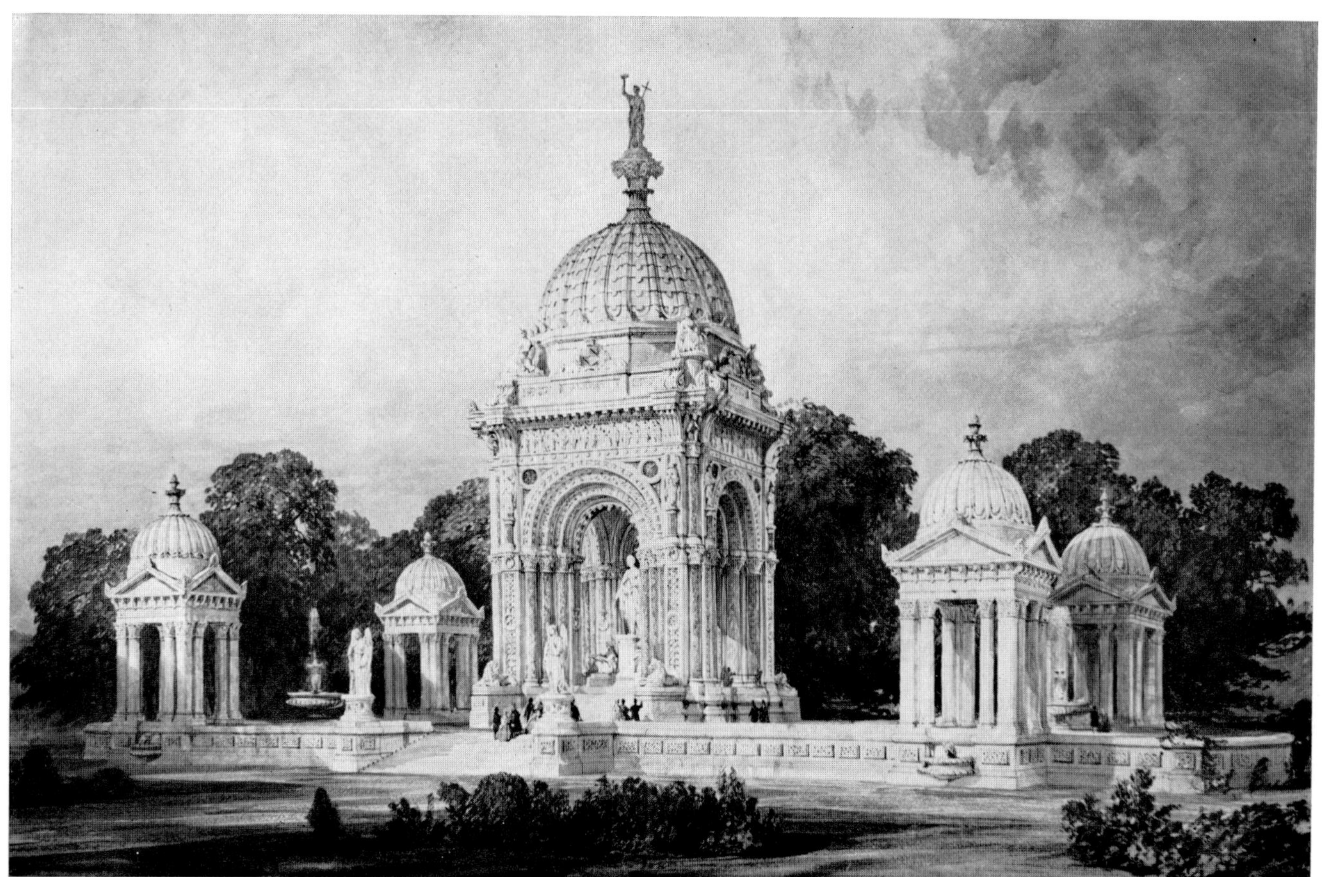

Fig. 150

*Figure 151 (right):*  Design for the Albert Memorial.
Pencil, $13\frac{1}{2} \times 10\frac{5}{8}$ inches. No. 9150F.

**151**   This drawing was bought from Mr. R. Jackson,
on July 9th, 1883, for 10 shillings.

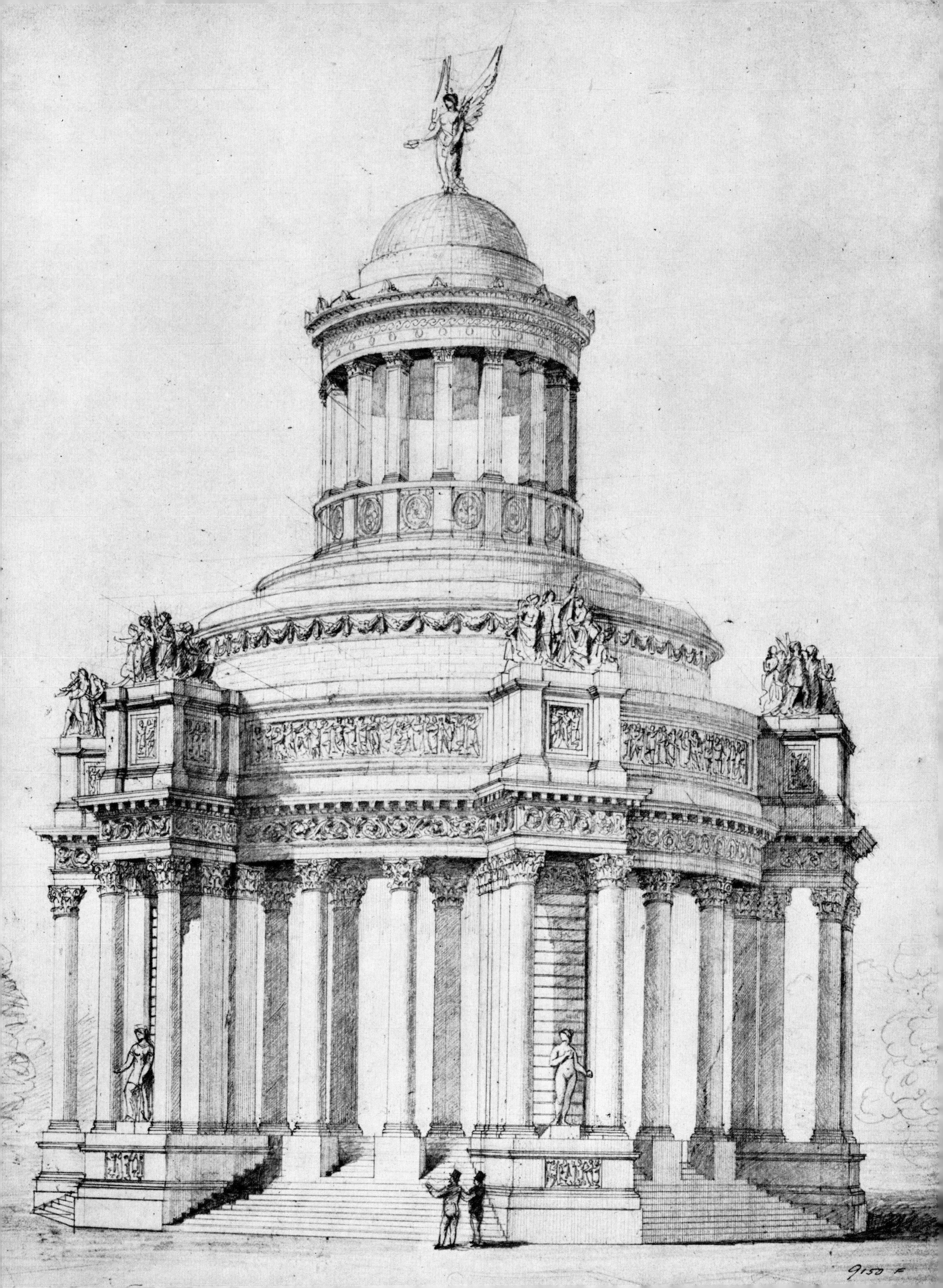

Aberystwyth: National Library of Wales 95
Ackermann, R. 21n, 84
Adam, Robert 11, 32n, 38, 142
Addington (Buckinghamshire) 30, 86, 87
Albert, Prince Consort 41, 42, 190–197
Aldershot (Hampshire) 183, 185
Alexander, Colonel Francis 116
Alscot (Warwickshire) 135
Amy, William 51
Angers (France), Royal Academy 68
Anne, Queen 27, 28, 113
Anson, Lord 123
Antigua (West Indies) 149
Antwerp (Belgium) 28
*Apollo* 42n
"Apollo" 54, 55
*Archaeologia* 4, 5, 7
*Archaeological Journal* 9
*Architectural Review* 32n, 75
*Architecture, Book of* (Gibbs) 22n, 75
Argyll and Greenwich, Duke of 30n, 33, 118–121
Arley (Cheshire) 46
Armstead, H. H. 42, 191, 193
*Art Journal* 10n, 43, 194, 195
Asheton, Hugh 4
Aubrey, John 52
Ayrton, Acton 186

Bacon, Annie 155, 157, 159, 163, 178, 179
Bacon, Elizabeth 136, 137
Bacon, John 20, 28, 38, 39, 79, 82, 147, 154–163
Bacon, John, the Younger 38, 39, 147, 161, 176–179
Badminton (Gloucestershire) 30, 98–100
Bailey, Bruce A. 23, 87, 97, 104, 111, 113, 127, 135, 137, 138, 149, 157, 175
Baily, Edward Hodges 41, 42, 181
Bambaia, Il 2n
Bandinelli, Baccio 2
Banks, Thomas 147
Barkby (Leicestershire) 17, 96, 97
Barry, Charles 191
Barry, E. M. 191
Bassett, John Pendarves 125
Bayne, Captain 146, 147
Beauclerk, Lord Aubrey 116, 117
Beaufort, 2nd and 3rd Dukes of 30, 98–100
Beaufort, 4th Duke of 95, 100
Beaufort, Lady Margaret *see* Richmond, Countess of
Beckford, Alderman William 140, 141
Bedborough, A. 194, 195
Behnes, William 41
Bell, John (painter) 7
Bell, John (sculptor) 193
Belton (Lincolnshire) 26n, 52
Belvoir (Leicestershire) 26n
Bengal, Bay of 177

Benson, Elizabeth 24
Bernini, Giovanni Lorenzo 24n
Biddick Hall (Co. Durham) 129
Biddulph, Sir Thomas 191
Bird, Francis 24, 27, 30, 32, 35, 61, 69
Bishop, Sir Edward 46
Blackman, Rowland 149
Black Prince *see* Edward
Blair, Captain 146, 147
Blake, Robert 173
Blake, William 41, 165, 168, 169
Blenheim Palace (Oxfordshire) 27, 37
Blore, Edward 84, 85
Blore, G. H. 173
Boca-Chica Castle (Colombia) 116
Boreham (Essex) 10
Borrett, John 127
Bottesford (Leicestershire) 10
Bouverie, Harriot 30, 33, 87
Boverton (Glamorganshire) 90
Bowyer, Lady 17n
Bowyer, Sir George 17n
Brasses, monumental 11, 12
Bray, Sir Edmund 68
Bray, Edward 27, 61, 66–68
Bray, Jane 27, 61, 66-68
Brayley, E. W. and Neale, J. P. 7
Brest (France) 147
Bristol, All Saints 22n
"Britannia" 40, 159, 165, 167–169
Brockett, Sir John 105
Brookmans Park (Hertfordshire) 111
Brownlow, Alice, Lady 52
Brownlow, Alicia, Lady 52
Brownlow, Dorothy, Lady 52, 53
Brownlow, Elizabeth, Lady 52
Brownlow, Sir John 52
Brownlow, Sir William 52, 53
Brownlow, William 52
Bruera (Cheshire) 144, 145
Buenos Aires (Argentina) 177
Burghley, Lord 10
Burlington, Earl of 28, 29
*Burlington Magazine* 28n, 34n, 58, 123
Burrell, Captain Percy 177
Burton, Decimus 42, 183
Burton-on-Trent (Staffordshire) 7, 9
Bury, Shirley 40n, 170
Busby, Jane 87
Busby, Rev. Thomas 30, 86, 87
Bushey Park (Middlesex) 56–59

"Calcutta" 20
Cambridge:
    St. John's College 4, 5
    Senate House 27
Campbell, Malcolm 169
Canons (Middlesex) 27, 30n, 68
Canterbury (Kent), Cathedral 1, 30, 87


# Index

**The references are to page numbers**

Capitsoldi, – 36n
Carew, John Edward 42
Carlini, Agostino 36n
Carpenter, 2nd Baron 127
Carpentiere, Edward 24n
Cartagena (Colombia) 109, 116
Carter, Benjamin 32
Carter, Thomas 32, 38
Cass, Christopher 27, 66-68
Cawalcant, John 5
Cavendish, Lady Margaret *see* Newcastle, Margaret, Duchess of
Chagre (Panama) 109
Chambers, Sir Robert 36n
Chambers, Sir William 36, 37
Chandos, Duke of 27, 30n, 68
Chantrey, Sir Francis 16n, 20n, 42
Charles I 27, 58
Charles II 27
Chatham (Kent) 179
Chatsworth (Derbyshire) 25, 26, 54, 55
Chaucer, Alice *see* Suffolk, Duchess of
Chaucer, Geoffrey 23
Cheere, Sir Henry 19, 28, 32, 34, 36n, 40, 122–129
Cheere, John 34n
Cheshunt (Hertfordshire) 65
Chester, St. John 23, 46
Child, Robert 38, 142
Chilham (Kent) 13
Chirk Castle (Denbighshire) 105
Chiswick House (Middlesex) 28, 30, 78, 79
Cholwick, John B. 175
Christie, Messrs. 91
Cibber, Caius Gabriel 24–27, 49, 52, 54, 55, 64, 65
Cibber, Colley 26n
Cipriani, Giovanni Battista 36
Clarendon, Earl of 191
Clayton & Bell 42, 193
Clayton, Muriel 12n
Cleopatra's Needle 181
Clifford Smith, H. 173
Clitherow, Christopher 48, 49
Coachmakers' and Coach-harness Makers' Company 36
Coade Artificial Stone Manufactory 38
Coke, Jane 150, 151
Cole, Sir Henry 191
Coleshill (Berkshire) 30, 33, 87
Colleton, Anne 114, 115
Collins, William 36
Collmann, Leonard William 181, 182, 186
Colston, Edward 22n
Colt, Maximilian 12
Colvin, Howard 10n, 21n, 24n, 46, 61, 68, 135
*Commemorative Art* 38n
*Connoisseur* 170
Cooke, Captain Edward 176, 177
Cooke, Sir George 28
Corbett, M. 12n
Coronation coach 36
Cotton, Sir John Hind 77
*Country Life* 16n, 26n, 38n, 42n, 43, 52, 68, 91, 128, 129, 173, 177, 183
Courtauld Institute of Art *see* London
Coventry (Warwickshire) 193
Coventry, 1st Earl of 16
Cox, Mrs. Anne 11, 19
Cox-Johnson, Ann *see* Saunders, Ann
Coysevox, Antoine 29
Craggs, James 19, 28, 29, 69-72

Craven, William, Lord 97
Crimean War 41
Croft-Murray, Edward 24n, 165, 173
Cromwell, Oliver 127
Croome D'Abitot (Worcestershire) 16
Crowley, Sir Ambrose 29, 75-77
Crowley, John 77
Cubitt, Sir William 191
Cuckfield (Sussex) 177
Cure, Cornelius 2, 6, 10
Cure, William 2

Dance, George 147, 169
Dashwood, Sir Robert 105
Deene (Northamptonshire) 22
Delvaux, Laurent 30, 36, 112, 113
Derby: Cathedral 8, 10
Derby, Earl of 191
Diana Fountain, Bushey Park (Middlesex) 56–59
*Dictionary of English Architects 1660–1840, Biographical* (Colvin) 21n, 24n, 46, 68, 135
*Dictionary of British Sculptors, 1660–1851* (Gunnis) 15
Digges, Lady 13
Digges, Sir Dudley 13
Donaldson, T. L. 191
Donne, John 23
Dorset, 3rd Duke of 152, 153
Douce Bequest (Ashmolean Museum, Oxford) 17n, 22, 152
Downes, Kerry 90
Drake, George Thomas 160
Dring, Robert 105
Dufour, Alexander 169
Duppa, Baldwin 30
Durisdeer (Dumfries-shire) 18, 24

Eastlake, Sir Charles 191
East India Company 20, 177
East Sutton (Kent) 12
Eckstein, John 32
Edgware (Middlesex) *see* Canons
Edward VI 6, 10
Edward VII 183
Edward, the Black Prince 1
"Eleanor Crosses" 191
Elgin (Morayshire): Cathedral 19
Elizabeth I 12, 42
Elmley Castle, (Worcestershire) 16
Enfield (Middlesex) 77
*English Church Monuments 1510–1840* (Esdaile) 12n
*English Monumental Sculpture since the Renaissance* (Esdaile) 15
Esdaile, Edmund 65
Esdaile, Katharine 12n, 15, 23n, 26, 34n, 119
Evelyn, John 58
Evesham, Epiphanius 2, 12n
Ewelme (Oxfordshire) 23
Ewen, Nicholas 7
Exeter (Devonshire): Cathedral 40, 174, 175

Faber, H. 54
Fane, Charlotte and Henry 91
Fane, Lady 83
Farington, Joseph 20n, 34n, 38, 41n, 147
Farmer & Brindley 191
Fergusson, James 186, 195
Fermor, Thomas 7, 9
Filmer, Sir Edward 12
Fisher, John, Bishop of Rochester 4
Flaxman, John 20, 21, 38, 40, 165, 167-175

Fleming, Richard 77
Florence (Italy) 36
Foix, Gaston de 2n
Foley, 1st Lord 30, 31
Foley, John Henry 41, 42, 191, 193
Fontana, Carlo 28
Fonthill (Wiltshire) 38
Fort, Thomas 61, 68
Foster, Rev. Thomas 19
Fox, Charles James 37, 165, 166
Fox, Richard, Bishop of Winchester 4
Franceys, S. & T. 42, 180
Fristobaldi, Peter and Leonard 5

Gage, John, Elizabeth and Margaret 11
Gahagan, George 152
Gainsborough, Thomas 36
Gainsborough, Wriothesley, Earl of 100
Gamble, James 187
"Ganymede" 28
Gascoign, Theodosia 77
Gay, John 20
George I 28
George III 34, 36, 38, 39, 147, 161
George IV 40
Gibbons, Grinling 16n, 26n, 61
Gibbs, James 17, 22n, 27–30, 32, 35, 61, 69, 70, 72, 74, 75
Gibson, John 41, 42, 180
Gidea Hall (Essex) 68
Girouard, Mark 129
*Gloucestershire, Monumental Effigies of* (Roper) 68, 100
Glynde (Sussex) 127
Goblet, L. Alexander 151
Godfrey, W. H. 11n
Gordon, Lord Adam 19
Gordon, Henrietta, Duchess of 19
Gould, Brian 79
Gravelot, Hubert 32n
Gray, Charles 191
Great Barrington (Gloucestershire) 27, 61, 66–68
Great Offley (Hertfordshire) 37n
Great Witley (Worcestershire) 30, 31
Green, David 26n, 61
Grenada (West Indies) 157
Gretna Green (Dumfries-shire) 142
Grigg, Elizabeth 43
Guadaloupe (Leeward Islands) 157
Guelfi, Giovanni Battista 22, 28, 29, 69, 71
Guernsey (Channel Islands) 123
Guilford, 2nd Earl of 41n, 147, 165
Gunnis, Rupert 12n, 15, 16, 19, 26n, 32n, 51, 54, 83n, 105, 138, 142, 165, 177

Hall, Sir Benjamin 41
Hallett, James 77
Hampton Court (Middlesex) 24, 56–58, 60–63, 68
*Hampton Court Palace, History of* (Law) 58
Handel, George Frederick 32
Handley-Read, Charles 42n
Hanover (Germany) 38
Hanway, Jonas 38, 130, 131
Hardwick, Bess of *see* Shrewsbury, Elizabeth, Countess of
Hardwick, P. C. 191
Hare-Naylor, Mr. 193
Hargrave, General 34
Harley, Lady Henrietta Cavendish Holles 61
Harley, Lord 29

Harpham (Yorkshire) 91
Harris, 1st Lord 22
Harris, John, 38n, 58
Hartshorne, Robert 34
Harvey, Captain 20n, 147
Haslingfield (Cambridgeshire) 15, 24
Hasted, Edward 2
Hatfield (Hertfordshire) 104–107
Hawke, Admiral Lord 38, 123, 132, 133
Hawke, Catherine, Lady 132
Hawkins, Philip 125
Hawksmoor, Nicholas 90
Hayward, Mary 36n
Hayward, Richard 34, 36
Henley-Ongley, Robert 113
Henry III 1
Henry VII 7
Henry VIII 2, 7
Herbert, Lord 4
Hereford: Cathedral 193
Heston (Middlesex) 38, 142, 143
Hildburgh, Dr. W. L. 141
Hoddington (Hampshire) 87
Hodgkinson, Terence 32n
Hogarth, William 129
Holland, Henry 39
Holles, Gertrude 127
Hollingbourne (Kent) 30
Hollins, Peter 40n, 181
Hone, Nathaniel 109
Hone, William 52
Hood, John 97
Horneby, Henry 4
Horsnaile, Christopher, the Elder 26
Hornaile, Christopher, the Younger 36n
Howard, Mrs., of Corby 44
Howe, Lord 147
Hughes, Rev. Mr. 20
Hulton, Paul 24n
Hussey, Christopher 128
Hussey, Sir Edward 97
Hutt, Captain 20n, 147

Imber, Lawrence 7
Ingram, Sir Bruce 137, 138
Ionides, Constantine A. 175
Irby, Mary 148, 149
Irby, William Henry 149
Ireton, Henry 127
Irish Georgian Society 19
Isham Papers 26
Isleworth (Middlesex) 105

Jackson, R. 164, 177, 180, 196
James II 27
Jansen, Garret *see* Johnson, Gerard
Jeavons, S. A. 9
Jeckyll, Dame Elizabeth 111
Jennings, Robert 7
Jersey, 5th Earl of 142
Johnson, Gerard 2, 10n, 11
Johnson, Nicholas 10, 11
Jones, Dr., Archdeacon of Hereford 160
Jones, C. P. 24n, 26n
Jones, E. Alfred 170
Jones, Inigo 30, 78, 79
Jupp, Edward 119
Jupp, Richard 39, 161

Katherine of Aragon, Queen 7
Keene, Henry 15

Kelk, John 191, 193
Kemeys Tynte, Sir Charles 87
Kent, Henry 17n, 22
Kent, William 16, 28, 78–83
Ketton (Rutland) 26n
Kilkenny (Ireland): Cathedral 11, 19
King, Peter, Lord 88–90
King, William 95
Kirkleatham (Yorkshire) 17, 74, 75
Knight, Mr. 83
Knoop, D. 24n, 26n

Lambton Castle (Co. Durham) 128
Lamport (Northamptonshire) 26
Landseer, Sir Edwin 181
Law, E, 58
Lawlor, John 193
Layard, Sir Henry 193
Leicester, Thomas Coke, Earl of 150, 151
Leighton, Lord 187
Le Neve, John 51, 65
Le Neve, Peter 113
Leoni, Leone 2n
Lewis, Mrs. Lesley 38n
Lichfield (Staffordshire): Cathedral 193
Limbrey, John 87
Lincoln, Cathedral 1
Linton (Cambridgeshire) 136, 137
Littleton, Sir Edward 101, 103
Liverpool (Lancashire) 42, 180
Lloyd, Rev. R. H. 16
Lobons, John 7
London:
    Albert Memorial 42, 43, 190–197
    Blackfriars 10
    British Museum 7, 24, 46, 56, 57, 83, 165, 173
    Burlington House 28, 69
    Churches:
        All Hallows-by-the-Tower 114, 115
        St. Alfege, Greenwich 27
        St. Anne, Limehouse 27
        St. Dunstan-in-the-East 64, 65
        St. George, Bloomsbury 28
        St. James, Hampstead Road, 178, 179
        St. Katherine's Chapel, Regent's Park 43
        St. Leonard, Shoreditch 24
        St. Luke, Old Street 27
        St. Martin-in-the-Fields 27
        St. Mary, Bromley, Poplar 50, 51
        St. Paul's Cathedral 2n, 23, 24, 27, 39, 41–
            43, 164, 186–189
        Westminster Abbey 1, 11, 12, 16, 19, 20,
            21, 24, 26, 28–35, 38, 60, 61, 69–72,
            80–83, 91–93, 108, 109, 116–125, 130,
            131, 146, 147, 154, 155, 159, 162, 163,
            165, 176, 177
        Whitfield's Tabernacle, Tottenham Court
            Road 79
    College of Arms 12
    Courtauld Institute of Art 17n, 24n
    East India House 39, 160, 161
    Euston Road 38n
    Fishmongers' Hall 36
    Foundling Hospital 101, 102, 131
    Great Exhibition of 1851 43
    Greenwich Park 40, 41n, 165, 167–169
    Guildhall 140, 141
    Hyde Park Corner 42, 183, 184
    Kensington Gardens 42, 190–197
    Mansion House 32, 119
    Marylebone Road 38n
    Monument 26
    National Monuments Record 1, 46, 65, 67,
        69, 71, 77, 89, 95, 103–107, 115, 129, 131,
        132, 142, 145, 151, 152, 159, 173, 177, 179
    New Road, The 38n
    Parliament Street, (No. 43) 128
    Public Record Office 36n, 56, 58
    Regent Canal 38n
    Regent's Park 43
    Royal Academy 41, 147, 152, 161, 169, 195
    Royal Exchange 28
    Royal Institute of British Architects 8, 10
    St. Martin's Lane Academy 33, 129
    Sir John Soane's Museum 12, 24, 41, 46, 58,
        69, 149, 169
    Slaughter's Coffee House 129
    Society of Antiquaries 20n
    Society of Artists 36n
    Soho Square 27
    Somerset House 37
    Stocks Market 27
    Tate Gallery 187
    Temple Bar 28
    Trafalgar Square 40n, 42, 181, 182
    Transport Museum, Clapham 20n
    University College 165
    Vauxhall Gardens 32
    Victoria and Albert Museum, Department of
        Architecture and Sculpture 22n, 33, 34n,
        81, 119
        Library 27, 42n, 79, 81
    Warburg Institute 24n, 63, 84, 85, 93, 109,
        116, 123, 125, 141, 147, 155, 163
    Whitehall Palace 27, 28
    Williams's Coffee House 69
*London, Greater* (Walford) 52
Lough, John Graham 42, 181
Lovell, Sir Thomas 4
Lyme Regis (Dorset) 26n
Lymington (Hampshire) 156, 157
Lyons (France) 32

Macclesfield (Cheshire) 52
Macclesfield, 2nd Earl of 52
MacColl, Dugald 187
MacDowell, Patrick 41, 42, 193
Malines (Belgium) 24
Mallet, John 179
Mann, Sir J. G. 1n, 10n
Manners, Lady Victoria 10n, 26n
Manners, Lord Robert 146, 147
Manning, Charles 39
Manning, Samuel 39
Mansfield, 1st Earl of 21
Margaret of Valois, Queen 1
Marignano, Marquis of *see* Medici, Jacopo de'
Marney, Sir Henry 4
Marochetti, Carlo, Baron 41, 181, 186, 193
Marshall, Edward 12
Marshall, Joshua 12
Marshall, William, 12n
Marshall, William Calder 41, 193
Martinique (West Indies) 157
Mary I 10
Mary II 56
Mason, Sir Richard 52
Mason, William 162, 163
Masons' Company 36n
Maynard, John 7
Medici, Jacopo de', Marquis of Marignano 2n
Mee, Arthur 13n
Merenda, Ippolito 24n
Middle Claydon (Buckinghamshire) 23

Milan (Italy): Cathedral 2n
Milman, Henry, Dean of St. Paul's, London 186
Milnes, Thomas 181
Milton Abbey (Dorset) 37
Mitcham (Surrey) 29, 75–77
Monconys, Duke of 58
Montagu, 2nd Duke and Duchess 34, 39
Montagu, Mary, Duchess of 38
Montague, Captain 20n
*Monumenta Anglicana* (Le Neve) 51, 65
Moore, John Francis 17n, 37, 130–133, 140, 141
Mores, Morgan 5
Morpeth, Lord 42n
Mortlake (Surrey) 5
Mount Vernon (Virginia) 36
Murray, Fairfax 145, 147, 149, 151, 152
Myddelton, Mary 34n
Myddleton, Robert 105

"National Cup" 40, 170, 171
National Monuments Record *see* London
Neale, J. P. *see* Brayley, E. W.
Netherton (Devonshire) 125
Newcastle, Margaret, Duchess of 61
Newcastle, John Holles, Duke of 32, 35, 42, 60, 61
Newsham, Ann 69
Newton, C. T. 193
Newton, Sir Henry 116
Newton, Sir Isaac 16, 80, 81, 83–85
New York, Columbia University 170, 175
Nicholls, Sutton 58
Nightingale Monument, Westminster Abbey 24, 34
Noble, Matthew 41
Nollekens, Joseph 11, 17n, 21, 34n, 36n, 37, 43, 44, 119, 144–153
*Nollekens and his Times* (Smith) 21, 36, 37, 151, 152
North, Lord *see* Guilford, Earl of
Northampton Records Office 26
North Mimms (Hertfordshire) 17, 110, 111
North Stoneham (Hampshire) 38, 132, 133
Norton, M. 12n
Nost, John 18, 22–24, 27, 42, 56, 57, 60–63
Nottingham 145
*Nottingham*, H.M.S. 123

Oakes, Helen 86, 87
Ockham (Surrey) 88–90
Old Somerby (Lincolnshire) 52
Old Warden (Bedfordshire) 30, 112, 113
Oliver, Isaac 10
Oman, Charles 42n
Ongley, 1st Lord 113
Ongley, Sir Samuel 30, 112, 113
Orwell, Francis, Lord 109
Osterley Park (Middlesex) 38, 142, 143
Otford (Kent) 19, 126, 127
Owen, Mary 77
Owlesbury (Hampshire) 127
Oxford:
    Ashmolean Museum 17n, 22, 24, 30n, 61, 75, 152
    Bodleian Library 6, 10, 18, 24, 60, 61
Oxford, Aubrey, Earl of 116

Paine, James, the Younger 164
Palladio, Andrea 79
"Pallas" 54

Palmer, Mrs. 37
Palmer, Susanna 65
Palmerston, Viscount 191
Panmure, Lord 41
Papworth, Edgar George 181
Parham (Sussex) 46
Paris, Exhibition of 1867 191
Parsons, E. 49, 79, 82, 111–113, 115, 116, 119, 125, 135, 161, 170, 175, 195
Parsons, Humphry 77
Paul III, Pope 2n
Pearce, Edward *see* Pierce
Pennans (Cornwall) 125
Pennethorne, Sir James 191
Penrose, F. C. 186
Peper Harrow House (Surrey) 37
Permoser, Balthasar 32
Pevsner, Dr. Nikolaus 24n
Philip, John Birnie 193
Phipps, Sir Charles 191
Physick, J. F. 3, 16n, 26n, 52, 68, 81, 119, 183
Picton Castle (Pembrokeshire) 128, 129
Pierce, Edward 23, 24, 46, 47, 58
Pigalle, Jean-Baptiste 36
Pinner (Middlesex) 48, 49
Pistrucci, Benedetto 181
Pitman family 2
Pitt, William 37, 147
Pitts, William 181
Pleshey (Essex) 40
Plymouth (Devonshire):
    City Museum and Art Gallery 30n, 81, 95, 119
    St. Andrew 123
Pochin, Charlotte 17, 96, 97
Pochin, Mary 17, 96, 97
Pochin, Thomas 17, 96, 97
Pocock, Sir George 158, 159
Polhill, Charles 19
Polhill, David 126, 127
Pope, Alexander 69
Porta, Guglielmo della 2n
Portobello (Panama) 109
Portsmouth (Hampshire): Dockyard 22, 24, 56
Potterne (Wiltshire) 17n, 22
Poulett, 4th Earl 160
Preston-on-Stour (Gloucestershire) 21, 38, 134, 135
Prideaux, Sir Edmund 124, 125
Prince and Co. 193
*Prince Frederick*, H.M.S. 116
Princeton University 169
Prior, Matthew 29
Public Record Office *see* London

Quaritch, B. 75, 90, 100, 123, 127, 131, 132, 141
*Quebec*, H.M.S. 157
Queensberry, Duke of 18, 24
Quellin, Arnold 24

Radcliffe, Dr. 95
Radley (Berkshire) 17n
Railton, William 181
Reade, Sir James 104–107
Reade, Sir John 104–107
Redenhall (Norfolk) 17n
Redfern, J. 193
Rennie, George 22, 181
Reynardson, Samuel 125
Rhodes, Anna 178, 179
Richardson, Charles James 46, 61, 62, 68
Richardson, Robert 115

Richmond, Anne, Duchess of 22
Richmond, Margaret, Countess of 2, 45
Rivers, 3rd Earl 52
Rivers, 4th Earl 52
Roberts, Dame Deborah 50, 51
Roberts, Sir John 50, 51
Roberts, Dame Mary 50, 51
Rockingham (Northamptonshire) 30
Rockingham Lewis, Earl of 30
Rodin, Auguste 187
Rodney, Admiral Lord 147
Rogers, James 157
Rogers, Captain Josias 156, 157
Roiley, Gabriel 9
Roiley, Richard 9
Rome:
    S. Giacomo alla Lungarna 24n
    St. Peter's 2n
    Vatican 28
Rook, Admiral 109
Roper, Ida M. 68, 100
Roubiliac, Louis François 32, 21n, 38, 39, 118–
    121
Rovezzano, Benedetto da 2
Rowe, Nicholas 20, 91–93
Royal Academy *see* London
Royal Commission on Historical Monuments
    15, 24n, 49, 51, 59, 189
*Royal George*, H.M.S. 132
Royal Institute of British Architects *see* London
Ruabon (Denbighshire) 30n, 94, 95
Rundell, Bridge and Rundell 40n, 42n, 170
Russell, Sir William 64, 65
Rutland, 5th Earl of 10
Rutland, 7th Earl of 26n
Rutland, 8th Earl of 26n
Rutland, Elizabeth, Countess of 10
Rysbrack, John Michael 15–17, 20, 22n, 28–34,
    69, 72, 73, 75, 79, 81–109, 119, 127, 131, 132,
    141

Sackville Monument, Withyham (Sussex) 26
Saighton (Cheshire) 145
St. Alban's, 1st Duke of 116
St. John of Bletsoe, 10th Lord 77
St. John, Sir John 4
St. Martin's Lane Academy *see* London
St. Quintin, Charlotte 91
Salisbury (Wiltshire): St. Martin 125
Saltaire, Shipley (Yorkshire) 181
Salusbury Monument, Great Offley (Hertford-
    shire) 37n
Salviati & Co. 193
Sandby, Thomas 15
Sausmarez, Philip de 122, 123
Saunders, Ann 38n, 161
Savage, Ann 52
Savage, Richard 52
Savage, Sir William 16
Saxton, William 10, 11
Scheemakers, Henry 34
Scheemakers, Peter 11, 15, 17, 19, 20, 28, 30,
    31, 34, 37, 38, 110–117
Scheemakers, Thomas 21, 38, 134, 135
Scott, Sir G. G. 42, 43, 190–193
Scott, R. S. 4, 5
*Sculpture in England, 1530–1840* (Whinney) 2n
Scutari (Crimea) 41
*Sepulchral Monuments Committee, Report of*
    20n
Serres, Dominic 132
Sevenoaks (Kent): Public Library 19

Seymour, Sir Charles 4
Seys, Richard 90
Shakespeare, William 28, 30, 31
Shelburne, Lord 147
Sherborne, 1st Lord 151
Sherburn, George 69
Shirley, Sir George 9
Shoreham, Kent 19, 126, 127
Shovell, Sir Cloudesley 109
Shrewsbury, Elizabeth, Countess of 8, 10
Shrewsbury, 7th Earl of 12n
Skidmore, F. A. 193
Sidnell, Michael 22n
Sidney, Sir Philip 10
Simcoe, General John Graves 40, 174, 175
Smirke, Sir Robert 41n
Smirke, Sydney 191
Smith, John Thomas 21, 36, 37, 141, 151, 152
Smith, Nathaniel 140, 141
Smythson, Robert 8, 10
Society of Antiquaries *see* London
Society of Artists *see* London
Somers, Lord 17, 110, 111
Somerton (Oxfordshire) 7, 9
Sondes, Sir Thomas 2, 3
Sotheby, Messrs. 69, 75, 137, 138, 145
Sotheby & Wilkinson 49
South Sea Company 113
Southwell, Hon. Edward 19
Sowerby (Yorkshire) 138, 139
Spearman, Sir Alexander 191
Spiers, W. L. 12n
Stamford (Lincolnshire) 26n
Standly, Peter 136, 137
Stanhope, Earl 16, 82–85, 193
Stannus, Hugh Hutton 187
Stansfeld, George 138
Stanton, Edward 26, 52, 64, 65
Stanton, William 14, 16, 24, 26, 28, 48–53
Staunton Harold (Leicestershire) 9
Steavens, Thomas 38, 134, 135
Stevens, Alfred 42, 181, 186–189
Stoke Bruern (Northamptonshire) 28
Stoke Park (Northamptonshire) 28
Stone, John 26
Stone, Nicholas 12, 23, 26
Stothard, Thomas 165, 166
Stratford Langthorne (Essex) 115
Stuart, James ("Athenian") 20, 21, 38, 134, 135
Stules, Sir Thomas 105
Suffolk, Alice, Duchess of 23
*Surrey, The Natural History and Antiquities of*
    (Aubrey) 52
Sussex, Earls of 10
*Sussex Notes and Queries* 11n
*Sutton and Cheam Herald* 52
Sutton (Surrey), St. Nicholas 52, 53
Swayne, Thomas 125
*Sybille*, H.M.S. 177
Sympson, John 30, 87

Talman, John 46
Talman, William 24, 26, 46, 58
Taloy, A. C. 75
Taylor, Sir Robert 28, 32n
Teddesley Hall (Staffordshire) 30, 100–103
Tehiddy (Cornwall) 125
Teniswood, G. F. 193
Theed, William 42, 193
Thompson, Francis 54
Thornycroft, Thomas 193
Throwley (Kent) 2, 3, 22

*Index*

Tillotson, John, Archbishop of Canterbury 138, 139
*Times Literary Supplement* 119
Tite, Sir William 191
Tittleshall (Norfolk) 150, 151
Torel, William 1
Torrigiano, Pietro 4, 5
Torrington, Lord 160
Torrington, 7th Viscount 191
Townroe, Reuben 187
Townshend, Colonel 32n
Trevor, Thomas 127
Trollope, Thomas 97
Tufnell, Samuel 40
Turner, Marwood William 17, 74, 75
Tweed, John 187
Twining, Rev. Mr. 20
Tyler, William 36n

*Universal Magazine* 132

Van Gelder, Peter Mathias 38, 142, 143
Vasari, Giorgio 2
"Venus, Triumph of" 61–63
Verney, Lady 23n
Verney, Sir Ralph 23n
Vernon, Admiral Edward 72, 108, 109, 116
Verskovis, Jacob Frans 79
Vertue, George 2, 10, 24n, 28, 29, 31, 83
Vertue, Robert 7
Vewike, Maynard 5
Victoria, Queen 42, 183, 191, 193
Victoria and Albert Museum *see* London
*Victoria and Albert Museum Bulletin* 32n, 33n, 81, 119
Voyers, – 36n

Wade, Field-Marshal 21n
Wales, National Library of *see* Aberystwyth
Walford, Edward 52
Walker, Humphrey 7
Walpole, Horace 79
*Walpole Society* (Volumes) 1n, 2n, 10n, 12n, 24n, 29n, 31n, 83n, 165, 173
Warburton, Diana, Lady 23, 46, 47
Warburton, Sir George 46
Warkton (Northamptonshire) 34, 38, 39
Warton, Dr Joseph 172, 173
Washington, George 36
Watson, Admiral 20
Watson, F. J. B. 30n, 159
Watt, James 20n
Webb, Mrs. M. I. 28n, 30n, 34n, 36n, 79, 95, 103, 123

Wedgwood, Josiah 38, 40
Weekes, Henry 42, 193
Welbourne (Lincolnshire) 97
Wellington, Duke of 41, 42, 183–189
Wells (Somerset): Cathedral 1
Wendy, Sir Thomas 15, 24
West, James, of Alscot 135
West Firle (Sussex) 11
Westmacott, Sir Richard 165
Westmorland, 10th Earl of 142
Weston (Warwickshire) 36n
Wetheral (Cumberland) 44
Whildon, James 54
Whinney, Dr. M. D. 2n, 24n, 43, 165
Whiston (Northamptonshire) 148, 149
Whitley, William T. 119
Whytell, Ann 28, 154, 155
William III 22–24, 26, 56, 57
Williams Wynn, Lady 94, 95
Williams Wynn, Sir Watkin 30n, 94, 95
Wills, John 43, 194, 195
Wilton, Fanny 36n
Wilton, Joseph 36, 91, 136–139, 147
Windsor (Berkshire) 26
    Castle 2
Winchester (Hampshire): Cathedral 172, 173
Winnington, Thomas 105
Winstanley, James 125
Wise, Henry 58
Withyham (Sussex) 26, 152, 153
Wogan family 17n
Wolsey, Cardinal 2, 7
Wood, Mary 65
Woodbridge (Suffolk) 2
Woodington, William Frederick 181
Woodstock (Oxfordshire): George Inn 27, 67, 68
    *see also* Blenheim Palace
Woodward, Edward 21n, 135
Works, Office of 20n, 186
Works, Ministry of Public Building and 22, 61, 68
Wray, Sir Christopher 10
Wren, Sir Christopher 24n
*Wren Society* (Volumes) 58, 61
Wrest Park (Bedfordshire) 23, 24, 56
Wrexham (Denbighshire) 34n
Wright, Ichabod 145
Wright, William 23n
Wroxton (Oxfordshire) 41n, 165
Wyatt, Emily P. 183
Wyatt, James, the Younger 42, 183, 184
Wyatt, Matthew Cotes 42, 183, 184
Wyatt, Matthew Digby 191
Wynnstay Papers 95